I DON'T CARE IF YOU LIKE ME, I LIKE ME

Advance Praise for
I Don't Care if You Like Me, I Like Me

"Bernie Mac had a way of telling it straight that made you listen and made you think. He was genuine, always positive, and truly cared if you were okay. *I Don't Care if You Like Me, I Like Me* is an undeniably funny and poignant strategy for reaching your fullest potential one day at a time."

—Courtney B. Vance, Multi-Award-Winning Actor of Stage and Screen

"I've never seen anything like *I Don't Care if You Like Me, I Like Me*. This book is self-help, Chicago-style. It's the perfect combination of comedy and truth, just like you'd expect from Bernie Mac."

—Sherri Shepherd, Award-Winning Actress, Comedian, and Talk Show Host

"*I Don't Care if You Like Me, I Like Me* is some straight-talking truth from the no-holds-barred Bernie Mac. His self-help approach makes you want to do exactly that—help yourself! His raw honesty will make you laugh, cry and possibly rethink your entire life."

—Kym Whitley, American Comedian and Actress

I DON'T CARE IF YOU LIKE ME, I LIKE ME

Bernie Mac
and Rhonda R. McCullouah

A PERMUTED PRESS BOOK
ISBN: 978-1-63758-404-0
ISBN (eBook): 978-1-63758-405-7

I Don't Care if You Like Me, I Like Me:
Bernie Mac's Daily Motivational

Cover Art by Tiffani Shea
Interior Design by Yoni Limor

Permuted Press, LLC
New York • Nashville
permutedpress.com

Published in the United States of America
1 2 3 4 5 6 7 8 9 10

Bernard, even though you’re gone,
you still give us inspiration.

Table of Contents

Foreword

I first met the Mac Man back in the early '90s. I was in Chicago to watch a taping of a new Comedy Central show being produced by my brother Mark Adkins called *Comic Justice*. This tall brother walked up to me and said, "What's up, Sinbad." There was something immediately magnetic about Bernie. He had that big smile and a presence you couldn't help but notice. We started talking about basketball and how he used to play for a semi-pro team owned by a potato chip company. It didn't take long to feel like we were old friends.

We immediately connected over our Midwestern upbringings. I grew up in a small town in Michigan called Benton Harbor, which is about ninety miles from Bernie's hometown of Chicago. I remember him saying to me, "They're not gonna get me in Hollywood, Sinbad. I'm gonna be too much for them. I'm bringing that Chicago swag." And that's what he did.

Whatever stage he was on, he brought that Chicago swag with him. That's part of what made Bernie so special. Even his name had style—Bernie Mac. It was made for show business. We would trade war stories about working the Chitlin' Circuit, performing in just about every club there was. When the '90s comedy scene became so hot, they were turning just about everything into a comedy club—a skating rink, a beauty salon—no matter what it was, it became a comedy club.

We were road dogs. Bernie, Steve Harvey, John Witherspoon, myself, and so many others, all of us putting in the time and paying our dues on the road. These circuits required us to spend a lot of time away from family. Family was as important to Bernie as it was for me. We would share stories about our families and how we had to keep pushing for them. He wasn't just a great comic, but also a good man.

Bernie's one of those comics you didn't want to follow because he worked the crowd into such a frenzy. He had a way of building up the crowd that was an art form. His style was unique and refreshingly honest. He was able to talk about the streets of Chicago and the truth of the Black experience and deliver it on stage in a way where anybody could understand, no matter their color or background. You could always count on Bernie to be unapologetically raw and real, a quality I always have and still admire to this day.

So much about him reminded me of Richard Pryor. It was the way he would offer advice and tell stories on just about everything in his own unorthodox way. He didn't concern himself with whether or not you understood him or if you got his style of comedy; he wasn't trying to conform to the idea of what a comic should be. I would tell him, "Don't change nothing. Just be you." We needed his voice.

I remember watching the *Kings of Comedy*. Bernie was up last, after D. L. Hughley, Steve Harvey, and Cedric the Entertainer. As a comedian, it's a hard job to follow even one funny comic, let alone three. But Bernie did it with no problem. He didn't just follow, he killed. He destroyed that stage. Who can forget the routine he did about his sister's kids coming into the kitchen saying, "I want some milk and cookies"?

Bernie was fearless. He would look you straight in the eyes, letting the audience know, "I'm not the one to mess with." When he was on *Def Comedy Jam*, I saw him do something I've never seen another comic do: he came straight at the audience. He came right out the gate and said, "I ain't scared of you, motherfuckers!" This was a powerful moment because he was letting them know, "You might be a rough crowd, but I don't care. I'm here to put in work and you all are gonna listen to me. I'm Bernie Mac." And he meant every word. I know every comic in the world probably wishes to this day that they would've said that first.

When he was on that stage, he wasn't scared, he wasn't worried. Bernie set the groundwork for a lot of comics that came after him. His boldness and bravery showed people you could just be yourself. Don't be scared about being Black or where you come from. Talk about it all. He showed us that it doesn't matter what color people are. If you're honest, they'll accept it.

I don't think Bernie ever had a dishonest moment on stage. This carried over into his show. Man, I loved that show. It was tough and funny and real. I loved how he invited us all in. By breaking the fourth wall, he was saying, "Pay attention. I'm here."

Bernie's in the same locker room with Richard Pryor, Redd Foxx, Robin Williams, George Carlin, and all the greats. He is truly one of the greatest in the game. I miss him. I miss that distinguishable voice and what he had to say.

No matter how hard they may try, there will never be another Bernie Mac.

—Sinbad

Introduction

Let me tell you somethin'. Helping yourself is the best thing you can do, because if you're not helpin' yourself, nobody else gonna be able to do a damn thing for you. Now, speakin' of doin' it yourself, I got a confession to make. Y'all know I passed away, so this ain't really me talkin' to ya'. It's more like me talkin' *through* some folks that know me like I know the back of my own got-damn *hand*. If I'm gonna trust somebody to be me, it's gonna be them. So, just go on and keep imagining it's me, 'cuz this here is the closest thing you gonna get to Bernie Mac. Now, here we go...

I started out a poor Black child. Yep, everybody's got a ghetto story, this is mine. I was poor growing up in Chicago in a little apartment above my granddaddy's Baptist church, holes in my britches and never a nickel for the ice cream man. But I didn't know any different. As a kid, we always had bologna in the fridge and a roast with chocolate cake on Sundays. My mama would say, "Don't nobody owe you nothin'." She was right. I got my first job when I was a teenager baggin' groceries at the local grocery store. I was the best *got-damn* bagger they ever had. Everybody wanted me. I made sure their bread didn't get squished and their eggs didn't crack...and I made 'em smile. I worked hard my whole life at every job I had, and I ended up doing exactly what I wanted and making money at it too. I always knew that everything you want in life, you got to work for it. You got to earn it.

What does that sentence start with? YOU.

If that means you got to get yourself out of a slump, make yourself better, you go on and do that first. I'm not some kinda therapist or shrink, ain't no doctor or playin' one on TV, nothing like that. I'm just a comedian and a father and a man that knows something about life, and I'm not afraid to tell it like it *T-I-Iz*. But there's a way to go about it, now. Me and my wife Rhonda, we're gonna make it easy for you to understand, easy to do.

Here's how we're gonna do it. We got twelve months chunked up into four parts to make it simple to follow, easy to understand, and even easier to implement. Here we go.

PART ONE: "All About You"

(January, February, March)

Fight your own fight, take responsibility for your life, and be the best *got-damn* version of yourself.

PART TWO: "Everybody Else"

(April, May, June)

You are part of this big community called "the world." Stop being selfish and see the big picture.

PART THREE: "Somebody to You"

(July, August, September)

Specific people come in your life and you have what we call a *relationship* with them. Thing about relationships is they take work sometimes. No, I got to keep it real. They take work all the time. You get out what you put in.

PART FOUR: "Plentitude"

(October, November, December)

You can have everything you want. It's there and God will give to you. You just got to make it happen.

At the beginning of each of these parts, my wife Rhonda is gonna break it down for ya'. Rhonda, she's good at that, you know? She's gonna tell you a story. She might tell y'all something embarrassing about me, but that's okay. I know who I am, and nothing's gonna make me blush up in here.

Now, you don't wanna go skipping that story. If you skip that story, it's like tryin' to figure out the Bible without the preacher or your mama, or your Big Mama, explaining what the hell them apostles was talking about:

> ***Matthew 18:19—Again I say unto you, that if two of you shall agree on earth as touching anything that they shall ask, it shall be done for them of my Father which is in heaven.***

What? Nobody knows what the hell that means except the preacher, and yo' mama, and yo' Big Mama. Maybe yo' granddaddy, 'cuz even if he doesn't know what it means, he's gon' make something up and you gon' believe him.

Anyway, read Rhonda's stories and you're gonna know what's *goings on*, that's all I'm saying to ya' now. You might also get to hear some funny shit about me that might make you laugh, might make you understand I'm not just up here spoutin' and *prophetilicizing* without walking the got-damn walk. You're welcome.

I got some good stuff on Rhonda too. But, you know, I'm not really in a position to tell it, if you know what I'm sayin'.

Now, go on and read from whatever date it says on your calendar, cell phone, computer screen, smartwatch, pibbity-pod, GPS.... *Whatever got-damn day it is, start on that date*. But read the introduction for that month first. Don't skip it. I'm tellin' you. Just read that introduction once through. You don't got to go and read it every damn time. Read it once for that month and then go on and just read your page a day. That's it.

Now, I know you thinkin' a *daily motivational* sounds like something Big Mama be reading out of that raggedy bible she got on her nightstand next to her wig and that glass of water with her false teeth up in it. Well...it *can* be that. *This one isn't.*

This is just a page a day of me tellin' you the shit you got to hear and nobody wants to tell you because you's raised in a world where y'all get a *got-damn* participation trophy when all you doin' is standing in the outfield pickin' your mothahfuckin' nose. Everybody tellin' you "that's great" and shit, when it ain't even good. I'm gonna be straight. I'm gonna tell you something you maybe don't want to hear, something good for you. Then you got something to think about for the day, something to do to make you a better person.

Everybody got enough attention span to read one got-damn *page a day*. If you do it, and you follow through, nobody can stand in your way ever again, not even your got-damn *self*. You about to change your life, get the kind of success I got in the same kinda way I got it. It works if you work it. Now, go on and do it.

PART ONE: ALL ABOUT YOU

*Fight your own fight, take responsibility for your life, and be the best **got-damn** version of yourself.*

Hey there, this is Rhonda. In each of my introductions to the four parts, I'm going to share the knowledge that I've acquired along the way and tell you a story about Bernard. That's what I always called him and always will—Bernard Jeffrey McCullough.

Bernard was never afraid to be exactly who he was. That's what gave him what he needed to succeed, because once you start questioning yourself and listening to all the naysayers instead of your inner voice, you won't ever get anywhere. Bernard knew it. Even when my daddy was tellin' him to get a real job, he knew it.

The other thing that happens when you are solid inside your own skin, is that you start taking full responsibility for yourself, your life, your circumstances. Why? Because when you have that perfect knowledge that you're exactly who you're supposed to be, you trust yourself and you trust God's plan, your plan, the Universe's plan, whatever you want to call it.

Then you start understanding something:

Nothing happens *to you*, everything happens *for you*.

Bernard was never one to be like, "Poor me," or, "I didn't get a fair shake," or, "It's so-and-so's fault," saying that's why he couldn't succeed. No. If something happened in life that knocked him down, or if someone treated him wrong, he learned from it and moved on.

Lessons, that's what life gives you. You can either choose to learn from them and grow or keep getting smacked in the head by them over and over again. But once you are able to take a good look at yourself, get solid on your own two feet, and take care of yourself and your business in the way you know best, you won't need to keep getting smacked. One time and you'll learn, and it will make you a better person.

Let me tell you a little story about a time that Bernard fell flat on his face, got knocked down real good as a comedian when he was just getting started...I gotta say, it wasn't pretty. In fact, I'm not sure I've ever seen him so down on himself.

This was back in 1980 or 1981. All our friends and neighbors knew Bernard was funny. He was always the one with the crowd around him at the barbeques, birthday parties, and church picnics. One of our friends was volunteering for some organization, and they were having a banquet and they wanted another comic to perform. He asked Bernard to come, said he'd get paid, and it would be at this place called the Condesa Del Mar. Of course, he said yes, he'd love to do it. We went home that night, and he was all excited because he was going to perform for money in front of a real audience.

Well, the week went by, and I started noticing something. He wasn't doing a dang thing to sharpen his skills. I asked him, "Are you gonna practice?"

He looked at me with that look he has, you know, and he said, "I don't need to practice."

I was like, "Practice on me, I'm right here!"

"Uh-uh," he said. "I don't need to practice."

I kept telling him to practice, and he kept telling me he didn't need to. Finally, I said, "Okay," and I dropped it.

Saturday night rolled around, and my mother and I went with Bernard. When we were walking in, he said, "I feel good." But once we were in the building, his face dropped. It was like, "Oh, no." He saw the crowd, and he said, "Wow, this is bigger than I thought." There were three hundred people, maybe more.

I looked at him, one eyebrow raised, and said, "You shoulda practiced."

He got himself together, and he said, "Naw, Imma be good."

He was going to be the second comedian on. We were sitting at one of those round tables with the nice white tablecloths, flowers in the middle, and silverware wrapped in cloth napkins. We were kind of near the back sipping our drinks, and the first comedian came up. You'll never guess who it was! ARSENIO HALL! Of course, nobody knew him just yet, but he had folks bent over in their seats laughing. He killed it.

Bernard looked over at me like, "Oh, my god." He stood up and made his way to the side of the stage. The audience was primed and ready to go. My mom and I were saying to each other, "I hope he does okay, because he sure didn't practice."

The announcer got up, took the mic, and introduced Bernard. "Here we have a treat for y'all! An up-and-coming new comedian, a very funny man,

Bernie Mac!" The crowd clapped and smiled. Everybody was having a good time except me and my mama. We were just waiting, holding our breath.

He stepped out onto the stage looking sharp with a big smile on his face and said, "Good evening, everybody." Then, he started telling his jokes.

Nobody laughed except me and my mother. Nobody else laughed at all. He kept telling his jokes and all those blank faces just stared back up at him. Finally, somebody shouted, "Get off the stage!" My mother and I were like, "Oh, lord," but no amount of prayer could help him, not anymore.

He came off the stage, walked up to me, and I just said, "Wow, that was tough for you."

He said, "I bombed real bad, didn't I?"

I looked at him and I knew I shouldn't have, but I said, "I told you to practice."

He bowed his head real low and said, "I know. Hmmm, wow, I did really bad." That's the last he said of it.

He didn't pick comedy back up again for a few years, but he didn't blame anybody but himself. He didn't come off that stage with a chip on his shoulder. He never said it was a bad crowd. He never blamed Arsenio for being so good. He never said he was tired, or the light was in his eyes, or the room was too hot, none of that. He knew that HE didn't practice. He knew that HE was responsible for everything that happened there that night. Maybe that's why he got so down on himself.

I think if he had to do it again, he would have picked himself back up quicker. But he still had a lot of lessons to learn. He was young then. Sometimes when you're young, your ego gets bruised easily.

When he did get back onto the stage, he used what he learned that night to make himself better. He'd practice on me, and I'd tell him if he wasn't funny. I had no problem with that. Better me than the crowd. It took a lot of work from that point to get where he was going, to make it as a comedian. But he was determined. He knew that's what he needed to be. It was who he was, and he made it.

Now, what do you think would have happened if he would have blamed everybody else for his failures? Think he would have become a better comedian? Think that would have made him funnier? Nope. But did he quit, throw in the towel, feel sorry for himself, and give up on his dreams? Not one bit. That's the point.

It's all about you.

January 1st

"I DON'T CARE IF YOU LIKE ME, I LIKE ME."

If you can look in the mirror and think, "I like you, mothahfuckah. You alright," then you gonna *be* alright. No sense in hating on yourself, getting all down and depressed wondering what the hell's wrong with you. No. Ain't nothin' wrong with you.

You got to like yourself, you got to love yourself, because you're the only one that's gonna be with you from the minute you're born until the minute you die. Better make sure you like who you're spending your life with.

The Bible says that everybody who lives has been born of God. You think God messed up? No. He did not, mothahfuckah. God's not up there makin' mistakes and shit. You better not go around sayin' God messin' shit up, and nobody else either, that's all I'm sayin'. Period.

> ***The minute you start caring about what other people think is the minute you stop being yourself.***
>
> —Meryl Streep

DO THIS TODAY: *Think about the last mothahfuckah made you feel like you weren't good enough, sexy enough, smart enough, funny enough, Black enough, White enough. You don't need to listen to a* **got-damn** *thing they say. In fact, whatever they say about you is none of your business. Remind yourself of that.*

January 2nd

"ONLY ONE YOU GOT TO BLAME IS YOUR OWN *GOT-DAMN* SELF."

This is about taking personal mothahfuckin' responsibility for your life, *got-dammit*. You can't go on and screw something up and then say, "Oh, that was Jimmy's deal, you know. He, uh, that mothahfuckah makin' us look bad and shit." No, man. No. It's your mothahfuckin' fault. And even if it was Jimmy's fault, if you in on it, it's your fault too.

But it's okay. Everybody screws shit up sometimes. We all human beings. So, yes, you got to blame yourself, but don't beat yourself up about it, either. Take the responsibility, then figure out what you need to do. It's not a self-pity kinda situation. It's an action item. Say to yourself, "Here's what I done, now how do I get back on track?" Boom. Do those things. Do something. Even if it ends up being the wrong thing, at least you're tryin' something instead of sitting around moaning about what so-and-so did to you.

> ***When you blame and criticize others, you are avoiding some truth about yourself.***
>
> —Deepak Chopra

DO THIS TODAY: *Ask yourself, "What did I do to fuck shit up recently?" Now, think real hard. Think about the last time somethin'* ***really*** *got fucked up. Figure out which part of that was on you. Own it. Say, "I did that shit." Figure out if there's anything you can learn from that experience or anything you can do to make it right, and then do it.*

January 3rd

"I THINK IF YOU GONNA REALLY BE WHAT YOU SAY YOU ARE, YOU GOTTA LIVE IT, WORK IT, PRACTICE IT, AND THINK IT."

You can't just talk the talk, you got to walk the walk. Can't go around tellin' people you a comedian when you can't even make Sister Bertha crack a smile at the church potluck.

I know this dude, used to tell folks all the time, "I'm the most humble mothahfuckah I know. I'm so humble, and I'm also the best." What? If you humble, you keep your mouth shut. That's the mothahfuckin' definition of humble. And if you the best, you don't need to say it. Everybody's gonna know it.

How do you get to be the best? You live it. Whatever that thing is, you practice it. You eat, drink, and breathe it. You learn from the folks better than you, 'cuz if you THINK you the best, you're wrong. There's always gonna be someone better than you. Knowing that is also the definition of humility.

> ***If your actions don't live up to your words, you have nothing to say.***
>
> —DaShanne Stokes

DO THIS TODAY: *Think about what you do. Maybe it's playin' guitar, shootin' hoops, or singin' in the choir at church. Maybe it's sellin' copiers. Whatever the thing is, find a way to learn somethin' new about it that's gonna make yourself better at it. How do you do that? Lemme tell you: watch a YouTube video, read a book or article about it, observe somebody who does it better, practice it, take a class on it, or listen to a podcast about it. There's lots of ways. Pick one and do it.*

January 4th

"WHEN I SAY SOMETHING, I MEAN IT."

A man's only as good as his word. Now, don't get all uppity on me, womenfolk. I was gonna say the same thing for you. A woman's only as good as her word too. The word don't *diffamentiate* between the sexes. Whether you're a man or a woman, a he, she, or they, if you say something, you better well mean it, *got-dammit*.

What happens when you say shit you don't mean? Ever hear the story of the boy who cried wolf? He cried wolf so folks would come, 'cuz he didn't wanna be all up in the meadow alone. Guess what? No wolf. He does it again and nothin'. Next time, when there *is* a wolf, folks get smart and they don't come. Kid gets gobbled up by the wolf.

I think this story is a bunch of bullshit. You can always find somebody new to believe your crap, and somebody's likely gonna come. Probably Big Mama, 'cuz she couldn't live with herself if you got caught up with the wolf, but then she gonna beat yo' ass all the way home with her slipper.

No. You do it 'cuz you gotta have integrity, or you won't be able to live with yourself. You go back on your word, nobody trusts you, then you feel like a lyin' mothahfuckah. You let yourself down. Why would you do a *got-damn* thing like that?

> ***Let your yea be yea; and your nay, nay.***
>
> —James 5:12, King James Bible

DO THIS TODAY: *Go the whole day without sayin' one thing that ain't 100 percent true. It's harder than you maybe think it is. Don't tell your girl she's looking sexy in that dress if it's looking like a muumuu on her. If you manage that for one day, then you can level up and think about a time you didn't keep your word on somethin', and then make it right.*

January 5th

"YOU GOTTA MEET ALL THE CHALLENGES, BIG AND SMALL, BECAUSE HOW YOU START IS HOW YOU FINISH."

You know what's a small challenge? When you go to Big Mama's and she been washing and scrubbing and cooking those dirty-ass chitlins all day, cookin' 'em up with some greens and cornbread, and you get yo' full ass up from the table when you done licked your fingers clean, and you wash up all the dishes so she can rest her bunions.

Small challenge, but how you meet that one is how you gonna meet them all. You build a pattern, if you see what I'm sayin' here, my friend. You are creating a pattern in your brain about how you're gonna do everything.

If you're sittin' in your chair, pretending to close your damn eyes and take a nap while Big Mama cleans up after she's been cookin' all day, that's how you're gonna do it when you go to work, when you get on the basketball court, when you raisin' your kids—you gonna let everybody else do the work, and you ain't gonna learn a got-damn thing in your life. You'll get no respect, 'cuz you wouldn't have earned any.

> ***No work is insignificant. All labor that uplifts humanity has dignity and importance and should be undertaken with painstaking excellence.***
>
> —Rev. Dr. Martin Luther King, Jr.

DO THIS TODAY: *Choose a small task, like washin' the dishes, mowin' the lawn, or foldin' the laundry. Do it like you gonna be paid one million dollahs if you do it better than anybody's done it in the history of everything. Do it efficiently, do it well, and do it with a smile on your face. You gonna feel joy, and you gonna feel proud of yourself.*

January 6th

"THE WORLD DON'T OWE YOU NOTHIN', MAN."

I'm so sick and *got-damn* tired of folks thinkin' that somebody owes them somethin'. Let me tell you something: your mama don't owe you nothin', your daddy don't owe you nothin', them rich folks don't owe you nothin', them White folks don't owe you nothin', yo' pastor don't owe you nothin', the Lord don't owe you nothin', your boss don't owe you nothin'.

You keep thinkin' everybody owes you somethin', you always be feelin' like you can't do it on your own, like you gotta walk around with your hand out all the damn time. How you gonna work hard at something if your hand's sticking out? How you gonna make yourself better?

I'm not sayin' you should never accept help at all. Sometimes we do all we can and we still need a little boost. But you want your friends, your family, your associates to help you out because they want to, because they believe in yo' mothahfuckin' ass, because they know you doin' right and workin' hard and you just hit a spot. *Not* because they feel sorry for your sad lazy ass, and not because you makin' them feel like they have to. This is about you takin' responsibility for yourself, right mothahfuckin' now.

> ***Nobody owes nobody nothin'. You owe yourself. Friends don't owe. They do because they wanna do.***
>
> —Rocky Balboa, *Rocky*

DO THIS TODAY: *Do something unexpected and kind for somebody. Pay the bill for that car behind you in the drive-thru. Surprise an elderly relative with their favorite dinner. Send a random thank-you card or email to somebody who's helped you in the past just showing your appreciation. Instead of thinkin' folks owe you, why not break the cycle and "pay it forward?"*

January 7th

"WHATEVER SUCCESS I'VE HAD, I ALWAYS LIKE TO TOP IT."

Always be working on yourself, trying to make yourself better tomorrow than you were yesterday. That's the key right there. Don't be lookin' at someone else and trying to be better than *them*. You ain't them. You're you. Try to do better than you, and feel it deep down, that's the one mothahfuckah you know you got to beat, 'cuz he's real good.

When I was at the top of my game, touring everywhere with my comedy, hitting all the late-night talk shows, I coulda stopped right there, got lazy, just soaked it up. But the problem if you're a sponge just soaking it up, is pretty soon you'll dry up. No, I had to keep doing more, so I started my own show and I done a few little movies. Maybe you seen 'em.

You got one chance. My granddaddy used to say, "Life is not a mothahfuckin' dress rehearsal." You don't get a re-do. You don't get to call out "line!" You don't get to reset to one and start over, and you're not performing the same damn story every single night. And it's a damn good thing, 'cuz that would get boring as hell. Keep uppin' your game. If you hittin' every free throw, move out to the three-point line.

> ***There is nothing noble in being superior to your fellow man; true nobility is being superior to your former self.***
>
> —Ernest Hemingway

DO THIS TODAY: *Ask yourself, "How can I up my game?" What's the next step? Take a few minutes to figure that out. Then, do somethin', anything. Send that email to your boss askin' to head an exciting new project. Enter yourself into that talent show. Tackle that French recipe they made on that White-lady cookin' show last night. Just get on your apron, clear the kitchen so nobody's trippin' you up, and do it.*

January 8th

"YOU GOT NOTHIN' TO LOSE BUT AN OPPORTUNITY."

How many times has somthin' come up, and you're like, "Naw, man. Pass." Maybe you turn it down because you think it's too hard, you can't do it. Or maybe it's gonna take you outside your comfort zone, shake up your routine. Could be something deeper...you're afraid of success, afraid to actually be better because that scares the fuck outta you.

What's gonna happen to your friends, your family, your girl, your boys, when they find out you doing somethin' different? How are they gonna feel when you make it doin' something you love to do? What's gonna happen to the old you? That's what you're thinkin', ain't it? Maybe not straight up, but that might be what's hidin' in the back of your brain. Well, here's my mothahfuckin' answer to that: Who gives a fuck? What you got to lose?

If they're your *friends*, if she's your *girl*, if that family's your true blood, you ain't gon' lose 'em. They're hoppin' up on that train you done jumped on and they're blowin' the *got-damn* whistle! And the old you, shoot, that's you, and he's gonna jump on with you no matter what, can't help that. But if you let that train pass, if you turn and walk away, you might never know where it woulda' taken you...coulda been exactly where you wanted to go.

> ***Within our dreams and aspirations we find our opportunities.***
>
> —Sugar Ray Leonard

DO THIS TODAY: *Make a list of your goals and dreams. Now, think of something you can do to help you get there, small or large. Did your girl say she knows a guy who works at a club, and you wanna stop messin' around and be a* professional *DJ? That's your goal. Ask your girl for the dude's number. BOOM! You took one step toward jumping on that train.*

January 9th

"KEEP YOUR NAILS CLEAN AND YOUR TEETH BRUSHED, 'CUZ YOU NEVER KNOW WHO'S LOOKIN'."

We all know that one mothahfuckah, he's got them raggedy fingernails with the dirt underneath. His teeth look like he just smeared some egg yolk up in there, got it in all the cracks. It's nasty, that's all it is. And then that crazy mothahfuckah thinkin' he's gonna be a famous rapper, get the girl, get a promotion? Mothahfuckah, please.

He puts on some cologne and some two-hundred-dollah sneakers when he's goin' up to the club, thinkin' he's real slick. But guess what? That fine girl in the tight dress he's got his eye on, she saw him when he's runnin' into the corner store the other day with his nasty teeth and his nasty fingernails and his dirty-ass T-shirt, and she already *formed* her opinion.

Maybe that's not just a good-lookin' girl, too. Maybe that's the CEO of a *got-damn* record label and you wanna be the next Dr. Dre. You don't know, mothahfuckah. Damn. Just clean yo'self up, look nice, feel good, be your best every time you step out the *got-damn* door, and you won't have regrets. Go to the nail salon, the barber, and the dentist almost as much as you go to church. I always did, and see how it worked out for me?

> ***You never get a second chance to make a first impression.***
>
> —Will Rogers

DO THIS TODAY: *You heard of Google, right? Well, sit down, look on your phone, and ask Google to locate the nearest barber shop or hair salon. Somebody who can untangle that rat's nest that's formin' on top of your raggedy head. Then go on and call 4 Star Nails up the street and make an appointment to file down those crusty-ass feet. DAMN! Get your nails trimmed too. Finally, brush and floss. Your smile's the first thing folks see.*

January 10th

"NOBODY CAN PREDICT THE *GOT-DAMN* FUTURE, REMEMBER THAT."

I been sayin' I'm gonna be a comedian since I was five years old. When I was little, everybody thought it was cute. I'd get up at church and make folks laugh. But then when I was a teenager, gettin' ready to be a grown man, everybody suddenly changed their mothahfuckin' tune. "You can't be a comedian, you won't make no money. You need a real job if you're gonna have a family. You're wastin' your time, Black." (That's what they used to call me back in the day, Black.) Since when did they become mothahfuckin' psychics, seeing in the future and shit?

Nobody can see the future but God. Don't forget that. Unless your cousin Laverne is God, she don't know what's gonna happen tonight when she get home from bingo, let alone what's gonna happen in your mothahfuckin' career. Don't let her get to you. You got to rise above that kind of negativity. You got to know with every ounce of your soul that you're followin' the right path, the one that's right for you, then nobody can tell you different. You got to keep chasing your dreams. Sounds better to have your head in the clouds than on the *got-damn* ground. Smells better too.

> ***If you can see the handwriting on the wall... you're on the toilet.***
>
> —Redd Foxx

DO THIS TODAY: *Think of a one-line response to use whenever somebody tries to shoot you down, tellin' you all the reasons why you gonna fail. Now, memorize it and use it.*

***Good Example*: "Thanks for your opinion, Grandad. I'll keep that in mind."**

***Bad Example*: "Shut the fuck up, man. Ain't nobody askin' you."**

January 11th

"YOU CAN'T CHANGE THE FUTURE BY WORRYIN' ABOUT IT. YOU JUST GOTTA KEEP MOVING."

Big Mama always told me that worry was a waste of time. You sittin' there, chewing your fingernail, shakin' your leg, doin' nothing but thinking about all the bad that *could* happen, if....

You gotta knock that the fuck off. It ain't helping one *got-damn* bit. All that time doing nothing but freakin' the hell out, you could be practicing, working, becoming better at whatever it is, or just becoming a better person. You know why you're anxious? Because you lack confidence. That's all.

How do you get confident? You know, and you know that you know. How do you know in the first place? You read, you listen, you learn, you practice... and no matter what, you keep moving. It's when you stop moving that the negative thoughts find you. Just plow forward and make mistakes if you have to. Do something, even if it's wrong. Sometimes wrong ends up being right. You'll hear more about that later.

> ***Worry is a prayer for something you don't want.***
>
> —Anonymous

DO THIS TODAY: *Take things step by step and inch by inch. Things is gonna happen in the right timin'. If you find yourself worryin' about the future, somethin' that hasn't even occurred yet, then wait a minute, take yourself to a sink, splash some cold water on your face, and then gently pat it dry. Do you feel a little better now? You feeling woke up now? Little bit of cold water will bring you right back to the present, that's for sure. Now that you're here, what can you change right now? Deal with that, 'cuz the future ain't happened yet.*

January 12th

"SOMETIMES WHEN YOU LOSE, YOU WIN. SOMETIMES WHEN YOU WIN, YOU LOSE."

You ever had that girl you really wanted to date? Oh boy, she's fine, good head on her shoulders, funny. You want to date her and you do the whole courtin' thing, then finally she says she'll go out with you! Oh, brothah. You got it MADE! Then all of a sudden, she's calling you all hours, tellin' you you got to wear this, talk like this, get a real job, stop hanging with your boys. You thought you won, but it turns out that, *hell no*, you lost.

Same goes for losing. Sometimes you don't get that thing you wanted. Leroy beat you out for that promotion, even though he always nappin' at lunch and cashing out early on a Friday. You don't think it's fair, right? But then he comes 'round a coupla weeks later and tells you how awful the job is, hates the boss, no air conditioning in the office. You dodged a bullet right there. See what I'm sayin'?

You got to trust that God's got a plan, and you got to lean in. No use gettin' angry when something doesn't go right. No use in celebrating too much when it does. Just be grateful, work hard, and keep moving forward.

> ***Everything negative—pressure, challenges—is all an opportunity for me to rise.***
>
> —Kobe Bryant

DO THIS TODAY: *Remember that everything happens for a reason. Sometimes you gotta take a step back for a step up. Think about a time when you felt like you completely failed. You were miserable, thinkin' you wanna give up, nothing's workin', might as well quit. You even cussed your own self out. You were one sad sack. Now, figure out one positive thing you can take away from that experience, somethin' you learned from it. That's your gift. Use it.*

January 13th

"I DON'T NEED TO PAT MYSELF ON THE BACK UNTIL MY ARM BREAKS. I DON'T NEED ANY OF THAT."

Tellin' yourself you done good when you done good, that's okay. Keeps your morale up. But telling it to yourself once is enough. "Bernie, you done good." Alright, move on now. You got more important shit to do. You keep sayin' it, talkin' about how mothahfuckin' amazin' you are, even to yourself, that's braggin', and all that does is make you look like a mothahfuckin' fool. It inflates your ego, and that's not good.

Only people that need to brag are the ones who don't do nothin'. All they got is talk, and talk ain't worth shit, but they're hangin' on to it like it means something. All I can do is shake my head. Thing is, if you're pattin' yourself up, you're convincing yourself that all you got is those mothahfuckin' words. It starts to work backwards on yo' ass. So, instead of runnin your mouth' about what you done, go *do* something else.

> ***Braggin' is when a person says something and can't do it. I do what I say.***
>
> —Muhammad Ali

DO THIS TODAY: *Refrain from braggin' on yourself. When you become a master at your craft, others will do the braggin' for you. Today, if you catch yourself braggin', stop and look at whoever you're talkin' to, and ask them something about themselves. "What's* goings on *with* you*, man? Lemme hear it." That keeps you humble and makes for better stories at the end of the day.*

January 14th

"ONLY WAY YOU CAN GET UPSET IS WHEN YOU EXPECTIN' SOMETHING."

When I was a little boy, I never saw my daddy. Then one day when I was about six years old, my mama told me my daddy's gonna come pick me up for a visit. I got all dressed up nice in my Sunday suit and I waited right there on the porch steps. He's comin' at eleven o'clock. Well, pretty soon it was eleven thirty, then two o'clock, then five o'clock. I sat there waiting and my daddy didn't come. Finally, seven o'clock come 'round and he pulls up in his car, said he's gon' take me for a ride but he just needed a little money for gas. I broke open my piggy bank and I gave him all my money, then my daddy made up some kinda lie and took off.

Boy, was I broken, disappointed as hell. I learned the hard way, don't expect nothin' of nobody. Don't ever expect a situation to turn out like you want it, or don't never expect somebody else to behave like you would behave. That's just settin' yourself up for disappointment. You just gotta do what you do, and see what happens. Hope for the best, but don't never count on it.

> ***Blessed is he who expects nothing, for he shall never be disappointed.***
>
> —Alexander Pope

DO THIS TODAY: *Don't focus so much on the outcome. Just do the very best you can, 'cuz that's really all you can do. Appreciate every step of the race, and if it's a relay, don't expect everyone to carry their weight. Maybe you win but maybe you don't, and that's okay. Everything's gonna fall into place, just like it's supposed to do!*

January 15th

"IF YOU A FRY COOK, BE THE BEST *GOT-DAMN* FRY COOK."

Let me tell you something. I was always a comedian, but I had a lot of what I like to call "survival jobs" until I started gettin' paid to make y'all laugh. I was a janitor, a furniture mover, an appliance delivery man, and I worked down at the steel yard. I coached community center basketball, drove a Wonder Bread truck, and I even spent a stint working as a cook at Doc's. Best *got-damn* fried fish you ever tasted. I made just over three dollahs an hour, and I was the best mothahfuckin' fry cook Doc's ever seen.

Why did I give a damn? 'Cuz it's about integrity. It's about being the best you can be, about how you act, because that shit translates over into everything else you doin'. If your ass bein' lazy on the fryer, you gon' be on that mothahfuckin' fryer the rest of your *got-damn* life. If you bein' lazy on the job, you gon' be lazy at school, lazy on the court, lazy in your relations... if you know what I'm sayin'. Plus, you ain't learnin' shit, ain't takin' a step up. You're better than that, mothahfuckah, and you know it, too.

> ***If you can't be a sun, be a star. For it isn't by size that you win or fail. Be the best of whatever you are.***
>
> —Rev. Dr. Martin Luther King, Jr.

DO THIS TODAY: *on Dr. King's birthday. Dr. King dedicated his life to justice. He led the charge so that you could have the same opportunities as other Americans and so that it would be possible for you to reach your own dreams. He worked hard, he sacrificed, now don't take that for granted. Instead, honor him by doing whatever tasks that lay before you today to the best of your ability.*

January 16th

"STOP GETTIN' SO DOWN ON YOURSELF. THINK BETTER, DO BETTER."

If you think you a failure, you a failure. If you think you a success, you gon' be successful. You got to have that right mindset, because whether you like it or not, you start to become whatever it is you're thinkin' about.

I knew since I was five years old that I was gon' be a comedian. I told my mama, "I'm gon' be a comedian, so maybe you never cry again." I just knew that's what I's gon' do, and I knew it was who I was. Ask me again when I was in middle school, same thing. "I'm gon' be a comedian." Ask me again in high school, "Comedian." I kept sayin' it. Even after folks knocked it out of me, I never let it go.

What if I'd been tellin' myself, "I ain't good enough to be a comedian"? Or what about, "I'm an amateur comedian, I'm just messin' around. It's a hobby"? Or maybe, "I'm a custodian, but I like to tell jokes." No, hell no. I'm a com-e-di-an. That's who I am, and it's what I do. Ain't no separating the two. I always knew I's gonna be a success, so failure wasn't even in my vocabulary. Lookit how it turned out for me. See what I'm sayin'? Think it, do it. Simple as that.

> ***As you think, so shall you become.***
>
> —Bruce Lee

DO THIS TODAY: *Start to visualize the outcome you want. If you can dream it, you can achieve it. You wanna get to the next rung in the corporate ladder and keep climbin'? Visualize what that looks like right there in your head. See it so clear it's like HDTV...new office with a window, nice paycheck so you can take your girl out to a fancy restaurant, new car. You're excited to go to work in the morning, puttin' on your tie in the mirror. Picture it in livin' color.*

January 17th

"THAT'S THE WHOLE KEY TO ANYTHING: DON'T BE AFRAID TO FAIL."

You know what some of the most successful people in the mothahfuckin' world have in common? They fail. Then they fail again, and again. Thing is, they don't get down on themselves for it. They get their ass back up and they try again a different way. My granddad used to say something funny. He say, "You don't fail if you don't try." Well, he mighta been onto something. Failure is a key to success.

How do you learn to hit the three if you don't miss a few times, adjust your throw, keep tryin'? Imagine if you missed a shot and walked off the mothahfuckin' court? "Naw, I'm done, boys. No good at ball." Hell NO! I shot hoops my whole life, and when I was a skinny little kid with no coordination, I never got picked for the teams. But the only way you get better is to miss a few and then miss a few more. It's okay. Keep playin'. I did, and sure enough, I got pretty damn good, grew a couple of feet too. Only thing that doesn't work is quittin'.

If I'd have quit comedy the first time I was booed off the stage, I'da probably been a custodian at the auto plant the rest of my life. Then I would have deprived all y'all of my spectacular jokes. Woulda been selfish.

> ***The moment you give up is the moment you let someone else win.***
>
> —Kobe Bryant

DO THIS TODAY: *Try on a new attitude. Think about one thing you tried and failed at, where you said, "Aw, fuck it," and just gave the fuck up. Maybe you had a business idea, or a little somethin' to help out your relationship, or even a small home renovation project. Now, go back and try again and finish what you started. It's the best* got-damn *feeling in the world.*

January 18th

"BAD DECISIONS MAKE GOOD STORIES."

Now, I'm not sayin' you should go out there into the world and make stupid choices. I'm not sayin' that. You still got to use your mothah-fuckin' brain, boy. I'm sayin' that sometimes you say, "Alright, I'll give that a shot," and maybe it doesn't go the way you thought it would go. But that's a story right there, and maybe you learn somethin'.

It's like the time I's riding in the back of a stretch limousine, had my boys for the night and we was doin' a little partyin', you know. Had my driver in the front, Dollah. That's what I called him, Dollah. He's the best *got-damn* driver I ever had. Anyway, it's maybe two, three o'clock in the mornin', and we just dropped off my last boy, and I'm sitting way in the back and I decide this is a good time to check the safety on my pistol. I always kept a pistol for my protection, you know? Well, the next thing I know, the gun goes off—BAM! My whole world freezes. I stare at Dollah in the driver seat, and he ain't movin'. "Dollah?" I say, my voice a little squeaky and shit. Finally, he answers, "Yeah, Mac?" I swear I let out a breath like I'd been holding it in my whole mothah-fuckin' life. Looked down, the hole in the floor is smokin'.

Bad decision. Good story. Turned out okay that time, could've been a hell of a lot worse, and I learned from that mistake. But you see what I'm sayin'?

> ***I'd rather regret the things I've done than regret the things I haven't done.***
>
> —Lucille Ball

DO THIS TODAY: *Get on your knees and thank God for savin' you from all the stupid-ass shit you've done in the past. It's just that plain and simple. Period! You've learned your lesson, now don't repeat that bullshit again.*

January 19th

"I'M NOT LIKE *ANOTHER* ANYBODY, I'M THE FIRST AND ONLY *ME*."

When I was in high school, I'd be at the parties or just riding on the L, makin' folks laugh. It's who I was, it's what I did. But I remember this mothahfuckah said to me, "Oh, you think you another Richard Pryor or something?" I said, "No, mothahfuckah. I'm the only Bernie Mac."

It's okay to learn from folks that done it before you. In fact, you *should* do that. I learned from Redd Foxx, Richard Pryor, Eddie Murphy, Sinbad, all the greats! But I never wanted to be like any one of 'em. It's called *inspiration*, not imitation. The harder part of that is that you got to figure out who you are. But you will, don't worry about that. Just tune out all those other voices and trust yourself, 'cuz the one mothahfuckah that knows you better than anybody else is the guy in the mothahfuckin' mirror. Listen to him. He knows how it *T-I-Iz*.

> ***Always be a first-rate version of yourself instead of a second-rate version of somebody else.***
>
> —Judy Garland

DO THIS TODAY: *What do you love to do? What are you daydreamin' about when you're supposed to be payin' attention to the teacher, your boss, your girl? I mean, somethin' you're so focused on that you can't even hear your dog whinin' at the door, and before you know it, you're steppin' in a puddle. You got that thing? Okay, good. Now, who's your mentor? Get a good image of that man or woman in your head. I want you to think about all the things you learned from them...got 'em? Good. Now, here's where it gets interestin'. Come up with at least five things, positive things, different about* **you**.

January 20th

"STOP TAKING EVERYTHING SO SERIOUS. BE THE BUTT OF YOUR OWN *GOT-DAMN* JOKES."

If I got angry every time somebody said something to me that cut me down, made fun of me, I'd be the angriest mothahfuckah on the planet. But I didn't have to fight nobody to take their power away, I just had to take the power back is all. How'd I do that? By taking their words for myself.

When I was a little kid, folks used to call me "Spookyjuice," or they'd call me "Black." I was the blackest little mothahfuckin' kid you know. If I come at you in the dark, all you made out was a couple of eyeballs and some teeth if I was smilin'. I'd come on stage as a comedian, and I'd start out by sayin' it, "I'm so Black, I leave fingerprints on coal." I owned it, made a joke, took away the power from anybody that was gonna use it to try and hurt me. Can't hurt me, 'cuz I already said it. And it ain't no fun going around feelin' *hurt* all the mothahfuckin' time. You got to stop that shit right there. Be a man and stop crying when someone call you a mothahfuckin' name or make some nasty remark on your Snipsnap or your Tokkitytalk, whatever that shit is. They're just words, boy. Shake 'em off and go run some laps or something. I'm not playin'.

> ***When you can laugh at yourself, no one can ever make a fool of you.***
>
> —Joan Rivers

DO THIS TODAY: *Make up one joke about yourself. Make it funny. What's funny about you? Lord, there's more than you think, and if you don't believe it, ask your brother, your sister, cousin, or Big Mama. They sure as hell know what's funny about you. Better you learn it from them. Now take it, own it, and make folks laugh with it. The best defense is a good offense.*

January 21st

"KNOW WHO YOU ARE, THEN DON'T LET NOBODY TELL YOU DIFFERENT."

I always knew who I was, and it didn't have nothin' to do with what I had or didn't have. I was poor growin' up, but it didn't make no difference to me. Sure, I wanted to give my daughter Je'Niece everything I didn't have, and eventually I did. But for a while, we scraped by, you know? Even way back then, before she even went to school, I was tellin' her, "You got to know who you are, and don't ever let nobody else dictate who you are." Because if you do that, you'll get confused, lost, and that's when bad shit starts to happen.

When Je'Niece was going into middle school, I was about to get famous. I ain't braggin', it's just the way it was. Done a couple of movies, makin' it bigger in comedy, my face was up on billboards and shit. I told her there's gon' be people who hate her for that, jealous folks, and she's gon' have to be solid in who she is. Sure enough, it happened. And boy, people started callin' her "Bernie Mac's daughter." She hated that. She'd be like, "I have a name! It's Je'Niece!" Boy, that killed me, but she was a strong kid. Smart too. Straight As and all that, worked hard. She was strong in who she was, so she did fine. If she hadn't a' been strong in who she was, she coulda' disappeared up in that, lettin' other people define her, you know? I'm proud of that. Today's my baby girl's birthday, and I'm proud of her.

> ***To be yourself in a world that is constantly trying to make you something else is the greatest accomplishment.***
>
> —Ralph Waldo Emerson

DO THIS TODAY: *Go wish my daughter a happy birthday. I'm serious. Then ask yourself this question, "Who the hell am I?" Define yourself right now and stick to it.*

January 22nd

"YOU GOTTA MAKE IT RIGHT WITH YOURSELF."

When I was young, we went to my granddad's church, the Burning Bush Baptist Church, where he was deacon. We'd go up in there and my Big Mama would tell me, "You got to make it right with God, Bernard. Whatever you done, you got to make it right with God." But the thing is, God's so forgivin' and all. I figure, 'fore you can make it right with God, you got to make it right with your damn self!

God can't hand you out peace of mind like he's handing out pieces of cake at Sister Bertie's retirement party. If you done something that's making you feel uneasy, something that's got you worked up, feelin' bad, you got to fix that shit. The sooner the better.

If you got to apologize for something, maybe you got to forgive somebody, tell the truth 'bout something, then mothahfuckin' do it. I promise you gon' feel better, gon' feel more at peace with yourself, and there ain't no better feelin' in the world than that.

> ***If you cannot find peace within yourself, you will never find it anywhere else.***
>
> —Marvin Gaye

DO THIS TODAY: *Forgive yourself. That's right, let go of past situations that you kinda screwed up. Don't pretend you don't have 'em, everybody does. Here's your chance to right those wrongs and fix them. Aren't you tired of living with that guilt? Do yourself a favor, forgive, let go, and move on so you can have some peace in your head. Trust me, you're gonna feel so good once you do this.*

January 23rd

"JUST MAC IT OUT!"

When I was on the set of *Ocean's Eleven*, I know Steven must have been real frustrated with me because I'd never say the mothahfuckin' line like it was s'pose to be. Always said it my way, you know? But it was funny. I had people laughin' all the got-damn *time*. I remember him finally throwin' his hands up and just sayin', "Alright, Mac it out!"

I had to smile, because there was a time when nobody wanted to hire me for the movies or even for comedy because they was like, "We can't understand what he sayin'," and shit. Now, we got bigwig Hollywood directors sayin', "Mac it out!" But that's what you gotta do. If you know a better way, if it feels right doin' it your way, stick to it. Don't let nobody tell you different. I'm not sayin' don't memorize the lines. Don't skip the part where you know what's expected of you. Doin' that would just be lazy. Nobody likes a lazy mothahfuckah. But if there's a way to make it better, to make it more authentic to who you are, then do it. That's what makes you stand out from the crowd, get noticed in a good kinda way. So don't be afraid to Mac it out once in a while.

> ***When you show up authentic, you create the space for others to do the same. Walk in your truth.***
>
> —Anonymous

DO THIS TODAY: *Pick up your phone, you know it's right there now, and take a selfie. Now look at that guy. Do you like who you see? You should, because that guy has a purpose to fulfill, no joke. Be bold, be assertive, but keep it real and authentic. No fakin' allowed. People see right through that bullshit. Flip Wilson, one of my own comedic mentors, used to say, "What you see is what you get!" So, you better be sure you like what you seein'.*

January 24th

"IT'S OKAY TO STRIVE FOR MORE. BUT AT THE SAME TIME, YOU GOTTA LEARN TO BE CONTENT WITH WHAT YOU ALREADY GOT."

When I was a kid, we was poor. You know you poor when you open up the fridge and all that's in there is some bologna. But you fry up that bologna til it's crisp around the edges, and you roll it up and you eat it slow, and it's so good. My granddad would make up some boiled eggs for a snack when we was hungry. He'd slice 'em in half and we'd each get a half, put some salt on it, and it'd fill our bellies, you know? I was poor, but I didn't know I was poor because I was happy with everything I had. I was fed, had clothes, had my family, and I was grateful.

When I was a kid at church I remember the preacher saying, "Do not covet thy neighbor's house, nor his wife, nor his manservant." Something like that. You know that don't just mean his house and shit, right? And it don't just mean your neighbor, neither. When you droolin' over somebody's fancy car, or their thousand-dollah suit, or their girl, or the way they look, well that's covetin'. When you comparin' yourself to what you see on the Snapchats or the Instagrams, that's covetin' and there's a mothahfuckin' reason it's in the Bible as a big no-no. See what I'm sayin'? If you lookin' at your neighbor's house, you ain't bein' content with your own accommodations. Yeah, you got to work hard to reach your goals, but be happy and mothahfuckin' grateful for what you got while you doin' it.

> ***Contentment is not the fulfillment of what you want, but the realization of how much you already have.***
>
> —Anonymous

DO THIS TODAY: *Go listen to the song "Be Thankful for What You Got" by William DeVaughn. As you listen, think of at least one thing someone else has that you feel like you want. Now, what do you have in its place? Can you be grateful for what you got?*

January 25th

"YOU AIN'T GONNA GET AHEAD BY FOLLOWIN' EVERYBODY ELSE."

If you're runnin' at the back of the pack all the time, how you ever gon' win? You can't. It's not physically possible. Back when I was in high school at Chicago Vocational, you kinda knew who was the leaders and who was the followers. The leaders were popular. Not in the sense that you might be thinkin' like "cool," but more like people liked 'em. They wanted to be like 'em, wanted to be around 'em. You know why? Because they knew who they were. They were solid, original, confident.

Now kids has got the social medias and everybody sees how many times somebody puts a heart or a thumb-up on their shit, photos, videos, whatnot. Everybody's doin' the same mothahfuckin' dance, wearin' the same clothes. Come on, now. Who do you think are the mothahfuckin' leaders? The one that made up the dance first. The one that wore the thing first. The one that came up with the idea. See what I'm sayin'? Use your head. Be creative. If I's tellin' the same jokes as Richard Pryor or Eddie Murphy, you think I'd have gotten where I did? Hell no! I learned from 'em, but I wasn't gonna try and copy 'em. That's what you gotta do, too.

> ***Use those brains that God put in your head.***
>
> —Moms Mabley

DO THIS TODAY: *Next time you go to the store, and you see a long line, don't even get in it. Instead, very calmly walk over to a closed register and ask a salesclerk if they can open up for you. Smile, make eye contact, be pleasant. I bet you ten dollars they open up...and pretty soon the rest of the folks will follow. Think outside the box and look what happens. BAM! You become a leader, and you're making other folks lives a little easier too.*

January 26th

"NO SENSE IN RUSHIN' EVERYTHING, THAT'S WHEN YOU START FUCKIN' IT UP."

You got a goal and you wanna get there. I know, I've been in your shoes. You're anxious. I get it. But the last thing you wanna do is try to hurry it up. You heard the saying, "Haste makes waste." That means a whole lot more than it looks. Let's say you decided to make it happen for yourself, and you made a call to somebody that could help do it for you...a mentor or a connection in the industry. What do you think is gonna happen if you callin' them every day askin' when it's gonna get done? When they gonna do it for you? That mothahfuckah's gonna snap and tell you to chill the fuck out. Then, you done just wasted that connection. See what I'm sayin'?

You got to trust that God has a plan for you, got to trust other people that they're doin' their job, and you got to take all the steps in between. You can't build a solid mothahfuckin' house on a crackety-ass foundation. Take your time, do it right, build good relationships with folks, and trust you're gonna get there 'cuz you ain't skippin' nothin'.

> ***A man who is master of patience is master of everything else.***
>
> —George Savile

DO THIS TODAY: *I know you're over there mumblin' and cussin' under your breath, thinkin' I don't hear yo' ass, when it takes a minute for your computer game to load. You can't stand it when you don't get a text back right away. You know that signal has to go to space and back, right? Develop some patience, please. Start by puttin' your phone, your laptop, your computer away for fifteen minutes, and occupy your mind with something constructive while you wait.*

January 27th

"IF YOU KNOW WHO YOU ARE AND YOU APPRECIATE WHAT YOU GOT, YOU AIN'T GONNA BE JEALOUS OF NOBODY."

Only folks that's jealous is the ones who want what somebody else got, or they wanna be like somebody else because they ain't comfortable in their own skin. But let me tell ya', jealousy is one ugly mothahfuckah. It will drive you crazy if you let it, push you to say and do ugly things...and God don't like ugly.

Here's the key to not being jealous: be grateful for what you got. That's all I'm sayin'. If you appreciate the family you got, the house you got, the ride you got, the body you got, the skills you got, you ain't never gonna be jealous of nothin'. Then, you can be really happy for the people who succeed, instead of wishin' you was them. You can pat them on the back, give 'em a genuine smile, and say, "I'm happy for you, brothah. I'm happy for you, sistah." And you know what? People gonna like you, you gonna feel good, build real relationships, and that's gonna come back around to you in a positive way.

> ***O, beware, my lord, of jealousy;***
> ***It is the green-eyed monster, which doth mock***
> ***The meat it feeds on.***
>
> —William Shakespeare, *Othello*

DO THIS TODAY: *Bein' jealous is human. I've felt it, I ain't gonna lie. But it don't do you any good. Jealousy can make you lose control, act like a straight up fool! Where does jealousy come from? Insecurity. The way you beat it is by makin' yourself secure. Focus on your strengths. What are you good at, what's good about you? Give me three things and focus on 'em today.*

January 28th

"THERE'S AN ORDER TO DOIN' THINGS RIGHT. YOU CAN'T JUST START IN THE MIDDLE."

You know when you get a brand-new piece of furniture, and you take it outta that box and there's that little white paper that tells you how to put that mothahfuckah together? You ever think, "Hmmm, let's start with step seven." No, mothahfuckah, you start with step one. You can't go putting in the screws when you ain't got the sides lined up with the front yet! How's that sonofabitch gon' stand up when you done? So, when we're talkin' about yourself and being a success, you got to start with step one: you. You got to know who you are first off. If you don't really know who you are, how do you really know what you want? You hear what I'm tellin' you? Once you know who you are, you know what you want, then you can start doin' shit to make it happen. That's when you're gonna get where you wanna go.

Can you imagine if you do it ass-backward, and you get everything you think you want, but then you realize that's not what you really want because you didn't know who you were before you started? How can you know what you want if you don't know who you are? Makes no mothahfuckin' sense. But it happens. That's how folks end up walkin' away from their school, their career, their marriage, throwing it all away because they realize they never wanted it in the first place. Don't do that shit. Follow the directions. Make somethin' that stands up.

> ***You have to be before you can do, and do before you can have.***
>
> —Zig Ziglar

DO THIS TODAY: *Think about babies. Do they come out of the womb runnin'? Of course not. There is a thing called* **divine order**. *They scoot, they crawl, they walk, and then they run. Life teaches us to build on each step. I told you the steps, now follow 'em. Remember, it's "YOU, DO, HAVE." Got it? Good.*

January 29th

"YOU CAN'T CONTROL EVERYTHING, JUST YOURSELF."

Only one that can control everything is God. So, unless you *God*, there's only one thing you can control and that's your own *got-damn* self. Thing is, folks like to think they in control. But that's just a fantasy world they livin' in. The real thing they can control is the one thing they think they can't. Let me break it down for ya'.

Your friend s'pose to come out and see you perform your comedy down at the club. That mothahfuckah doesn't show. You say that makes you feel bad, hurt, angry. Then you go out there feelin' some kinda way, and you blow your act. Now you blamin' the friend, get mad, maybe say you ain't friends no more. See, here's where you goin' wrong. You could never control your friend and if they come or not. Maybe they got in a car accident, you don't know. Then, the one thing you *can* control, how you *react* to it and how you *feelin'* about it, you don't! Yep, you heard me right. You can control your mothahfuckin' feelings. At the end of all of that, you didn't take no *got-damn* responsibility for your own mothahfuckin' actions, going on and blamin' your friend 'cuz you got booed off the mothahfuckin' stage. All you had to do is understand what you can control and what you can't, and then take responsibility. That's what it's about.

> ***I do know that I'm responsible not for what happens, but for what I make of it.***
>
> —Sidney Poitier

DO THIS TODAY: *You want to control your emotions so that your emotions don't control you. Sometimes that takes a little practice. Here's how you gonna do it. You gonna figure out what works best for you. Maybe you count to ten and take some breaths. Maybe you think about "Mad" being a little ticked-off man inside your head, and you gotta tell him to chill the hell out. Maybe you need to go for a walk. Whatever it is, figure out what works for you, then practice it. This way, you won't let little things upset you, take your power away, messin' with your happiness and your peace of mind. I'm tellin' you, nobody's got time for that shit, especially you.*

January 30th

"ONLY WAY TO FIGHT BACK IS TO GET BETTER."

When you an entertainer, you put yourself up there to get ridiculed, razzed, yelled at, booed, criticized. And Black folks, they don't give a *got-damn*, ain't gon' be polite and shit. They'll boo your ass right off the mothahfuckin' stage. I know Rhonda told you about the time I got booed off the stage at the banquet, time I went on after Arsenio Hall. Man, I took that hard, but I learned something. If I'd have got angry, yelled back at them, or if I'd have tried to *tell them* I was funny, that wouldn't have mothahfuckin' worked. I don't care how smooth you talk, you can't convince nobody that a pile of chicken shit is chicken salad. They can see it, they can smell it, they can stick their finger in it, and they could mothahfuckin' taste it if they wanted to.

Nope, the only way to fight back is to get better. Boy, I studied all the greats. I practiced on Rhonda, and I listened when she said, "No, that ain't funny." I worked my craft, and now all of them that booed me off the stage back then, they like, "Damn, that Bernie Mac funny." I know it takes work, takes humility, you gotta throw back your ego. But it's the only way you gon' win, you know what I'm sayin'?

> ***First, they ignore you, then they laugh at you, then they fight you, then you win.***
>
> —Nicholas Klein

DO THIS TODAY: *What's the fastest way to developing a better you? You're gonna give yourself a little pep talk. Some folks are calling this* **positive affernashuns**. *It doesn't matter what you call it, you're gonna do it every day, when you're in the shower, riding the L, cooking up some chicken...that's right, you're gonna say, "I am the best at what I do." You're gonna say, "I have what it takes. I am successful." Say it enough, and it starts to become real. I'm not telling you what I heard, I'm telling you what I know. Facts.*

January 31st

"SOMETIMES YOU GOTTA CHANGE YOUR MINDSET TO CHANGE YOUR OUTCOME."

You know the definition of insanity? When you do the same thing over and over again expectin' different results. Let me ask you something. Are you mothahfuckin' insane? I didn't think so. So, why you keepin' doing the same thing, acting the same way, thinking the same thoughts, just prayin' this time it's gonna work?

Let's say you been goin' to work the same way every day, and every day traffic so backed up on the Dan Ryan it looks like the lineup for Big Mama's fried chicken at the church picnic. Every day, you stuck in it and you late for work. Don't you think at some point, you gonna figure out a different route, or maybe leave twenty minutes earlier?

Don't get so stuck in your ways that you can't figure out a different, better route, one that will get you where you wanna go when you wanna get there. Maybe if you do that, you'll end up on time, get in good with the boss, get a raise...you hear what I'm tellin' you?

> ***A problem cannot be solved with the same level of consciousness that created it.***
>
> —Albert Einstein

DO THIS TODAY: *Sometimes, the best way to get out of a rut is to shake it up, find yourself a new routine. What are you needin' to upgrade? Is the first thing you pick up in the mornin' after you wipe the crust out of your eyes your phone, checking your social media? Maybe pick up this book instead, read a page, then drink a glass of water and take a stretch. Maybe to let go of the old you, you gotta stop usin' that same old stanky cologne from ten years ago, smellin' like my granddad's aftershave. You still wearin' nothin' but basketball jerseys and sweatpants?* ***Got-damn****. Change it up, change your style, change your mindset, change your life.*

Black History Month

February is the annual observance of Black History Month, so I want to define what this beloved month means to me as a Black man. Now, I'm not one to get political, but if you don't already know February is mothahfuckin' Black History Month, you the exact *got-damn* reason we need Black History Month. I want you to pay attention, now.

This twenty-eight-day month serves as a constant reminder of, and appreciation for, the ancestors that paved the way so that we could have opportunities that they never could. Without their hard work and sacrifice, I know I couldn't have even attempted to get where I got in my lifetime. We got to remember that and be grateful for it.

Black History Month also acknowledges and uplifts all forms of Blackness while transcending its people to a place where the hate can no longer feel permeable. It is an assertion of the strength of the African American people and an understanding of the trials and tribulations that were fought and overcome by those who came before us. Nowadays, we got different trials, but understanding that Black leaders accomplished what they did in the past helps us push forward with hope for a better future.

This month is a time for us to acknowledge the history and confront the problems of today with confidence and in solidarity with our brothers and sisters. It also celebrates the fact that we are more than our struggles. It's continuous recognition of the leaders of the past and present and helps encourage the Black youth of today to be excited about their lives. It's so important, that excitement, you don't even know. So, throughout the pages of the book this month, we're spotlighting events and leaders that may have been missed. We're grateful for the past and hopeful for the future, because even though we're doin' pretty good here in America and in this great big colorful world right now, we can always do better.

February 1st

"THE HARD WORK YOU PUT INTO SOMETHIN', NOBODY CAN EVER TAKE THAT AWAY FROM YOU."

I never once said to myself, "Damn, Bernie, wish you wouldn't have worked so hard on that." Workin' hard on something, no matter what it is, won't ever be something you regret. When you're working hard with your own two hands, your own brain, your own God-given talents, it makes you feel good about yourself. Even if you don't get as far as you wanted with it, the sweat and the effort you put into it, that's worth something on its own.

There was this time I was workin' as a furniture mover. I'd get up early before the sun came up, call in to the boss and see if there was work for me that day. I'd get on the bus and get myself to the job, move heavy cabinets and beds and shit all day, bustin' my ass, then I'd come home tired, hot, sweaty. But man, that shower never felt better. That dinner Rhonda or Big Mama cooked up never tasted so delicious, even if it was just sausage and beans. Then I'd sleep like a baby. How you think I'd have felt if I was sittin' my ass at home all day doin' nothin'? We s'posed to be workin' at something. Man was not designed to hold no couch down all mothahfuckin' day. Work hard, do good, feel good. That's it. Makes you appreciate what you got.

> ***Just don't give up trying to do what you really want to do. Where there is love and inspiration, I don't think you can go wrong.***
>
> —Ella Fitzgerald

DO THIS TODAY: *Think about the Bible quote, "To whom much is given, much is required." It means anything you* **receive** *comes with* **responsibility***. I'm not sayin' you should deny those gifts, but it's your responsibility to appreciate 'em. Take care of 'em and keep workin' hard so you can know what it feels like to accomplish something. What have you been given recently that you been takin' for granted? Figure out how many hours you'd have to work to buy it. I bet you'll appreciate it a little bit more.*

February 2nd

"YOU DON'T GET YOUR LIFE, YOU MAKE IT. IT'S A CHOICE."

A lot of folks are whinin' and cryin' sayin' they was handed a short lot. They maybe didn't come into this world with as much as somebody else. Maybe they don't have no mama, no pops. Maybe they don't have no money. I get it. I grew up in an apartment up over my granddad's Baptist church. My dad was out of the picture. My older brother kicked my ass on the daily. But I never felt down on myself, never blamed God, never got angry about any of that shit. 'Cuz there's one thing everybody's got the same, and that's *choices*.

Everything's a choice. Opening your eyes in the mornin' is a choice, which socks to wear, which job you gonna do, whether you gonna smile or scowl, who you gonna kiss goodnight. All choices, and every one of 'em leads to a consequence. What you do today will determine what you'll be able to do tomorrow. Remember that, and make better choices.

> ***This is the world you have made yourself, now you have to live in it.***
>
> —Nina Simone

DO THIS TODAY: *Stop reacting first and thinkin' about it later. That kinda shit will fuck up your marriage, your job, your future, everything. How do you slow down and make smarter choices? Practice. The very next thing you do is a choice, including where you put this book when you done readin' this page. Are you gonna leave it on the couch for someone else to move, or are you gonna place it on the table for tomorrow? Think about how each choice is gonna set off a chain reaction. Then, go ahead and decide what you gonna do.*

February 3rd

"LOSING IS NOT IN MY VOCABULARY."

I have played basketball ever since I was big enough to run. I always loved it, but I wasn't always so good. I spent a lot of time gettin' my ass kicked on the court. I had two left feet and two left hands until I was in junior high. But I kept at it, kept playing, kept losing, and kept smilin'. Even when I was losing, I loved the game. Nothin' was gonna put me off of it.

All the time I spent ballin', I seen a lot of other guys lose too. Some of 'em were sore losers, stompin' off the court, taking their ball and going home. Sometimes, they'd even start a fight over it. All I could do was shake my head. They didn't know what I did. Losin' is just a chance to learn something. Maybe you learn that you got to practice your pivot or work on your left-handed layup. Or, maybe you learn who you wanna play with and who you don't. That's a valuable lesson, too. There's always something to learn in every situation. Losing isn't really losing when you gain something from it.

> ***I never lose. I either win or learn.***
>
> —Nelson Mandela

DO THIS TODAY: *Whenever I lost out on something, I just knew it wasn't meant for me. I'm not gonna trip, because I know something better is coming. You gotta have that mindset. When I look back, so many of my losses turned into wins in the end. You got outbid on the house you wanted, but the next house you found had that den you wanted. Didn't get the job? Turns out the boss is a mothahfuckah. Remember. you don't lose, you grow. Now, think about something you lost. What did you gain, and what did you learn?*

February 4th

"YOU KEEP REACHIN' LOW, YOU'LL NEVER GET TO THE TOP."

What do you want out of your life? Maybe you say, "Oh, I just wanna be able to pay my bills," or you say, "I just wanna graduate." Just? Stop sayin' *just*. Take that word right outta your mouth. If you *just* want that low-hangin' fruit you ain't never gon' get the big, juicy peach up at the top.

Instead of setting your sights low, set 'em so high you gotta keep working your whole life to reach 'em. I feel like once you do everything you wanna do in your life, that's it, might as well exit. That's why you gotta set your sights so high you don't reach all of your goals for a long, long time. Maybe never. So, when you think you wanna say "just," say what you really want instead. Then that "just" becomes a step on the way to gettin' there. I always said, "I want to be a comedian." To get there, I gotta pay my bills. I'll get that job and work hard. Now that job isn't the "just" anymore, it's one rung on the ladder. Makes a difference how you think of it. Then if you do happen to reach your goal, you got to set a new one straight away. Comedian—got that. Okay, now—movie star. Check. Bestsellin' author...see what I'm sayin'?

> ***I set my star so high that I would constantly be in motion toward it.***
>
> —Sidney Poitier

DO THIS TODAY: *Raise the bar on your thinking and create some new goal for yourself that most folks could only dream of, some high-end Elon Musk, Jay-Z type of shit. Remember: big thoughts equal big accomplishments. The bigger, the better. If you already reached your goal, maybe that goal was too small. Get a new one, a bigger one. You think Will Smith is like, "I already done some movies, I'm good?" Hell, no. He's settin' a new* **got-damn** *goal. You can do it too.*

February 5th

"STOP SMACKTALKIN' YOURSELF. YOU GOTTA BE YOUR NUMBER ONE FAN."

How would you like to have somebody following you around all mothahfuckin' day, callin' you names, tellin' you that you can't do nothin' right, tellin' you to give up, sayin' you ain't smart enough or ain't handsome enough? My guess is after about an hour of that shit, you'd smack the hell outta that mothahfuckah. I know I would. But what if that mothahfuckah is YOU?

Listen to me. If you wouldn't tolerate someone slingin' insults at you day in, day out, why you gonna say that shit to yourself? You gotta cut that shit out right now. The one person who spends the most time with you is you, so you got to make sure that guy is cool. You gotta be your own biggest fan. Now, I'm not sayin' to overdo it. Don't start givin' yourself a big head. You gotta be your biggest fan, but you also got to take stock of yourself sometimes too. The best fans don't just hype you up for no reason. They gonna tell you if you fuckin' it up, but in a chill way. They gonna say, "Hey, man. You a little off tonight. But it's alright, you'll get it back next game! I know you will." They gonna say it like that because they know you got it, just slipped a little this time. That's how you got to talk to yourself inside of your head.

> ***If you have no confidence in self, you are twice defeated in the race of life.***
>
> —Marcus Garvey

DO THIS TODAY: *Start to create some storage space in your mind. I call it, Shut the Fuck Up Storage. Start filling this space with positive thoughts about you.* ***I feel great about who I am. I am capable of achievin' success. I believe in myself and my power. I deserve to be loved****. Now, whenever a negative self-thought pops into your brain, tell yourself to* ***shut the fuck up****, then take one of those positive thoughts out of storage. Do this enough and a change is gonna come.*

February 6th

"FIND SOMEBODY THAT'S BETTER THAN YOU, AND WATCH WHAT THEY DO."

I don't care who you are or who you think you are, no matter what you do, there's always somebody can do it better. I'm not sayin' that to put nobody down. I'm sayin' it to help you. If you can find those people doin' it better, being' successful at it, watch them carefully. That's how you gonna learn. That's what I did. I started out watchin' *The Andy Griffith Show*. That's some good stuff right there. Then there's Jackie Gleason, Redd Foxx, Richard Pryor, I watched 'em all. But I didn't just watch 'em, I studied 'em careful, you know. I learned what they did and how they made folks laugh.

Doesn't matter if you wanna be a CEO, a barber, a rapper, or a mothahfuckin' lifeguard, you find somebody that's great at that job and find out how they got there. What did they study? What habits do they have? How did they achieve their success? You don't gotta do everything exactly how they done it, but you should know how they done it. Then you can try it out. Maybe some of what they do works for you, maybe some doesn't. That's good. You don't want to *become* them, you just wanna get to where they are.

> ***The greatest education in the world is watching the masters at work.***
>
> —Michael Jackson

DO THIS TODAY: *Tiger Woods is one of the greatest golfers on the* **got-damn** *planet. I love golf, and I like to learn from the best, so I studied that mothahfuckah hard. I watched how he held his club, how he stood, his classic swing. That's how I beat him at his own* **got-damn** *game. No, I'm just fuckin' with you. But I do love golf and I respect Tiger Woods. Who's the master at whatever game you playin'? Learn one thing about how they got where they did.*

February 7th

"I DON'T CARE ABOUT HOW I LOOK. I'M DEDICATED TO THE LAUGHS."

I do care about how I look. I like my nails nice and trim and buffed. I like my teeth white and my shoes shined. That's about self-respect. That ain't what I'm talkin' about here. What I'm talkin' about is not doin' something because you don't want to look a fool. When I'm up on that stage, I know I look like one crazy mothahfuckah. But I get the audience laughing, forgetting about their problems for a minute, and that's all I need.

You ever been at the club and you get the music up in your bones, and you wanna let loose, but that little voice in your head says, "No, don't. You gonna make a fool of yourself. Sit yo' ass down"? You know what I'm talkin' about. Or maybe you stop yourself from asking out the girl you like, asking your boss for a raise, or learning how to mothahfuckin' crochet because you too afraid to embarrass yourself. Hell, no. Don't let that shit stop you from doin' the things you want to do. You gotta stop livin' in fear. Stop carin' what folks think. What do you got to lose? If they don't like your crazy-ass dancing, they don't have to watch. But chances are, you gonna make folks smile. Might even give someone the courage to get out on the dance floor and do it too.

> ***The soul that is within me no man can degrade.***
>
> —Frederick Douglass

DO THIS TODAY: *Try something outta the box, something that makes you a little bit uncomfortable. For instance, I've always wanted to do a flash mob dance to Michael Jackson's "Thriller." Don't laugh. I like to dance, and I'd do that shit and kill it too. Y'all couldn't tell me a* got-damn *thing. What have you always wanted to do, but you were afraid of how people would react? Make a plan to do it.*

February 8th

"YOU GONNA FAIL SOMETIMES, BUT DON'T BE A FAILURE."

Everybody's gonna fail sometimes. Hell, I've failed many times myself, and I ain't ashamed to admit it. You gotta fail if you ever wanna learn anything. But there's only one time I let myself feel like a failure. I worked a lot of different jobs when my baby girl was young, kinda had a string of bad luck. I knew I wanted to be a comedian, but I let everybody tell me I had to do *what's right*, get a real job, take care of my family. Of course, I wanted to take care of Je'Niece and Rhonda, so I was working them jobs. Worked at the steel yard, then at the auto plant as a custodian. I drove delivery vans and even worked for the UPS. Well, I got fired from one of them jobs because this crooked mothahfuckah stole some money and blamed it on me. I got into a slump, and I couldn't get myself out. No work, couldn't pay the rent, had Rhonda supporting us. Boy, did I feel low. I had to go and get food stamps, head hangin', lookin' at the floor.

But I got myself out of it, 'cuz I realized I let that feeling change me, let it affect my relationships, let it get up under my skin. I didn't like who I was, so I decided to change. I learned something valuable from that experience. I'd had some failures, but that didn't have to define who I was. When you win, that doesn't define who you are, either. You just are you who are, and that's it. All your wins and failures do is teach you somethin'.

> ***You will face many defeats in your life, but never let yourself be defeated.***
>
> —Maya Angelou

DO THIS TODAY: *Pick up where you left off. If you were sidelined by a failure, something just didn't turn out right, do something now to pick it up and keep it movin'. Raise your hand to your shoulder, dust yourself off, and try again. Ask yourself, "What's next?" and keep it movin'.*

February 9th

"IT ALL STARTS WITH LOVIN' YOURSELF."

I know this sounds a little hippity-dippity and shit, but there ain't no other way to say it. If you don't love yourself, you won't care enough to accomplish a *got-damn* thing. I know I talk about likin' myself, and that's important too. But "like" is different from "love." I *like* my barber, but I don't love him. I *like* the guy that owns the hot dog stand down the corner. Boy, he's funny. Makes me smile...but I don't *love* the man. I might have a beer with him, but I probably wouldn't give him my kidney. You see the difference?

Think about the people you love most in the world. Maybe it's your mama, your brother, your ride or die. Is there anything in the world you wouldn't do for them if they need it? Hell, I'd give my left eyeball if my little girl need it. Give the shirt off my back to Big Nigga. (That's what we always called him. Can't barely remember his real name, now.) If Rhonda be needin' somethin', I'd bust my ass to get it for her. Now, are you doin' that for your own got-damn *self* too? You got to treat yourself like you treat the people you love most in the world, then see how things start to change for you.

> ***You really have to love yourself to get anything done in this world.***
>
> —Lucille Ball

DO THIS TODAY: *You always doin' shit for other folks, so turn the page on that book and spoil yourself today. Get a massage. Invite your friends to your favorite restaurant but go Dutch when that* **got-damn** *bill comes, for real. Get some new kicks or try a new cologne. Maybe you just buy yourself some ice cream if that feels right. Or take some time to read a book for an hour or watch your favorite movie with a big bowl of popcorn. You get the picture. When you love yourself, it causes a chain reaction, and others will love you even more.*

February 10th

"TRY SOMETHING NEW. IF YOU DON'T LIKE IT, AT LEAST YOU'LL KNOW YOU DON'T LIKE IT."

I don't wanna hear none of this, "Ew, I'm not tryin' that. I don't know if I like it." Of course, you don't know if you like it, you ain't never had it before! How are you gonna expand your horizons, grow up, get better, if you keep doing the same *got-damn* thing every day for the rest of your life?

What if you never tried fried chicken? Never put your toes in the water at the community pool? Never watched a new movie when it came out at the theaters? What if you never ever talked to someone you didn't know before? You'd be hungry, bored, and lonely, that's what.

Besides, you might learn something about yourself. You put your toes in the water, might learn you're a really good swimmer. Then again, maybe you don't like it, and that's okay. You can check that one off and move on. Boy, if I never stepped on a stage 'cuz I's afraid I wouldn't like it, no tellin' where I'd be right now. I do know I never woulda realized my dreams, that's for sure. You can't let fear of the unknown stop you, 'cuz fear only exists in your own mind, and you can flip that switch right now if you want to.

Never say what you will never do or don't want to do because the very thing you dislike is most likely the thing you would become most successful in doing.

—J. J. Williams

DO THIS TODAY: *Take a leap of faith and try something out of the ordinary. Maybe you been wantin' to test drive that new Bentley. Nothing's stoppin' you. Go home and put on some fly threads, then take your ass right to that dealership, hold your head high. Push yourself to do it, even though you maybe can't afford it right now. The folks at the dealership don't know it, and maybe you find out you can afford more than you think. But you won't know it 'til you try.*

February 11th

"ALL YOU CAN DO IN LIFE IS DO YOUR BEST, AND YOUR BEST IS NOT ALWAYS 100 PERCENT."

If you were going at it 100 percent all the time, you'd be wiped out, knocked down, dragged out, tired. Of course, you wanna do everything to the best of your abilities, but sometimes you got other things *goings on*. You need to reserve a little bit of yourself for them. And sometimes when you got other things *goings on*, you still push yourself your hardest and maybe you don't get it perfect. You don't get an A+ on that test because you also spending time takin' care of your grandmama at home. You don't get the lawn mowed perfect with the criss-crosses and shit because you got to get it in before workin' your double shift. That's okay. If you're trying the hardest you can at the time, then you can be proud of yourself.

My daughter Je'Niece loved school and she's smart. I remember one day she come home with her head down sayin', "I failed, Daddy. I failed." Me and Rhonda, we's like, "Oh, no. You failed?" Didn't sound like her. "Yeah," she says. "I got a ninety-three." I start shaking my head. I told her if she worked her ass off for that ninety-three, that's better than a one hundred percent that come easy. As a matter of fact, I'd take a *hard C* over an *easy A* any day.

> ***Whatever the activity in which you engage, do it with all your ability, because there is no work, no planning, no learning, and no wisdom in the next world where you're going.***
>
> —Ecclesiastes 9:10

DO THIS TODAY: *Say this to yourself right now. The best is yet to come. How many times have you heard that before? You gotta open your mouth and speak it into existence, then believe what you just said. Everything ain't gonna be perfect all the time. Get that outta your head. But when you done your absolute best, you can be proud of yourself, 'cuz you went as high as you could go in that situation. That's better than perfect any day.*

February 12th

"FIGURE OUT WHAT'S RIGHT AND DO IT."

You always gotta do what's right. Big Mama taught me that. Mama, too. Granddad preached it. Problem is, maybe you don't always know what's right. You gotta figure that out first. Folks might say the right thing is subjective. I agree with that some of the time. For me, it's not about "right and wrong." That's too black-and-white, and life ain't no black-and-white. It's all kinda shades of gray in between. What's right is how it sits with your soul.

You make the wrong choice, do somethin' to hurt somebody else, that shit will sit in your gut like a batch of my auntie's cornbread. I *swear* she makin' that shit outta sawdust and *glue*. You know that feelin', though. It feels heavy on your gut, heavy on your mind, heavy on your soul. Problem is, you can't rise up if you got all of that weighing you down. Do what's right, and you gonna feel light. You gonna feel like you can fly! You know that feelin' too. Feels like buzzin', like your feet ain't touchin' the ground. That's how you wanna feel all the time. All you gotta do is do what's right.

> ***The time is always right to do what's right.***
>
> —Rev. Dr. Martin Luther King, Jr.

DO THIS TODAY: *Have you ever had that feelin' deep in your belly that tries to guide you in a certain direction? That's called a gut feeling, intuition, or your first mind, and it's tryin' to tell you God's plan, but you can only feel it when you quiet yourself down. That means shutting your laptop, putting your phone on silent, and turning off that old school Mary J. you got blastin' in the background. Turn it all off for a minute and put a situation in your mind. What is your gut tryin' to tell you?*

February 13th

"DO IT NOW, 'CUZ YOU DON'T KNOW WHAT'S GONNA HAPPEN LATER."

"I'll do it later." "Maybe tomorrow." "After I lose ten pounds, I will." C'mon now, I know you heard yourself say some of this shit, but all these are just mothahfuckin' excuses. What are you doing right now that's so important that you gotta wait until later?

You ever do this? You sittin' around in your raggedy-ass sweatpants because you got no other clean clothes. You sittin' there on the couch eating cereal watching TV, thinkin' you'll wash that laundry tomorrow. Then your phone rings. Yo' boys wanna go to the club, meet up with some girls. They wanna pick you up in twenty minutes. DAMN, you got nothing to wear! There you are, smellin' like Homeless Eddie. How you gonna go to the club like that? All you had to do was wash your mothahfuckin' clothes, but you gonna "do it later."

Pull your shit together. Stop wasting time, putting shit off, *procrasternatin'*. You're smarter than that. What you do right now will determine what you can do in the next minute, hour, day, rest of your mothahfuckin' life. Your mama didn't raise no fool. Start actin' like it.

> ***It always seems impossible until it's done.***
>
> —Nelson Mandela

DO THIS TODAY: *Beep, beep, beep! You hittin' the snooze on your alarm three, four, five times? Why can't you get your ass up outta bed? Oh, you were talkin' on the phone 'til three in the mornin' with your new girl? Stop puttin' off priorities. Today, you gonna figure out how much sleep you need. Eight hours is good. Count backwards from when you need to get up tomorrow, and set an alarm for your bedtime tonight. You need that sleep so you can get shit done in the morning. Take care of your business first!*

February 14th

"NEVER SKIP A CHANCE TO SHOW SOME LOVE."

Today is Valentine's Day. Some people say it's not a real holiday, not a religious holiday, so they don't celebrate. I'm tellin' you something right now. I ain't never met a girl that didn't feel some kinda way if you don't do nothing for her on Valentine's Day. She might say, "That's cool, don't mean nothing." She lyin' through her teeth. However you look at it, Valentine's Day is a reminder for us to show some love. We sometimes get so caught up in our routine, just keepin' our heads above water, that we forget to show the folks we love how much we appreciate 'em. It don't have to be expensive, no five-star restaurant or two dozen roses. Could just be a foot rub and some chocolates. Or maybe you do something nice, like take her car up to the car wash and make it sparkle.

Maybe you ain't got no significant other right now, and that's okay too. Do something nice for your mama or your Big Mama, your sister or brother, cousin, aunt, friend, the waitress that always smiles and gets your order just right. Tell 'em how much you appreciate 'em. Making them feel good will make you feel good too. I promise you that.

> ***Love recognizes no barriers. It jumps hurdles, leaps fences, penetrates walls to arrive at its destination full of hope.***
>
> —Maya Angelou

DO THIS TODAY: *Make a list of all the most important people in your life. I know this shit sounds corny, but go all out for them this year. If you're on the social medias, make a video tellin' them how much you love 'em, and say their names in it too. Then, post it and tag 'em. Like Spike Lee said, "Do the right thing." Spread the love today!*

February 15th

"THIS AIN'T JUST MILK AND COOKIES."

You think life is supposed to be easy? Shoot, I don't know where you got that idea from. Some folks might make it *look* easy, but that's 'cuz they got some shit figured out about how to do it. They lived a bit and learned it. Life ain't easy. It's *got-damn* hard sometimes, but it's worth it.

When you stop and think about all the shit you got to do just to keep going, just to be

somebody in this world, it's a lot of movin' mothahfuckin' parts! Damn, you got to pat yourself on the back just for keepin' all of your shit together. You got to get enough sleep, put the right food in your body, and don't fuck it up with drugs and alcohol. You gotta use your brain, exercise it just like you exercise your muscles. You gotta talk to folks, build relationships, and don't fuck them up, neither. Then on top of all of that, you gotta make money and pay your *got-damn* bills on time so you don't get your mothahfuckin' heat turned off. Brothah, I been there. Negative twenty degrees, no heat. I guess I must've let one of them parts slip, but I learned my lesson. Gotta keep all of them parts greased up and clackin' along. And I'm gonna tell you again, it ain't no milk and cookies. But man, when it's workin', whizzing along and everything runnin' smooth, it sure is sweet.

> ***Success is to be measured not so much by the position that one has reached in life as by the obstacles which he has overcome while trying to succeed.***
>
> —Booker T. Washington

DO THIS TODAY: *Take a deep breath. Now, relax. Take another deep breath and exhale slowly, like you doin' some kinda cigar-smoke trick. That's right. Ahhh, doesn't that feel good to slow down some? Just breathe. Repeat when needed. It's free and you can take it with you anywhere, maybe keep you calm when you startin' to get worked up.*

February 16th

"YOU WANT SOMETHING, ASK FOR IT. WHAT HAVE YOU GOT TO LOSE?"

Don't ever be afraid to ask for what you want. Shoot, you want some milk and cookies? You ain't gonna get some if you don't ask. Might not get some if you do, neither. But that's okay, at least you tried. You had a fifty-fifty shot of walkin' out of that kitchen with a tall glass of ice-cold milk and a plate of chocolate chip cookies. What's your chances of gettin' some if you never ask? Zero. I'll take fifty-fifty over zero any day. Now, I'm not sayin' you should go around with your hand out. That's annoying as a mothahfuckah, and a good way to lose friends. Hell, family won't even answer your calls no more if you doin' that shit. I got a cousin, every time he come by, we shut the shades and turn off the lights, nobody movin', nobody breathin' til we hear his janky-ass car drive off the curb. You don't wanna be that guy. That's not what I'm talkin' about. I'm talkin' about asking for a raise when you deserve it, asking for a chance to go on stage, asking for somebody to believe in you, asking for help when you done all you can do.

Sometimes asking might be just askin' God. When you close your eyes, or you put your palms up to the sky, or you kneel down in the church pew, you ask God to deliver you that opportunity you lookin' for. You heard the phrase, "Ask and thou shalt receive"? That's what I mean. Then you open your eyes and watch for the signs, work hard, and see it happen for you.

Ask, and it will be given to you; seek, and you will find; knock, and it will be opened to you.

—Matthew 7:7

DO THIS TODAY: *Babies will make you understand what they want in every way they can. They'll have you on your hands 'n' knees, crawling up under the couch lookin' for the pacifier. I'm not sayin' throw no baby tantrum, but if you want something, be like that baby and ask for it. What do you want that you can ask for right now?*

February 17th

"ALWAYS BE THINKIN' AHEAD."

My granddad was quick. Boy, I'd step into the room, he'd take one look at me and make his eyes all squinty, point his finger, and he'd say, "Don't you dare. You gonna to get your ass whooped, son." He knew it when I was up to no good, 'bout to swipe the sugar cubes Big Mama bought for her coffee or gonna sneak the comic books into bed. He knew. My granddad was always one step ahead, never missed a beat. That's how you gotta be to make it, always thinkin' ahead.

When you act on your *got-damn* impulses, thinkin' just about right now in this minute, it's a good way to go fuckin' shit up. We all done it. I'm not comin' down on you. But I've learned my lesson. We've all cashed in a paycheck straight away before we even went home. Feels good to have that money in your pocket. You thinkin', "Damn, that new stereo is on sale." Walk in, drop the cash on the counter, feelin' like a king. You walk out and you grinnin' like a *got-damn* fool. Remember that feeling, 'cuz it's only gonna last until you get to your front door. Your wife's gonna shake her head, make you turn around and take it back. But it's on sale, so you can't. Final sale and shit. Next week rolls around and you can't pay your mothahfuckin' rent. Use your brains. Every choice you make sets off a chain reaction. Think ahead, one step, two steps, maybe even more if you can. That way, you gonna end up with better results.

> ***A wise man thinks ahead; a fool doesn't and even brags about it!***
>
> —Proverbs 13:16

DO THIS TODAY: *Always have a plan B. Plan C can't hurt, either. You need to stay focused on plan A, but no matter what situation you're in, sometimes things just get fucked up! So, stay ahead of the game. It's better to be prepared for a change and not need it, than to be unprepared when a change hits. What's your plan B?*

February 18th

"YOU GOTTA GO THROUGH IT TO GET TO IT."

Nothin' in life is free. You ever hear anybody sayin' that? Well, that ain't exactly true. You sometimes gettin' a free side of fries with your fried chicken, free perfume samples in the mail, a nickel's worth of free advice. But I'm gonna tell you something right now. If you just go through life takin' what's free, all you gonna have is what everybody else wants to give you. How you ever gonna get to where YOU wanna go that way?

Takin' the easy route will probably not take you to the top of the moth-ahfuckin' mountain. Take the easy job 'cuz your cousin needs help up at his corner store. Keep the girlfriend because she into you, but she's crazy and you don't really love her. Take the room at your grandmama's house because you don't gotta pay no rent. Once in a while, to help you get through a spot, it's okay to take what's offered. That's a gift. But you gonna do that the rest of your *got-damn* life? Hell, no. Might be hard if you move out and get your own place. Might be lonely a bit if you set that girl loose so you can find the right one. But that's the kinda shit you got to go through to get what you *really* want.

Don't be afraid to go through it. If I can do it, you can do it too. You just gotta know what you want and go after it, even if it's hard. That struggle ain't gonna last forever.

> ***Smooth seas do not make skillful sailors.***
>
> —African Proverb

DO THIS TODAY: *Be honest with yourself. Take your eye off of what someone else might have. That's their blessing and, truthfully, you don't know what the hell they went through to get it! What do you need to do to get what you want? Are you ready for the challenge?*

February 19th

"DON'T EVER BE ASHAMED OF WHERE YOU ARE ON YOUR PATH."

When I was a kid, we was poor. Didn't have no new clothes, wore hand-me-downs and shit. Didn't have no board games, video games, no color TV. We played kick the can out in the street, chased dogs, made up our own *got-damn* games. But I didn't know no different. I was always proud of who I was, didn't matter where I lived or what I didn't have that maybe other kids did. I musta' known from a young age that where I was at the time wasn't where I was gonna end. It was just one step toward gettin' there.

The key to not bein' ashamed is to have gratitude. If you appreciate what you got, that's what's gonna shake that feelin' that you ain't good enough. Maybe you wanna own a restaurant, but right now you bussin' tables. Shit, that's okay. Say it proud, 'cuz you know you the best *got-damn* busser in the city. And while you pickin' up dirty plates, you be watchin', learnin', studyin', and makin' connections. Better to say, "I'm a busser," with pride than to lie and say you somethin' you're not. People find that shit out fast. If you do whatever you do with all of your effort, people find that out real quick too, and you might get the break you need. It don't matter if you a busser or a CEO. It don't matter if you live in the projects or in a mothahfuckin' mansion. People will respect you if you're honest, if you take pride, and you work hard.

> ***It isn't where you come from; it's where you're going that counts.***
>
> —Ella Fitzgerald

DO THIS TODAY: *What's one thing you been ashamed of in the past? Think about what you gained from it. Maybe it taught you a valuable lesson, it served a purpose, or it was the result of hard work. Is there some way to be grateful for it?*

February 20th

"STOP LOOKIN' AND START DOIN'."

Everybody's talkin' about lookin' for happiness, lookin' for love, lookin' for success. Where the hell you lookin'? Not like it's hidin' and you gotta find it. You don't *find* happiness, you *create* it. I know, that puts it back on you. Makes you take responsibility for your own *got-damn* life, makes you have to get up off your ass and do something. But once you understand that it's not about searching, it's about buildin', you can get right to work.

I had this friend, Louis. Now, Louis was always lookin' for a girl. He was one lonely mothahfuckah. He'd go out to the club lookin', go to church lookin', go to the mothahfuckin' grocery store lookin'. He thought if he found the right girl, he'd be happy. Well, 'course he'd never find a girl, 'cuz soon as he'd look, they'd be lookin' away. Why? 'Cuz that mothahfuckah reeked of desperation, drippin' off him like sweat. I told him to pull his shit together. Start getting some exercise, get a haircut, clean yourself up. Work hard at your job. Take care of your business. That shit will give you confidence, then you won't have to go lookin'. You'll be happy just with yourself. Sure enough, coupla years later, I run into Louis and he's a manager at a sportin' goods store and he's engaged to be married. He listened. He done the work, focused on makin' himself better, and pretty soon, there she was, lookin' for a pair of boxing gloves and instead she found Louis, and he looked like a catch. See what I mean? All you gotta do is put in the work, and everything around you will start to fall into place.

> ***A productive and happy life is not something you find; it is something you make.***
>
> —Rev. Dr. Martin Luther King, *Jr.*

DO THIS TODAY: *Pay close attention to the person you are right now. It's time to stop lookin' for somebody or something to help you live a happy and productive life. You're changing that shit today. Now, think about something you want. What work do you need to do to become the kind of person who has that in their life?*

February 21st

"IF YOU DON'T LIKE SOMETHING, WAIT A MINUTE. IT'LL CHANGE."

A lot of young folks think whatever they're goin' through is gonna last forever. Nothin' could be further from the truth. Everything changes. It's the only mothahfuckin' thing you can count on. That can be good, and it can be bad too. If things are good, you got a good job and your relationships is good, you got to appreciate that while you have it 'cuz something could happen to change it up real quick. I lost more jobs than I can count. Lost a lot of folks dear to me too. I'd be startin' the day with a skip in my step and end it with my head down. Boy, it hit me real quick that anything can happen at any time, and there's not a *got-damn* thing you can do about it.

But the flip side of that is that change don't discriminate. When something's bad, you think it's the end of the mothahfuckin' world. Then you remember that it ain't gonna last. Even better, how long it lasts depends on *you*. It all depends on your attitude and your actions. I remember I was in a real slump, then outta the blue my cousin called me up and said they's an opening for a driver up at the UPS! I took it with a smile on my face, happy for that change.

Change is good. It keeps you on our toes, keeps you learnin' your lessons, gives you hope when you feelin' down. But if you feelin' stuck in that dark spot, remember that once you take personal responsibility, you can make the change happen that's right for you. See what I'm sayin'? Control what you can, accept what you can't. It's God's plan, not yours. Trust it.

> ***This too shall pass.***
>
> —Persian Adage

DO THIS TODAY: *Make a list of what you can control and what you can't. Keep it somewhere you can see it and check it often.*

February 22nd

"KNOW WHAT YOU WANT AND INSIST ON IT."

I knew I wanted to be a comedian ever since I was five years old. Now, I'm not sayin' you need to know what you want to do for a career when you're in kindergarten. Lots of young folks strugglin' with that, feelin' like they a little bit lost, not sure what they're passionate about quite yet. It's okay. You'll figure that out just by livin' your life and trying lots of different things, not being afraid to try something new. You never know, you might figure out you're good at chemistry or you love workin' with animals, or maybe you love fixin' up cars. That's cool.

Whenever you do figure it out, don't ever accept anything less. That's called "settling," and once you settle, it's hard to get back up again. Kinda like granddad after Sunday dinner. He settles down into that old ratty-ass reclining chair, got the television on, maybe watching a game. Ain't no way he's getting up. He's done for the *got-damn* day. See what I'm sayin'? When you have that vision for yourself, what you want to do with your life and how you want to live it, work hard to get there. Don't ever get comfortable with a life you don't want. That's a good way to find yourself stuck, depressed, and angry at the whole mothahfuckin' world.

Have a vision. Be demanding.

—Colin Powell

DO THIS TODAY: *Where there is no vision, the people perish (Proverbs 29:18). You see, God is tellin' you to stop being content with what life throws at you. You got to get up off your ass and create a vision for yourself. What's your vision? Focus on it today. Focus on it every day, and that tiny thought, that tiny vision that started in your head, will eventually become a reality.*

February 23rd

"ALWAYS BE UPPIN' YOUR GAME."

I remember when I was a little kid, if I did somethin' wrong, screwin' up or screwin' around, my mama would tell me, "Bean...." That's what she used to call me, Bean. "Bean," she'd say, "you know better." And she was right. I usually did. But I went on and did it anyway. That's when I'd find myself in a world of hurt. Because you can't blame someone for doin' wrong if they don't know any better. That's how we learn, by makin' those mistakes. My mama would never punish me for that. But Lord, if I knew better and did it anyway, I'd be shakin' in my shoes 'til my Grandpa Thurman got home.

Thing is, once I knew better, I could do better. That carries through your whole *got-damn* life, not just when you're a kid. Every single mothahfuckin' thing you do is a chance to learn somethin'. So, you got an *infinitude* of opportunities to keep uppin' your game. I'm not talkin' just in your job, not just in makin' money or shit like that, I'm talkin' about bein' a better mothahfuckin' human being. Talkin' about bein' better to yourself and others, bein' a better you. No matter how good you get, you can always be better.

> ***Do the best you can until you know better. Then when you know better, do better.***
>
> —Maya Angelou

DO THIS TODAY: *When you think about steppin' up, you gotta do it like Junior's singin' in his song, "Mama Used to Say." Stop what you're doing right now and go listen to it, especially that part where Mama says to take your time. It's sayin' do it, but don't rush it and do it halfway. What's one small thing you can do better today to up your game?*

February 24th

"WHEN ONE HOUSE IS ON FIRE, YOU DON'T HOSE DOWN THE WHOLE *GOT-DAMN* BLOCK."

A big problem I see with folks today is they tryin' to do it all at once. They tryin' to get fit and work out. They tryin' to switch up their diet and eat nothin' but kale and shit. They tryin' to work on their relationship. They tryin' to get better grades. They tryin' to work on their career. They tryin' to be a better brother, son, friend, uncle...they tryin' to do it all at once, and sometimes that can make your head spin, make everything go out of focus. It's kinda like hosing down the whole block when only one house is on fire. That shit can be overwhelming, and it's unnecessary, you hear what I'm sayin'?

Sometimes, you gotta work on the one big thing that's blockin' you from risin' up. You got to do that first. Maybe your health is a *got-damn* mess. Maybe your head ain't straight. Maybe you come home fightin' with your girl every day. Maybe you can't pay your bills. Any one of them things could be the thing that's blockin' you from really being able to get where you're going. Roadblocks is what they are, and you got to move 'em if you wanna drive down the road. So, when you're feeling a little fuzzy, things is gettin' kinda blurry, and you don't know which way to turn, you got to try to pick that one thing that seems to be trippin' you up the most, and just focus on that thing until it's all cleared up. You might be surprised to see the other things kinda fallin' into place along with it.

> ***When life gets blurry, adjust your focus.***
>
> —Anonymous

DO THIS TODAY: *What setback are you finding yourself in right now? Look carefully at the situation. What's the roadblock and how can you go around it or get through it successfully?*

February 25th

"I AIN'T GONNA TELL YOU NOT TO BE SCARED. JUST DON'T LET IT STOP YOU."

Fear is a natural mothahfuckin' thing. When you feel your heart racin', feel your stomach drop and your legs go weak, that's tellin' you that you better get yo' ass outta there! Fear told cavemen to run from the saber-tooth tiger or to back the fuck up away from that cliff. Now, that feelin' tells you to steer clear of the dark alley or to drive the *got-damn* speed limit on a twisty mothahfuckin' road. Fear is a good thing. But you got to know when to back the fuck up, slow the fuck down, and when to push through it.

You see, that fear response, it don't know the difference between the saber-tooth tiger and your fear of being embarrassed in front of folks. Fear is nothin' but a chemical reaction in your brain. You gotta go on and feel it, and then think to yourself, "Is anybody gonna die from this?" If the answer is, "No," then go on and do it! Do you know how many times I was nervous early in my career? Backstage, I'd be sweating, stomach hurtin'. The anticipation is what got me the most. But man, once I walked on stage, I was in my element, laughin' at my own *got-damn* self. Had the audience laughin', too, and I forgot I was ever afraid at all. When you start facing your fear and walkin' through it, pretty soon, you won't be afraid no more. That's called confidence. The more fear you overcome, the more confident you become. Remember that!

> ***I learned that courage was not the absence of fear, but the triumph over it. The brave man is not he who does not feel afraid, but he who conquers that fear.***
>
> —Nelson Mandela

DO THIS TODAY: *Do it afraid! What's one thing that you were scared to do, maybe even when you were a little kid, that you did anyway? How did you feel about it right before you did it? How do you feel about it now?*

February 26th

"AIN'T JUST ONE WAY FROM POINT A TO POINT B."

You're startin' out on a trip and you got the route planned out and it's gonna take you so many hours to get there. You got your bags packed, some cold chicken for the drive, and you ready. You get in the car and it's goin' alright, got some music on the radio, and then, "What the hell is this?" Traffic stopped. Construction. Accident. Far as I can see, you got three choices: wait, go back, or find another *got-damn* way to get there. You wait, you could be stuck there for hours. Do that if you want a good exercise in patience. Go back? Well, that depends on how bad you wanna go where you goin'. If you really don't care, maybe you go back.

But if you really want to go, you excited to get there, you get off at the first exit, get out your map (if you're old school like me) or click "alternate route" on your GPS, and you take a different mothahfuckin' way. Look at all them streets, all them highways, all of them back alleys and country roads. You could probably find a hundred different ways to get where you wanna go. Might take a little bit longer, sure. But you might also see some stuff you wouldn't have seen if you stayed on Route 20, stuck behind the pickup truck with the bumper sticker that says, "The closer you get, the slower I go." *Got-damn*, don't nobody take pride in themselves no more?

What I'm tryin' to say is, it don't matter if it's a career goal or a trip to see your cousin, learnin' to swim or becomin' a mothahfuckin' astronaut, if you wanna get there bad enough, you'll figure out a way.

> ***I have discovered in life that there are ways of getting almost anywhere you want to go, if you really want to go.***
>
> —Langston Hughes

DO THIS TODAY: *We have options in everything we do. What's one thing you wanted to do that got roadblocked? Now, list at least three different ways to try to tackle it again.*

February 27th

"YOU CAN'T MOVE FORWARD IF YOU'RE ALWAYS LOOKIN' BACK."

You ever try to walk down the sidewalk with your head turned around lookin' behind you? Pretty soon you gonna crash right into something. You can't walk straight lookin' back, it throws off your balance, you know what I'm sayin'? Plus, can't mothahfuckin' see unless you got eyes in the back of your head. Which, unless you're my grandmama, I don't think that you do.

Listen, I'm not sayin' you can't be proud of what you done. You should be, but *got-dammit*, don't stay there...and definitely don't keep reliving it because you think them was your glory days, thinkin' that's the best you ever gonna get. That's a bunch of bullshit. Man, if I'd have been workin' at the auto plant or bustin' my ass movin' furniture and all I did was keep on thinkin' about how I was the mothahfuckin' *king* of Chicago Vocational, class of 1975, you think I'd ever have become a King of Comedy? Hell no. I'd have been sitting on my ass, drinkin' beers with the fellas, talkin' about how great life used to be.

Shit, you can do better than that. You can do better than you ever thought you could if you just keep your eyes on the road in front of you, quit checking the rearview mirror, and press on the *got-damn* gas pedal.

> ***I don't live in the past. I don't play my records for that reason. I make a statement, then move on to the next.***
>
> —Prince

DO THIS TODAY: *Get on YouTube and find the song "Wake Up Everybody" by the legendary soul group Harold Melvin & the Bluenotes. Or ask Alexa, she maybe knows it too. Listen to it right now, I'll wait.... You know how they talk about not thinkin' backwards and it's time for you to think ahead? I feel ya' singin' it in your head right now. Keep doin' that and think about those lyrics as you go about your day today.*

February 28th

"YOU CAN'T FORCE ANYBODY OR ANYTHING TO CHANGE, EXCEPT YOURSELF."

I know what it's like to wish somebody would change, would do better, or to wish that some kinda circumstance would change. But here's what I found out: all the tryin' in the world can't change somebody if they don't wanna change. So, the best thing to do is just work on yourself.

Here's one example that lots of folks go through. You got someone you love, maybe your mama, someone like that. You know they're not healthy, not eating right and not gettin' enough exercise. You're worried about their health. Diabetes runnin' in the family. So, you talk to 'em, tell 'em you're concerned. Maybe you give 'em a healthy cookbook. Maybe you sign 'em up for a gym membership. Fool, you know they ain't gonna use that shit! Now, you gonna start a *got-damn* fight. Nobody likes to be told what to do, especially when they don't wanna do it. Best thing you can do for them is change yourself.

Don't eat the fried chicken and mashed potatoes when you tellin' them to eat the salad. Don't take the car two blocks to the corner store when you got two legs and you can walk. Ask if they wanna go for a bike ride instead of out for an ice cream. You change yourself, you start feelin' better, lookin' better, and then maybe they wanna jump on that train. Even if they don't, what did you lose? Nothin'. You got yourself healthy, feelin' good, and that's a win-win situation right there. So, just worry about yourself, 'cuz you're the only one you can really change.

> ***There is only one corner of the universe you can be certain of improving, and that's your own self.***
>
> —Aldous Huxley

DO THIS TODAY: *Selfish ain't always a bad thing. Sometimes it just means that you gotta focus on your* **got-damn** *self in order to get the ball rolling. Who's that person in your life you been tryin' to help, tryin' to change? Make a commitment right now to let it go. Stop tryin' to force a change on somebody who ain't ready.*

February 29th (Only on Leap Years)

"JUST BECAUSE YOU DON'T UNDERSTAND SOMETHING DON'T MEAN IT'S WRONG."

Today is a mothahfuckin' bonus day. We only get twenty-nine days in February every four *got-damn years*. I don't understand it, but that don't mean it's wrong. Somebody understands it, and they figured if we don't do this, pretty soon our seasons and maybe our days and times would start gettin' all fucked up. I got to *trust* them, right? 'Cuz they know something I don't even pretend to know. Sure, I could learn it. Maybe I will. But for now, I'm just gonna trust the mothahfuckin' scientists because they're probably smarter at this particular thing than me.

But sometimes, you don't understand something and it makes you frustrated, makes you scared, maybe even makes you angry. That's when you got to learn more about it. My mama always told me that the key to *peace* is *understanding*. You angry? What is it you're *actually* angry about? For example, one time I was waiting for my boy to pick me up. He was gonna drop me at the Cotton Club for Open Mic Monday. I was waiting for thirty minutes, forty minutes, and he doesn't show. I gave up waitin' and ran to catch a bus, walked seventeen blocks, showed up sweating and mad as a mothahfuckah. Got home about two in the morning, had a message for me—his girl had gone into labor and he was rushin' her to the hospital. He's a daddy of a baby girl, and all that night I spent pissed off, assumin' he just found something better to do. Man, did I feel bad. So now, before I lose my shit I ask myself, "Do I know for sure? And do I know why?"

> ***The beginning of wisdom is this: Get wisdom. Though it cost all you have, get understanding.***
>
> —Proverbs 4:7

DO THIS TODAY: *What's one issue that makes you angry, frustrated, afraid, confused? Take a few minutes and learn something about it that ain't from a tabloid, TikTok, Facebook post, Instagram, or a meme. You gotta grasp the whole situation. Remember, understanding comes through communication and education. Through understanding, you can find your way to a peaceful conclusion.*

March 1st

"YOU ONLY GOT ONE BODY, SO DON'T FUCK IT UP."

I'm not gonna lie. I didn't always do the best I could by my body, but I sure as hell didn't fuck it up like some folks do. I was never one for drugs. I tried marijuana once. That shit was laced with somethin' and I ended up in the hospital. Scared me straighter than I already was. Yeah, I avoided drugs. I did my best to stay away from the gangs, too. 'Cuz if there's one thing that will fuck you up as quick as drugs, it's gangs. I drank a few beers, smoked a few cigars, maybe ate one too many sausages from Jimmy's Red Hots downtown...but I digress.

My point is, you only got one body. It's not like you can replace it if it breaks the fuck down. This ain't no car, ain't no motor home. Yeah, modern medicine is a mothahfuckin' miracle, but it can't fix everything. And even what doctors can fix, sometimes livin' with the consequences ain't no life at all. My grandmama used to tell me, "Don't put anything in your body that God didn't want there." It's a good rule of thumb.

Take care of yourself. Exercise. I always played ball, and sometimes I even went to the gym. Whatever feels good for you, makes you move your body, do that. Drink water. Eat your greens. Get some *got-damn* sleep. You treat your body right, it'll take care of you. Pretty soon you'll see that you're thinkin' clearer, feelin' good, feelin' motivated. It's all connected.

> ***Take care of your body. It's the only place you have to live.***
>
> —Jim Rohn

DO THIS TODAY: *Do you realize that your body hears everything your mind says? Your body achieves what your mind believes. So, you gotta say shit to trick it, like, "I* **love** *waking up early every morning to work out." It's a small change, but it's a start. Now, reframe one thing you wanna do for your health in a positive way. You'll start to believe it and your body will respond.*

March 2nd

"DON'T HOLD GRUDGES. LET THAT SHIT GO."

You know what it feels like to hold a grudge. Man, it'll eat you up inside. It's all you can think about, all you can talk about, and pretty soon it's takin' over your whole *got-damn* life. Maybe you even start to plan some kinda mothahfuckin' revenge. Grudges like that, they can change who you are, take you down a notch, make you one angry mothahfuckah. Why in the hell would you want that? So, somebody does you dirty. Okay, it happens. But when you hold on, it's like you're letting them keep on beatin' you up over and over again. Do you think that shady mothahfuckah is still thinking about it? Hell no. They don't give a shit. You stayin' all torn up ain't affecting them one mothahfuckin' iota. Only person you're hurtin' is your own *got-damn self.*

Here's what you do instead of holding the grudge: *you think about* what you learned from that experience. Maybe you learned to guard yourself a little bit better. Maybe you learned who you ain't ever gonna work with again. Maybe you learned to do your research before takin' a big risk. Whatever the lesson there is in it, take it! That's your mothahfuckin' gift. Grab onto it and move the hell on.

> ***Holding on to anger is like grasping a hot coal with the intent of throwing it at someone else; you are the one who gets burned.***
>
> —Buddha

DO THIS TODAY: *You can't keep livin' in the* **got-damn** *past. What grudge have you been holdin' onto? Remember, the best revenge is success. Take that thing that happened to you and turn it into a lesson that will help you grow, then let it go.*

March 3rd

"IT'S HARD TO CLIMB A LADDER WITH A BAG OF ROCKS ON YOUR BACK."

There's lots of things that will hold you down, stop you from livin' your best *got-damn* life. Grudges are one, then you got jealousy, anger, hate, anxiety, fear, grief, pity, resentment, hostility, even boredom. Man, even just sayin' those words makes you feel bad. These feelings are heavy. They're like stones. Why would you wanna keep carryin' those mothahfuckahs around? Ain't doin' you no good. And the more you carry 'em, the heavier they get, and then they start changin' who you are.

We all got that one friend shows up at the barbeque and everybody kinda turns their head, pretendin' like they deep in a conversation. You got to avoid eye contact with that mothahfuckah, 'cuz he's angry at the *got-damn* world. Everything he says, he's spoutin' about something or other. Or you got that one cousin always pity-postin' on Facebook, makes you feel bad inside. Nobody wants to be like that, and nobody wants to be around that. That shit's heavy, and if you wanna rise up, you got to dump all of them rocks outta your bag. You see what I'm sayin'? You gonna find out real quick how much easier it is to climb without 'em.

> ***You wanna fly, you got to give up the shit that weighs you down.***
>
> —Toni Morrison

DO THIS TODAY: *Go through your friends list on Facebook, Snapchat, TikTok, Instagram, and whatever else you on. Delete, block, unfollow, or unfriend anybody who's constantly posting negative shit. My guess is you'll feel a whole lot lighter.*

March 4th

"MARCH FORTH, BUT BE CAREFUL WHERE YOU STEPPIN'."

This is the only day of the year that's also a sentence: March forth. You know what that means? The day itself is tellin' you to keep moving forward, to go out there and make it happen. I get it. Takin' those first steps can sound a little bit terrifying. Do it anyway, and do it the right way. What's the right way? Well, it sure as hell ain't supposed to involve tramplin' up on other folks' backs. It's already gonna be lonely at the top, the last thing you want is a trail of enemies left behind you. You don't have to *conquer* nobody else in this world in order to go forth on your own mothahfuckin' path. In fact, if you're doin' it the right way, you're gonna end up having a whole *got-damn* crowd of folks walkin' behind you. You'll have your feet solid on the ground, and they'll just wanna be followin' you because you treatin' everybody with respect, honorin' what they bring to the table. You'll be marchin' forth with passion, and you'll have that energy all around you that other people just wanna be near to, because that's what happens when you doin' what you s'posed to be doin'. When you doin' it right, you end up leadin' the march and you wasn't even tryin'.

> ***This, then, is the test we must set for ourselves; not to march alone but to march in such a way that others will wish to join us.***
>
> —Hubert H. Humphrey

DO THIS TODAY: *Think of something you really want to attain. Now, listen to "Ain't No Mountain High Enough" and imagine Diana Ross singing just to you, right in your ear. no wind, rain, cold, or anything is gonna stop you from reaching your goal. You know she got that whisper in her voice, and her goal is your goal. Yeah, that's right, you got this.*

March 5th

"IF YOU START SOMETHING, FINISH IT."

Are you a fifty-percenter? You know, the kinda guy with half-done projects all over the house? Maybe you refinished the floor but you never put the trim up. You took apart that classic 1977 Chevy but it's still sittin' on blocks in your garage, 'cuz you never put it back together. You had a big idea for a business, started gettin' everyone excited about it, designed the logo, and never did another *got-damn* thing on it. Sound like you? Yeah, you're a fifty-percenter, and there's a coupla different reasons maybe why.

One, maybe you get distracted. I understand that. You doin' this thing and it gets to a boring part and there's this new thing over here that looks excitin'! Oh, man, that other thing's so shiny. So, you drop what you're doin', and you go to something new. Problem is, there's always gonna be something shiny danglin' in front of you. Two, could be that you just *got-damn* lazy. Somethin' starts to get hard, and you gettin' tired, you wanna go sit on the couch and watch reruns of *Fresh Prince* instead, take a nap. Maybe it's not your fault. Maybe you were handed everything you ever wanted, and you never learned how to work for nothin'. It's okay. We can fix that. Three, it's possible that you afraid of success. Why in the *hell* would that be? Well, 'cuz when you finally get what you been working hard toward, you don't know how it's gonna change you. That shit can be scary, deep inside. Maybe you addicted to the struggle. But here's the deal. Once you start finishin' what you started, you gonna feel so good. Feels like a rush, and pretty soon you get addicted to that feeling instead, and you're gonna wanna keep going.

> ***Don't do nothing halfway, else you find yourself dropping more than can be picked up.***
>
> —Louis Armstrong

DO THIS TODAY: *Do you drive halfway there and walk the rest of the way? Do you get half-dressed for work? Do you put on one shoe and walk barefoot with the other? Hell, naw. Today, you're gonna take the time to finish one thing you started. It don't have to be a big thing, just something. Bring it to fruition, got-dammit. It's gonna make you feel accomplished.*

March 6th

"YOU CAN'T MAKE YOUR DREAMS COME TRUE IF YOU AIN'T DREAMIN'."

I remember when I was in school, I'd be starin' out the window when the teacher's tryin' to get me to pay attention to some kinda numbers addin' up to this or that on the chalkboard. She'd snap her *got-damn* ruler and say, "Mister McCullough?" Why they callin' you mister when you seven years old? "Mister McCullough, your work is in here, not out there." I knew what she meant. She was sayin' my work was in the classroom and not out the window, but here's how I like to take it. My work is *in here*, inside my head. Not *out there* on the *got-damn* chalkboard, or on the computer screen, or anywhere outside of my head.

You see, I wasn't really lookin' out the window all that time. I wasn't watchin' nothin' outside on the playground. I was all up in my daydreams, thinkin' about stories and jokes and shit like that. I could see myself on stage in there, clear as I seen George and Weezy on the TV screen. I was buildin' my vision, that's what I was doin', and I didn't even know it yet. You got to have dreams like that, dreams so big and so clear they're like videos playin' in your head. You got to start dreamin' like a little kid bored in class. Not small dreams, either. You need dreams so big they scare you. It's time to reignite your *imagination*, 'cuz that's what drives *motivation*. If you can dream it so clear it seems real, you'll do everything you can to make it happen.

> ***Every great dream begins with a dreamer.***
>
> —Harriet Tubman

DO THIS TODAY: *Talk show host Wendy Williams always says, "How you doin'?" What I wanna ask you is, "How you dreamin'?" The key is to dream big. If your dreams don't scare you, they ain't big enough. All you need is some imagination. What do you want? Imagine it clearly, all the details. Just make sure your dreams are bigger than your fears.*

March 7th

"NO SENSE IN LYIN' TO YOURSELF. PRETTY SOON, YOU'RE GONNA FIND OUT."

Everybody knows lyin's a sin. When I was a kid, it was punishable by a smack upside the head. That was my granddad's way. My mama's way was even worse. She'd look at me and shake her head, sad as hell. Then she'd say, "Oh, Bean. Now, I can't trust you." Boy, did that kill me. If my mama didn't trust me, who would? If you think that's painful, try lyin' to *yourself* and findin' out about that. Damn, that hurts like a mothahfuckah, 'cuz that one person you should always be able to trust, no matter what, is you.

What the fuck you keep lyin' to yourself for? Your girl done left and she ain't comin' back. You keep tellin' yourself she is, but you gotta let that shit go. You tellin' yourself you doin' everything you can to get a job. No, you been playing video games for seventeen hours. Maybe you even gone so far as to pretend you *are* something, *got* something, *done* something that you *aren't*, *don't*, or *haven't*. Trust me, now, that shit will come back to bite you in the ass so hard you won't be able to sit down until you're ninety-seven. Even if nobody else finds out, when you realize you been a fraud your entire mothahfuckin' life, that shit hurts. Or maybe your lyin' is the other way around. You ain't good enough. You ain't smart enough. You ain't got what it takes. Knock it the fuck off. Those kinda lies can hurt you as bad as the other ones.

Now, I'm different on stage than I am at home, different in church than I am playin' cards with the boys. I get that. It's okay situationally. But real authenticity means you ain't tryin' to *become* something you're not. It's about *accepting yourself* exactly as you are in the present moment, whatever the hell that looks like.

> ***You never find yourself until you face the truth.***
>
> —Pearl Bailey

DO THIS TODAY: *In the past, have you lied to yourself or pretended to be someone you're not? Think about why you did so, and how you might approach the situation in a more authentic way.*

March 8th

"IT DON'T MATTER WHAT NOBODY ELSE IS DOIN', JUST DO WHAT YOU GOTTA DO."

I don't care what your daddy told you, what them sneaker ads tellin' you, what your high school basketball coach told you, life ain't no competition. There's room for everybody at the top. But we are so mothahfuckin' conditioned to think we got to beat the guy next to us if we wanna make somethin' of ourselves. That's why we always lookin' at him, tryin' to one-up him, feelin' some kinda way if we ain't got what he got.

That's just a bunch of *got-damn* bullshit, that's what it *T-I-Iz*. The possibility for success in this mothahfuckin' world is endless. It ain't like there's a handful of spots up at the top and we in a race to get 'em. Hell, as far as I'm concerned, there ain't even no top. So why you lookin' at what he's or she's doin' next to you? It don't matter. This ain't no football game. You don't have to tackle him to get where you wanna go. Y'all can run right beside each other and maybe even help each other, slap each other on the back when you got some little victories, you know. Then, when y'all get there, you gonna see a whole helluva lot of other folks there too! Yeah, that's amazing, 'cuz you gonna be in great company.

> ***When you are content to be simply yourself and don't compare or compete, everyone will respect you.***
>
> —Lao Tzu

DO THIS TODAY: *Today, make an extra effort to help and encourage someone. Use your gifts and time to help them to reach* **their** *goal. When you do that, you will realize that life is about workin' together to empower each other.*

March 9th

"DEAL WITH YOUR PROBLEMS, 'CUZ THEY'RE NOT GOIN' AWAY ON THEIR OWN."

We all got problems. That's just a factual part of life. You could have the best plan in the world, be prepared, and then you get hit with a curveball. It takes you off guard, but turnin' away is a good way to strike the fuck out. You gotta keep your eye on the ball and swing. I ain't gonna lie, sometimes you don't feel like dealin' with no damn problems. You at home chillin' when all of a sudden, the toilet's overflowin'. Ain't that a bitch? Now, we gonna let that toilet keep flowin'? Hell naw, that'll only gonna make me a bigger problem to clean up later. See what I'm sayin'?

I've had my share of problems, and they sure as hell didn't go away without me payin' them some attention. When I was a kid in junior high, there was a gang had their eye on me, intimidatin' me, wantin' me to join 'em. Well, I knew better. I wasn't gonna join no mothahfuckin' gang, good way to get yourself killed. Thing is, not joinin' a gang when they want you is no picnic, either. They started harassin' me and shit, but I'd rather take my chances with that. I made it clear that I wasn't gonna join. Next day, a few of 'em tried to jack me up. I threw a few punches, hit hard. But when I ran, they chased me. Good thing my brother Darryl was comin' up on us, and he was one scary sumbitch. He stopped 'em, said he'd let me fight 'em if they wanted, but one at a time. Boy, they backed the hell off and didn't bother me no more. Sometimes it's good to have a scary sumbitch for a brother. Anyway, if I had just let 'em keep pushin' me, they never woulda stopped until I gave in or they hurt me bad. I had to stand up to 'em, no matter what, and I thank the Lord every day that I did. Changed the course of my life.

> ***Not everything that is faced can be changed, but nothing can be changed until it is faced.***
>
> —James Baldwin

DO THIS TODAY: *What challenges are you facin' that you been avoiding? Pick one, and work on cleanin' it up now. See if you feel a little bit lighter when you done.*

March 10th

"GIVE WHAT YOU CAN, WHEN YOU CAN. IT MAKES YOU FEEL GOOD."

How would it have gone down different if Jesus woulda turned five pieces of bread and two fishes into thousands and kept it all for hisself? Sittin' there eatin', washin' it down with wine he made outta the jug of water, actin' like he's all of that while thousands of folks around him starvin'? You think folks woulda followed him like they did? No, they wouldn't. But Jesus multiplied the bread and fishes and he fed everybody. Everybody. I know this ain't the same exactly, but I remember when we wasn't doin' so good. Me and Rhonda and Je'Niece, we were livin' with Grandpa Thurman and Big Mama and my aunt too. I was out of work, livin' off of Rhonda's check and what my grandparents had. I remember I finally got food stamps, and I went to the store and I filled up my shopping cart. I stocked the fridge and cupboards with all kinda good stuff...and I didn't go writin' my name on shit. Everybody gets to eat whatever is there. You see what I'm sayin'?

Lots of folks have come to me for help since I started makin' money. If they're good, if I see 'em workin' hard, they're humble, I help 'em out, no strings attached. Why? It feels good. That's how you connect with folks. That's how you get respect too. But I always did that, even when I didn't have two nickels to rub together. You always got something to give, even if it's just your time. It feels good to bless somebody else, and that's how you *get* blessed.

> ***From what we get, we can make a living. What we give, however, makes a life.***
>
> —Arthur Ashe

DO THIS TODAY: *Think of someone you'd like to surprise or help. Now, when you ready, silently give it to 'em, no strings attached. Remember, real giving is doin' something nice for someone without praise or reward.*

March 11th

"DO WHAT YOU GOTTA DO FIRST, THEN YOU CAN MOVE ON UP."

You got to have food, water, a roof up over your head, clean air to breathe. You gotta feel safe. Then, you gotta have your family, or at least human connection, 'cuz without that life ain't worth much in my opinion. These are basic human needs. You gotta have all of these things taken care of, solid, 'fore you can go on and really chase your dreams right. Why? I'm gonna tell ya' why. How you gonna focus on visualisin' your dream if your stomach growlin', you malnourished, weak? You gonna be dreamin' about some chicken, vegetables, and potatoes, not your comedy career. You can't help that, it's your mothahfuckin' body tryin' to stay alive. So, whatchyou gotta do to take care of those things? Go to work, make some money? Okay, do that, then. That's what's necessary.

Then, after you come home from your shift, shower up and relax, do whatever you possibly can toward your goal. Sometimes, for me, after I worked the second shift at Doc's Fish, it was just watchin' *Saturday Night Live* and takin' notes. That's what I could do. Pretty soon, I could do a little bit more and a little bit more. Before I knew it, I didn't have to work the fryer just to keep food on the table no more. I was livin' my *got-damn* dream.

> ***Start by doing what's necessary; then do what's possible; and suddenly you are doing the impossible.***
>
> —St. Francis of Assisi

DO THIS TODAY: *Make a list of all the things you accomplish daily just to meet your basic needs. My guess is you can't be feelin' down on yourself when you gettin' all that done every damn day! Now keep goin' and set some new goals you can work through a little bit at a time.*

March 12th

"SOMEBODY TRYIN' TO HOLD YOU BACK, IT'S ONLY BECAUSE THEY THINK YOU MIGHT WIN."

You only gotta hold something back if it's moving forward. So, if you got somebody tryin' to stop you from doing what you doin', it's probably because they think you gonna win. Sometimes it don't even matter to them if they're tryin' to do the same thing as you or not. Some folks just get jealous, don't wanna see you succeed at anything. Or maybe they don't wanna see you succeed before they do. They don't wanna be beat. Those kinda people are small-minded, caught up in their own ego. They feel threatened by folks who are solid in who they are and where they goin'. But that's not your problem, it's theirs. It's not your fault they ain't livin' up to their own *got-damn* potential.

If you got somebody at your work or in your family, maybe one of your friends, who always seems to have a negative attitude about your little victories, don't get mad. Instead, smile real big and thank 'em. They just paid you a mothahfuckin' compliment. They just told you they think you gonna succeed. Damn, jealous people are a trip. Like the sayin' goes, "Don't worry about those who talk behind your back. They're behind you for a reason."

> ***Nobody would bother to beat you down if you were not a threat.***
>
> —Cicely Tyson

DO THIS TODAY: *If you're doing somethin', moving forward, chances are you got some folks jealous of you right now. Here's how you deal with 'em: just keep on movin', keep doin'* **you**, *and don't change a* **got-damn** *thing.*

March 13th

"WHAT YOU THINK ABOUT IS WHAT COMES ABOUT."

Prayers are good. I said a great many of 'em myself in my day. When you say that prayer, you're sending a message up to God, or out into the Universe, however you wanna think about it, and God answers it best He can. But prayers ain't always said in church with your hands folded up, or on your knees at the side of your bed, or at your dinner table. Sometimes, prayers are more like the conversations goin' on in your head. God can hear them, too, and he's makin' your life happen accordingly. Proverbs, chapter 23, verse 7: "As a man thinketh in his heart, so is he."

That's why you got to keep it positive. Your thoughts, your prayers, don't let yourself dig into the "woe is me" type of shit, even if it's somethin' you needin' help with. Here's what I'm talkin' about. Let's say you need some money. Don't go saying, "Lord, I'm so broke. Ain't got no job. Can't feed my family. I'm desperate. Please send me some money." Shoot, you walkin' around sayin' you're desperate and broke, that's how you gonna be. Try it this way instead. "Lord, I appreciate all the blessings you've given me. I know I can work hard, and I know there's a perfect job for me out there. I know that you'll help me find it." You see the difference? That's a positive prayer, a positive thought. That's how it's done.

> ***Once you start replacing negative thoughts with positive ones, you'll start having positive results.***
>
> —Willie Nelson

DO THIS TODAY: *Watch your thoughts today. When you start to frame something in a negative way, instead fill your mind with positive prayers. Force yourself to do this all day no matter what the situation and see if your prayers get answered.*

March 14th

"YOU WON'T RISE UP IF YOU'RE FOCUSED ON KEEPIN' OTHER FOLKS DOWN."

Whatever anybody else is doin' is none of your *got-damn* business. Why in the hell would you wanna spend your energy holdin' another sumbitch down when you got your own shit to do? It ain't gonna help you at all. In fact, all that's gonna do is keep you both on the mothahfuckin' ground! You don't wanna be down there with him, pressin' your foot in his *got-damn* back. You need them feet to carry you forward. You get me?

I got some stories from the entertainment business about folks gettin' sabotaged. When I was workin' the clubs, one comic showed up an hour late, too late to get on the list for the open mic. New guy, and he was frustrated 'cuz another guy told him the time and he wrote it down right as he said it. Turns out, there was a talent agent in the audience that night, and the guy who told him the wrong time was another mothahfuckin' comic who didn't want the competition. Boy, you don't think word got around about that? That sumbitch was so busy tryin' to hold back somebody else, that he got himself blacklisted. You heard the sayin', "What goes around comes around"? All he had to do was stay in his lane. Damn shame. Me, I like to see the guys around me making their dreams come true. There's room enough for everybody at the top.

> ***You can't hold a man down without staying down with him.***
>
> —Booker T. Washington

DO THIS TODAY: *Jealousy comes as a result of self-doubt. Instead of tryin' to keep somebody else back, I want you to say this to yourself: **I appreciate my own uniqueness. I have something to give that no one else can**. Feel free to press the repeat button as needed!*

March 15th

"YOUR EGO DON'T ALWAYS STEER YOU RIGHT, ESPECIALLY IF IT'S TOO *GOT-DAMN* BIG."

Everybody's got an ego. I'm not sayin' everybody's arrogant. That's not what that shit means. Your ego is kinda like how you see yourself and this world, you know? It's your idea or opinion of yourself and your own importance, kinda like a filter between what is and how you see it. Problem is, some folks got an ego so big they can't see around it. They get stuck in their ways and won't listen to nobody else. Those guys are the sumbitches nobody wants to be around.

If you feel offended when someone challenges your opinion or corrects you, then yo' ass has a mothahfuckin' inflated ego. You got to tone that shit down right now or it's gonna make your life a livin' hell, probably your afterlife too. Here's how you do it: things ain't goin' your way, don't throw your mothahfuckin' hands up and say "fuck it." If I'da done that shit, I'd still be workin' my jokes on the mothahfuckin' L train. Then, you gotta get outside your *got-damn* self and help somebody else sometime. See how it feels. Finally, you get in a disagreement, quit judgin' the other guy so quick. Find the good in their differences, 'cuz everybody's got something good about them if you look hard enough. You can get those things down, man, you'll go a long way to thinning out that ego that's been stoppin' you from being your best self.

> ***Ego is the enemy.***
>
> —Ryan Holiday

DO THIS TODAY: *What issue do you feel strongly about? Come up with three good pieces of support for the* **opposing** *viewpoint. That should help you understand where they're coming from, even if you still don't agree.*

March 16th

"KEEP DOIN' WHAT YOU'RE DOIN' AND IT'LL HAPPEN BY ITSELF."

Whenever I hit a roadblock, if my grandmama knew that I was doin' everything right, she'd tell me, "Bean, you just keep doin' what you doin' and it'll happen. Don't you worry." I didn't always listen. Sometimes, I would try to push it when it wasn't time, or I'd beat myself up over something that I could not change. That ain't gonna do you no good.

When I was just startin' to make a name for myself, I got a call from the legendary Robin Harris. Man, was I excited. He wanted me to open for him. I said yes and I showed up backstage, but there was this other comic waitin' to open for him too. This mothahfuckah was spittin' mad, throwin' a *got-damn* fuss. I just stepped back, said I wasn't tryin' to steal nobody's thunder, but he wouldn't let up. Finally, Harris walked in and greeted me with a big smile. Said he was a big fan of my work, and would I open for him at his *next* show? I said of course, and I stepped back. I'm sad to say, there never was a next show. Robin Harris died before it could happen, and the world lost a great man. Good thing I kept my head straight that day, or my last memory of him woulda been a regret.

I just kept doin' what I was doin', and I made up my mind I was gonna carry his torch. I think I done a pretty damn good job of it too. Everything turned out fantastic for me. That comic that had a tantrum...I won't even mention his name 'cuz it don't matter no more.

> ***Do the right things and the right things will happen.***
>
> —Anonymous

DO THIS TODAY: *Keep doin' what you're doin', and trust that it's gonna work. Don't dwell on what went wrong, instead focus your energy on what to do next and move in that direction toward an answer.*

March 17th

"TOO MUCH OF ANYTHING'S GONNA FUCK YOU UP."

Good things, bad things, it don't matter, too much of 'em will do you more harm than good. Oh, you probably sayin', "Bernie, what about money? What about love?" Hell, too much money'll fuck you up quicker than anything else. It can make you arrogant, gluttonous, greedy… and too much money can make you afraid of losin' it. Love? You ever been smothered to death by a girl that wants to love up on you all the *got-damn* time? Makes you ill in your stomach. Alcohol is another one. I like a good cold beer on a hot day, but drink a whole mothahfuckin' case and you gonna fuck up yo' liver and make some stupid mothahfuckin' decisions. I know it's St. Paddy's Day, just make sure you're drinkin' that green beer responsibly.

How about work, though? Work is good, right? You gotta work hard to get where you need to go in life. Of course, you do. But what if all you do is work? That sumbitch is called a *workamaholic*, and they got a mothahfuckin' twelve-step program for his ass. He gonna work himself into the grave and miss out on all the good stuff. You gotta have balance, that's the key. You work hard, play hard, get plenty of rest. Balance.

> ***Everything that exceeds the bounds of moderation has an unstable foundation.***
>
> —Seneca the Younger

DO THIS TODAY: *Moderation is supposed to be a small helpin', and maybe you sample a little bit of everything that way. You're not supposed to take it all or do it all. Damn, that's selfish. Start working on eliminating excess in small ways right now. For instance, if you carry too much change, it'll weigh down your pockets, maybe even pull your pants right off. So, eliminate some of it. Give a handful of quarters to a stranger, a homeless man, a little kid, or throw it in the tip cup. You get my drift? Moderation in small things leads to moderation in all things.*

March 18th

"THERE'S ALWAYS SOMETHING TO BE THANKFUL FOR, EVEN IF IT'S JUST TO BE ALIVE."

I've been down so hard in my life, felt like I couldn't have gotten any lower. Lost my job, lost my apartment, felt like hell. Started goin' into the places in my mind I never wanna go again, thinkin' I was worthless, couldn't even take care of my wife and daughter. But then I realized something important. I had a family that loved me. I was alive and breathin'. I had a capable body that could serve me when I needed it. I thanked God for those blessings, and that gratitude there, it turned everything around.

That's when we moved back in with my grandma and granddad. Man, was I thankful to have them, thankful for that roof over our heads, that's for sure. Didn't mean I didn't want to get the hell outta there and get my own place again, but you can want more and still be grateful for what you got. Even after my mama died, brother died, my best friend Billy died too young, I kept gratitude in my heart, and that's what got me through that kinda pain. It's hard to stay down when you're filled with gratitude, that shit's like helium.

> ***No matter what the situation is...close your eyes and think of all the things you could be grateful for in your life right now.***
>
> —Deepak Chopra

DO THIS TODAY: *Take a deep breath and relax. Inhale. Now, exhale. Again, inhale. Now, exhale. Damn, did you bring those breath mints? Just messin' with you. Okay, now that you're relaxed, let's start your day with a positive thought. Try saying the following affirmation:* ***I am grateful today for a healthy, happy, and prosperous life. I'm moving in peace and stillness as I focus on the good****. Say that shit with feelin' and authority. It works if you work it.*

March 19th

"I AIN'T GONNA PUT MYSELF DOWN TO LIFT SOMEBODY ELSE UP."

Sure, you got to help folks along on their path. Makes you feel good, you know. But let me tell you something, you can't go sacrificing your own *got-damn* dreams, your own reputation, your own work, or your own happiness to do it. If you start doin' that shit, you won't be able to get where you wanna go. Pretty soon, you gonna start feelin' resentment toward the folks you was tryin' to help in the first place.

You've heard the saying, "Put the oxygen mask on yourself first." You know, when you on a plane and the air pressure droppin', those masks come outta the ceiling. The flight attendant tells you to put yours on first and then help whoever needs it, 'cuz you can't help nobody else if you can't breathe your *got-damn* self. Now, how you gonna do that in real life, not just on a literal mothahfuckin' plane? Start by creating some emotional space so you can preserve your own values, well-being, your sanity. Damn, when I started on my rise up, I had folks comin' outta the woodwork looking for my mothahfuckin' help. I helped some, the ones I knew was doin' their best, workin' hard, had a good attitude. Other folks, though, they be messin' with my mental health, and I don't do no mothahfuckin' drama. Had to cut them loose to save myself.

> ***When you give someone something you need for yourself you make the other person a thief. True giving does not require self sacrifice.***
>
> —Iyanla Vanzant

DO THIS TODAY: *Who do you know that's wearin' your ass down emotionally? Time to put the oxygen mask on yourself, first. If you can cut them outta your life, good. But if you can't cut their asses out completely, just establish some limitations around your relationship. Those limitations often lead to mutual respect.*

March 20th

"LYIN' IS ONE OF THE WORST THINGS YOU CAN DO TO YOURSELF."

There's big lies and little lies and all kinda lies in between. Sometimes, you think them small ones don't matter. For example, you tell your buddy you sick and can't go to his place for dinner, but really you can't stand his *got-damn* kids. No harm, right? He probably will never know the difference and you sparin' his feelings. Naw, man. That ain't how it works. You keep tellin' those little lies like that, what you doin' is trainin' your own mothahfuckin' brain to lie. Do you really want lyin' to be your natural instinct? Hell, no. Why?

Well, first of all, lyin' is one of the seven deadly sins. Think about whether or not whatchyou sayin' is worth burnin' in hell for all of mothahfuckin' eternity. Think about whether it's worth the whoppin' karma you gonna get back too. Secondly, somebody gonna find out eventually, then you'll be in a world of hurt. Might get your ass whooped, but even worse, ain't nobody gonna trust your word anymore. That shit hurts worse than an asswhoopin'. You got nothin' if you don't got your word. Third thing about lyin' is that it's hard to keep that shit up. You got to remember what you said and who you said it to. Can't keep it straight, starts cloggin' up all your brain cells, and some of y'all don't have a ton to spare. You know I'm kiddin'.... But if you been hearin' yourself sayin', "Naw, man, that's the truth for real," you probably been lyin'. Those words right there clue folks in, and they won't trust you. You need to fix this, quick. Just tell the *got-damn* truth, it ain't that hard to do.

> ***The way to right wrongs is to turn the light of truth upon them.***
>
> Ida B. Wells

DO THIS TODAY: *Think back to the last time you told a lie, and correct that shit right now. You may be shocked at how easy it really is, and how good it makes you feel once it's done.*

March 21st

"SOMEBODY RUBS YOU WRONG, YOU GOTTA HAVE SOME SELF CONTROL."

Imagine this. It's Caesars Palace in Las Vegas, the lights are shinin' in the center ring. The world heavyweight boxing championship is about to begin. Then right before the main event the announcer steps in and hollers, "GENTLEMEN! TO YOUR CORNERS, PLEASE!" BAM! You feel that energy rushin' through you. That's what I'm talkin about, sometimes folk make you wanna jump in the ring with their ass, but that's where self control comes in. It causes you to pull back on reacting in a foolish way 'cuz they upset you. Take a step back, chill out, and count to three. The more you exercise self control on a consistent basis the stronger you will get!

I'll be the first one to admit it, if somebody comes at me, I'm gonna get in my feelin's at first. Might start hopping side to side a little bit, hands up, fightin' position. There might have been a time in my life I woulda taken a swing, but those days are long gone. I learned to let that shit go, and you can too. You just gotta realize that what's making them rub you wrong is their own mothahfuckin' insecurities, and you don't wanna be like that too. You got to be the better man, and then see who actually comes out on top.

> ***Should you ever find yourself the victim of other people's bitterness, smallness, or insecurities, remember, things could be worse... you could be them.***
>
> —Unknown

DO THIS TODAY: *Think of somebody that makes you feel like you wanna fight 'em. Now, list all the reasons you can be grateful you ain't like 'em. That kinda of gratitude goes a long way to keepin' your cool.*

March 22nd

"SUCCESS AIN'T NO SECRET, JUST STOP TALKIN' ABOUT IT AND DO IT."

A'right now, listen up real good. People who talk about money tend to be people that are broke as hell, or they want people to believe they have more than they got. People who have confidence don't talk about confidence all the damn time, they're too busy doin' shit with mothahfuckin' confidence. People who have talent don't talk about talent, they just use it. People who are successful don't talk about being successful, they demonstrate it. Ta-dow, see what I'm sayin'?

It's not about what you say, it's about what you do. There's no trick. It's simple and anybody can do it. You start actin' successful, doin' the things that successful folks do, soon enough you're gonna see the same kinda success. You think I woulda got where I got if I was just goin' around tellin' folks I was funny instead of spending my time watching, learning, practicing? Pretty soon, they're gonna be like, "Okay, mothahfuckah, tell us a joke." What woulda happened if I didn't have no joke, if I couldn't kill it when I was called out? I'd have been laughed at, ridiculed, shut down and shut out. Better to shut your *mouth* and let your actions speak for themselves.

> ***You wanna be a boss, you gotta make boss moves.***
>
> —J. J. Williams

DO THIS TODAY: *Open up the sound recorder on your phone and brag hard on yourself. Play it back. How does that sound to you? Now, shut your mouth and go do something that will actually help push you closer to your goals.*

March 23rd

"YOU DON'T EVEN KNOW."

I was backstage at Def Comedy Jam in New York, and all I could hear was the crowd tearing up the comic in front of me. They were some ruthless mothahfuckahs. He was out there sweatin', stumblin', and they booed him the hell off the stage and maybe outta his career. Black audiences are some harsh sumbitches. He stepped by me and gave me a look like he pitied my very soul, like I was walkin' the mothahfuckin' plank. I straightened my shoulders and walked out there, groovin' to the music. I cut it, took the mic, and I said, "I ain't scared a' you mothahfuckahs. You don't even know." I was about ready to give them an *edumacation*.

Everybody has their own experiences, and those mothahfuckahs didn't know mine. They didn't know shit about who I was, how I was feelin', or what I was about to say. But that ain't just for me up on that stage, it ain't just between me and an audience. It's for everybody everywhere in the *got-damn* world. Even if somebody livin' in your own house, you don't know what it's like to be them. So, don't assume that you do. My granddaddy used to say, "*Assume* makes an *ASS* of *U* and *ME*." You don't know something, ask. Somebody doesn't know something about you, and you think they need to know, tell 'em. This way, everybody has the information they need to empathize with each other. Everybody learns something.

> ***You must never be stupid enough to say, or smart enough to admit, you "know" what someone else is talking about. The moment you do, your learning stops.***
>
> —Awo Osun Kunle

DO THIS TODAY: *Ask somebody you think you know really well to tell you one thing about themselves that nobody knows. Maybe it will help you appreciate 'em in a different way.*

March 24th

"GET OVER IT."

I've had my fair share of pain and mothahfuckin' loss. I've fought some battles that didn't come out my way. But one thing I learned is that the longer you dwell in it, the deeper it gets, and the harder it is to get yourself out. That shit's like quicksand. I'm not gonna tell you not to feel sad if you lose somebody you love. Won't tell you not to feel disappointed if you fail at something you hustled your ass off for. Go on ahead and feel them feelings, nobody gonna tell you that's wrong. But pretty soon you gotta flip that switch and turn the lights on again if you wanna see where you goin'. You gotta let go to move forward.

I realized that after my mama died. Man, I lost my best friend the day she left this earth, and I felt it something fierce. But then I heard her voice in my head tellin' me it's gonna be okay, tellin' me she wanted me to live my life and make it the best *got-damn* life I could make it. I knew then and there that if I stayed in my grief, I wasn't even givin' myself a chance. My mama woulda hated that. So, I moved forward and I carried that lesson with me in everything. When I lost a job, had a bout with someone in my family, missed out on a movie role, when my *Midnight Mac* show on HBO was cancelled, or lost out on a gig...I felt it, got over it, and kept on going. That perspective changed my life.

> ***Getting over a painful experience is much like crossing monkey bars: you have to let go at some point in order to move forward.***
>
> —C. S. Lewis

DO THIS TODAY: *What was that "flip of the switch" moment that permanently changed your life or perspective? Did you feel the gravity of it at the moment, or did it become clear later?*

March 25th

"QUIET YOURSELF AND LISTEN, AND YOU MIGHT JUST HEAR WHAT YOU NEED TO HEAR."

One thing most successful people have in common is that they've learned how to just sit quiet and listen. Maybe they're listenin' to someone talk to them, or maybe they're listening to their inner voice, or maybe it's God. You can call it meditation if you want to, or you don't have to. You can just call it quiet, and it's one of the best *got-damn* gifts you can give yourself, just spending a little bit of time every single day with no mothahfuckin' noise. When you do that, you can start to really hear what your gut's tellin' you. You start to hear God answerin' your prayers. You start to pay attention better when folks are talkin' to you. And you know what happens, then? You calm the fuck down and you start to make your dreams happen.

Where do you think I got all my jokes, all my material, from? Shuttin' my mouth and listening to the folks around me and the masters of my craft. Where do you think I got my answers, learnt my path? Listening to my gut and to the voice of God answering my prayers. All I needed was a little bit of quiet, and that's a good start for you too.

> ***The quieter you become, the more you are able to hear.***
>
> —Rumi

DO THIS TODAY: *Find five minutes to turn everything off and sit quietly just focusing on the natural sounds around you, even the sound of your own breath. Then, if you wanna up your game a little bit more, you could ask someone to tell you a story about their life or even just their day, then listen without interrupting.*

March 26th

"WHEN YOU'RE COOL WITH YOURSELF, NOBODY CAN TAKE AWAY YOUR JOY."

When you an all-star, you gonna get a lot of haters. Here's one thing I know about them: Their hate comes outta their own insecurities. Have you ever met a hater that has more than you? My point exactly. You can't worry about people who have a damn problem with yo' ass. They'll hate you if you fine as hell, and they'll hate you if you an ugly sumbitch like me. They'll hate on you for what you don't have, and for what you do. You got slick moves? They hatin' cause they can't keep up. Somebody stole their joy and now they wanna steal yours.

I gotta tell you, I've had plenty of folks come at me, especially once I started gettin' some attention. I'd be goin' along on my day, a smile on my face and a skip in my step, and some Jealous Joe come along and try to knock me down. Maybe they hit me with a heckle. Or maybe it's worse, maybe they try to smear my name or swindle me. Other times, they might just start some shit, tryin' to break down my spirit. You wanna know the best way to stop those mothahfuckahs from gettin' to you? Keep smilin'. Be so full of joy, so confident in yourself, that nothin' they can say or do could possibly shake you. Those sumbitches hate it when they tryin' to rile you up and you just standin' there smiling. 'Cuz they know they can't get under your skin, and that makes you untouchable.

> ***Don't let anyone steal your spirit.***
>
> —Sinbad

DO THIS TODAY: *Think about a time somebody riled you up. Now, remind yourself that whatever they goin' on about is their problem, not yours. Maybe even pray that they fix their shit so they can be a better person.*

March 27th

"DON'T CONTINUE TO BEAT YOURSELF UP OVER MISTAKES YOU MADE. FORGIVE YOURSELF."

Believe it or not, Bernie Mac is not perfect. There, I said it. I've got flaws, and I sure as hell have made some mistakes, but I don't sit here and relive 'em. The past is the past, and you can't change nothin' by re-playin' it. Does the movie come out different when you rewind and watch it over again? No, it does not. Only reason you should be thinkin' about your mistakes is to figure out what you got to learn from 'em. Once you got that, you're done with it. Forgive the past you and move on. There's a better version of yourself on the way.

I'm gonna tell you a story. When my baby girl Je'Niece was in kindergarten, I was workin' the late shift and it was my responsibility to pick her up from school right about lunch time. Well, this one night I went out with the boys late, had too many beers, and I slept through my alarm. I woke up fifteen minutes after I was s'pose to get her. Boy, I ran all the way to the school, snow comin' down, wind whippin', and there she was sittin' all by herself on the bench, teeth chattering. She looked at me with them eyes and for a minute, I couldn't forgive myself. But I got her home, got her some of her favorite candy from the gas station, you know.

Once everything was cool, I did forgive myself, and I changed. I didn't want to be like that no more. I made a commitment right then to be the best *got-damn* father I could be, and that meant being the best man I could be, first. If I'd have stayed down there, feelin' bad, I never woulda been able to pick myself up, and that wouldn't have done nobody any good.

> ***Forgiveness is for yourself because it frees you.***
>
> —Louise Hay

DO THIS TODAY: *What's one thing you've done that requires self-forgiveness? Forgive yourself for it, and really truly let it go.*

March 28th

"IF THINGS FEELIN' CRAZY, LOOK FOR THE OPEN DOORS. NOT FOR THE WAY OUT, BUT FOR THE WAY UP."

Life gets crazy sometimes. It ain't your fault, it just happens. As much as we want peace and mothahfuckin' quiet, *BOOM*, it just explodes like a *got-damn* firecracker. You got your manager bookin' you gigs across the country, you be movin' to the city and tryin' to unpack, your car breaks down, your boy needs your help real bad, and suddenly you got your sister's kids standin' in your kitchen askin' for some milk and cookies. Seems like nothing's ever spread the fuck out, all happenin' at once, makes your head spin. I know sometimes in all that chaos you wanna pick up your shit and head outta Dodge for real, but then nothin' gets solved. The faster you run, the faster the problem runs right beside you, puttin' on new disguises along the way. So, how do you deal with it?

In the middle of it all, stop and open up your eyes, and you gonna start seein' opportunities you didn't have before, like little rays of light peekin' through the cracks. Sure, when my niece and her baby girl moved in with us for a little while, it changed the family dynamic, and it was hard for a second. But I turned it into one of my most popular comedy routines, and then it kinda jump-started the storyline for my show. You see what I'm sayin'? Even that friend that needs your help is an *opportunity* to think about somebody other than yourself, give your time or talent. All of that makes you grow, be a little bit better.

> ***In the middle of chaos lies opportunity.***
>
> —Bruce Lee

DO THIS TODAY: *Create opportunity out of the chaos. Identify at least one thing in your life that feels a little crazy right now. What kind of door can you build from it?*

March 29th

"YOU MOVIN' SLOW, YOU STILL GONNA GET THERE. KEEP GOIN'."

We are livin' in a time where everything is fast, fast, fast. Shit, if it takes more than a half a second for your show to load, you're already screamin' for your mama to fix the ***got-damn*** internet! What's wrong with you? Nothing. That's the world, now. It's all lightning cables and five gig, then we wonder why kids got no mothahfuckin' patience no more. Y'all graduate high school, go to college, don't have no six-figure job when you walk out, and you already wondering, "What's wrong with me?" Gettin' all depressed and down on yourself. Knock that the fuck off. Good things take mothahfuckin' time. You just got to keep at it.

You ever heard of *The Little Engine That Could*? Maybe your mama read it to you when you's a little kid? "I think I can, I think I can..." That little train kept on chuggin' and chuggin', slow but sure, til he made it to the top of the ***got-damn*** mountain! You got to be that train.

When I was gettin' started, I was workin' the open mic nights at the Cotton Club. I was showin' up in my borrowed ***got-damn*** suit, too big for me, and I was killin' it week after week. No pay except the feelin' I got makin' folks laugh. Pretty soon, I was attractin' a different crowd—Michael Jordan and Scottie Pippen sittin' up in there rollin' with laughter. Damn, I knew then and there that even though I was in the same place, I musta been chuggin' along in some kinda direction, slow but sure. I was right, 'cuz I got where I wanted to go.

> ***Be not afraid of growing slowly; be afraid only of standing still.***
>
> —Chinese Proverb

DO THIS TODAY: *If you don't know the story of* The Little Engine that Could, *find it and read it. Then, repeat in your mind today: slow and steady wins the race.*

March 30th

"Y'ALL NOT GONNA STRESS ME OUT TODAY."

There's certain people you just know is gonna do their mothahfuckin' best to stress you the hell out. You know those people. They talk real fast, frantic. They gotta do this, gotta do that, gotta do it right now before the *got-damn* world falls apart. Those folks gotta sit the fuck down, that's all I'm gonna say. When I approach somebody like that, I tell it to 'em straight before we even get started. I tell 'em, "Y'all are not gonna stress me out today." You know why I can say that? Because stress is a mothah-fuckin' choice.

Those frantic folks that let themselves get all worked up, they do that because they don't trust the process. They don't believe in themselves or anybody around them, and they ain't grateful for where they're at. Thankful folks, on the other hand, are not frantic all the *got-damn* time. They've learned to remain calm and appreciate what they got, who they got, and they're confident they're gonna get where they're going. I've learned that in my life. So now whenever a difficult situation arises or a frantic person tries to stress me out, I can just say, "Okay, I'm not gonna let this get to me. I'm gonna work it out or *kick them* out, whichever the situation requires." It's your responsibility to protect your peace.

> ***If you're feeling a lot of stress, it's because you're choosing to accept that stress.***
>
> —Mark Divine

DO THIS TODAY: *Who or what is stressing you out right now or recently? Take a few minutes to breathe slowly, calm your heart rate down, and tell yourself that you will not allow that person or that situation to cause you stress.*

March 31st

"SOMETIMES SHEER DETERMINATION IS THE ONLY THING'S GONNA GET YOU THROUGH."

You ever grit your teeth, put your head down, and push through somethin' that feels like it's killin' you? I have, and lemme tell you, no victory ever tastes as sweet as that. Don't matter if it's big or small, once you cultivate your drive, pretty soon you don't need it no more because pushing through just becomes part of who you are. For instance, one time I went to the gym to work out with my boys, and I knew damn well I was bench pressin' more than I should. I'm layin' there tremblin' and sweatin' and shit, just showin' the hell out. But on the inside I was thinking to myself, *Oh, shit. How the hell do I get outta this?* Well, I ain't gonna never let myself fail without tryin'. I ain't no punk! Yeah, I pushed through that shit like a big dog, and I did it. Man, did that feel good. Next time I came to the gym, I did it again. Pretty soon, I was benchin' more than Big Nigga, not that it's a competition or nothing, you know.

When you push yourself, you come back stronger. You can't stop when you're tired, you stop when you're done. Just gotta be persistent till somethin' happens. Keep your focus on the end result. You gotta think like a champion if you gonna be a champion. You start doin' that in little things, it transfers over to bigger things you got goin' on. Life won't be able to knock you down, 'cuz you'll be ready for it.

> ***The germ of success in whatever you want to accomplish is in your will power.***
>
> —Paramahansa Yogananda

DO THIS TODAY: *What have you done in your life that has required sheer determination? How did you feel when you completed this task? If the answer is, "I feel good," then you're on the right track.*

PART TWO: EVERYBODY ELSE

You are part of this huge community called "the world." Stop bein' so got-damn self-centered and see the bigger picture.

One of the things that I always loved about Bernard is that he never thought he was an island. Even after he started to get famous, he never made it all about him. We were a team, Bernard, Je'Niece, and myself. He was by nature a family man, always looking out for relatives and friends. Let the circle expand further, and you see that Bernard paid close attention to what was happening in the world and always wanted to make a difference when and where he could. He wasn't political, and he certainly wasn't politically correct, especially on the stage. But he genuinely loved all people and wanted to use his gifts to help make a real difference. I know, he had lots of big dreams, but he wasn't just a dreamer. He was a doer. That's how we're all supposed to be.

I will never forget this one afternoon when Bernard was sitting in the living room watching the news. He was pretty sick with his sarcoidosis, having a hard time breathing, so he was spending a little more time relaxing at home. He had this very serious look on his face. I said, "What's the matter?" He shook his head slow and said, "I'm tired of seeing young Black faces up there." He gestured toward the TV screen. "Gettin' into trouble. Gettin' shot. Fightin' each other. Droppin' outta school. I gotta do something." I asked him, "What are you gonna do?" He turned off the television, stood up, and he said, "I'm gonna talk to the mayor." I smiled and shook my head. Talkin' to the mayor, okay. I walked away thinking nothing of it.

Days later, he was sitting in Mayor Daley's office brainstorming about how he could use his celebrity to help the youth of Chicago. I'm not kidding. When Bernard McCullough said he was gonna do something, he did it. He always knew that he would never be completely at peace, fully successful, if he wasn't using his gifts to make a difference in the lives around him. That's why he got into comedy in the first place, to make folks smile when they've got a million worries, to take their minds off of their troubles, even for just a few minutes. He did that, and so much more too.

Bernard was the go-to for so many folks for advice, for leadership, and yes, for help when they needed it. He didn't always just hand it out, sometimes you had to work for it, and other times he'd assess if somebody was worthy of it…especially when it came to money. Folks can get greedy, and he wouldn't have any of that. But when he helped, he didn't do it for any kind of reward. He did it because it was the right thing to do.

Here's a story about another one of those instances, just a little more personal. Phil, the band leader of the Mac Man Band, told me about when he went to Bernard looking for some help. He needed a bit of money to record his CD, twenty-five hundred dollars. Phil and Bernard had a real good relationship. Phil is talented and always worked hard. He was part of the team, and Bernard respected him. He gave Phil the money he needed, said he wasn't worried about getting paid back, he knew Phil would do what he needed to do, and that was that. Then one day, Phil walked into Bernard's office, and he was sitting at his desk kinda grooving in his seat. That's when Phillip realized Bernard was listening to his album! All he said to Phil about it was, "I like that. That's smooth." He was just so thrilled that Phil was putting his talent out into the world, that he did what he said he was gonna do, and Bernard didn't expect anything more than that. It's Bernard's way, giving without a promise of anything in return. Giving just for the sake of giving, that's how he did it.

As you go through this process of becoming your best self, remember that you're not doing it in a bubble. You can't really be your best self if you're not aware of your place in the world, unless you understand that you're an important part of God's creation and that everything you do affects every other part. Even the small things count. One tiny act of kindness can change someone's whole perspective, and they'll pass on that joy. One tiny act of cruelness can damage someone deeply, and then they go on to spread darkness.

In the pages of this section, Bernard's gonna show you how to take responsibility for your part in all of this, how to use your gifts for the greater good, and how to shine your light so everybody else can see it and shine theirs too.

April 1st

"DON'T BE A ***GOT-DAMN*** FOOL."

You know what a fool is? Somebody who acts unwisely. Lots of times somebody's actin' a fool because they're so focused on the moment, what they can get out of it right then, that they don't think it through all the way. Other times, they're makin' stupid choices because they don't know no better. Of course, there's the instances that something silly like "love" makes you act a fool, but that's a different kinda foolish than I'm talkin' about here.

Thing is, we're all gonna act a fool like that at some point in our lives. We're gonna make snap decisions, embarrass ourselves, make mistakes. Can't nobody be on it all the *got-damn* time. It's okay to act foolish once in a while, but for God's sake don't ***be*** a fool. A real fool, he's the one that's always talkin' smack, always bitchin' and moanin', puttin' folks down, and blamin' everybody else about shit that happens. That kinda fool ain't takin' no personal responsibility, and he's fuckin' up the vibe for the folks around him. He's foolish 'cuz he's wasting what God gave him. Don't be that kinda fool.

Today is April Fool's Day, the one day of the year when you can pull a practical joke and get away with it. I want you to think about the root of a practical joke, though. You're actually convincing someone that something exists when it doesn't, or that something don't exist when it does. That's powerful stuff, right? You fool folks into your version of reality. You gotta make sure you use that power wisely.

> ***Any fool can criticize, condemn, and complain—and most fools do.***
>
> —Dale Carnegie

DO THIS TODAY: *Check your thinking to make sure it's not coming from a foolish mindset. Then, go on ahead and have a little April Fool's fun. Pull a silly and harmless prank, step outside your comfort zone, and get folks to smile a little.*

April 2nd

"WORK AT YOUR PASSION."

It's not good enough to settle for just "not bein' unhappy." Man, that kinda livin' ain't no livin' at all. You need moments of pure joy, as many as you can, 'cuz that's what life's all about.

I don't know if you got your career yet or not, or you're workin' a job to make ends meet. Wherever you're at right now, it's okay. We gonna start there, 'cuz there's no place else you can start. When you're lookin' for a job, or when you *were* lookin', maybe you hear someone say, "Well there's a high demand for this job or that job right now." They're sayin' you to do that so you can get hired and make some money. Lemme tell ya', that's the wrong *got-damn* approach. Instead, ask yourself what makes you really *got-damn* happy. What makes you wanna jump outta bed in the morning? What are you really good at? That's a gift that you're meant to use. Now, try to figure out how you can make some money doin' it, 'cuz you gonna spend at least eight hours a day, five days a week, for most of your life, working at a job. Damn, you don't wanna spend all those hours doin' something that brings you down, something that doesn't excite you, or worse, somethin' you hate. Can you imagine if everybody was excited to go to work doin' something they love? Everybody would be smilin', happy, content. That's a world I wanna live in.

> ***Don't ask yourself what the world needs, ask yourself what makes you come alive. And then go and do that. Because what the world needs is people who have come alive.***
>
> —Howard Washington Thurman

DO THIS TODAY: *Decide that today is gonna be a great day! Take your lunch break outside, go for a walk, paint, make music, write poetry, go play with some dogs at the shelter...or even just treat yourself to that smokin' outfit you saw in the store and post yourself up on Instagram. Focus on living any one of your passions today by doing something that truly makes you happy.*

April 3rd

"WHEN YOU STOP BEIN' AFRAID AND CHOOSE LOVE INSTEAD, FOLKS AROUND YOU WILL TOO."

A lot of folks think the opposite of love is hate. I think that the opposite of love is fear. When you afraid, it causes a chain reaction that can turn into hate real easy. Fear causes anxiety, depression, anger, and all kinda other bullshit. Fear starts wars and can stunt your growth as a human being. Now, sometimes it's good to fear, I'm not gonna lie. The fear of your ass gettin' burned will keep you safe from fires or hot stoves. The fear of your mama beatin' your ass will cause you to listen next time when she says don't run out in the road or talk to a mothahfuckin' stranger. Sometimes fearing failure can make you try harder so you won't. That's the good kinda fear. That's the fear you need to keep.

But when you stop fearin' what other folks think, stop fearin' the joy that you deserve, start lovin' yourself for exactly who and where you are, that energy is gonna spread out around you like radio waves, and whether they can see it or not, the folks around you are gonna receive it. And they're gonna receive that feeling a helluva lot quicker than they're gonna hear the words you're preachin', 'cuz folks go by what you do, not what you say. So, don't be a talker that's spouting loud and doin' nothing. Put action behind your mothahfuckin' words, or even better, just do without sayin' nothing, and you're gonna lead by example. That's the best kinda leader, one that spreads love just by living it.

> ***And as we let our own light shine, we unconsciously give other people permission to do the same. As we are liberated from our fear, our presence automatically liberates others.***
>
> —Marianne Williamson

DO THIS TODAY: *Start today by keepin' your light bright so others can follow. What do you need to do to flip on your switch this morning? Do it.*

April 4th

"WE CAN ALL GET ALONG. WE JUST GOTTA SHARE THE SAME DREAM."

What do you think my dream was when I was a kid? If you said it was to be a comedian, you'd be partly right. That was a dream of mine, but I had lots of dreams. Bein' a comedian was about doin' what I love every *got-damn* day of my life, not havin' to hold onto no "survival job" to make ends meet. But I had so many other dreams too. One was to take my girl to Disneyland, which I did, by the way. Another one was to have my own television show, which I also did. Sure, I had a lot of personal dreams, then they turned into goals, and I accomplished a lot of 'em.

But I also had bigger dreams about how I wish the world could be. Wish it could be fair and equal. Wish there weren't so much hate. Wish folks would be able to get along better between religions, between races, between the rich and the poor, between countries. Damn, just between people. You know? The more folks that share them kinda dreams, the more folks who add their goals to help reach 'em, the quicker we're gonna get there.

> ***Nothing happens unless first a dream.***
>
> —Carl Sandburg

DO THIS TODAY: *Dare to dream! One of the greatest speakers of all time told you how to do it. Today, say out loud, "I have a dream." Then follow that shit up with somethin' you want to achieve. For instance: I have a dream that I will graduate college debt free. Now, stop hittin' up the casino on payday and put that* **got-damn** *money toward that dream. See how your dream becomes a goal? Think about it real good, then go ahead and fill in the blank.*

I have a dream today that ____________________________________

April 5th

"YOU GOT AN IMPORTANT PLACE IN THIS WORLD. DON'T FUCK IT UP."

You think you the only one on this mothahfuckin' planet? You think nothin' you do affects anybody else? Well, you got another thing comin', 'cuz everything you do affects everybody else in some kinda way. So, pay attention to what you do, what you say, how you think, how you treat folks. It's a little bit like a game of poker. You make one wrong move and you could be fuckin' up your game and changin' the game for everybody else at the table too. Might be good for 'em, might be bad for 'em, but either way it's gonna shift everything.

Let me give you an example. When I was a kid, one of my chores was to take the garbage out every week. Man, I hated touchin' that nasty-ass garbage can. I would try my best to fake sick on garbage day, or I'd try to pull a slick move on my brother and offer to pay him to take it out, but he'd pop me upside my head every time. Then one day I pitched such a fit, he did it for me. But it was icy outside and damn if he didn't slip and crack his head. He laid up with a nasty headache all damn night, my mama had to come home from work, and I felt bad as hell. If I'd have just taken out the *got-damn* garbage, none of that woulda happened.

> ***Humankind has not woven the web of life. We are but one thread within it. Whatever we do to the web, we do to ourselves. All things are bound together. All things connect.***
>
> —Chief Seattle

DO THIS TODAY: *Everybody has a place in multiple "organizations," like family, a team, work, or a club. Think about why your place in each of those is crucial to the entire "operation," and what would happen if you dropped the ball.*

April 6th

"KEEP YOUR EYE ON WHAT'S HAPPENIN' IN THE WORLD, THEN DO SOMETHING TO HELP IT."

I never like to get involved in politics and other kinda bullshit. Feel like that shit divides folks more than it helps 'em. But I watch the news and I keep up with what's *goings on* in the world. You live on this *got-damn* planet, you better know what's happenin' in it! I know sometimes the news can get depressing. Folks gettin' shot and killed, wars, one group attackin' the other one, folks homeless on the streets and other folks dyin' of diseases and starvation. All of that can weigh on your mind and make you tired, make you weary, make you angry. I'm not sayin' you should be consumed in all of that all the time. Just know about it, feel how you feel about it, then do something about it. 'Cuz when you get up off your ass and do something about it, the most amazing thing happens. The feelings don't weigh on you so heavy anymore.

> ***This is a dark time, filled with suffering and uncertainty. Like living cells in a larger body, it is natural that we feel the trauma of our world. So don't be afraid of the anguish you feel, or the anger or fear, because these responses arise from the depth of your caring and the truth of your interconnectedness with all beings.***
>
> —Joanna Macy

DO THIS TODAY: *Turn on the news and look for one story that you can react to. For instance, a kid's tryin' to raise money for a new wheelchair for his dad, you can react by sendin' a donation. How about that new hot dog stand started by high school students? Go buy a wiener or two and show 'em some support, help 'em believe in their dream...and you know those Chicago-style hot dogs ain't no joke.* ***Maxwell Street, I miss you fo sho!*** *The point is, no matter how big or small, do somethin' to make a difference today.*

April 7th

"EVERYTHING THAT MAKES A DIFFERENCE STARTS WITH AN IDEA."

You got an idea to make something better, easier, more fair, you gotta share it with someone and keep sharin' it until somebody listens. And if nobody will listen, you gotta push it until they do, or you gotta make it happen yourself. It might be something small to upgrade how you're doin' things at work or in your household. Or maybe it's gonna make something more efficient, or it's an idea on how to bring folks together. You gotta share that shit. It ain't just your right, it's your mothahfuckin' responsibility.

Lemme tell you how a crazy idea changed everything for me. I was at my granddad's funeral, and of course everybody wanted me to stand up and say a few words. I stood up there and looked at all those sad faces, and I decided to make 'em laugh. I talked about my granddad like a standup routine, even did my imitation of him, how he'd repeat things four times. "Bernie, go on and get my slippers. Get my slippers, boy. You know where them slippers at? Go on and get 'em, now." Had folks rolling. Afterward, a member of the church comes up to me and asks if I'd come to her cousin's funeral next week and make folks laugh, she'd pay me. Some of y'all mighta thought that's a crazy idea. But I listened, and I did a whole lotta funerals after that. Made me remember why I wanted to do comedy in the first place...to make folks smile through their pain. That's how I got my groove back on and got myself back into comedy after I went through a funk. That woman's crazy idea changed my life, my family's life, and now that you're reading my book, maybe your life too.

> ***No matter what people tell you, words and ideas can change the world.***
>
> —Robin Williams

DO THIS TODAY: *What's one idea you have about how to improve something? Tell it to as many people as you can today. By the time you done, they gonna be just as excited as you! Then you can sit back and say, "Now, that's alright! You just showed me who ya' wit!"*

April 8th

"IF YOU LET IT HAPPEN, YOU'RE PART OF THE PROBLEM."

You know when you're a kid, and your big brother has a really good idea. You go on along with it because you want him to think you're cool. Then when you end up with a burn hole in the carpet and the fire department knockin' at your door, you try to point your finger at your brother. You know that shit ain't gonna fly. You gonna get an ass-whoopin' same as him. That's 'cuz your mama knows you just as much at fault for not stoppin' him.

Same goes for any kinda situation. I remember this time I was in junior high. Some kids were always pickin' on this gangly girl, callin' her names and followin' her around. One day, I saw them chasin' her, and they caught her and they were knocking her around and shit. I had enough. I ran right over with my fists flyin'. I didn't know her. Didn't know anything about her, but I knew the way she was bein' treated was wrong. After that day, them boys never bothered her again. I came home and my mama asked how I got all banged up. I told her, and she just nodded her head with a little smile on her face. She knew I had to do what I had to do. Like my Grandpa Thurman used to say, "If you're not part of the solution, you're part of the problem."

> ***The world is a dangerous place, not because of those who do evil, but because of those who look on and do nothing.***
>
> —Albert Einstein

DO THIS TODAY: *Roll up your sleeves, get ready to go for what you know. Pick a cause that is near and dear to you and get busy. Maybe choose a charity for the homeless where you can volunteer your time. Become a mentor to youth in underserved communities or step up to coach a peewee basketball team. Whatever you decide to do, be proactive and sign up now!*

April 9th

"NOBODY CAN TELL THE MOTHAHFUCKIN' FUTURE, SO MAKE THE BEST OF TODAY."

Nothing in life is a mothahfuckin' guarantee. You can do everything right, and with one accident, one wrong move, one asshole gettin' in the way, one slip, it could all crash down around your ass. On the other hand, you could do just about everything *wrong*, and get mothahfuckin' lucky. You have no idea. That means all you got is right now.

You ever find yourself sayin', "I'll do that tomorrow." What if you walkin' down the sidewalk and a mothahfuckin' bus drives off the road and flattens your ass? All of that amazing shit you was savin' for "tomorrow" don't mean shit now, does it? Life is shorter than you mothahfuckahs even know. Last thing you want is to be takin' your last breath thinking, "I wish I woulda...." Only thing you can take with you to the grave is regrets, and you don't want none of that taggin' on in the next level.

> ***Life is about not knowing, having to change, taking the moment and making the best of it, without knowing what's going to happen next.***
>
> —Gilda Radner

DO THIS TODAY: *Make a list of all the things you wanna do in your life before you die. That's your bucket list. Start today by doin' just one of 'em. Go take those flight lessons, travel across the scenic USA on an old-school Amtrak train, or finally get your groove on and learn that new line dance everybody's doin'. It's real simple, just get yo' ass up and move!*

April 10th

"YOU KNOW WHAT EMPATHY IS? LEARN IT AND PRACTICE IT."

I ain't sayin' you should be a *got-damn* punk or no sissy, or that you should take on everybody's emotional bullshit. But, it's a good idea to try and understand folks and what's *goings on* with them. You ever hear someone sayin' you wouldn't know what it feels like to be someone else unless you walk a mile in their shoes? Well, first off, ain't no way in hell I'm walkin' in somebody else's stank-ass shoes. Also, you're *never* gonna know exactly what it's like to be somebody else. But you can try to understand where they're comin' from a little bit. You ain't gotta be so mothahfuckin' cold. See what I'm sayin'?

Maybe one of your boys got an attitude. Instead of comin' off all gangsta on his ass, use these three words that will catch him totally off guard: "Are you okay?" Use them words on him, and let him tell you what's up, maybe you both feel better. Those three mothahfuckin' words are like magic, takin' folks out of their anger for a minute and lettin' 'em know you care. Use 'em often on friends, family, coworkers, or even the disgruntled drive-thru lady. You're gonna be surprised at how those easy words diffuse the situation and make everybody feel a little better. There's more about usin' this phrase on July 16th, so check that out when you get there.

> ***I wanted a life in which there was a constant oneness of feeling with others, in which the basic emotions of life were shared.***
>
> —Richard Wright

DO THIS TODAY: *Perform a task or do a chore that isn't usually yours. Maybe your woman always cooks. Tonight, you do it. Maybe your coworker always makes the coffee, but this morning, you beat 'em to it. See how it feels to be them just for a few minutes.*

April 11th

"LEAVE THE PAST IN THE PAST, OR IT'S GONNA KEEP TRIPPIN' YOU UP."

Thing that's crazy about the past is that it doesn't exist. Not really. It's gone. You can't touch it, can't change it, can't do nothin' about it. So, why the hell you holdin' onto it? You're usin' your mothahfuckin' energy carryin' around something that does not even exist. That's not too bright, now, is it? On top of that, how you gonna build something new if you got one arm around that kinda dead weight? Imagine you got an armload of bricks and you're tryin' to put up a wall. You gonna have to lay the grout, smooth it out, then put down the trowel and take a brick out of your other arm, lay it down, and do it all again. It's gonna take you seventeen years to build that mothahfuckin' wall. You gotta let that shit go.

Now, I'm not sayin' you should forget it all, because the man who ignores history is doomed to repeat it. Of course, we gotta understand. When we're talkin' about big things that affect us all, like the history of Black oppression in this country, it's important to know the details of how we got to where we are today. We got to know 'em and learn from 'em, but we can't hold onto 'em and let 'em keep weighing us down. You see the difference?

> ***The secret of change is to focus all your energy, not on fighting the old, but on building the new.***
>
> —Dan Millman

DO THIS TODAY: *What are you still holdin' onto from your past that makes you feel some kinda way when you thinkin' about it? That shit's blocking your forward momentum. Let it go right now. Even if you have to throw away actual physical shit, like letters or old pictures and whatnot. Do it and feel better. I know you will.*

April 12th

"DON'T GO SECOND-GUESSIN' GOD'S PLAN."

You can't go through each mothahfuckin' day saying shit like, "That's not how it's supposed to be." Or, "That ain't fair." Or, "The world's against me." The world ain't against you. Get a handle on your ego, mothahfuckah. God's doin' his thing. He ain't got time to mess around fuckin' your shit up. If you keep havin' one bad day after another, it means you ain't listenin' to what he's tryin' to teach you. There's lessons in there, you just gotta pay attention. Find the *got-damn* lesson, learn it, and pretty soon you gonna start havin' good days. But if you don't learn the lesson and you try to blame God, the Universe, or anybody else, you're giving away your power. Most folks are doin' that because they don't want the responsibility. Easier to blame somebody else and sit around and moan and groan about it. But guess what? That ain't gonna work for long. Pretty soon the dark days are just gonna pull you down.

Keep in mind that God and the Universe are never wrong. Y'all know I don't believe in no *got-damn* coincidence. Everything happens for a reason. You may wonder why you're dealin' with a certain problem or situation right now. Whatever it is, it's happenin' to teach your ass to prepare you for something comin' up. Once you look at it that way, you'll be able to handle it, no matter what. When you get the bad days, remember that there's hope for better. When there's good days, take 'em and run with 'em as fast and hard as you can. Pretty soon, every day is gonna look brighter than the last.

> ***I find hope in the darkest of days and focus in the brightest. I do not judge the universe.***
>
> —Dalai Lama

DO THIS TODAY: *I know you got a lot* **goings on**, *like tryin' to finish that big presentation that's due in an hour or pickin' up a last-minute anniversary gift for your partner cause yo' ass forgot about it. One of these situations could have the real ma-kin's of a bad day. That's when you gotta quiet your mind, take a deep breath, and ask yourself, "What is it that I can learn from this that's gonna help me down the road?"*

April 13th

"GET ANGRY ABOUT INJUSTICE, BUT DON'T LET THAT SHIT MAKE YOU AN ANGRY SUMBITCH."

I know lots of folks really mothahfuckin' angry about what's been *goings on* in the world. We got plenty of hate spewin' out from ignorant folks like slobber from a Great Mothahfuckin' Dane. If you ain't angry about some of the shit they're sayin', and some of the shit that's happening, then you got no heart. Be angry. Anger is a good thing. It pushes folks to do something about it, pushes for change. But what you can't do is let your anger change *you*.

Anger is a mothahfuckah. It will eat you alive if you let it hold onto you too long. It'll turn you into a dark soul. Those kinda folks suck the joy outta the room. So, you got to feel the anger and then let it the fuck go, then go on and do something about it. You angry because folks is starving and homeless in your city while other folks livin' high on the hog? Good, you're mad 'cuz you feelin' something for humanity. That's a good thing, and you can turn it into a positive force if you channel it the right way.

Let's use teachers as an example: Monday morning at 8:00 a.m., teachers who are pissed as hell show up for the picket line with spit and venom about 'em. But visit their classroom and you can almost hear the violins playin' as they teach the youth with enthusiasm and compassion. That's how you do it.

> ***Rage—whether in reaction to social injustice, or to our leaders' insanity, or to those who threaten or harm us—is a powerful energy that, with diligent practice, can be transformed into fierce compassion.***
>
> —Bonnie Myotai Treace

DO THIS TODAY: *What's one issue that sets a fire in your soul? Think about it, take deep breaths, and focus on lettin' the thought of it ease itself away from you. You can still see it, you can still work on solvin' it, but it's no longer a part of who you are.*

April 14th

"THE BETTER THE ATTITUDE, THE BETTER THE RESULTS."

You ever see that guy who maybe is workin' at the hardware store, and he's smilin' while he's stockin' the paint cans and shit. Maybe he's whistling a little tune to hisself? Makes you wonder what's up with him. I tell you what's up with him. That mothahfuckah has a positive mothahfuckin' attitude! His energy is infectious. Pretty soon you decide you gonna paint your mothahfuckin' bedroom even though you just did the whole *got-damn* house last year. You wanna get some paint just to be next to the man, get a little feel of what he's feelin'. That gentleman right there has figured ***somethin' out***. Attitude is everything. He's runnin' on a high vibration right there. He's maybe feelin' a tiny touch of the Holy Spirit in him.

When you approach life like that, things just seem to fall into place easier, and the bonus is that you're happier while you're goin' through it. You remember those seven little shorties stuck up in that cottage in the woods with the girl that was White as a mothahfuckah? They was singing about whistlin' while you're workin'. That's exactly it right there. Pretty soon you're attracting all kinds of help—birds, rabbits, squirrels, Bambis and shit comin' to clean your floors. It's not always about what you do, it's about how you do it. Work positive and get results. That's the mothahfuckin' truth.

> ***There's a direct correlation between positive energy and positive results.***
>
> —Joe Rogan

DO THIS TODAY: *Head to your personal playlist on your phone. Hit that play button and go to town singin' and dancin' while you doin' your chores. Do the "Cha Cha Slide" with the broom. Get funky. Really get into it! If you live with other folks, watch how they react. If you live alone, check how you feel while doin' it.*

April 15th

"PUT YOUR ENERGY INTO SOMETHIN', THAT'S WHAT'S GONNA GET BLESSED."

Lots of folks like to talk about blessings, saying, "You blessed, and you blessed, and I'm blessed. Everybody blessed." Sister Berta over there, she got the diabetes, can't even walk, got varicose veins and emphysema and cataracts. I gotta help her go to the meeting house to get her coffee and donuts after service, but she even sayin' she's blessed. Here's the mothahfuckin' truth—blessings don't just fall down random on folks. You gonna get your blessings wherever you're puttin' your mind and your *got-damn* work. God ain't up there just sprinkling favors willy-nilly. He ain't got time for that. It's more like a garden. The plants you feed and water and prune are the ones gonna pop up tall, healthy, and give you some plump and juicy vegetables. The ones you ain't waterin', those ones is gonna wither up and die.

So if you got something you wanna change, you gotta put your time into it. It ain't just gonna change while you're being distracted with something else. Whatever you're distracted with, *that's* what's gonna mothahfuckin' grow instead. But if you're payin' attention, you tending to that garden, God's gonna provide the sunshine and the magic...and that little seed of an idea, it's gonna grow up big and tall and healthy.

> ***Energy flows where attention goes.***
>
> —James Redfield

DO THIS TODAY: *What seeds do you want to grow? Get 'em in your head or write 'em down, then stay focused. Sometimes, there's folks intentionally distractin' you in order to serve their own purpose. You gotta have that tunnel vision. Don't look to the right, left, or behind. Just keep it movin' straight ahead.*

April 16th

"SOMETIMES MAKIN' A DIFFERENCE IS EASIER THAN YOU THINK."

With all kinds of shit *goings on* in the world weighin' on your shoulders, sometimes it feels like there's nothin' you can do to help nothin' at all. You feel small as a mothahfuckah, and the problems of the world feel too mothahfuckin' big. Thing is, you ain't gotta solve it all. Don't get me wrong, it's a noble cause. I see whatchyou tryin' to do. But thinkin' that way's gonna make yourself feel like a mothahfuckin' failure before you even try. The problem is, your goal's too *got-damn* big. Dream big, that's alright. But set your goals where you can reach 'em.

Here's the truth. You don't gotta heal the whole *got-damn* world. Maybe just start with changing somebody's day. I remember this time when I was stuck in the *got-damn* secretary of state office. Place was packed, and my number was in the triple digits. Folks in there was tired, frustrated, hot as a mothahfuckah. I coulda moaned and groaned too. But instead, I started crackin' jokes. Pretty soon, everybody was roarin' laughin'. Maybe one of them dads went home and instead of bein' in a foul mood, he took his boy outside to play catch, made his kid smile. Then the kid does something nice for his sister 'cuz he's in a good mood. You see where I'm goin'? Makin' folks smile is a really good *got-damn* way to start toward bigger change.

> ***I am only one, but still I am one; I cannot do everything, but still I can do something; and because I cannot do everything, I will not refuse to do something that I can do.***
>
> —Edward Everett Hale

DO THIS TODAY: *Go out of your way to make someone laugh or smile. If it makes you feel good, do it more than once! Open that door for the lady holdin' all those* got-damn *bags, return the grocery cart for a senior at the grocery store. Little things mean a lot, and they all add up.*

April 17th

"IF YOU WANT SOME PEACHES, YOU GOTTA SHAKE UP THE TREE."

Change ain't easy, especially when we're talkin' about changing shit that's been the same for a long, long time. I know I can get up on the stage and talk about how White folks and Black folks, we the same, we just do things different. I can make everybody laugh about it, but all them laughs are a little nervous. White folks lookin' around, surrounded by Black folks maybe for the first time in their lives. Anyway, I knew way back when I was gettin' started that once White folks were comin' to see my show, I made it. Boy, I crossed over from the Chitlin' Circuit, and White folks liked my comedy just as much as Black folks. I was blessed, but I know it took a lot of strong Black mothahfuckahs comin' before me to shake things up so I could.

Thing is, change don't usually come peaceful. So, look around you and pay attention. If things seem like they're all shook up, dark, maybe a little chaos *goings on*, that might just mean we about to have a change for the good. You can't get no peaches if you don't shake the tree. And when you do it, you might get knocked on the head with some fruit, might even get stung by a bee. But when you take a bite of that juicy, sweet peach pie, it's all worth it in the end.

> ***Any change, even a change for the better, is always accompanied by drawbacks and discomforts.***
>
> —Arnold Bennett

DO THIS TODAY: *Try changin' somethin' small that might make you a little uncomfortable at first. Do sixty sit-ups before you get ready for your day. It might shake up your routine of drinkin' coffee and checkin' email when you wake up, but you'll get used to it and start feelin' better. Organize your messy-ass closet, or harder yet, tell a family member you have a better way to do something that's different from how y'all have always done it. See how it feels to get through that momentary discomfort and consider the potential reward.*

April 18th

"WHAT IF WE WERE S'POSE TO BE ONE BIG-ASS TEAM TRYIN' TO WIN THIS GAME?"

We keep lookin' at each other like we're opponents, like we gotta be better than the other and we gotta beat everybody else. Sure, we got teams when we go play ball, teams on the job maybe, the family's a team. But what if we're ALL s'pose to be a mothahfuckin' team. Like every got-damn one of us everywhere in the mothahfuckin' world workin' together? Maybe we here to be one big-ass team. How's that gonna work if you're tellin' the guy next to you he ain't on the team because you don't like his beard and shit? But he's s'pose to be the *got-damn* wide receiver. You gonna lose, that's what I'm sayin'. Imagine if the quarterback looked at his right tackle and talk some shit like he's not part of his team and never was? He gonna look at you like you lost your *got-damn* mind. You'd never do that shit. You wouldn't see Reggie White doin' that shit on the field. Wouldn't see Shaq doin' it out on the court. So, we gotta stop doin' it in the most important game of all time—the game of mothahfuckin *life*.

Okay, so I don't give a good *got-damn* about your color, gender, your faith, or what country you comin' from. I don't care what language you speak, how old you are, or how much money you make. We're all on this mothahfuckin' planet together tryin' to survive and maybe even level up, and that makes us a mothahfuckin' team. Let's act like it.

> ***Talent wins games, but teamwork and intelligence win championships.***
>
> —Michael Jordan

DO THIS TODAY: *Pick somebody who you think is exactly the opposite of you. Maybe you're a Black Baptist millennial from the city, so you pick a White baby boomer Jewish lady from the suburbs that you know from work. See what I'm sayin'? Lots of differences, probably. I don't care about that. List all the things you got in common. I bet there's more than you think.*

April 19th

"NEVER GIVE UP A CHANCE TO TEACH SOMEBODY SOMETHING."

Whenever shit happens in life, you can either let it knock you down or you can learn something from it. And when someone makes a mistake and it fucks your shit up, far as I'm concerned, you got two options. You can let it make you angry, let it change you into the kinda person you don't wanna be when you punish them in some kinda way, or you can use it as a teachable moment. Now, I'm not sayin' that punishment is never an appropriate response. There's some nasty sumbitches that need to be mothahfuckin' punished for the shit they did, so we gotta do somethin' and then let God punish them again. But mostly, if there ain't no mothahfuckin' murder involved or no sick and twisted shit, there's teaching opportunities, even if that just means you're teaching by example. I know I say I'll smack them kids 'til the white meat shows. But y'all know I'm just joking around about that...generally speaking. *Eh hem. Y'all know I'm just sayin' whatchyou all wanna say but won't*. The thing is, when you punish somebody, they don't do that shit again 'cuz they're scared of getting punished. If you take a minute to teach them why what they did was wrong, or show them by example how to behave, they're gonna take that into their *got-damn* soul. That's how you gonna change a life, not by smackin' 'em upside the head. "Bend a tree while it is young, because when it is old, it will break." This proverb means you got to teach your children the right way when they are still bendable, the way that's gonna sit right with their soul, because tryin' to do it when they get older might be too fuckin' late for them and for yourself.

> ***Educate the children and it won't be necessary to punish the men.***
>
> —Pythagoras

DO THIS TODAY: *Think about how you might be punishing the people in your life who make mistakes. How can you teach them something in a compassionate way instead? When you punish, you harm. When you teach, you heal.*

April 20th

"ALL KINDS OF MESSAGES OUT THERE, BUT YOU CAN CHOOSE WHICH ONES TO BELIEVE."

Seems like nowadays everybody's tellin' you what's what. You got ABC, CBS, NBC, PB&J, FUC, and whatever TV news tellin' you that *this* is the thing or *that* is the thing. You got folks on the *Tikkitytak* and the *Grammadam* tellin' you what to think about this or that. It's got to the point where nobody can think for their *got-damn* self. Now, I'm not tellin' you not to listen to those folks. Listen to 'em. Some of them are smart folks, and you should know what they're sayin' even if it's just so you know why other folks are believin' what they're believin'. But don't stop with one. Listen to more than one, then go do some mothahfuckin' research yourself. Find out if what they're sayin' is factual. If it seems off, it probably is. And if what they sayin' is makin' you uncomfortable, like it's just not sittin' right in your soul, turn that sumbitch off.

Lots of folks, lots of companies, out there tellin' you that you ain't sexy enough, you ain't smart enough, you ain't tall enough, you ain't White enough, you ain't skinny enough. You gonna listen to those sumbitches? No. Pick another *got-damn* message to listen to. Maybe from your preacher or your friends or your mama, but not those mothahfuckahs tryin' to steal your joy for a dollah. That's some *got-damn* bullshit. Your joy's at least worth three damn dollahs. I'm kiddin'. It's worth everything, and don't you forget that. Believe a better message.

> ***My doctors told me I would never walk again. My mother told me I would. I believed my mother.***
>
> —Wilma Rudolph

DO THIS TODAY: *What are two opposing messages you're receiving about yourself right now? Choose the one that sits right in your gut and believe that one.*

April 21st

"YOU WANNA BE STRONG? STICK TOGETHER."

You ever try to rip a mothahfuckin' phone book in half? Wait, do they even make *got-damn* phone books anymore? With the yellow pages and shit? If you never heard of a phone book, you at least heard of a ream of printer paper, three hundred sheets, about four inches thick. Pick that shit up and try to rip it in half. You strainin' your neck and shit, usin' your mothahfuckin' foot, and you still can't do it, can you? Now, take out a sheet and rip it? Easy as slicin' butter. You could rip every *got-damn* one of them in less time than it takes to read this page. You see what I'm sayin'? Strength in numbers.

"Divide and conquer" ain't got no place in my *vocabellary*. Why? Because it mothahfuckin' works. You pull them sheets apart, they gonna rip up easy and blow away in the *got-damn* wind. You start pittin' one family member against another, the family gonna get stressed and break. "Divide and conquer" is used by folks who believe the only way to get ahead is to hold somebody else back, tear somebody else up. But the secret is that if we all stack up together, we become so mothahfuckin' strong that nobody can break us. You heard, "It takes a village to raise a child?" It means everyone plays a part in the success of our children.... You know growin' up in the Black community you got at least four mamas on your block ready to beat yo' ass if you get outta hand. That's what I'm talkin' about, and even more than that, we all God's children, so we need that village 'til the day we die. Unity. That's what that means.

> ***Unity is strength, division is weakness.***
>
> —African Proverb

DO THIS TODAY: *Who do you see as your "competition?" Now, think of them as part of your team instead. How can you work on risin' up together?*

April 22nd

"BE CAREFUL WHAT YOU LOOKIN' AT AND HOW YOU LOOKIN'."

You think you can change something just by lookin' at it? You think you Harry mothahfuckin' Potter, shootin' the old stank eye and makin' some biddy turn into a *got-damn* toad and shit? No, that shit ain't real. C'mon, now. But what *is* real is that you can change shit by *how* you look at it. I don't mean it actually morphs into a different mothahfuckin' shape, ain't no Transformer. But it changes because how you lookin' changes how it is. Believe it if you wanna, or don't, I don't give a fuck. I'm just tryin' to give you an *edumacation*.

I had this comic I was seein' a lot at the venues and shit, and he was makin' me all kinds of mad. He'd try and throw me off, try and do me wrong, and I didn't like him. Every time I saw his ass, I'd get jumpy and shook up. Boy did I hate that cocky mothahfuckah. Then somebody told me to make a list of all the things I appreciated about him. Not that I "liked" mind you, but that I appreciated. Damn, that was hard at first. But then I started thinkin', mothahfuckah's a snappy dresser, got good teeth and nice shoes. He stands up straight and looks folks in the eye. I saw him be good to his mama when she came in to watch. Pretty soon, I started lookin' at him a little different and I'll be a mothahfuckah, soon enough he stopped harassin' me, started askin' me to sit with him for a drink. Hmm, hmmm...who woulda thunk. But that's what I'm sayin', change your viewpoint and shit you lookin' at changes.

> ***Change the way you look at things and the things you look at change.***
>
> —Wayne W. Dyer

DO THIS TODAY: *Make a list of things you appreciate about someone you're feelin' some kinda way towards. Recall the list whenever you see 'em or think about 'em.*

April 23rd

"ANYBODY CAN BE A HERO. JUST PUT ON THE MOTHAHFUCKIN' CAPE."

Everybody lovin' Superman, Batman, Black Panther. Of course we love 'em, they're mothahfuckin' superheroes. All they do is save folks, riskin' their lives and shit to do it. These guys are some badass mamajamas, and we all kinda secretly wanna be like them, you know. Well, lemme tell you somethin'. You *can* be like them. All you gotta do is put on the mothahfuckin' cape. Now, now, I'm not talkin' literal. Don't go on and cut up your curtains and shit and put that around your neck, you gonna choke your *got-damn* self.

One time when I's about six years old, Sticky Jonnson from down the street put on a mothahfuckin' cape made outta his mama's apron. He was ridin' around on his bike with his fist out and shit, tryin' to show everybody he's Black mothahfuckin' Superman. I swear to God he got the *got-damn* apron strings stuck in his spokes. THWAP-WHAP-CRASH! Sticky's on the ground, cryin' like a mothahfuckin baby, all the kids laughin' askin' where the *got-damn* kryptonite at. Ya' see, Sticky made the mistake of wearin' his cape for other folks to see it and cheer and shit. That's not why you wear the cape, for real. And I know you know I'm talkin' about a *methaphillical* type of cape. It's like you gettin' ready to do some epic shit, so you put on this imaginary cape and what that is, it's just your power to do good. Nobody needs to see it but you, but they gonna feel it when you out there doin' good in the world.

> ***I think a hero is any person really intent on making this a better place for all people.***
>
> —Maya Angelou

DO THIS TODAY: *Do good. Legendary Motown diva Diana Ross sang about making the world a better place in "Reach Out and Touch (Somebody's Hand)." Challenge yourself to do one good thing for somebody else today without them knowin' it was you.*

April 24th

"STOP FIGHTIN' OVER EVERY *GOT-DAMN* THING. THERE'S ENOUGH FOR EVERYBODY."

One of the reasons everybody steppin' on one another, steppin' over one another, knockin' each other down is 'cuz they all thinkin' there's only so much to go around. Get rid of that "crab in the barrel" mentality. Y'all know what the hell I'm talkin about, all them damn crabs in the mothahfuckin' barrel, one crab tries to escape and makes it to the top of the barrel for a better life that doesn't involve boilin' in a pot, and what do the other crabs do? They reach up and pull that mothahfuckah back down into the barrel. Those *got-damn* crabs were thinkin', "Shit, if I can't get up there, neither can you." Or maybe they thinkin', "Imma hold onto that mothahfuckah and push myself up over the edge when he gets to the top." Lemme tell you, that's a bunch of bullshit. Imagine if all them crabs in that pot pushed against the side of it together, or if they made a *got-damn* chain and pulled each other one at a time? See what I'm sayin'?

You think the Universe only got so much of whatever it is you lookin' for? Love, money, fame, peace, freedom from that pot of water? Whatever it is you think you want, you don't think God can make more? Who do you think you're dealin' with up in here? You gotta stop bein' a stingy sumbitch and learn how to share. Learn how to share, *got-dammit*. God blesses those that help each other. As kids we're taught that sharing is good, and yet competition is what it sometimes turns into. Learn to share by not tearing others down, tryin' to block 'em, and keepin' the goods for yourself.

> ***People who wonder if the glass is half empty or full miss the point. The glass is refillable.***
>
> —Simon Sinek

DO THIS TODAY: *Stop bein' jealous of other folks' success. When you do this, even if you never receive a thank you, the world will thank you for it, and you'll know in your heart that you've done some good. Who are you jealous of right now? Go tell 'em that you happy for 'em or proud of their success...and mean it, for real.*

April 25th

"GOD WANTS YOU TO SUCCEED, AND THE UNIVERSE IS TRYIN' TO HELP MAKE IT HAPPEN."

God did not put you here to struggle. I'm gonna tell you that straight. He's not up there tryin' to throw obstacles and shit in your way. He wants you to be happy and successful, and he's doin' his *damndest* to help you out. Sometimes, you see it and you take his help. Other times maybe you're too preoccupied, you ain't payin' attention, and you miss what he's throwin' you. But if you always sittin' there thinking life has to be a struggle, that you got to claw your way to the *got-damn* top all the time, well, that's a bunch of bullshit. The right path is gonna feel easy, it's gonna bring you happiness, and it's just gonna flow like a river to the mothahfuckin' sea. Sometimes you might have to paddle a little, but you don't mind, 'cuz you enjoyin' the ride. That's when you know everything's comin' together to help you, that you on God's path.

No matter how much structure you try and create in your life, no matter how many good habits you tryin' to build, there's always gonna be somethin' you can't control that's gonna affect all different parts of your life. That's when you gotta go with the flow. Accept it without getting angry or frustrated, or you gon' be a cranky-ass mothahfuckah all the time, and you gonna miss out on the lesson God's tryin' to teach you.

> ***The whole universe is working in your favor. The universe has got your back!***
>
> —Ralph Smart

DO THIS TODAY: *Think about a time something threw a wrench in your careful plan, screwin' shit up. How did you feel? Did you learn a lesson, find a new path, end up with something better? Can you see God's plan at work?*

April 26th

"WHAT YOU DO TODAY'S GONNA DETERMINE WHAT A WHOLE LOTTA FOLKS CAN DO TOMORROW."

My granddaddy used to tell me this when I was young, but it was a little bit different. He used to say, "What you do today will determine what you'll be able to do tomorrow." It works, and I always got what he was sayin'. He meant that you gotta prepare yourself and you'll be able to do anything you wanna do when you're ready to do it. But now that I'm grown and I've lived a little, I like to change it up this way, 'cuz I know that what I'm doin' right now is gonna affect a lot more folks than just me.

When I made the push to be a professional comedian, my family got behind me, and they made sacrifices too. I knew back then that what I did with my career was gonna have a major effect on my wife Rhonda's life and my little girl Je'Niece's too. Man, did it ever. That first check I got from the Miller Lite Comedy Search, it went straight to my daughter's college education. And I told Rhonda once we made our first million, she could quit her nursin' job. We moved on up, just like the Jeffersons. But it didn't stop there. Me gettin' successful at what I wanted to do rippled out to Rhonda's sister's kid and her baby who stayed with us for a while, out on to the Mac Band members and the Macaronis. I s'pose I paved the way for other young comedians too. Maybe helped some kids just with the advice I was givin' out on my show. Thing is, you can try, but you can't even see all the effects of your choices.

> ***Someone is sitting in the shade today because someone planted a tree a long time ago.***
>
> —Warren Buffett

DO THIS TODAY: *Toss a stone in a puddle today, or even just drop a bar of soap in the tub, and watch the ripples spread out. Think about somethin' you've done and how it's affected others. Was it a positive or a negative thing?*

April 27th

"GET RIGHT WITH YOURSELF AND BE RIGHT WITH THE WORLD."

Congratulations, you are already takin' a step to gettin' right with yourself by reading this mothahfuckin' book. That's good. You're makin' yourself strong from the inside out. As you go through it, you'll realize that there's parts of yourself fightin' with each other like my sister's husband's cousins at a family barbeque—nails scratchin', toes kickin', wigs trippin'. Each one of 'em thinks they're right and both of 'em feel like they have a right to be there. I know you're thinkin', "Bernie, what does your fucked-up family have to do with my *self*?"

Hold on, I'm gonna tell ya'. All of them contradictin' thoughts in your head's like my sister's husband's cousins. Maybe one voice in your head is sayin' you gotta make a lot of money because that's what society is tellin' you. But your heart says you don't need much, you just wanna live in a tiny house in the middle of nowhere and sell fruit by the road and don't bother nobody. You got a struggle *goings on* insida you. That's gonna make you touchy, stressed, and make you lose your mothahfuckin' patience with everybody. If you're a normal human being, you got lots of those conflicts in your soul. It's time for you to face 'em head on. Be solid in the outcome. Know yourself and be set in your choices, and you won't give a good *got-damn* what's comin' at you out there. You'll be a pillar of mothahfuckin' peace and serenity.

When there is no enemy within, the enemy outside cannot hurt you.

—African Proverb

DO THIS TODAY: *Learn more about your inner self. Figure out your purpose, your values, what motivates you, your goals and beliefs. What have other folks been tellin' you about yourself that you don't feel is true? Don't believe 'em, just focus on what you have discovered for yourself.*

April 28th

"YOUR MIND IS A POWERFUL TOOL, SO OPEN IT UP AND USE IT."

First of all, you can't use the tools if the mothahfuckin' toolbox is shut. You gotta open up your mind to new ideas, new experiences, new thoughts, new possibilities. A shut mind, boy, all it will do is get dusty, old, dry, and shrivel the hell up...and nothin' gonna get fixed. But when you got it open, it's like all fresh air pours in and it makes you wanna be alive. When you got it opened like that, you can come up with ideas to do anything. You think George Washington Carver woulda come up with three hundred uses for the peanut if he was like, "Naw, we gotta just keep doin' shit the way we do it. Peanuts is for Cracker Jack. I know what I know," and that's it? Hell, naw. That Black mothahfuckah was like, "Peanuts could be soap," and a lot more shit, and now he's part of mothahfuckin' history.

Lemme tell you about a brothah at my granddad's church, Mr. Raymond Conrad. He was an old curmudgeonly mothahfuckah, had them deep wrinkles in his face look like he could stick his hanky right in there and lose it. He sat in the front *got-damn* row every Sunday with his arms crossed over his chest. All other folks is singin', swayin', shoutin' "Hallelujah!" Not him. Not Mr. Ray, 'cuz he was mad that they changed up the music and the order of the service...seventeen mothahfuckin' years before. I always thought the way he was sittin' like that, he was blockin' the Lord's blessings, blockin' the preacher's lessons. Damn, I was right!

> ***For things to reveal themselves to us, we need to be ready to abandon our views about them.***
>
> —Thích Nhàt Hanh

DO THIS TODAY: *Be mindful of how you hold yourself. If you notice your arms crossed, ask yourself what it is you're closed to at the moment? What signal are you givin' off during a face-to-face conversation when you keep lookin' at your phone? Not interested, right? Body language reflects your inner self. Open up, keep your shoulders back, your eyes up, and pay attention.*

April 29th

"I WOULDN'T HAVE DONE WHAT I DID IF YOU HADN'T HAVE DID WHAT *YOU* DID."

The quicker you realize that luck don't mean shit, the quicker you'll start feelin' lucky. Thing is, if you think luck has anything to do with why you're getting' blessed or why you ain't got shit, then you're takin' away all your mothahfuckin' power. You leavin' it up to fate? Why the hell would you do that? You gotta take control, take responsibility, then you start makin' your "luck" happen. And I put that in quotations because luck ain't dumb, it ain't random. Luck is when your actions line up with God's plan, then BOOM! Blessings. And not *sometimes*, but *always*, there's a long chain behind you of what other folks done that rippled out to what you done.

I think about how I crossed over from the Chitlin' Circuit to the mainstream, then onto film. I know I couldn't have done it if my mentors hadn't have paved the way—Richard Pryor, Sinbad, Eddie Murphy, Redd Foxx. And they couldn't have done that if it weren't for Dr. King, for Emmett Till and Mamie, for Rosa Parks, Bob Moses, Harriet Tubman. The list goes on and on. When you realize that, it makes you one humble sumbitch, and that's a good thing, for real. Humility actually makes you stronger.

> ***Shallow men believe in luck. Strong men believe in cause and effect.***
>
> —Ralph Waldo Emerson

DO THIS TODAY: *Think about something great that you done recently. Now, break it down. What had to happen first for you to be able to do it?*

April 30th

"WHAT YOU LOVE TO DO, THAT'S YOUR GIFT. DON'T WASTE IT."

Everybody comes into this world with a gift. Mine was makin' folks laugh, maybe a few other gifts, too, but that's the big one. When God was puttin' me together, he sprinkled that in there, and he intended that I use all the mothahfuckin' ingredients when I came out into the world. He knows what the world needs, he ain't no fool, and he's doin' his best to deliver it. You see, each gift is supposed to come together to put the world straight. But if you're ignoring your gift, it's wasted, and it throws off God's plan. You really gonna look at God and say, "Uh, God, I don't like this. I won't use it, so...can you take it back?" Hell, naw. You turn your head at a gift from God, you gonna get a bigger lickin' than when you told Aunt Bunny that the hand-sewn rooster quilt she made you for your twelfth birthday was ugly.

This is why you gotta use your gifts as much as you possibly can, 'cuz they were designed especially for you! Your gifts are gonna be things you love to do anyway, so it's no sweat. You hear what I'm sayin'? If you use your gifts, and Joe Dingle next door uses his, and Little Louie over on Fenkel uses his, and everybody in the mothahfuckin' world did the same, boy, I can't even tell you what would happen. It'd be like heaven on earth.

> ***Our passion is our strength.***
>
> —Billie Joe Armstrong

DO THIS TODAY: *Think of three people you spend a lot of time with. See if you can identify one or two things they're gifted at. You should be able to come up with at least one. Now, flip the script on yourself. What do you love to do when you don't have to do nothin' else? Make a list of those things, 'cuz those are your gifts. Are you usin' 'em?*

May 1st

"YOU CAN'T JUST PRAY, YOU ALSO GOTTA DO."

You got those folks in your life, when you goin' through some shit, they're all, "Oh, Bernie, I'm gonna pray for you. I'm gonna start a prayer chain and pray all day. Bernie, I'm keepin' you in my prayers." Okay, okay. That's wonderful, Sister Pearl, but whatchyou gonna *do* for me? I ain't sayin' that 'cuz I want folks to help me out all the time, it was just a *got-damn* example. Maybe you got Sister prayin' for all those sad homeless souls sittin' on the sidewalk beggin' for spare change, but she walks on by 'em and does not drop in a dime. She don't go help out at the soup kitchen, she don't give her household items to the shelter thrift shop, nothin'. But hold up, she prayin'. Now, don't get all uppity on me. I know I said you gotta pray, and it's good. Prayer is gonna help you focus, help God hear what you need. But you follow that up with action, you'll get God's attention and you gonna see things start to shift for real.

It's kinda like when you a kid and you really really want that View-Master for Christmas—you know, the plastic goggles and you put in the little round disk and the pictures click-click-click around and it's like mothahfuckin' magic. You want it so bad, you askin' and askin' and askin' your mama. Maybe she get it for you. But, if you also takin' out the trash, washin' the dishes, sweepin' the floors extra clean, she gonna notice, and your chances just shot way the hell up of gettin' what you want under that Christmas tree. You see what I'm sayin'? That's how prayers work too. You gotta pray and then *do* if you wanna see results.

> ***Prayer is where the action is.***
>
> —John Wesley

DO THIS TODAY: *What do you wanna ask God or the Universe today? Say a prayer and then do one small (or large) thing to move on it.*

May 2nd

"WHENEVER YOU CUTTIN' SOMEBODY DOWN, YOU CUTTIN' YOURSELF TOO."

My granddaddy used to tell me, "Whenever you pointin' your finger, you got three fingers pointin' back at you." Then he'd repeat it, sayin', "Three fingers pointin' back. Hear me, boy? Pointin' back at you, them fingers." He always said things three or four times. Anyway, what he meant was that when you're findin' stuff in other folks that you don't like, you probably got that same kinda shit in your own *got-damn* self. 'Cuz guess what? We all a part of one big-ass creation, so really you pointin' at both of y'all at the same mothahfuckin' time, kinda like you pointin' at your whole self even when you just pointin' at your nasty corned toe.

Lemme put it another way. What if you sayin' your sister got a mama that's all fucked up on drugs and shit? Damn, that's *your* mothahfuckin' mama too. You pointin' at your damn self, not just your sister. Now, don't be lookin' at me that way, we all got one of them in our *got-damn* families. Nothin' to be ashamed of, you know. It is what it is. We all one big *got-damn* family up in here, so quit pointin' and start actin' like your Big Mama's watchin'. Preacher, too, maybe, if that helps. 'Cuz whether you like it or not, we all in this together, every single mothahfuckin' one of us.

> ***My humanity is bound up in yours, for we can only be human together.***
>
> —Desmond Tutu

DO THIS TODAY: *Think about someone you've "pointed a finger" at recently. Maybe you've been talkin' about your coworker cause they're gossipin' again. Why are you singlin' them out? Can you find similar "ugly" characteristics in yourself? Think about it. Do you need to make a change?*

May 3rd

"YOU GOTTA PEEL OFF ALL THE BULLSHIT IF YOU WANNA SEE YOURSELF FOR REAL."

You got stuff holdin' onto you like *got-damn* wet towels. You know, when you go to the beach and you get outta the water, go to grab a mothahfuckin' towel and your girl already used all of 'em. So, you pick 'em up and you got 'em wrapped around you, heavy, drippin', coverin' you up, each one weighin' like forty-seven pounds per square inch. You think it's maybe helpin', but that shit is really just makin' you wetter and colder, makin' it so you can't move, can't even see too good. You lookin' like *Nephrotitty* up in here, nobody can tell it's you. That's what it's like when you hold onto all the bullshit that's not workin' for you no more. You got anger, grudges, old hurts, anxiety, fear, you got an attitude of lack, you got hate and doubt...all of that's another wet towel. You gotta take each one of those, peel 'em off, throw 'em down, and let the *got-damn* breeze air-dry your ass.

It's kinda like sheddin'. If you ever had a pet, then you know about the *got-damn* sheddin'. It's a mothahfuckin' mess, but it has a purpose. Healthy dogs and cats shed away the old unneeded and damaged hair of their undercoat, all that fur that's doin' nothin' but weighin' 'em down and makin' 'em hot. See where I'm going with this? Time for you to shed the old, unneeded, and damaged goods in your life. It might be a little messy at first, but you gonna be lighter and happier once you done it.

> ***Whatever is bringing you down, get rid of it. Because you'll find that when you're free... your true self comes out.***
>
> —Tina Turner

DO THIS TODAY: *What are you holdin' onto that no longer serves you? Maybe it's a copin' mechanism, like not trusting anybody because somebody hurt you with their lies once. You don't need that no more, 'cuz that person ain't around, now. So, let it go. Whatever "undercoat," whatever "wet towels" you got, pick one and make a decision to shed it right now.*

May 4th

"WORRYIN' IS LIKE PRAYIN' FOR THE SHIT YOU DON'T WANT."

Why you gonna worry about some shit that ain't happened yet? Y'all know that constant worrying and negative thinking can affect your emotional and physical health. It can give you headaches, make you restless, make it hard to concentrate.

Listen, I had a friend in high school, always worried that the other kids was lookin' down on him because he didn't have no money. He'd be walkin' down the hall, lookin' for kids who's lookin' at him funny. Mothahfuckah was wound up tighter than my cousin La'Toya's weave. Well, let me tell you, the hallways was always packed with kids, so of course somebody's gonna look at him. I told him once, "Hey, Slim, slow your *got-damn* roll. Folks can't walk around with they mothahfuckin' eyes closed. They just lookin' around." He didn't believe me. He was so worried all the *got-damn* time, he sure as hell was gonna see what he's lookin' for.

One day he thought some punk-ass was lookin' at him funny, so he gave the kid a nasty look back. That kid says, "What the fuck you lookin' at?" Slim says, "You, mothahfuckah. You got a problem with me?" The kid did have a problem, it was his shitty *got-damn* attitude. That's when the fight started. I tried to pull him off, but that sumbitch had a switchblade. Slim got suspended from school, ended up on the street, in a gang. Fucked up his life. All I kept thinkin' was, "Damn. I ain't got no money, neither. But if folks is lookin' at me, it's 'cuz I'm the finest Black man they ever saw." Slim, though, he kept worryin' all the mothahfuckin' time, and guess what? His "prayers" were answered. They always are in some kinda way.

> ***Stop talking about the things that are bothering you so much.***
>
> —Abraham Hicks

DO THIS TODAY: *Take a deep breath, now release it slowly. Do that two more times. The key word here is "RELEASE." What are you worried about? More importantly, how can you change that worry into a positive prayer?*

May 5th

"BE CAREFUL WITH HATE. IT TAKES A CHUNK OUTTA YOU EVERY TIME YOU USE IT."

"Hate" is a strong mothahfuckin' word. I never liked it, but I wouldn't say I *hated* it. You got to reserve that word for things and folks that cut you so deep, they punch a hole in your very soul. That's a rare kinda folk, a rare kinda thang. So when you say, "I hate cooked cauliflower." Does it really cut your soul? I mean, that shit smells like Baby Peg's diaper, so full it's draggin' down on the mothahfuckin' ground, her ass-crack showin' and shit. I know it smells nasty like that, but it does not require such a strong word. You gotta use your language precisely. You say, "My mothahfuckin' taste buds repel that nasty shit." But you don't hate it. You *hate* that some *got-damn* coward came outta nowhere and pushed your disabled brother off his bike and stole it right in front'a you for apparently no mothahfuckin' reason. You *hate* that folks is sufferin'. You *hate* Satan, you *don't care for* cauliflower. You see the difference?

Don't go throwin' that word around like its nothin'. 'Cuz if you do, it loses its meanin' and it tears you up. The more you hate, the darker a shadow it's castin' on your soul, smothers your *got-damn* light, you know. It ain't worth none of that.

> ***The price of hating other human beings is loving oneself less.***
>
> —Eldridge Cleaver

DO THIS TODAY: *Go the entire day without usin' the word "hate." I know the level of anxiety y'all gotta deal with today is unreal, with all of the* **got-damn** *drama* **goings on** *in the world. But you gotta take your life into your own hands and say no to hate. Maybe you can get creative and come up with a list of other phrases to use instead, just so you're prepared.*

May 6th

"YOU GOTTA HELP OUT IF YOU GONNA BE LIVIN' HERE."

When I was a kid, we lived in the apartment above the church where my granddaddy was deacon. It was me and my mom, my brother Darryl, Big Mama, and Grandpa Thurman. Plus, we always had a whole lotta cousins hanging around there too. The adults in my house, boy, they did not tolerate no freeloadin'. I'd be four years old, and Big Mama'd tell me to earn my *got-damn* keep. "You gonna live here, child, you gotta work for it. Ain't no free rides. You can pedal a bike, you can push a broom." We all pitched in. We might have moaned and groaned, but lookin' back I realize it made us feel like we was worth something, like the family needed us to run right, you know?

Same thing for the bigger picture. You livin' here on this planet, you can't just sit around freeloadin'. You got to be here, so it's your responsibility to chip in a little somethin'-somethin'. You can't pay no *got-damn* rent. What's God gonna do with cash money? But give a little to somebody who needs it? Now, you're talkin'. Take it up a notch, too, and donate that money to a group that's doin' the work to make folks' lives better. Or even better, go help out at that organization. Give your time, your talent, and your energy. That's all the rent you need.

> ***Activism is my rent for living on the planet.***
>
> —Alice Walker

DO THIS TODAY: *Get off your ass, roll up your sleeves, and help somebody, anybody. Don't just sit there lookin' around askin', "What do I do? Where do I go?" Ask Siri to locate the nearest Boys & Girls Club and become a mentor. Find the closest senior center and go visit the folks there. You CAN help make someone's life better. Helpin' one person may not change the world, but it could change the world for one person.*

May 7th

"IF I DON'T DO IT, IT WON'T GET DONE."

You gotta stop relyin' on everybody else to do what you can do your got-damn *self*, because when you lay it on other folks, it's a good way to get yourself disappointed. If you got a job to do, you see somethin' that needs fixin' or changin', don't sit there and think, "So-and-so is gonna do it, I'm sure, so I'll just let them take care of it." If I came into your kitchen with a sweet potato pie and set it down on the counter, you ain't gonna say, "Oh, somebody else is gonna eat it, I'll just let them eat it. I'm good." Hell naw, you gonna jump in there with your plate and a scoop of mothahfuckin' vanilla ice cream. You jump in there 'cuz it's good and you want it. But if I asked you to take out the trash...don't lie, you know you gonna hesitate. Especially if I don't ask, and the trash is just overflowin', you gonna think, "Somebody else will take it out." Be honest with yourself, you know you done that shit before. But what if everybody was sayin', "Somebody else will do it?" Naw, you gotta assume *nobody* else is gonna do it, and then you do it your own *got-damn* self or the whole house is about to smell like stank.

Same principle applies to your career, your goals, your family, and the *got-damn* world you livin' in. You see somethin' needs to be fixed, do it. If you need some help, get some other folks on board to do it too. Basketball great Shaquille O'Neal said it best when he said, "There are seven days in the week and *someday* isn't one of them." Now that's facts.

Assumptions are quick exits for lazy minds that like to graze out in the fields without bother.

—Suzy Kassem

DO THIS TODAY: *Press the start button for yourself. Stop waitin' on everybody else to do shit before you do. Remember, your future is created by what you do today, not tomorrow. How are you gonna jump start yourself today?*

May 8th

"AS SOON AS YOU STOP GROWIN', YOU START DYIN'."

I heard somebody say this when I was young, and it stayed with me ever since. It means that you gotta keep learnin', you gotta keep gettin' better, because if you don't, you're maybe not dyin' on the outside but you're dyin' on the inside. Kinda like the water that sits in the bottom of an empty dumpster. It ain't flowin', just sittin' in the hot sun, and before long it starts to fester, starts smellin' foul. That's what's happenin' to your mind, it's what's happenin' to your *got-damn* soul, if you get stuck in your ways.

How do you keep growin'? You watch and you listen. Everyday something else is gonna be *goings on* around you that you can learn something from. It could be a mistake and you gotta learn a lesson. It could be a big event that everybody's talkin' about, maybe you start diggin' up your own information on both sides. You study some ways to calm your mind and let shit go that ain't servin' you. You help other folks and learn how to empathize with 'em. Or maybe you read all kinda books and newspapers, listen to podcasts, go to the mothahfuckin' theater or the opera. You keep learnin' and keep growin', and it's good. But sometimes your growth can scare some folks whose own sense of security depends on your stagnation. Those folks might try and hold you back, but you can't let 'em. You gotta just leave 'em be scared, 'cuz you gotta stay focused on yourself, your dreams, your goals. That's how you do it.

> ***A man who views the world the same at fifty as he did at twenty has wasted thirty years of his life.***
>
> —Muhammad Ali

DO THIS TODAY: *Look for opportunities to learn and grow. If you see somethin' interesting pop up, even if it's outside of your box, say yes and expand your horizons a little bit.*

May 9th

"HURRY UP AND SLOW THE HELL DOWN."

I know I'm always talkin' about "do it now," and "don't wait." What I'm talkin' about there is not putting shit off sayin' you gonna do it later. What I *don't* mean is that you gotta be *frantic* about shit. What I also don't mean is that you gotta try to do everything at once. That's a good way to overwhelm yourself. What are you racin' for? How can you possibly give all your attention to so many things at once? That's ridiculous. You're gonna half-ass stuff, nothin' will receive your full efforts, and nothin' will be done right. You can only take one step at a time, carry one load at a time, and that's all you gotta do as long as you keep movin' forward.

I had this buddy when I was young. Man, he had about seven jobs. He was always runnin' from one place to the other, always frantic. "Shit, I'm gonna be late, gotta go." He was so desperate to make somethin' of hisself. He was savin' money, but he was always tired, never had any fun, never laughed. He didn't realize that it's not a mothahfuckin' race. You ain't gotta be at a certain level at a certain age. That's some made-up bullshit that keeps kids in a state of mothahfuckin' frenzy, feelin' like they ain't movin' fast enough. Who says you gotta be outta the house by eighteen, gotta have a nice car and your career by twenty-two, gotta be married with kids by thirty? That's just a buncha bullshit put into place by human beings. God got an individual plan for everybody, and their mothahfuckin' idea can't trump God's. So, slow the hell down. Focus on doin' shit right the first time, takin' care of your health and well-being while you doin' it, and you gonna get in the right flow. When you're in that right flow, it's never ever gonna feel frantic.

> ***There is a time for everything, and a season for every activity under the heavens.***
>
> —Ecclesiastes 3:1

DO THIS TODAY: *Slow yo' ass down. You want a bunch of fucked-up projects that could be way better if you had just taken your time? Today, figure out your priorities and come up with a plan on how you gonna tackle first things first.*

May 10th

"YOU'RE NOTHIN' MORE OR LESS THAN THE STORY OF WHAT YOU BEEN THROUGH."

You ever think about what makes you *you*? Maybe you think it's your body, but it ain't. Them cells that make up your body, they shed off and get replaced more often than Big Mama's wigs. You know you got new fingernails every coupla months, completely new hair every few years, but *got-damn*, you even got a whole new skeleton every mothahfuckin' decade! Once you're graduatin' from elementary school, you ain't even the same *got-damn* body at all. So, what makes up *you* if it ain't your body? Your mind, okay. That sounds about right. But what makes up your mind? Memories of the experiences you gone through.

You are your mothahfuckin' story, and every event writes itself on a new page, and every new page is gonna influence who you are and what you do next in your life. It's like you can imagine every day like it's part of your own autobiography, and you're writin' right now. What do you want folks to read in your mothahfuckin' autobiography? The good news is, you're still writin' it! You can put whatever the hell you want on them pages. Man, you got the opportunity to write a *got-damn* bestseller. Better get to it.

> ***Life is not what you alone make it. Life is the input of everyone who touched your life and every experience that entered it. We are all part of one another.***
>
> —Yuri Kochiyama

DO THIS TODAY: *Think about your story like it's a book. Who are the main characters? Who's the hero and who's the villains? What's the plot? Is it a book you'd want to read? If not, start changin' it right now.*

May 11th

"WHEN SHIT'S GETTIN' HARD, THAT MEANS YOU ABOUT TO LAUNCH."

Remember when you was a little kid at the swimming pool. You'd wriggle your little arms and legs, water gettin' all up in your nose, eyes open even with the chlorine, and you'd force yourself to get all the way down to the bottom and touch it. Then what did you do? That's right, you rolled around, touched your feet down on that rough concrete, and pushed yourself up. Man, you'd go rocketing up through that water and come busting through the surface like mothahfuckin' Shamu! You'd come out takin' a deep breath with a smile on your face. You did it! And that push off the bottom, that's what shot you up so *got-damn* fast.

I hit the bottom myself, and I pushed myself off too. I was in a slump. Couldn't get no jobs, quit comedy, got on food stamps. Man, was that a low point for me. I felt like a got-damn *failure*. Up until then, I always felt like I could do anything I wanted, reach all my mothahfuckin' goals. I didn't like that feelin'. It was heavy, dark, cold, like the bottom of the *got-damn* pool. That's when I realized that I didn't wanna keep feelin' that way, so I put my feet down and I pushed off. I found a job, got back on the stage, and everything took off again. It's like I needed to touch my feet on the bottom to realize that I needed to push.

> ***When everything seems to be going against you, remember that the airplane takes off against the wind, not with it.***
>
> —Henry Ford

DO THIS TODAY: *Listen to the '70s classic by the Steve Miller Band, "Fly like an Eagle." Damn, that's a smokin' cut, but it's also speakin' facts to you. That eagle is a cold mothahfuckah. When it rains, most birds head for shelter, but the eagle feels the rain comin' and soars above the* **got-damn** *rain clouds. How are you gonna get up above your own rain clouds?*

May 12th

"THINGS CAN GET BAD, BUT IT AIN'T THE END OF THE MOTHAHFUCKIN' WORLD."

The planet we livin' on is over four billion years old. You think because you got some mothahfuckin' problems it's gonna stop spinning? Human beings have been walkin' around here for like...well, at least a couple hundred thousand years or something. Shit, you're just a blip on the timeline. Life on Earth ain't gonna stop because something's not going your way. The planet, the Universe, does not give one single fuck.

Kids nowadays be walkin' around, hoodies up over their heads, actin' like everything's so bad they don't even wanna come outta their rooms. What's so bad? You sittin' up in there with your smartphone, laptop, HDTV, your mama bringin' you snacks and shit. Now, I ain't belittling the folks who has real problems. I get it, bad shit happens all the damn time. But I can pretty much guarantee if you readin' this book, there's some shit happenin' to someone somewhere in the world that's as bad or worse than what yo' ass is facin'. I know, it's not a competition, but it's just a little perspective so you don't feel like your shit is worse than everybody else's. You got a problem; you deal with it. Get proactive, because in every situation there's about a million different choices about what you can do. It's when you do nothin' that shit starts to feel hopeless, and you need hope to get you through it.

> ***In three words I can sum up everything I've learned about life: it goes on.***
>
> —Robert Frost

DO THIS TODAY: *Think about the successful people you know. More than likely, these folks went through some jacked-up shit just like you. Was it their talent and skill that made them successful? Naw, but they all got somethin' in common—resilience. They just keep on tryin' and they bounce back. I said this shit before, and I'll say it again: a setback is a setup for the next level.*

May 13th

"YOU SMILE, FOLKS GONNA SMILE WITH YOU."

You ever sittin' in a room with a lot of folks, and one of 'em lets out a huge jowl-poppin' yawn? You look at 'em, and you ain't tired at all, but pretty soon you feel your jaw quiver, eyes pop, and there it goes. You yawn, and you see everybody else yawn too. That's what I mean about the energy you put out. The yawn is mothahfuckin' contagious. Same thing goes for a smile. You walk into work, folks can be grumpy as hell, you smile real big, twinkle in your eye, and say, "Good morning!" You're gonna notice it spread around you like a *got-damn* yawn. It's like magic. The downside is that the same thing goes for a frown, for anger, for laziness, or for any other kinda energy you projectin'.

Listen, we all got that one member of the household that sets the whole *got-damn* mood for the whole family. In my house, it was Big Mama. Boy, you walk in the door, and you can tell what kinda mood Big Mama's in. If she's feelin' tired, down, folks is layin' around with their heads down, eyes droopin'. Dinner that night's boiled cabbage, smells like nasty feet. Kids is fightin', no good. But if Big Mama just had her hair did or somethin', she done spent the day with the girls at the beauty parlor, she's got a big smile and everybody's happy. Maybe we even get some chocolate puddin' for dessert. You see, that kinda shit is contagious. So, be careful what you puttin' out there, and protect yourself from the energy other folks is puttin' out too.

> ***Energy is contagious, positive and negative alike.***
>
> —Alex Elle

DO THIS TODAY: *Watch the company you keep. Who you hangin' around with? What kinda energy are you allowing in your circle? Check yourself. Do you like what you seein'? If not, then create a new got-damn crowd.*

May 14th

"IF FOLKS WANNA BE AROUND YOU, THEY GOTTA VIBE WITH YOU."

Breakin' off a relationship is the hardest mothahfuckin' thing on the planet. I don't care if it's a romantic relationship, business, professional, just a friendship, or hell, even family. You been around with somebody a while, it ain't easy to walk away when you realize they don't give a good *got-damn* about you, 'cuz you got comfortable with them. Or maybe you realize they're just bad folks, bringin' you down. But once you learn how to walk away from that kinda bullshit, your life is gonna get blessed. Once you feel that blessin', it's gonna get easier and easier to cut off the folks that block it for you.

I understand that sometimes you can't really cut off somebody. Maybe it's your mama makin' you feel some kinda way. Maybe it's your brothah or your boss. Now, you can *always* cut somebody off, but there's times you don't wanna make that kinda sacrifice, so you gotta learn how to "bubble up." That means you gotta put like a force field around yourself when you get near those kinda energy vampires, suckin' you dry all the time. It could be as easy as repeatin' to yourself, "My energy is stronger than yours." Or, "I won't let your nasty-ass comments affect me." Whatever works, sit for a minute before you gotta be around 'em and put up your mothahfuckin' bubble. If that don't work, maybe you need to reassess the pros and cons of keepin' 'em around.

> ***Positive things happen when you distance yourself from negative people.***
>
> —Boonnaa Mohammed

DO THIS TODAY: *Fam, I want you to be honest with yourself. Who do you know that's suckin' your energy, blockin' your blessings? Can you cut 'em off? If not, practice puttin' up your negativity force field. You got this.*

May 15th

"YOU GOTTA HELP OTHER FOLKS, BUT DON'T LOSE YOURSELF DOIN' IT."

I know I'm always sayin' to help others 'cuz that's how you get your blessings. But you can't help everybody else so much that you kinda disappear behind 'em. You ain't nobody else's shadow. You don't wanna let nobody else *consume* you, neither. Some folks are just so hungry that they gonna suck you down quicker than my brothah Big Nigga suckin' down a fish & chips basket at Dock's, and they still be wantin' some more. Them kinds of folks will suck you dry, make you feel like nothin', worthless, even when you been doin' so much to help 'em. Them kinda folks let you slip into the background while they stealin' the show.

Now, I ain't talkin' about givin' up what you want for a little while to give what you need to give to your children, or a family member that's sick or somethin'. We can do that temporarily, you know. That's called sacrifice, and God looks kindly on that. We can all sacrifice at times, and that teaches us humility. But you can tell the difference. Mostly when you sacrifice like that, folks is grateful for it. The ones that suck you dry ain't never grateful. Don't go spendin' your time and energy on them folks. Bottom line is, you gotta give, but only give what you can and only to the folks that appreciate it. That's blessings all around, and you wanna live in that kinda energy. That's when givin' actually builds you up.

> ***You are not just here to fill space or be a background character in someone else's movie.***
>
> —David Niven

DO THIS TODAY: *Who do you have in your life that's suckin' you dry? Decide right now if you can cut 'em off or if you gotta figure out how to step back so they can't get their fangs in ya'.*

May 16th

"KEEP LOOKIN' AT THE WORLD LIKE A CHILD DOES."

Why's everybody takin' everything so serious all the time? *Got-damn*, we need room for *livin'* in between all the *responstabilities*. You remember when you was a kid in the summertime? You'd wake up, eyes pop open, you look over at your cousins all sleepin' next to you, shake 'em awake. "Hey, let's go!" They wake up, wipin' sleep outta their eyes. "What we gonna do?" You say, "I don't know yet! But let's go!" That's the kinda excitement and joy and wonder we need to keep havin' in life. Even when we're old as a mothahfuckah.

There's been a lot of mornings in my life that my *got-damn* alarm goes off, beepin' in my ears, mornin' radio announcer soundin' way too happy, and I swear I wanna throw the *got-damn* thing across the room. First off, it wasn't the clock radio's fault. Second off, whatchyou got to be upset about? Your alarm's goin' off, so at least you got somethin' to get up for—a job, school, somethin'. Be excited about that! Think about all the possibilities, all the choices you get to make. Man, when I was a janitor, I used to push around my mop and broom, smilin', thinkin' about all my new jokes, and then I'd get home and practice 'em. Every new day there was new material just in livin'. Then, when you get done with that job or that school, maybe you sit with a pencil and draw out your new invention. Maybe you go for a ride on one of them electric scooters. Or maybe you whip up some kinda new dessert creation and share it with your neighbors. That's how you do it, like you still got a little bit of that summertime kid in you.

> ***I have a lot of growing up to do. I realized that the other day inside my fort.***
>
> —Zach Galifianakis

DO THIS TODAY: *It's cool to be happy for no fuckin' reason at all. I heard this sayin' and it's so true: "We don't stop playing because we grow old. We grow old because we stop playing." Get your play on today. Do somethin' fun that you'd do when you was a kid and haven't done for a long-ass time.*

May 17th

"DON'T KEEP YOUR VISIONS TO YOURSELF. SAY 'EM OUT LOUD AND THEY START TO COME TRUE."

Y'all remember when you had phones that stuck to the wall with long-ass twisty cords? You'd be sittin' on the floor in the *got-damn* coat closet, door pulled shut as far as it would go, cord stickin' out and running down the hall to the kitchen. You're talkin' to your girl, gettin' all sweet, then your granddad coughs and he says, "C'mon, now, boy. You can do better than that. Tell her she sweet like molasses." Yep, everybody on the same line. Before we had that, we was even more hooked up to each other 'cuz they had them party lines and shit. What I'm gettin' at is that all our minds work like that. They all on the same mothahfuckin' *system*, and if we'd all pick up at the same time, we'd hear each other's business. That's why it's important to affirm your vision out loud, just in case there's other folks on the line that can help push it forward.

I remember goin' into meetin's with executives and shit, sayin' I'm gonna have my own show. Even when I got turned down, I kept sayin' it. Guess what? *The Bernie Mac Show*, that's what. I kept sayin' I was gonna be a Hollywood movie star way back when I was still doin' stand-up. I'd tell it to my family, tell it to my manager, my publicist, anybody. Guess what? Movie star. That's how you do it. The more folks that know your vision, the more gears get in motion to make it happen.

> ***Because of the interconnectedness of all minds, affirming a positive vision may be about the most sophisticated action any one of us can take.***
>
> —Willis Harman

DO THIS TODAY: *Start your morning by saying, "I am happy with who I am and who I can be." Now go on into the day and tell your visions, your dreams, to as many folks as will listen to 'em. You gonna start to feel the positive energy buzzin' around you. Bet on that.*

May 18th

"YOU DON'T KNOW SOMETHIN', ASK. AIN'T NO SUCH THING AS STUPID QUESTIONS."

My wife was just like everybody else's wife. We'd go on a drive somewhere, maybe to a picnic, and we turn down the wrong street or somethin', end up somewhere we don't wanna be. She'd be naggin' at me, "Bernard, stop up at that store and ask for directions. Bernard, there's a gas station, you can ask them for directions." But like every man in the *got-damn* world, I'd hush her up and tell her I knew where I was goin'. Yeah, we'd finally get there…three hours late, and missed all of Auntie Mabel's potato salad. I'll admit, I was stubborn, but I learned my lesson.

It takes a bigger man to ask the questions when he don't know somethin', don't know which way to go, or how to solve somethin' that's he's been workin' at. There's folks that's been through it, been there before, and they got wisdom you don't have yet. Then, there's some times you got big questions you feelin' like you can't get a solid answer for, so you ask God. Then you quiet yourself down and you listen for an answer. This way, you gonna get on your path quicker, and you gonna stay on it. Nobody should ever be travelin' alone…also, listen to your *got-damn* girl when she's tellin' you to ask for directions. She's ridin' shotgun for a mothahfuckin' reason.

> ***Ask and it will be given to you; seek and you will find; knock and the door will be opened to you.***
>
> —Matthew 7:7

DO THIS TODAY: *See that quote above? God already told you what to do. Stop being hard-headed and follow His directions. What are you gonna ask for today? Humble yourself and do it.*

May 19th

"BE CAREFUL IDENTIFYIN' YOURSELF WITH A GROUP, IT CAN MAKE YOU LAZY."

Everybody today's joinin' shit left and right. You gotta be part of an organization to feel like you doin' somethin', gotta put that badge on your *got-damn* profile. But half the time, folks join this group and that group and they ain't actually doin' jack to help the cause. Okay, so maybe you share a mothahfuckin' meme on your social medias, or maybe you bring the lemonade for the meetin', but are you diggin' in your heels and doin' the real shit it takes to make change? Okay, it helps a little to make a post on the Instagram—lets folks know how you feel, puts it out there. But if that's where you stop, if you don't do nothin' more, then you ain't really doin' the work to make no mothahfuckin' progress. It's real easy to say "I stand for this" or "this is bad and has to go." It's a lot harder to do somethin' about it.

Here's a way to look at it. When I was a kid, we didn't have a lot, but we always got some food on the table, that's for sure. I didn't always like it, but we almost never complained, 'cuz Big Mama said, "You don't like it, either starve or fix yourself somethin' else." Sometimes, if I dislike that meal enough and I's hungry enough, I'd get on up and go fry myself an egg and a piece of bologna. It was work, but boy I did not like the taste of boiled cabbage. What good would it have done if I'd just sat at the table and kept on sayin' "I don't like boiled cabbage?" You guessed it—I'da starved half to death.

> ***The activist is not the man who says the river is dirty. The activist is the man who cleans up the river.***
>
> —Ross Perot

DO THIS TODAY: *You're either gonna shit or get off the pot. So, stop talkin' about it and* **be** *about it. Contact your group and see what you can do. Remember, action speaks louder than words.*

May 20th

"KNOW WHAT YOU BELIEVE, OR YOU'LL FALL FOR ANY OLD BULLSHIT THAT COMES ALONG."

You go through life not knowin' what it is you believe in, and you end up easy pickin's for all of them crazies that wanna convince you to do what they want you to do. You end up latchin' onto any old idea that floats by, 'cuz human beings need to believe in something. It's part of our mothahfuckin' nature. That's how folks end up joinin' cults, givin' away all their shit and drivin' off to the desert in a van with no seats, wearin' tin-foil hats and changin' their name to Stardust Chitlin' and shit. They're so mothahfuckin' desperate to believe in somethin'.

Me, I was raised up in the Baptist church. My mama, my granddaddy, my Big Mama, they all taught me what they believed, and I stuck to it. Got me through some tough times. Now, I ain't sayin' you necessarily gotta stick with what your folks taught you. That's up to you. I ain't caught up in all the rules and all of that. But what my faith taught me was how to treat folks, how to be a good man, how to talk with God. That's what's important. Whatever way you find your beliefs, that's okay, just find 'em. Hold onto 'em, and believe in yourself, and you won't go on and do nothin' foolish.

> ***If you don't stand for something, you will fall for anything.***
>
> —Gordon A. Eadie

DO THIS TODAY: *Have your own* **got-damn** *thoughts. The most common way you can give up your power is by thinkin' you don't have any. Practice gettin' your power back. Start by writin' down one thing you firmly believe in and remind yourself of it throughout the day.*

May 21st

"EVERYTHING YOU DO, EVERY WAY YOU FEEL, IS A CHOICE."

There's nothin' in life left to chance. You hear me? Nothin'. Not one thing is a mothahfuckin' accident. God don't make accidents. Plus, you got control over it too. Maybe you think that sounds like a contradiction, but I'm gonna tell you how it works. God puts situations and folks into your life for a reason, to teach you somethin' maybe or to open up a got-damn *opportunity* for you. Then, you choose how to react to that. It's called free will. You see what I'm sayin'? You got free will to do what you want with what comes your way. Not only "do," but "feel" too.

I hear folks sayin' all the time, "So-and-so made me mad" or, "What's-his-face hurt my feelin's." Nobody can make you mad without your permission. Nobody can hurt your feelin's without your permission. You can just say, "Naw, man. Not gonna happen. I'm good." Then you take that information, that nasty comment or that mean thing they done, and you figure out what you gonna do with it. Other times, we might be tempted to say, "Aww, damn, why does all this bad shit happen to me?" Mothahfuckah, whether you like it or not, that shit's happenin' *for you*, and it's happenin' as a result of everything you done and thought about in your lifetime. So, if that bad shit's happenin' *for you*, it's time to figure out why. What did you learn? What new door's openin' up now? How is your life maybe *better* from that experience?

> ***Choice, not chance, determines your destiny.***
>
> —Aristotle

DO THIS TODAY: *Take a step back and actually look at your situation right now. Are you happy with what you see, or do you need to fix some shit? You can start small right now and take steps to change what needs fixin', or you can simply say "fuck it" and leave it as is, your choice.*

May 22nd

"TAKE WHAT YOU NEED AND LEAVE THE REST."

When I'm talkin' about this, I mean it in a way that's bigger than just "sharing." We all know our mamas taught us to share when we was kids. You got twelve cousins and one mothahfuckin' cupcake, you gonna split it a dozen ways, that's for damn sure. But this ain't about sharin' your cupcake or sharin' your money or nothin' like that. This is about how you *are* in the *got-damn* world. You meet folks and you walk into situations every day, and it can get overwhelmin' sometimes. Thing is, you don't have to take *everything* in all the *got-damn* time. You'd be on mothahfuckin' overload, your senses drained, your brain hurtin', tired. You gotta learn how to take what you need and let the rest slide off.

Let me tell it to y'all this way. You got this coworker, and she's great at work, efficient, gets shit done. You like workin' on projects with her 'cuz she knows what the hell she's doin'. But then she wants to meet you for a drink. Maybe you go one time, and man, she's dumpin' everything about her *got-damn* relationship, she's havin' trouble with her family, her dog's dyin'. Damn, she's a hot mess and she just dumped it all on you. You go home and you feelin' exhausted, then the next day she wants to do it again like y'all are best friends or some shit. Don't feel like you gotta do it. You can draw the mothahfuckin' line. You need an excellent workin' relationship, you don't need an emotional vampire suckin' you dry. Period. Take what you need. It ain't selfish, it's self-preservation.

> ***Taking on too much of other people's drama is just a poor excuse for not taking ownership and control over your own life.***
>
> —José N. Harris

DO THIS TODAY: *Who or what do you have in your life right now that ain't servin' you? Figure out what you need from that relationship or experience, and let the rest slide off.*

May 23rd

"IF WHAT YOU'RE DOIN' AIN'T WORKIN', DO THE OPPOSITE."

When we're born, we come out having instincts that are supposed to keep us on the right path. But somewhere along the line, most of us are gettin' our natural instincts all fucked up. We learn bad habits. We learn to trust advertisements, social media, and everybody else before we listen to our own *got-damn* gut. That sometimes turns into some bad habits, some bad ways of thinkin'. So, if you're feelin' like life ain't workin' out how you want it to, try doin' the opposite of what you been doin'!

There was this time when I hit a hard place. I started stayin' up real late, having some drinks with the boys, sleepin' in until it was time to get up and get my daughter from her half-day of kindergarten. Man, was I a mothahfuckin' mess. But when I started tryin' to straighten myself out, I did the *got-damn* opposite of what I was doin' before. I set my alarm for early in the mornin'. Gettin' up early, goin' to bed early, skippin' the drinks, and that little shift made a helluva lotta impact on the rest of my day. I had more energy, got more shit done, and it made my wife happier too. All of that gave me more confidence in myself. Made me feel good. See what I'm sayin'? One switch to the opposite, gettin' up early instead of late, changed a whole lotta other shit. It worked, and I was finally gettin' myself together.

> ***What assistance can we find in the fight against habit? Try the opposite!***
>
> —Epictetus, *Discourses*, 1.27.4

DO THIS TODAY: *Think about what habit has got you stuck. Why do you want to change it, and what good can come from it if you do? Now, how can you do the opposite of that bad habit?*

May 24th

"BAD SHIT HAPPENS. DON'T KEEP TALKIN' ABOUT IT."

I remember one time after a shift at Dock's, I was sittin' waiting' for my ride, and I was sittin' with one of my coworkers who was talkin' about when his brothah done run off with his girl...*and* his mothahfuckin' car. Kid's name was Gerald, and boy, he was bent about that shit, goin' on and on sayin' how it wrecked his mothahfuckin' life. He even got a tear in his eyes. I was like, "Okay, man. It's gonna be okay. Time will heal." Then he says, "Yeah, you right. It's only been about three years. I just gotta give it time." THREE YEARS?! Three mothahfuckin' years of his life gone to hell 'cuz he just keeps relivin' that nasty part, just keeps askin' why all of that shit happened to him. He never took no personal responsibility, never looked for the *got-damn* lesson. He just kept whinin' and cryin' all the damn time. Guess what? It wasn't gettin' his girl back. It wasn't gettin' his brothah back, and it sure as hell wasn't gettin' him his car back.

Relivin' the past over and over, all it does is hold you in the pain of it. Why you wanna keep pickin' at that scab? Let it heal, *got-dammit*. The more you keep pickin' at it, the bigger the scar. Figure out your lesson and then let that shit go. If Gerald woulda done that, then he maybe woulda had a new girl, a new car, and maybe he woulda been happy. Instead, I think he's still workin' at Dock's livin' at home with his mama. It's a damn shame.

> ***You can't discover light by analyzing the dark.***
>
> —Wayne W. Dyer

DO THIS TODAY: *Listen, nobody's perfect. We've all made stupid-ass mistakes. However, you can do one of two things: you can remain in a rut of guilt and shame, or you can accept the past for what it is and be willing to move on and enjoy today. What mistake or dark spot in your past do you keep talkin' about? Make a vow to stop right now.*

May 25th

"YOU CAN BE SMART AS A MOTHAHFUCKAH, BUT YOU STILL NEED COMMON SENSE."

I'll take an ounce of common sense over a pound of *got-damn* smartness any day. I know some folks that's really *got-damn* smart. They know a lotta facts, must have an IQ like Einstein. They got these brilliant ideas, and they know how it's all gonna work. They can play the stock market, and they can take apart shit and put it back together, but the same mothahfuckah can't hold down a job, can't keep a relationship, can't pay his *got-damn* bills on time. All of them brains wasted, you know, 'cuz he can't get along in life. My granddad used to say, "He's an educated fool. Smart as a whip but no common sense." Thing is, you gotta know to bring an umbrella if it's rainin', take a different route when there's construction, don't put your *got-damn* fork in the toaster or buy no Rolex off a shady character. Common mothahfuckin' sense.

I do not pretend to be a genius. Naw, I'm just a regular guy with a spectacular job. I didn't use no brilliant brain to get where I got, I used my common *got-damn* sense. I was good at makin' folks laugh, so it's common mothahfuckin' sense to use that gift that God gave me. Why go lookin' for another kinda gift when you already got one perfectly good one? That's like holdin' the flathead screwdriver in your hand and goin' to look for another flathead screwdriver. Makes no sense. The one you already got is gonna be able to put in that screw just fine, and quicker too. See? Common mothahfuckin' sense.

> ***Common sense is genius dressed in its working clothes.***
>
> —Ralph Waldo Emerson

DO THIS TODAY: *Here's how to build some got-damn* **common sense**. *Take a look at the tools you already got. Think about what you done right and wrong. Be aware of your actions and who you are, and pretty soon you'll learn what you need to do and not do to get along in life.*

May 26th

"THE WISEST MEN ASK THE MOST QUESTIONS."

I can't tell you how many times a day I'm sittin' there thinkin' "I wonder if…" or "I wonder how…." Damn, it's probably more than I can count. Now, I'm not sayin' I'm the wisest mothahfuckah on the planet, but I'm getting a little bit wiser every day 'cuz I'm stayin' curious about the ***got-damn*** world, the Universe, my own mind, everything. You ever sit there eatin' a red hot on a bun at the stand downtown, and start wonderin', "Damn, I wonder who's the first mothahfuckah to put ground-up meat in a tube." Or maybe somebody's got an idea, and you ask, "How is this or that gonna work?" Then there's the bigger shit, like, "Where do I fit into this *ginormous* Universe?" You gotta stay fascinated. You gotta ask the questions.

Check this out. I had this fly pair of snakeskin boots, and I was zippin' 'em up one day and I thought to myself, *Who the hell came up with the idea for a zipper?* So, I start lookin' it up. Turns out the guy that invented the sewing machine, Elias Howe, first thought of it in 1851. But his design didn't work too good. Another guy, W. L. Judson, patented the "clasp-locker" in 1893, but it kept poppin' open. Then in 1914, a Swedish engineer named Gideon Sundback took a job with the Automatic Hook and Eye Company because he fell in love with the owner's daughter. That's who invented the zipper, and now we don't have to waste our time buttonin' up our boots or our flies because good ole Sundback got smitten with a girl. Ain't that somethin'? Now, go on and talk about that at your next company picnic and see if you get your boss's attention. Curious mothahfuckahs is the ones that come up with new ideas, tell great stories, fix problems, and make big changes. Remember that.

> ***Wisdom begins in wonder.***
>
> —Socrates

DO THIS TODAY: *Children are so inquisitive. They never stop askin' questions. One of a child's favorite words (that can bug the hell out of you) is "Why?" But that's how they grow. Same with you. So, today I want you to ask "Why?" at least a half dozen times and see what you learn from it. The more you ask, the more you grow.*

May 27th

"STOP THE *GOT-DAMN* GOSSIP. FIND SOMETHIN' BETTER TO TALK ABOUT."

Thing is, folks will always be talkin'. Nothin' they like better, especially folks that's got nothin' better to do. We all know it's just gossip, but the thing you gotta understand is that gossip *goings on* between small-minded folks can make big things happen. And that can be scary as a mothahfuckah. You don't wanna be any part of that bullshit. So, you gotta disengage and find some better *got-damn* topics. You can talk about your vision, discuss your dreams, get excited about possibilities or inventions, or even talk about interesting shit you read about the history of mothahfuckin' shoelaces. You hear what I'm tellin' you? Talk about big ideas and give that brain of yours somethin' to chew on. And if you aren't in the mood, then talk about some current events, but only in a way that you're diggin' into the issues, maybe even tryin' to think of solutions. The one thing you don't wanna do is chitter-chatter about other people's business. If you startin' to do that, then it's better to shut the hell up. Just sit quiet. Ain't nothin' wrong with that. In fact, it'll probably do you some good. My mama always used to say, "If you can't say somethin' nice, don't say nothin' at all." Well, I don't know about that. Not everything's gotta be nice. It's more like, "If you can't say something more interesting than talkin' about Yeezy's ranch in Wyoming, then shut the hell up."

> ***Great minds talk about ideas, average minds talk about events, and small minds talk about people.***
>
> —Anonymous

DO THIS TODAY: *Remember, gossip is a conversation about other people that's none of your* **got-damn** *business. You don't want folks talkin' about your shit, so stop talkin' about theirs. Go all day today without talkin' about nobody else's business—not one time. You hear me?*

May 28th

"YOU HAVE NO IDEA WHAT GOD HAS PLANNED FOR YOU."

You think you got a plan? Good, have a plan, but don't be so stuck in it that you get all busted up when God's plan is different from yours. You might have the *got-damn* map, but God laid down the roads. He knows where you're goin', and he knows the best way for you to get there. So, the best thing you can do is keep drivin' and pay attention to the signs.

You ever had your heart set on somethin', maybe you wanted a relationship with somebody or some kinda job, and you wanted it so bad you could taste it? You'd be gettin' frustrated 'cuz it was always just outta reach? Or maybe you had it for a second and you lost it. Damn, that shit hurts. You feelin' like you been kicked in the guts and can't get up. But hold on, look at the road, watch for the signs. You bet yo' ass God's gonna send you some, and he's gonna take you where you *actually* need to go. But he can't get you there if you're all broken up and stopped on the side of the *got-damn* road. Listen, there was a girl I was datin' before I met Rhonda. Sure, I thought she was what I wanted, but I was young and foolish and I didn't know. She broke it off with me and at that time, I had this friend...name was Rhonda. You see where I'm goin' with this. Rhonda married me. She got on the Bernie train and never got off, she was my rock and my life. You see, God knew better than me and he always does.

> ***Sometimes, the plans in your heart aren't God's plan.***
>
> —Katie Taylor

DO THIS TODAY: *Be flexible. In life there are twists and turns. The road is never straight and narrow, but as long as you're open and receptive, chances are God will exceed your expectations. Think about what you really want in your heart right now. Are you willin' to let it go if God reveals a different plan for you?*

May 29th

"ANSWER YOUR *GOT-DAMN* PHONE. YOU NEVER KNOW WHO IT'S GONNA BE."

Man, when I was a kid, we *ran* to the phone when it was ringin'. We'd knock each other down gettin' to it too. The one who got it would be clawin' their way to it, another one grabbin' his pants tryin' to pull him back. Then you'd grab it and calm yourself and say, "McCullough residence, Bernard speakin'." You had to answer it nice and polite, or you'd get a smack upside your head, right outta nowhere. THWACK! Maybe that was Grandpa Thurman's slipper, you know. But we answered the telephone 'cuz it was like a mystery. It was excitin'! The possibilities were endless, and of course we was all prayin' it was for us...or at the very least, that it wasn't *about* us. You know, the dreaded call from school or from Billy down the street's mama tellin' that we done made Billy "share" all of his bag of licorice. So, there was always that little bit of thrill when we heard the *bringg-bringg* comin' from the kitchen. Now, we look at the number on our cell phones and if we don't recognize it, we don't answer. "Oh, if it's important they'll leave a message." What kinda bullshit is that? Everybody's too afraid, playin' it too safe. Where's the excitement of pickin' it up and just for a second, it could be anyone? It's time to step outside your comfort zone and answer your got-damn phone. You might end up with an unexpected opportunity.

> ***Be gracious in your giving for as long as you're living. The blessings will come back on an unexpected day and present themselves in an unexpected way.***
>
> —Joan Marques

DO THIS TODAY: *Answer your phone all day, every time it rings. If it's someone tryin' to sell you somethin', be polite. They're people too. It's a good opportunity to practice your empathy.*

May 30th

"WHEN TRAGEDY HITS, LOOK FOR THE FOLKS THAT'S DOIN' GOOD."

When bad things happen, it's sometimes too easy to get down in the dumps. You start to wonder if there's good in the world. You know? Like when there's an earthquake, or a *got-damn* tornado hits, or there's a flood and folks' homes are drownin', you wonder if there's any kinda good in the world left at all. Even wonder if God's good. But then you see 'em, the helpers. You see folks out there doin' what needs to be done: diggin' through rubble to pull out survivors, droppin' into fires by parachute, paddlin' rubber rafts around flooded streets to help save swimmin' dogs. You see folks rebuildin' roads, see 'em makin' room on their couches, openin' up their churches, usin' their gifts to help do what they can for the ones that can't do for themselves. Those are the helpers. But the helpers ain't just there when the big shit happens. They're around all the time, you just gotta be able to look past the ugliness to find 'em. Hell, if you really wanna do somethin', maybe you can *be* one of 'em.

> ***When I was a boy and I would see scary things in the news, my mother would say to me, "Look for the helpers. You will always find people who are helping."***
>
> —Fred Rogers

DO THIS TODAY: *Open your eyes and really see. When you look for the best in others, that energy turns into a real positive vibe. The folks you interact with will feel it too. This is cool 'cuz you can use this energy whenever you want to. Try it today with the lady across the counter, your package delivery man, your professor, your mama. Show genuine appreciation for everyone that's doin' their little piece to help somebody else, and they'll appreciate you for it.*

May 31st

"WHAT YOU WANT AIN'T ALWAYS GONNA BE WHAT YOU GET, BUT IT'LL BE WHAT YOU NEED."

A lot of folks give up faith 'cuz they're thinkin' God ain't listenin'. Trust me, He's listenin', but He knows better than you. He hears what you want, but sometimes you don't know exactly how you're supposed to get it. He also knows that sometimes what you think you want ain't actually what you really want, or maybe He knows you ain't ready for what you're askin' Him for. That's right, God can see deeper than all of that. Let's say you think you want that new Cadillac Escalade. Damn, that's a cold-ass ride. But maybe God knows what you *really* want is to have the kind of money that will take care of your bills and have enough to get whatever car you like. You don't just want a car, you want some mothahfuckin' stability. So, He might not give you the car right now, but He's gonna start showin' you the way you gotta go to get to it.

Once you start to understand that your prayers are always gonna be answered, you'll start to look for the answers in places you maybe weren't before. You thinkin' you want that car, so you see that advertisement for a little bit better job as an answer, and that gets you even more excited. You get that job, then maybe your cousin asks if you wanna learn how to work on cars with him. Damn, that's another answer. Do that and see if it gets you closer. That's how it works. Prayers get answered in bits and pieces, and you gotta put 'em together.

God answers prayers, but he doesn't always answer it your way.

—Lou Holtz

DO THIS TODAY: *Make yourself a grocery list. Ask yourself, "Is this a want or a need?" So, you* **need** *toilet paper, but you* **want** *rocky road ice cream. What do you get? Lots of times we let the want win over the need, or we think it's a need but it's a want. It's the opposite with God. He will fulfill your needs first. Then if yo' ass acts right, you can look forward to receivin' the rest.*

June 1st

"SOME PROBLEMS ARE FOR YOUR FUTURE SELF."

You don't gotta take on the mothahfuckin' world all at once. That's how we get all bent outta shape, anxious, depressed. If you got a problem that don't need immediate attention, that's for *tomorrow you*, or maybe even *next week you*. Hell, that might even be for *old as a mothahfuckah you*. I mean, that guy's gonna have problems you never even dreamt of yet, so let him have it. Again, if it don't need your immediate attention today, it ain't today's problem.

I had this friend after high school. He was always talkin' about how he's gotta have enough money to fix his car when it breaks down, pay the insurance, keep it gassed up and all that shit. He was stressin' about it every mothahfuckin' time I saw him. Finally, I looked at him and said, "Yeah, it's gonna be a problem...when you get a *got-damn car*, mothahfuckah." That sumbitch was still ridin' the *got-damn* bus. The problem that was eatin' him up, it was for his *future you*. Let *that guy* take care of it when the time comes. *Today you* gots other things to think about, like earnin' enough money to get a mothahfuckin' car in the first place. Or maybe even, "How am I gonna get to work today?" You see what I'm talkin' about here? 'Cuz chances are, once you get to the version of you that has to deal with the problem, the answer will be there waitin' for you.

> ***Therefore do not worry about tomorrow, for tomorrow will worry about itself. Today has enough trouble of its own.***
>
> —Matthew 6:34

DO THIS TODAY: *Why are you jumpin' the gun? Slow down. Whatever it is that's worryin' you, ask yourself, is it a problem for today or tomorrow? If it's today, deal with it right away so you can get it off your mind. If it's tomorrow, let that shit go.*

June 2nd

"GET YOURSELF A LITTLE BIT OF PEACE AND QUIET."

Meditation. *Got-dammit*, that word's everywhere. Used to be, you'd only hear it when folks was talkin' about monks and nuns. Now, everybody talkin' about meditation. They got meditations to do at your desk, new mom meditations, meditations on how to stop eatin' cake, walkin' meditation, meditations to do in your car. You wanna know *why* they got all these different mothahfuckin' meditations? Because we can't get any *got-damn* peace and quiet no more. My mama used to say, "Bean, it's so loud in here, I can't hear myself think!" Now I know what she's talkin' about. You got all kinds of beepin' and buzzin', all kinda lights flashin' and folks talkin' at you. You got a million distractions up in your face all the day long and mostly half the night, and my mama's right. You can't hear your own *got-damn* thoughts. That's why you gotta clear out all the clutter, take some quiet time to get your brain right.

When I was a kid, this was just built into everyday livin'. You didn't go to bed with no radio on or no movies playin'. You didn't pop in your EarPods and listen to your jams while you's on the bus. You didn't have shit beepin' at you all the *got-damn* time. We played games with balls and cards, not plastic laser guns with real exploding sound effects. We wrote shit down in notebooks, we didn't click and drag and make PowerPoints in kindergarten. We was still playin' with playdough and finger paints. Now it's so noisy, you gotta "meditate" to reset yourself. Well, okay, then do it. I promise, you gonna start to hear yourself think again.

> ***When the mind is calm, how quickly, how smoothly, how beautifully you will perceive anything.***
>
> —Paramahansa Yogananda

DO THIS TODAY: *Find a quiet spot, take three deep breaths, and sit still and silent for a while. Get out the clutter from your head and see if you feel a little clearer when you're done.*

June 3rd

"YOU GOTTA CARE ABOUT NATURE, 'CUZ IF YOU FUCKIN' IT UP, WHERE YOU GONNA LIVE?"

Now, I'm not gonna get all tree-huggin' on yo' ass. That ain't me. I like nature. I like to go out and play eighteen holes of golf in the beautiful sunshine. I like to walk down the street and be able to breathe the *got-damn* air. I like to sit on my back deck and look at trees and grass and shit, you know. It's nice. But that's not what I'm talkin' about. We live on this big-ass planet that was created to the exact specifications it needed to be healthy. It's like God put everything for our perfect habitat on here, and then He put us here to live a good got-damn life. But if we keep goin' like we goin', we gonna fuck it all up. Then where we gonna live? We gonna get on spaceships and go out to mothahfuckin' Mars and shit? I don't think so. Not me. Seems shady. I prefer to stay in my own *got-damn* neighborhood.

Okay, even if movin' to another planet is a possibility, it's not gonna be for a long time, and you don't wanna go countin' on it, anyway. Why would you use up a perfectly good planet just 'cuz yo' ass wanted to be lazy and selfish? That's one way to end up in a world of hurt. Thing is, it's easy to take care of it. You just gotta start with the small stuff. You got one of those green *got-damn* bins with the arrows on it? Yeah, you do, so recycle your shit. Walk yo' ass to the corner store instead of drivin' all the time. Maybe don't buy so many mothahfuckin' Happy Meals. Small stuff, but it makes a big difference if we're all doin' it.

> ***We need to reach a balance where people, habitat, and wildlife can coexist. If we don't, everyone loses...one day.***
>
> —Steve Irwin

DO THIS TODAY: *Remember, small things can make a huge impact. Gather a group of non-lazy family members and friends and go pick up litter. Switch your bank account to paperless statements. Maybe just take a* **two***-minute shower. What can you do to help the Earth today?*

June 4th

"WE GOTTA START TOGETHER AND FINISH TOGETHER. THAT'S HOW WE GONNA WIN."

You know, I ain't never gone to a Bulls game where they started with five players on the court and ended with one. How the hell you expect to win like that? I mean, Michael Jordan's a maniac on the court, but he ain't gonna win one on five. Here's the thing; when we're talkin' about basketball, you can see how it's makin' sense. But what about when we talkin' about life? Like all of the *got-damn* human existence? I know, that feels like a real big situation. I'm not askin' you to strain your brain thinkin' about it, but what I'm tellin' you is that the only way we are gonna succeed as a mothahfuckin' species is if we do it together. Otherwise, we'll have one group of folks over here tryin' to make things good and another group comin' in behind and fuckin' it up.

I used to have this friend when I was in about the second grade. Name was Twigger. He was a skinny mothahfuckah with a smile full of teeth and sparks in his eyes. Them sparks was probably 'cuz that kid was already a pyromaniac. One time I come in the lot behind his buildin' and he had all these little piles of torn-up shit all over the place and he had about four lit already. I was goin' on and stompin' 'em out, and he kept lightin' 'em. I could barely get to the next one 'fore he had another one lit. That's what it's like when we goin' against each other, both on the side of progress and on the side of regress. That's why we gotta see each other like a *got-damn* team. It's the only way it works.

> ***Coming together is a beginning; keeping together is progress; working together is success.***
>
> —Henry Ford

DO THIS TODAY: *Teamwork requires you to play off each other for a solution. Start in your own home. Grab whoever's livin' there and do a project together, start to finish. The results are happiness and success.*

June 5th

"NOT TODAY."

Maybe someday you're gonna be doin' the exact thing you said no to yesterday or datin' that girl you weren't quite into at the time, and that's okay. "No" now doesn't mean it's gotta be "no" forever. Let me break it down for ya'.

Let's say your brother-in-law comes around and he's got this amazing mothahfuckin' opportunity, he just needs you to invest a couple thousand smacks. No big deal, right? A couple thousand and you gonna make a hundred thousand dollahs back. He's tellin' you this deal is so good, it's *almost* guaranteed. He's investin' all he's got into it, and he's excited, but you're lookin' like you ain't so sure. It kinda looks like a pyramid scheme to you, and there are some details that just don't add up. He ain't doin' too good at answerin' your questions neither. Plus, you gotta pay that utility bill you keep forgettin' to pay, so money's tight. You're not gonna do it. Instead of goin' off and tellin' him to take a hike, that's some bullshit, and you don't want no part of it, tell him, "Not today. The timing's just not right, you know?" And that's the truth. That way, you ain't slammin' the door in his face or knockin' down his dreams, and you're leavin' the door ajar for the future, just in case his scheme pans out and you're also in a better situation later on. Never say never. Better to say, "Not today."

> ***You can relax into knowing that what is meant for you is always yours. Trust yourself with a yes or a no answer, and that can be your full answer.***
>
> —Jennifer Renée Bouteiller

DO THIS TODAY: *It's okay to say no to anything that drains you. You just can't be givin' energy away, ain't nobody got time for that. Instead, show up for what really matters, and say no to the stuff that's not currently in your flow. What do you need to say "not today" to today?*

June 6th

"DANDELIONS GROW ANYWHERE, EVEN IN THE GHETTO."

Dandelions ain't just weeds. You ever seen a big, beautiful, yellow-headed dandelion poppin' up outta the crack in the janky-ass broken-up concrete out in back of your apartment building? That mothahfuckah's the prettiest *got-damn* flower you ever gonna see. And here's the truth—it didn't need no waterin' and no fertilizer. Dandelions don't even need no other dandelions. It's the only mothahfuckin' flower that can reproduce by itself. Did you hear that? *By itself*. Ya' see, the dandelion don't know it's stuck in a crack in the ghetto. That's just where the seed dropped. It felt the warm sun, got a little rain on it, and it just pushed itself up toward the sky. It's stronger than everything around it that's tryin' to hold it back.

I grew up on the South Side of Chicago. It wasn't no walk in the park, but it was home to me, and I loved it. I found everything I needed to grow there. I reached for the sky just like them kids growin' up in them cushier neighborhoods, maybe even reached a little higher. And I grew up just fine, 'cuz the same sun is shinin' on the South Side just like it is everywhere else. I was a mothahfuckin' dandelion, and you gotta be one too. Underestimated, strong as hell, and pretty soon you're fillin' a whole *got-damn* field full of flowers all by yourself.

> ***The soul is stronger than its surroundings.***
>
> —William James

DO THIS TODAY: *Most folks don't have the perfect conditions to help 'em grow. Everybody's got obstacles. Today I want you to identify yours and start thinkin' about how you gonna use the tools you have at your disposal to start to overcome 'em.*

June 7th

"IF YOU CAN'T SEE THAT THERE'S BEAUTIFUL THINGS EVERYWHERE, THEN YOU AIN'T LOOKIN'."

Oh, man, if you ain't blown away by the beauty that's everywhere, I'm thinkin' you must have your mothahfuckin' eyes closed. I swear, I can be anywhere and just look up, just listen for a second, and there's somethin' that's gonna take your breath away. Maybe it's the sound of the breeze rustlin' some dry leaves on the sidewalk. Or it could be a raindrop makin' a trail down the car window. Ooohhh, or it's the smell of some chicken fryin' in the kitchen. At the very least, you got the sun risin' and settin' every single *got-damn* day. You got the sound of your own heart beatin', and *damn* that's a beautiful sound.

I'm not tryin' to get all sappy on y'all, but if you're feelin' some kinda way about your life, gettin' down, noticin' the little bits of beauty that God put here can go a long way to turnin' yourself around. I think most of us go through life in a kind of a blur, so we're not seein' it, and that's what's makin' folks depressed and shit. Keep your face in your phone all the time and you don't see the way the sunlight hits the backside of every leaf on that maple tree, and it's actually about a million different shades of green. You gotta watch life like it's in HD and you checkin' to see if it's as clear a picture as everybody sayin' it is, then you'll see it for real.

> ***Think of all the beauty still left around you and be happy.***
>
> —Anne Frank

DO THIS TODAY: *Today, I want you to put your phone away unless it's absolutely necessary. Don't walk with it, don't stare at it while you're in line at the store, just put it away and notice all the beautiful, free things around you. If you see a flower, stop and smell it. Live now, enjoy the moment, be present, be grateful for life, 'cuz all the best things are free and available if you're payin' attention.*

June 8th

"ONE STICK ON FIRE GIVES OFF MORE LIGHT THAN A PILE OF WOOD WITH NO MATCH."

Damn, it's a lot of knowledge kids gotta cram into their brains these days. Probably a hell of a lot more than I had to learn when I was in school. Maybe that's 'cuz now there's more to know. With the internet and all of the advances in technology, the world is filled up with more information than any computer ever invented could ever hold. The thing is, a brain ain't like a computer. It ain't even like a robot. Computer's got a massive amount of storage for all kinds of facts and data. So does your brain, but your brain is special. No, your brain is mothahfuckin' amazing—it's alive and it's connected to your soul. It doesn't just pile up and regurgitate zeros, it wants to light up with new ideas. You can't just dump facts into your head and expect to solve nothin', expect to grow as a person, expect to heal and make positive changes.

What if Benjamin Franklin just filled his head up with facts, but he could only spit 'em out when he was asked to choose between A, B, and C? He would have never gotten excited about tyin' a key to a mothahfuckin' kite and flyin' it in a lightning storm. Then, where would we be? Sittin' in the *got-damn* dark. He needed to have that fire to light up that load of facts that was piled up in there. That fire's what turns smart folks into change-makers.

> ***The mind is not a vessel to be filled but a fire to be kindled.***
>
> —Plutarch

DO THIS TODAY: *Think back to elementary school when the teacher caught your ass daydreamin' in class. You were really just firin' up your imagination. I bet Elon Musk, Jeff Bezos, and Jay-Z daydreamed too! Imagination takes us to places that we've never explored. What have you been daydreamin' about lately? Write it down. The best ideas happen because one person let their imagination fuel their fire.*

June 9th

"PRIDE BREEDS DESTRUCTION."

Be proud of your accomplishments, celebrate your success, but don't inflate it so that other folks start feelin' some kinda way about you. Don't go and puff out your feathers and strut. Doin' that shit don't make other folks admire you more, it just makes you a target for all of their insecurities. There's a difference between bein' proud of the things you've done and bein' prideful. Pride with a capital *P*, that's about ego-boostin', and you ain't gotta do that shit. Big egos equal big problems. Pride separates you from the rest of the folks around you, sayin', "Look at me. I'm better than all y'all." If you're "little *p* proud" of yourself, that's okay, be proud of everything and everybody that contributed and got you where you are. Be proud of your team, and proud that you've done somethin' to make positive changes and advance on your chosen path. Be "little *p* proud," but be grateful and stay humble at the same time.

For real, I had this friend that was so full of himself, he thought he was God's gift to women, men, the mothahfuckin' world. I swear to you, he actually said, "I am the humblest mothahfuckah I know." We all looked at him and busted down laughin'. He got mad, couldn't see the irony. He couldn't even be humble about bein' humble. That's the kinda pride that'll knock you down, burn your bridges, disconnect you from the rest of humanity, and stop you from fulfillin' your potential.

> ***We are all one. Only egos, beliefs, and fear separate us.***
>
> —Nikola Tesla

DO THIS TODAY: *Is it always your way or the highway? If so, you're a prideful sumbitch. It comes from fear of embarrassment or shame, and it can stop your growth. You don't know everything. Next time you feel yourself shuttin' someone down before they even finish a sentence, take a breath and make yourself focus on what they have to say. Watch how many new things you learn by doing this, and how much more respect you're gonna get.*

June 10th

"PAY ATTENTION TO YOUR INTENTION."

First, I gotta say, the English language is a mothahfuckah. The word "intention" has two definitions. First, it means what you aim to do or what something was designed to do. But it also means the process of a wound healin'. Ain't that somethin'? And I think you gotta pay attention to both of those things if you wanna be content in this world. You gotta pay attention to your aim, and you gotta pay attention to your healin' too. If you ignore one of those, you ain't gonna stay right on the path and maybe it takes you a little longer to get yourself right.

Wherever you're at in your life right now, it's safe to say that you're goin' somewhere and you've already been through some stuff to get to this place. Where you're goin', that's your aim. It's like the legendary Walter Payton racin' toward that end zone. Then whatever tore you up on the way so far, whatever cut you deep or hurt you, that's your healin'. You gotta watch that too. Imagine when Payton had a bum knee. If he didn't go through some PT and fix that shit up, he'd be sidelined before his career even had a chance. You get what I'm sayin'? If you got your eye on both your healin' and your aim, givin' your attention to both of those intentions, you gonna be on a fast path to a mothahfuckin' touchdown.

> ***Our intention is everything. Nothing happens on this planet without it.***
>
> —Jim Carrey

DO THIS TODAY: *What are your intentions for this year? Something you really want and plan to do. Maybe you've decided to start researchin' that take-out restaurant idea, or you're finally ready for jujitsu classes. Whatever your intentions, write them down and start small. Settin' intentions is the best way to achieve your goals. You just do it one step at a time.*

June 11th

"YOU GONNA KNOW THIS BOOK IS WORKIN' WHEN YOU UNDERSTAND THAT YOU ARE ENOUGH."

You go through life sometimes feelin' like you ain't complete, like you got some part of you that's missin' or like you need somethin' more to be satisfied. I'm gonna tell you a secret: you are, and you don't. You are 100 percent complete just how you are right now, and that's all you need. Thing is, we've been raised up in this world to think we need somethin' else, somethin' more, in order to be happy or be successful. If you wanna be cool, you need this kinda edge gel or those vintage kicks. If you wanna be happy, you need to have this kinda damn job and that kinda car. The message you're hearin' all the time is you gotta constantly strive for more, more, more. You gotta be like a Hungry Hungry Hippo gobblin' up them balls. But when is enough enough? I'm gonna tell you, it's enough right now.

I know you maybe don't realize it yet, but you keep on goin' like you're goin', you keep on learnin' and movin' in the right direction, pretty soon you will know it deep down in your soul. You are enough just exactly as you are, mothahfuckah. Just exactly. That's what this is all about, gettin' you to the point that you don't just know it, you feel it. That's when you're gonna be completely content in a way you ain't never felt before.

> ***Our whole spiritual transformation brings us to the point where we realize that in our own being, we are enough.***
>
> —Ram Dass

DO THIS TODAY: *Be honest, do you sometimes feel that you don't live up to expectations? Not the expectations others set for you, but the expectations you set for yourself. If so, cut that shit out. Stop being so* **got-damn** *hard on yourself, beatin' yourself up, feelin' all unworthy. You are enough already, mess and all. Know it. Say it. Mean it.*

June 12th

"SOMETIMES IT AIN'T JUST ABOUT SPEAKIN' THE TRUTH, IT'S ABOUT HOW AND WHY YOU SAYIN' IT."

You goin' around speakin' the truth all the *got-damn* time, you're gonna get your ass whooped and be sittin' alone at the mothahfuckin' lunch table. You know what it's called when you just blurt out the truth all day? It's called rude or snitchin', one of the two, dependin' on what you're talkin' about. You tell the bus driver that he smells bad and his teeth's whacked out, you gonna be walkin' yo' ass home. That's rude. You tell your boss that your associate took an extra half hour at lunch to take a nap, you ain't gettin' no office cake on your mothahfuckin' birthday. You a snitch. I remember I told my mama on my brother Darryl one time, told her he was skippin' out on his chores and takin' off to go see this girl. I did it 'cuz I wanted him to spend the day with me and take me to the movie. All I remember is the look he shot me when Mama told him she's disappointed in him. He said he was gonna do the chores later, but I jumped the gun 'cuz I was bein' selfish. He didn't speak to me for weeks. Boy, that didn't work out how I wanted it to.

Finally, if the truth you're speakin' is gonna cause more harm than good, if it's coming' from a nasty place, you best just keep your *got-damn* mouth shut. Your hate-filled or greedy-ass truth don't trump the greater good for humanity. It's time for you to shut the hell up and re-analyze yourself and your intentions.

> ***When words are both true and kind, they can change our world.***
>
> —Jack Kornfield

DO THIS TODAY: *Watch the words you speak. If you don't have nothin' good to say, then sit your ass down. Try this, find one positive and true thing to compliment on someone today. For instance, "Hey, I really like your style." Or "Wow, that's the best cup of coffee I've had all week." Sharing a compliment can really make someone feel good, and they'll pass it on.*

June 13th

"YOU ALWAYS GONNA ATTRACT THE SAME KINDA ENERGY YOU PUTTIN' OUT."

You gonna naturally hang with folks that's got the same vibes as you. It's like that sayin', "Water seeks its own level." You an ice cube, you gonna float to the top with the other ice cubes. You light and airy, you gonna rise on up outta there with the other steam particles. You cold water, you gonna fall down to the bottom of the mothahfuckin' pond. Warm water, you at the top by the surface—unless you be swirlin' around Freckles Rufus at the pool, then you ain't water, if you know what I'm sayin'. He was always swimmin' by hisself. Anyway, the different states of water, they group together naturally. That's how it works. And you can see this happenin' everywhere, not just with water, that's why it's a good metaphor. You understand me?

I could see the same kinda thing happenin' on the playground at my elementary school, in my high school, on my block, and later on in life too. But this time, it's with people. You look out at the playground and the kids start to split off and find their friends; same thing at the jobs. Seems easy to notice that the pretty chill kids hang together, the bad ones, the happy ones, the "angry at the world" ones, the ones with their pants hangin' off their ass. Somehow, they find each other. That shit ain't random. It's how it works. You gonna attract other folks by the energy you puttin' out there. Just be aware of that.

> ***Water seeks its own level.***
>
> —Fact

DO THIS TODAY: *You know the old sayin', "Birds of a feather flock together." It's a scientific fact that you become like the average five people you spend the most* got-damn *time with. So, how you flockin'? Take stock of those five people in your life. Are they a positive influence? If not, maybe start puttin' out some new vibes and attract yourself a new tribe.*

June 14th

"START GIVIN' YOURSELF A LITTLE MORE CREDIT. YOU'RE SMARTER, BRAVER, AND STRONGER THAN YOU THINK."

One of my least favorite words is "can't." *Got-damn*, I hate it when I hear folks sayin' it. Never let my little girl say it, neither. That word takes away your mothahfuckin' power. Most of the time folks is usin' it, what they really mean is, "I don't feel like it," or, "I don't wanna try," or maybe even, "Not right now." They just use that word as a *got-damn* excuse for why they ain't gonna do it. Excuses have no place on your path to success. You gotta start lookin' at yourself like you look at your own best friend. You give that mothahfuckah the best *got-damn* pep talks. You ain't gonna let him fail, let him stop before he's finished. You'd never smack-talk him like the way you been smack-talkin' *yourself* all of those times.

So, it's time you start treatin' yourself like you are your own *got-damn* best friend. 'Cuz if you ain't rootin' for yourself, sittin' up in the stands with that big-ass foam finger, screamin' your guts out even when your team's ten points behind at the buzzer. You gotta believe in the tiny chance that you can pull it off. You only know the smallest part of what you can do.

> ***If we all did the things we are capable of, we would literally astound ourselves.***
>
> —Thomas Edison

DO THIS TODAY: *You're about to hype yourself up like you are your got-damn* ***best friend****. Either look in the mirror or get out your phone and make a recording. Pretend you're talkin' to your friend that was gettin' down on themselves. Hype 'em up for a solid minute. If you recorded that shit, play it back to yourself when you're feelin' like you ain't got what it takes.*

June 15th

"SOMETIMES HOPE IS HARD, BUT IT'S ALWAYS WORTH IT."

It's true, sometimes it's hard to keep hopin' for change when you feelin' stuck, but that's kinda the point of hope in the first place, ain't it? You wouldn't need the hope if everything was goin' your way. Hope is for the times when you feel like you got nothin' else to grab on to.

Now, I ain't talkin' about the kinda hope here that you seein' on them mean-girl movies, where the stuck-up blonde chick is sayin', "I hope she chokes on a chicken wing and dies." Naw, that ain't at all what I'm talkin' about here. That ain't hope, that's just some kinda fucked-up wish. Hope is what you got when you seein' a tiny ray of light, but you surrounded by darkness. Hope can get folks through when they feelin' like they got no place else to turn. Hope is like optimism. It's like when you can see that there's a chance even in the face of a lot of some serious *got-damn* obstacles. It takes a lotta mothahfuckin' courage to have hope, 'cuz hope means you ain't gonna give up. You gonna keep on the full court press even if you down by four with seventeen seconds on the clock. That's some got-damn *hope*. It means you believe in yourself, and you believe in the plan that's set out for you. It gives you the motivation to take the actions necessary to follow through. I learned it from my church and from my mama who kept on even when she had no husband, no money, even when she had cancer. She kept her head high and a smile on her face. That's hope, and that shit takes some serious got-damn *strength*.

> ***Keep hope alive.***
>
> —Rev. Jesse L. Jackson, Sr.

DO THIS TODAY: *If you can look up, you can get up. When life's problems got you down, it's easy to feel a loss of hope. Family and friends encourage you, but sometimes it ain't enough. But gratitude can bring it back. Practice by writing down three things you're grateful for. Do it every day and read that list in the mornin' then again before you go to bed at night.*

June 16th

"YOU GOTTA BE BRAVE TO FIND PEACE."

Peace don't come just by sittin' there doin' nothin'. Even monks don't just sit, even yogis, nuns. They study, eat bowls of rice and porridge, go for walks, help folks that's needy. Peace ain't about nothin' happenin'. Peace ain't about never havin' a problem. Peace is all about bein' calm through the ***got-damn*** storms. Peace is about knowin' you are exactly who and where you need to be and that you're movin' in the right direction, and it takes a lot of mothahfuckin' courage to really believe like that. Remember *The Wiz*? I loved the one with Diana Ross, Michael Jackson, and Richard Pryor. Toward the end, the Cowardly Lion finally gains his courage and becomes king of the jungle. You see that? All it took was a little courage and, ***got-damn***, look at that, he had it all the time. My point is, don't let fear block your blessin'.

You ever see somebody that's frantic all the time? They're anxious, always questioning their choices, askin' everybody else to decide for 'em. They don't know what the hell they want because they don't know who they are, for real. It's like they're all jumpy and shit, make you nervous just to be around 'em. It's those folks that end up suckin' on to your dreams and holdin' you back. They do that shit 'cuz they're afraid—afraid to make a choice and for it to be wrong, afraid to claim their mothahfuckin' place in the world, afraid to fail. That ain't no way to live. Once you start bein' brave, it's all gonna come quicker and you gonna find the kinda peace in your life that makes you confident, the kinda peace that brings success.

> ***Courage is the price that life exacts for granting peace.***
>
> —Amelia Earhart

DO THIS TODAY: *Courage is when you decide to do something difficult, even though you may be afraid. For some folks, that might be just answerin' the phone. Today, do it afraid. Just one small thing, jump through the jitters and do it. You'll feel like, "Damn, I got this!" Then you gonna feel real calm when it's done.*

June 17th

"IF ALL YOUR DREAMS CAME TRUE, WOULD THE WORLD BE BETTER, OR JUST YOU?"

It's important to have dreams for yourself, and to have visions that will help you turn those dreams into a reality. Plus, I've been tellin' you to dream big, then dream bigger. When I say that, you gotta know what I mean. I'm not sayin' to dream of a bigger mansion for yourself, a sweeter ride, a taller stack of cash. I'm sayin' to expand your dreams wider, broader, and make 'em encompass more of humanity. It's like you gotta start to think bigger, that's what folks is meanin' when they tell you to expand your mind. When you do that, you're gonna be able to fly higher than you would if you just keep dreamin' of a bunch more shit for yourself.

It's like if you have a balloon and you're fillin' it up with helium. Dreams like a nice car, a new job, those are tiny puffs. They might lift the balloon a tiny bit up off the ground, but that's it. When you start pumpin' it with bigger dreams, like providin' homes for the homeless, they get in there and they heat up and they expand. The edges of that latex start to stretch wider and rounder, and pretty soon that old balloon lifts up. You tie a bunch of 'em together, and *got-damn*, they're flyin' all the way up 'til you can't even see 'em no more, reachin' heights you can't even imagine. That can only happen when your dreams expand to include humanity, the future, the greater good. You catchin' what I'm layin' down?

> ***Pray till prayer makes you forget your own wish and leave it or merge it in God's will.***
>
> —Frederick William Robertson

DO THIS TODAY: *If you dare to dream big, you gotta push yourself beyond your current limits. How can you start to include them big ideas in your dreams, the ones that's gonna make an impact on more than just yourself, the ones that could change the world?*

June 18th

"SAY YES AND EMBRACE THE POSSIBILITIES."

How many times a day do you think you say no? I don't blame you. It's not your fault. The fact of the matter is that your folks did that shit to you when you's just a baby. Most toddlers hear the word *no* about four hundred times a day. That's a lot of *no*. It ain't your mom and pop's fault, they heard it when they was a kid too. Can I? No. Will we? No. Gimme? No. No. No. No! *Got-damn*, when you think about it like that, it's a little bit sad, ain't it? Babies hearin' "no" all the damn time, right when they're learnin' how to be in this world. Well, now you know all about this world, and it's time to start sayin' yes.

When you start sayin' yes, that means you're accepting the gifts that God has put right there in front of you. Now, it don't mean acceptin' every crazy mothahfuckin' thing that crosses your path. You still gotta say no to some shit: drugs, jumpin' off a train, cheatin' on your wife...you get what I'm sayin'. Use your *got-damn* brain. But start sayin' yes more than you say no, and see how your life is gonna get a lot more interesting.

> ***Everything in the world began with a yes. One molecule said yes to another molecule and life was born.***
>
> —Clarice Lispector

DO THIS TODAY: *Take a risk. Be willing to open yourself up and be vulnerable. There are as many ways to say yes as there are to say no. Think about when you were presented with an opportunity at work, or socially, or tryin' some new machine at the gym. Did you jump right in, or did you say "not yet" or "no thanks"? Start turnin' no into yes. It could even be "I'll try" or "Tell me more!" You just gotta say, "I ain't scared of you, mothahfuckah!" Then do it.*

June 19th

"LAUGHTER RESETS YOUR SOUL."

I've understood the power of a laugh, ever since I was a little boy. You see, my mama was real sad. She was carryin' the weight of a burden she never shoulda had to carry alone, and it was makin' her tired. She was up late one night, and I could see the flickerin' light of the TV screen on the livin'-room rug, so I shuffled my sock-feet in there and my mama was sittin' on the big armchair with tears rollin' down her face. I climbed up on her lap and Bill Cosby was on there, and he made her laugh right through the tears. Her face lit up and it was like that laugh hit a reset button in her soul. That's what laughter does for folks.

I remember I was ridin' the L back in high school and there's this man, and he had a look in his eyes like he just lost his job, wife left him, and his cat died all at the same mothahfuckin' time. He was one sorry-lookin' sumbitch. Nobody's even lookin' right at him.... But I look in his eyes and I say, "Sir, you look like you could really use a sandwich." He looks at me like I'm crazy, but I reach in my bag, and pull out a big fat ham sandwich. I hold it out to him, then I pull it back and fake like I'm about to take a bite. He shakes his head, then I hold it out again. He takes it and I fake a tear in my eye. "I'm not sad," I say. "I'm happy cryin', 'cuz when you take a bite of that sandwich you gonna forget whatever kicked you in the ass today." He hesitated, then he laughed, and before we knew it, all the folks around us was laughin' too, and it felt good. We all needed it in some kinda way. 'Cuz no matter how hard we try to stay optimistic, life can get rough sometimes. When that happens, we gotta use that easy reset button.

> ***A good laugh heals a lot of hurts.***
>
> —Madeleine L'Engle

DO THIS TODAY: *Laughter strengthens your immune system, boosts your mood, diminishes pain, and protects you from the damaging effects of stress. Shit, why not start laughin' now? Turn on a stand-up comedian, maybe even some old Bernie Mac, and get poppin'! See how that laugh flips your mood.*

June 20th

"IT IS WHAT IT IS."

Just because something happens you're not sure about, that don't mean it's bad. God don't judge. He never said that dark is bad and light is good, never said that pink is for girls and blue is for boys, never sorted folks out by their color or the language they spoke. Human bein's did that. God never told the shark and the snake that they was evil, but the fuzzy bunny rabbit is good. People did that. God ain't assignin' good and bad to shit. Everything just is what it is.

The same goes for all of the shit that you go through in your life and every emotion you're feelin'. Maybe you gettin' anxious about somethin' that's *goings on*, and you feel your heart racin', sweat formin', you feel yourself gettin' worked up. That ain't "bad," it's just your *got-damn* body's reaction that's happenin' there. You don't gotta label it, just feel it and acknowledge it, and then let it pass. The emotion ain't bad or good and feelin' it don't make you bad or good. It just is what it is.

Same goes for your experiences in life. Somebody hurt you, or maybe some kinda shit happened and you feelin' upset by it. Was that experience bad? Well, you don't know, do you? Maybe in the long run it's gonna open a door, so best not to label it. If goin' through somethin' teaches you an important lesson, does that make it good? I know it's hard to think like this, but the more you detach from the labels of "bad" and "good," the more you gonna be able to step back and look at it for what it is, and the easier you'll be able to learn and grow from it.

A day without sun is like, you know, night.

—Steve Martin

DO THIS TODAY: *You live and you learn. Go through today takin' it all in without judgment. See if that gives you a sense of calm and a new kind of clarity.*

June 21st

"WHEN YOU'RE CRAMMED IN A BOX FOR A LONG TIME, IT MIGHT BE A WHILE FOR YOU TO WALK RIGHT AGAIN. BE PATIENT WITH YOURSELF."

You ever sit all cramped up in the backseat of a car, or maybe ridin' the L all the way to your cousin De'Shawn's place up on the north side? When you get there, you pull your legs out from under yo' ass and you step down, it feels like you steppin' on Legos. Your feet pitch over, legs buckle, and you feel like they turned into rubber. You're walkin' all bow-legged like a mothahfuckin' toddler, and it takes you a minute to work out the kinks and walk right.

Same thing applies when your mind has been crammed up for too long, stuck in one place. When you finally unbend and stretch, you maybe gonna stumble for a few steps. You gonna learn somethin' new, you shift on some important position, or you make a big leap on your path, and maybe you don't get it exactly right at first. Maybe you say the wrong thing sometimes or you slip up. Be patient with yourself and just keep walkin'. Before long, the pins and needles will go away and it'll feel natural again. In fact, you'll be walkin' taller and faster than you ever had before. Then pretty soon, you gonna take that box you was crammed up in, and you gonna stomp on it. You gonna hack at it, and you gonna throw that piece of shit in the dumpster, 'cuz you got no use for boxes no more.

> ***Have patience with all things, but first of all with yourself.***
>
> —St. Francis de Sales

DO THIS TODAY: *What are you workin' on changin' right now? Give yourself some credit for tryin'. God didn't build the world in a day. Remind yourself that you're growin' in the right direction, and that's all you need to do.*

June 22nd

"IF YOU GOT A HEADACHE, TAKE SOME ASPIRIN. IF IT'S ACHIN' NONSTOP, FIGURE OUT WHY AND FIX IT."

Nothin' worse than hearin' somebody you love cryin' all the time that they're hurtin'. Maybe it's headaches, maybe a stomachache, or maybe it's emotional pain they're goin' through. As a man, of course I'm always wantin' to fix it. You know that's how we do. "Oh, baby, I can't see you cryin'. Lemme fix it." Of course, sometimes your girl be like, "Damn, I just want you to hold me. I don't need you to fix it." Then she's mad on top of it. But it don't make no sense. Okay, you get a headache one time, maybe it's just stress. You take some Tylenol and lay down. But if you got a headache every *got-damn* day, there's somethin' wrong, and you gotta find out what it is or you just gonna keep on sufferin' with the mothahfuckin' affliction, and makin' life miserable for everybody around you too. That's just common got-damn *sense*.

Of course, this ain't just for headaches. I'm talkin' on a bigger scale, here. If you got one mothahfuckah that does some fucked-up shit, well you can deal with him and be alright about it. But if more and more mothahfuckahs doin' it, it's affectin' everybody around 'em and it ain't stoppin', there's a bigger problem and we gotta get to the cause of it so we can make it stop. Otherwise, it's like a cancer and it'll just keep on growin' until it takes over. At that point, it's hard as a mothahfuckah to get rid of. Better to stop it before it gets that far.

> ***An ounce of prevention is worth a pound of cure.***
>
> —Benjamin Franklin

DO THIS TODAY: *What do you have* **goings on** *with you that seems to be a constant problem? Maybe it's physical, maybe it's a situation or an emotion, or maybe it's your mother-in-law. Whatever it is, take a look at it and make a plan to address it today. Also, she wouldn't want you to make a fuss, but today's Rhonda's birthday. So, just appreciatin' that she was born, that's all.*

June 23rd

"GET YOUR HEART RIGHT AND IT CAN HELP HEAL THE WORLD."

You wanna change the world, change your heart first. That's where it all begins, you know. Your heart is at the center of everything. That's why there's so many different sayin's about it. If you have a deep talk, it's a heart-to-heart. You lose your love, heartbroken. Your mama is the heart of the family. You understand what I'm gettin at, right?

You ever see a great athlete or an amazing singer, think about Michael Jordan and Stevie Wonder, and folks will be sayin', "Man, that sumbitch has got heart." There's a quality that comes from that place, and it radiates through to everything that you do, and then it goes out into the world like a mothahfuckin' radio signal. You can feel it when somebody puts their heart into somethin' they doin'. But if somebody got a cold heart, boy you can feel that shit too. Makes you shiver. That kinda energy is gonna block up progress, block your blessin's. If you feelin' cold-hearted at all, if you feelin' stingy or self-centered, you gotta right your heart before you can change anything at all. You gotta put a little bit of love into everything you're doin', everything you're thinkin', because when it comes from that place of love, it's got no choice but to succeed, 'cuz love is the compass and you've got the map.

> ***Center of your heart is the center of the Universe. Go to that center and radiate positive vibration for the well-being of the humanity.***
>
> —Amit Ray

DO THIS TODAY: *Go listen to that old-school cut from the soul group Atlantic Starr, "If Your Heart Isn't in It." Ain't that the truth? When your heart is really in it, you can make the ordinary extraordinary. What do you pour your heart into? That's your gift.*

June 24th

"REFRAME YOUR PAST."

We've all got baggage. Some of us have so much we had to check a few cases at the gate. At fifty bucks a pop, that's quite a chunk of change. You might be tempted to pack light, save that cash for a new boat or a set of golf clubs. But what if you gotta take it all with you 'cuz you got no choice? That's how the baggage of our past works. You gotta take it with you, but you can try to think about it a different kinda way instead of like somethin' you'll be draggin around for the rest of your *got-damn* life, takin' chunks of money outta your wallet.

Instead of thinkin' about the weight of them bags, think about what's in 'em. You got all of this stuff crammed up in there, all of these experiences, and it all taught you somethin'. All of that stuff, the challenges you got yourself through, that's what got you to where you are right now. So, you don't *have to* drag them bags around, you *get to* drag them bags around as a reminder of the gifts they brought you and the lessons you learned. That's how you reframe the past so you can be strong enough to carry it all forward. Shit, that ain't baggage. That's CrossFit, and the more you carryin', the more ripped you gonna get.

> ***The language we use is extremely powerful. It is the frame through which we perceive and describe ourselves and our picture of the world.***
>
> —ben Dissing Sandahl

DO THIS TODAY: *What kinda baggage are you carryin' with you right now? Does it make you feel some kinda way when you thinkin' about it? How can you reframe and look at them experiences like a positive?*

June 25th

"THE FOLLOW-THROUGH IS AS IMPORTANT AS THE PLAN."

You know when you go to the doctor and he prescribes you some antibiotics, you been havin' burnin' pee. It's a UTI, or what we used to call a bladder infection. Seven days of them big-ass horse pills, gotta gag 'em down with a whole glass of water. He says seven days, but, you know, you startin' to feel better after about forty-eight hours. It's funny, you wanna take 'em when you can't stay outta the toilet and you're screamin' in *got-damn* pain like a knife's stabbin' you in the bladder like a mothahfuckah. Then you shovin' 'em in, whatever it takes. But once the pain is gone, you just sorta forget about the nasty-ass horse pills. Outta sight, outta mind, right?

Well, the problem is, the prescription is the plan, and you just bailed on it. Ya' see, a prescription, it ain't just what to take, it's how long to take it and when. You gotta finish it, the whole mothahfuckin' thing, if you want it to work. And you can't go and skip it for days and then expect it to come back and work the same. Naw, mothahfuckah, you gonna have to go back and start it all over again. If you'da taken the whole *got-damn* thing the first time, you'da been done and healed by now. You see what I'm tellin' you? Start what you finish, and you gonna keep yourself on the right track.

> ***In golf as in life, it's the follow through that makes the difference.***
>
> —Ben Wicks

DO THIS TODAY: *Short-term decisions can have long-term consequences. So, when you make a commitment, follow it through to completion. You can't stop halfway. If you half-ass shit, you'll get half-ass results. What commitments have you made? Are you followin' through? Pick one and make steps toward completion. It's gonna make a huge impact on your sense of self worth.*

June 26th

"EVERYTHING YOU GET IN LIFE, YOU GOTTA BE RESPONSIBLE WITH IT."

If you been given gifts, wealth, talent, knowledge, then you are required to use them gifts well. You are required to do right by 'em. Don't mess around and fuck this shit up, I'm tellin' you right now. You are held responsible for what you have. I don't wanna hear any excuses. Think about it this way. Let's say you got a box under the tree on Christmas mornin', a box with little holes punched in the top. You open it up, and it's a *got-damn* puppy. That puppy's cute as hell, and you always wanted a puppy. Best gift ever, and you spend all day showin' that puppy off to everybody. Now, what's gonna happen if you don't take care of it when the newness of it wears off? You just wanna play with it but you don't let it out, don't brush it, don't feed it, don't give it some water? That's right, you know where I'm goin'.... But we don't talk about dead puppies, that's a no-no. So let's say if that happens, your mama and your pops gonna give it to somebody that's gonna take care of it. You didn't take mothahfuckin' responsibility.

Same goes for when God gives you a gift. Let's say you got talent comin' out your ears—the best mothahfuckin' singer anywhere in Chicago. Let's say you even practice a bit, and you land a record deal. Nice, now you got even more gifts. You got money, you got some fame, but you screwin' around with drugs and you makin' stupid statements on your social media, leadin' kids off in wrong directions. You bet yo' ass that gift, that talent you was given, and all of that wealth, it's gonna be taken the hell away from you. God don't play.

To whom much is given, much will be required

—Luke 12:48

DO THIS TODAY: *What do you have that you ain't usin' right? Maybe it's books collectin' dust. Give 'em to somebody who'll read 'em. If it's your talent, start usin' it. It's your responsibility.*

June 27th

"YOU GOTTA LIVE IT UP WHILE THE PARTY'S STILL HOPPIN'."

If you been sleepin' through the whole *got-damn* party, you can't pitch a fit when you wake up and wanna dance with a lampshade on your head, but everybody's already cleared out. You gonna be standin' there lookin' around feelin' some kinda regret. Thing is, life is kinda like that party. You only got the time that you got, but you don't know when the party's gonna end, right? So, get out the *got-damn* lampshade right now.

You can tell how well a man lived by how many folks show up at his funeral...and what kinda stories they got to tell about him. Well, I've been to a lot of mothahfuckin' funerals. My family, one of my best friends Billy, and a whole lotta folks that I don't know—'cuz for a minute I was workin' what I called The Funeral Circuit, gettin' paid to go in and tell some stories and make folks laugh through their tears. One common thing I kept hearin' is, "Oh, his life was too short," and, "We didn't expect it." Why, *got-dammit?* We all gonna end up in that place at some time, so why ain't nobody expectin' it? Thing is, once you come to grips with it, you can let loose and start livin' it up right now! The folks that done that, whew, their funeral was standin' room only and their loved ones had stories that'd make you laugh, cry, stand up and clap, or praise Jesus. That's a life well lived, right there. Ain't nobody showin' up like that for the guy that sat on his couch his whole mothahfuckin' life, missin' the *got-damn* party. It ain't about the time you got, it's what you do with it.

> ***Not how long, but how well you lived is the main thing.***
>
> —Seneca the Younger

DO THIS TODAY: *The mighty O'Jays said it best with their legendary hit, "Livin' for the Weekend"! Open up those windows and let that sunshine in. Pick up that phone and call your crazy-ass friend, you know, the one that always makes you laugh. Go do somethin' today that makes you feel alive, give 'em somethin' to talk about.*

June 28th

"YOU'RE GONNA BE SMACKED UPSIDE THE HEAD WITH THE LESSON UNTIL YOU LEARN IT."

We all got that one friend always moanin' and cryin', "Why does this keep happenin' to me?" Every car they buy breaks down. They're getting' into relationships that fall apart, or maybe they get taken advantage of over and over again. The thing is, them folks tend to blame everybody else but themselves. The sorry thing is that when they're doin' that shit, they're blockin' their lesson, so they gotta keep gettin' it thrown in their face, louder and louder, until they learn it. When shit's happenin' to you, it means that God's tryin' to give you a lesson, tryin' to teach you something you gotta know so you can grow and be a better person, live a good and happy life. If you keep turnin' away from them lessons, they gonna smack you upside the head again and again until you can't see straight.

It's kinda' like when I's a kid and ducked Grandpa Thurman's backhand. Boy, he'd come around harder the second time. And if you duck that one, too, you better watch yo' ass, 'cuz you about to get a whoopin'. God's got a whoopin' for ya' if you keep turnin' your head on His lessons. He's tryin' to teach you somethin'. You best pay attention. Remember, you can learn great things from your mistakes once you quit denyin' 'em.

> ***Nothing ever goes away until it teaches us what we need to know.***
>
> —Pema Chödrön

DO THIS TODAY: *It's time for you to start takin' responsibility, so you can stop getting' smacked upside the head. What do you got* **goings on** *in your life that seems to keep repeatin' itself? Ask yourself what you can learn from it right now.*

June 29th

"GRACE IS LIKE GOD'S LOVE, AND IT WILL SET YOU FREE."

If y'all have gone to church at all, you've heard about grace. "By the grace of God, so shall it be" and all of that. But do you know what it really means? Yeah, that's what I thought. Lemme tell ya'. Grace is kinda like when God says to you, "Alright, I know you messed up. But you learned your lesson and I'm gonna forgive you on this one." Man, when you receive that, it feels like the weight of the world done slid right off your shoulders. It feels good.

But the thing is, God ain't just goin' around givin' just anybody His grace for no reason. You got to catch His attention. It's not like you gotta earn it in the way you earn a reward, 'cuz God can give grace whenever He wants for whatever reason He wants, He's God. However, if you're out there doin' your best, you're learnin' and you're growin', and you're givin' your own kinda grace to other folks, He's gonna see that. It's kinda like when outta the blue, Big Mama hands you a cookie. Your eyes get big and she's smilin'. She just says, "I seen you helpin' out Mrs. Jenkins with her groceries." Then she winks at you. That cookie never tasted better. Like Big Mama, God's payin' attention all the time, and if you be doin' good, He's gonna come in with His grace when you least expectin' it.

> ***Amazing grace, how sweet the sound, that saved a wretch like me.***
>
> —Hymn, John Newton

DO THIS TODAY: *Grace has the potential to change lives and turn negative situations into positive ones. Think of a time when you felt overwhelmed with good, like something saved you when you's sure you wouldn't be saved. That's grace, and you can keep feelin' that as long as you keep followin' your path and doin' good.*

June 30th

"WHAT WORKS FOR YOU MAYBE DON'T WORK THE SAME FOR EVERYBODY ELSE."

Ain't nothin' more annoying than some mothahfuckah who's got his shit figured out and he's all up in your grill about how you should do it just like him. "You gotta do this program, eat this food, say this prayer, do this dance, wear this watch that tracks everything you do, and then you'll be just as successful as me." *Got-damn*, makes you wanna kick a mothahfuckah's teeth out. It's not that you ain't happy for him, but it just rubs you some kinda wrong way. Maybe 'cuz it draws attention to the fact that you ain't tryin' to get your own shit together. Man, when folks hold a microscope up to your insecurities, it hits you in the gut.

My point is that when you gettin' your groove on, shut the hell up about it, for two reasons. One, your friends and family gonna know you gettin' your groove on 'cuz they're gonna see all the good shit happenin' for you. If they ask what's up, then you got a green light to tell 'em. Two, what you're doin' might not work for everybody. We all got different experiences that we bring to the table, different genetics, different goals, different *got-damn* needs.

Not everything works for everybody.

—Chamillionaire

DO THIS TODAY: *I like to help people. It's a rewarding feelin' we get by helpin' others, but it's not our job to "fix" nobody else. You gotta let folks find their own way. Now, you can give 'em a copy of this book, but maybe they don't get the same thing out of it you did, or maybe they don't wanna get fixed. Different strokes for different folks. It's time for you to let go and let God.*

PART THREE:
SOMEBODY TO YOU

Specific people come into your life, and you have what we call a relationship with 'em. Thing about relationships is they're work sometimes. No, I gotta keep it real. They're work all the time.

Bernard's always been the type of man that folks gravitate to. I don't know if it's because he's so confident, because he's funny and handsome, or if they can sense that he really cares about them. Maybe it's a little bit of all of that. Either way, he's been a good friend to a lot of folks over the years, given some of the best advice, done real honest business, and he's got so many people in this world grateful to him for it. Everywhere he went throughout his career, everything he did, he was making connections and building relationships, because he knew that's what it's all about.

You know how folks say that it's not always about *what* you know, it's about *who* you know? That's true, and it works both for business and for life in general. But it's not *just* about who you know, it's how you *treat* the folks you know. It's also who you choose to be around, and how well you put up your boundaries. When Bernard started getting famous, he had to learn to do that real quick. He had folks coming at him out of the woodwork, wanting favors, wanting money. He always gave what he could and helped when he could, but never to somebody who didn't deserve it. And he always treated folks, from the bus driver to Steven Soderbergh, with the same respect. People could feel he really cared about them, and that's what I think endeared the world to Bernard.

Bernard had the same driver for many years. His name was Bill. Wherever he went, he always had Bill pick him up. They did a lot together, and Bill quickly became more than just a driver to Bernard, I think because they just clicked. Bernard knew he could trust Bill. Now, you knew that you meant something to Bernard when he gave you a nickname. He called me Red and Je'Niece is Boops. His close friend Morris was Big Nigga. His band leader Phil Seed was Shorty Ruff, and his friend and singer Adrienne Locke was Ride. Well, the nickname Bernard gave Bill Hawthorne was Dollah. That's what he called him, never Bill, always Dollah. Anyway, Bill told me this story about how he drove Bernard to a meeting with some big-wig film people up at the Peninsula Hotel, and Bernard wanted Bill to go in.

"I didn't want to go in," Bill said. "But Bernie says, 'Naw, come on in. You ain't gonna wait in the *got-damn* car. Come in and have some lunch.' He'd almost always invite me in wherever he went, but this was a really nice restaurant, and I wasn't so sure. But Bernie insisted, so of course, I went in." Bill shook his head. He knew he was gonna do what Bernard asked. That man had a way with people like that. "We walk in there together," Bill said. "Bernie goes to the table with the businesspeople, and the hostess gives me a seat at a table across the other side of the room. I'm not part of the meetin', you know, but I'm over there, and the staff is treatin' me like royalty. They surrounded me like I was a star. It felt kinda good. So, I was over there eatin', enjoyin' myself, when all of a sudden, I hear a shout. 'Hey, Dollah! You okay over there?' I look up, and Bernie's sittin' there all the way across to the other side of the room, the folks at his table lookin' at him, and he had a big smile on his face. He just wanted to make sure I was bein' taken care of. I was fine. He just took that minute to ask me, and it was great." Bernard has always been that kind of man.

Now, Bill drove all of us for a lot of years, but most importantly, he was *Bernard's* ride...and I know they did a lot more than riding. Bernard would take him to the golf range, the gun range, and to get their nails done and pedicures. One time, Bill said they went to a gun range about an hour outside of Chicago where you could shoot anything. He said the guys had Gatlin's and everything, it was unreal. "It sounded like a war zone," he said. "And it was ninety percent White people." That took some trust on Bill's part right there. It made him a little nervous. But Bill did trust Bernard. That's how it worked between them, because you have to trust somebody if you're gonna have any kind of relationship with them at all.

Trust is the foundation, then there's a lot of bricks that go on top of that. First off, you've got to have the same kind of energy. When I got serious with Bernard, I knew he had something about him, a magnetism that drew folks to him even when they resisted. I remember when he first came to my house, I tried to prep my mama. "Now, mama," I said to her. "He's real dark. Like he's dark, dark. So, please, don't say anything to him." She promised, and I prayed. He came to the door and I opened it.

My mama came in behind me and she just couldn't do it. "Oh, Rhonda. You said he was dark, but you didn't say he was that dark."

Bernard just grinned his big smile, and he said, "Yeah, but you never seen a man pretty as me." Well, that endeared my mama to him from that moment. He knew who he was, and he knew where he was goin'. He was gonna be a comedian.

I know we could not have lasted if I'd ever tried to stop him from shooting for the stars, or if I tried to change him, and I didn't want to. He never tried to stop me from doing what I wanted to do or from reaching my goals either. You've got to be each other's biggest cheerleader and their voice of reason too. You've got to be real with one another and be open with your communication. That goes for all kinds of relationships, including friendships and professional, not just the intimate and family type.

I think Bernard has understood the value of his connection with other people from a very young age. It got him real far in life, and it can do that for you too. Once you start creating meaningful relationships, and you learn to protect yourself from the toxic people that are blocking your path, you're going to really start to soar. Trust me, you'll see.

July 1st

"IF YOU WANNA RIDE WITH ME, YOU BETTER HOP ON THIS TRAIN."

I remember when Rhonda and I was datin', I told her I was gonna be a comedian, and I was gonna be rich, and I asked her if she was gettin' on that train. She did and she never got off. That's the kinda person you want to be with, not somebody who's tellin' you to get off at the next stop. You gotta be selective, make sure you're "equally yoked." My old heads know what I'm talkin' about. But for you new schoolers, "equally yoked" means choosing your mate wisely. Choose someone with the same set of beliefs and values as you, someone who's movin' at your pace. If not, your life together can be fucked up, a livin' hell, on thin ice, and there ain't no way that relationship is gonna last. Either you'll be rushin' them up or they'll be slowin' you down and holdin' you back. Either way, you gonna end up resentin' one another.

This goes for whoever's gonna be your partner in life, but also anybody that you're associatin' yourself with: friends, employees, business partners too. What if I had a manager that only wanted me to keep workin' the Chitlin Circuit, only thought I should focus on my stand-up, didn't want to take big risks? Hell, no. That shit wouldn't work, 'cuz they woulda been holdin' me back. You see what I'm sayin'? If they can't keep up with you, they gotta drop off.

> ***When you walk with someone, something unspoken happens. Either you match their pace or they match yours.***
>
> —Sidney Poitier

DO THIS TODAY: *Do an inventory of the folks that's around you. Are they walkin' beside you, behind you, or in front? Decide if you need to match their pace or let them drop off.*

July 2nd

"YOU CAN'T BUILD YOURSELF BY BEATIN' SOMEBODY ELSE DOWN."

If you successful, folks will know it without you havin' to tell 'em all the *got-damn* time, and they sure as hell won't give a good *got-damn* about your success if you been walkin' all over somebody else to get it. 'Cuz that shit gets around fast, and you gonna end up lonely and at the bottom real quick. Even more than that, you know success breeds success and there's room for all y'all at the top. Think about that for a minute. Successful people learn from each other. They motivate each other to reach higher. They don't waste time turnin' up their noses and purposely tryin' to hurt some-damn-body. They don't put their time or their energy into no vendettas, no kind of jealousy, no revenge and shit. They're too busy bein' successful.

You ever hear Will Smith smack-talk Kevin Hart or vice versa? Hell no. Damn, them guys is so happy to see each other rise up, they're the kinda guys that say, "Oh, damn, you funny and everybody loves you. We should make a mothahfuckin' move together." Why? Because the more stars and talent in a movie, the better it is! They know that, and it's the same for anything. Get all the successful folks together and they're like a train that even mothahfuckin' Superman can't stop. That's how you gotta be, celebratin' one another and liftin' each other up.

> ***If you have to hurt other people in order to feel powerful, you are an extremely weak individual.***
>
> —Bobby J. Mattingly

DO THIS TODAY: *You got somebody that you tryin' to keep down in some kinda way, even if it's just smack-talkin' 'em behind their back? I want you to think of somethin' positive about 'em right now. Then, next time you wanna flex or keep 'em down, compliment 'em or find some way to include 'em instead. You're buildin' your own dream team.*

July 3rd

"YOU CAN SEE THE UGLY INSIDE OF FOLKS IF YOU JUST PAY ATTENTION."

I always try to see the best in folks. It's a good way to look at the world and all that. But you can't let folks blind you, neither, 'cuz the ones that got all kinda ugly inside 'em have real sneaky ways of hidin' it. It's kinda like them girls you see at the club, and they got thick eyelashes and sexy cheekbones. They got a bang-bang-bang figure, you know. They sweet as honey, but then you see 'em the next morning and you're like damn, fake eyelashes off, makeup smudged, got they Wonderbra and the damn corset off, and you thinkin', *Who's that? She bring her mama?* Now, I ain't sayin' a good woman's gotta be lookin' like that, I'm just sayin' it's false advertisin'. That's what folks doin' that covers themself up with fake promises, boosted-up tales about themselves, secret agendas, and all the other stuff they hidin' up under their mothahfuckin' lies. It's gonna come out at some point, and when it does, it's gonna be ugly as hell.

I had this happen to me once. I was blindsided, too, and that shit hurt. I had somebody workin' for me I found out was stealin' from me. He was s'pose to be on my side, but that mothahfuckah was bookin' gigs and takin' fees for shit I was never notified about in the first place. He was makin' a bad name for me and tryin' to fill his own *got-damn* pockets. I learned real quick to be a little bit more cautious, to dig a little deeper, 'cuz the ugly don't sit too far underneath the skin.

> ***Beauty may be skin deep, but ugly goes clear to the bone.***
>
> —Redd Foxx

DO THIS TODAY: *Have you noticed in life that the more "fake" people are, the larger their circle will be? They got a lot of people maybe, but they keep 'em all at arm's length. The opposite is also true. The more "real" folks are, the smaller and tighter their circle. Check yourself. Are you bein' real or puttin' up a front? How big is your circle?*

July 4th

"ALWAYS TELL THE *GOT-DAMN* TRUTH AND STAY THE HELL AWAY FROM LIARS."

Didn't your mama teach you not to lie, *got-dammit*? That's one of the first mothahfuckin' things I learnt when I was a boy. Hand to God, as soon as a word came outta my mouth my mama was tellin' me, "Now, don't you lie to me, child." Anything came outta my mouth sideways, I'd get a thwoppin', you know what I'm sayin'? It made me honest, and it almost made me understand how to detect a mothahfuckin' lie. All you go to do is watch their face, eyes shiftin', too much smilin', playin' with their *got-damn* fingers and shit. I can tell, and sometimes I'm wishin' I could give 'em a good thwoppin'. But since that is generally frowned upon, I just walk away from those lyin' mothahfuckahs. 'Cuz I'm gonna tell you somethin' right now, if they're lyin' once, they'll do it again. And if they're lyin' to somebody else, they won't have no trouble lyin' to you too. So, get the hell away from those shady-ass mothahfuckahs fast. You don't want nothin' to do with 'em, and you sure as hell don't want nobody to think you're with 'em, 'cuz folks will think you a liar too. And if they already done you dirty, and they're out there throwin' their lie up against the truth, don't worry, that lie won't last too long. They gotta try and remember that shit, and they gonna slip up eventually. Worst thing in the world to be called is a liar, but the second worst thing is to have somebody sayin' you a liar when you tellin' the truth. I get it. Just know that the truth will come out soon enough. The truth will set you free.

> ***Lies run sprints, but the truth runs marathons.***
>
> —Michael Jackson

DO THIS TODAY: *Try tellin' the truth. You don't have to remember what you said, and you'll earn folks' trust and respect too. You got somethin' you lied about, even just a little fib? If it won't hurt nobody to do so, go correct it right now. You're gonna feel so free from that burden.*

July 5th

"PAY ATTENTION TO HOW SOMEBODY'S TREATIN' OTHERS, 'CUZ BEFORE LONG, THAT'S HOW THEY'LL BE TREATIN' YOU."

I had this slick mothahfuckah I was workin' with once. I won't tell y'all his name, 'cuz I don't wanna get my ass sued. But he starts actin' shady. He's talking about, "I don't know if Jimbo Johnson is really that good at his job. I know he's had our back since we started, but maybe we should replace him." Or he's goin' off sayin' shit about another team member, then cuttin' 'em out without givin' 'em no reason. But damn, he's talkin' to you about *loyalty* and shit. Now that's cold. You don't think he's sayin' that shit about *you* behind your back too?

You gotta watch out for them kinda folks. I call them assholes. Thing is, they don't show their true colors 'til you already knee-deep workin' with 'em and you feelin' like it's too late to cut the damn ties. I'm gonna tell you right now, it's never too late. No decision is ever final, and you can change your mind, get the hell out, and you gonna start to feel everything openin' up for you 'cuz they blockin' your blessings. Then next time, you can avoid this kinda situation by doin' one thing before you get in with 'em: watch how they treat strangers. How they actin' to the waiter, the taxi driver, their secretary, that'll show you their true nature, and maybe give you a glimpse of how they'll treat you, too, once they feel like you're in their way or they don't need you no more. That's why you take 'em out to lunch before you sign the *got-damn* contracts. It ain't to be nice and socialize, you on a mothahfuckin' *recognisance* mission.

> ***Learn to be quiet enough to hear the genuine in yourself so that you can hear it in others.***
>
> —Marian Wright Edelman

DO THIS TODAY: *Think about somebody you maybe wonder about. Have you noticed any of their behaviors toward folks they encounter? Make a plan to take 'em out for lunch or coffee before you get in any further, and pay close attention, especially when somethin' ain't goin' their way. If it feels wrong, don't walk away, run!*

July 6th

"TREAT ALL YOUR PEOPLE RIGHT ALL THE *GOT-DAMN* TIME."

Nothin' I can't stand more than folks that'll treat you good when they want something from ya', but then turn around and act like you nothin' when they don't. Let alone try and help you out when you might be needin' somethin'. *Got-damn*, I can't stand that, so I gotta make double sure I don't ever do that to none of the people that I love. The thing is, time goes by and once it's gone, you can't get it back. I remember them times when Je'Niece was small and we'd play wrestle on the rug, rough-housin' and just horsin' around. I used to make her lunch after school, same thing every day—a ham sandwich, Pepsi, and a Hostess CupCake. That's right, we's livin' large and havin' fun. And I wasn't always a perfect dad, but I loved my girl at every age and every stage. Same thing with Rhonda. I loved the new love, and the new-parent kinda love, and the love that makes you feel like you comin' home. So, I made sure I was treatin' 'em right all the *got-damn* time—as well as I knew how, anyway.

Same thing goes for my friends, my other family members, my business associates. Why'd you wanna go treatin' anybody any way less than you'd want somebody to treat you? Didn't you learn that golden rule when you's just a little kid? Luke 6:31, "Do unto others as you would have them do unto you." If you go by that, you can't go wrong.

> ***Cherish every moment with those you love at every stage of your journey.***
>
> —Jack Layton

DO THIS TODAY: *Take a minute to reflect on how you treat the folks around you. Are you doin' and sayin' to them how you'd want them to act and speak to you? If not, how are you gonna try and change that?*

July 7th

"IT'S NOT ALWAYS WHAT YOU SAY, IT'S HOW YOU SAYIN' IT."

Let's start this out with a little exercise, okay? Think about the question, "Whatchyou doin'?" I can say that in a coupla different ways, and you gonna know right away it means some different mothahfuckin' things by how I do it. So, let's say I trot into the room, my eyes wide open, shoulders open, big smile, and I ask, "What y'all doin'?" You gonna smile back and tell me what y'all doin', maybe invite me to join you. But if I stomp in there, hands on my *got-damn* hips, eyebrows all bent, and I shout, "Whatchyou doin?" Damn, you gonna be scared and maybe get a little bit defensive. Then there's another way too. I come in there, squint one eye and peer at you all suspicious, and I whisper, "Whatchy'all doin?" You might get a little nervous and shit. See, it's not what you sayin', it's how you sayin' it. You gotta watch your tone. You can try to clarify, justify, or apologize all you want, but once you say it like you do, it can't be undone, and you might just have a huge mothahfuckin' fight on your hands that was not at all necessary.

So, maybe you really are upset or suspicious, whatever it is, but if you go on in there with a fire in yo' pants, you ain't gonna get very far—unless what you tryin' to do is make folks scared and angry. Why would you wanna do that? Instead, you gotta take a breath, get your head straight, calm yo' ass, and talk in a reasonable tone of voice. You might be surprised that doin' so will get you more respect in the long run.

> ***The tongue can paint what the eyes can't see.***
>
> —Chinese Proverb

DO THIS TODAY: *Check your tone. Every time you speak today, right yourself before you open your mouth so you can communicate clearly and calmly. See how folks respond to you.*

July 8th

"THE FIRST RELATIONSHIP YOU GOTTA MAKE RIGHT IS WITH YOURSELF."

Sometimes we treat ourselves so badly. We listen to our inner critic, get involved in fucked-up relationships, and dwell on old shit, and it gets to the point that we don't even wanna be alone with ourselves. Damn, that's harsh, 'cuz you are the only person that you gonna be alone with for absolute sure for the rest of your *got-damn* life. You are cuffed to that mothahfuckah like my cousin Louis was cuffed to that fender after he told his brothah, "Here, hold my beer and watch this." That's right, your "self" ain't goin' nowhere, so you gotta start bein' civil to him, or he's gonna be a mothahfuckah to live with. In fact, you gotta start treatin' him more than civil, you gotta love him, for real. 'Cuz if you don't love yourself, you don't take care of him, you don't help him be healthy and grow, you ain't gonna really know how to love anybody else. It's gonna be hard to do it, and you gonna try, but you're strugglin' and you won't have much left of yourself to give.

You gotta start treatin' yourself with the same kinda love you tryin' to give others. At least keep a little bit of it for yourself, and once you do that and you're lovin' who you are, the love for other folks is gonna come so much easier, and they're gonna feel it too.

> ***If you don't love yourself, how the hell are you gonna love somebody else?***
>
> —RuPaul

DO THIS TODAY: *Are you a people pleaser? Do you find it easier to love others than to love yourself? Today I want you to write yourself a "love" letter, or just a reminder note if you don't wanna call it that. Tell yourself all the things you love about you, all the things you appreciate, even if they're just small right now.*

July 9th

"YOU CAN'T MAKE NOBODY ELSE HAPPY. THEY GOTTA DO THAT SHIT FOR THEMSELVES."

I'm so sick and tired of hearin' folks say, "Oh, I had to dump so-and-so, they just weren't makin' me happy." That's some bullshit right there. Nobody can *make* you happy, and if you lookin' for that out of a *got-damn* relationship, well, you best just stop lookin'. 'Cuz if you ain't happy all on your own, ain't nobody gonna be able to do it for you. Oh, they might make you laugh a little, make you smile, or make you forget about your mothahfuckin' misery for a day, a week, a month...but they will not be able to make you happy deep inside of your soul. Nobody can do that shit but you. And if you're countin' on somebody else to do it for you, it ain't gonna work out. Trust me on that one.

Same thing goes the other way too. If you got somebody in your life, and they're usin' you to help them find happiness, that shit's gonna get exhausting fast. They're askin' you to do an impossible thing, and that's not fair, is it? Best thing you can do is work on yourself so that you radiate mothahfuckin' happiness. I don't mean you gotta walk around with a goofy-ass grin on your face all the damn time, but just get content with your life and who you are. Then you gonna meet folks that are doin' the same thing, and y'all can be happy together. That's how it works, and that's the kinda relationships that last.

> ***You can't make another person happy: they have to make themselves happy.***
>
> —Kate Kerrigan

DO THIS TODAY: *Do an about face. Are you lettin' somebody else put their happiness and fulfillment on your "to do" list? It's not your damn job to lift them up if you feel like it's pullin' you down. When it comes to your happiness, be selfish and take care of you first.*

July 10th

"IT'S LONELY AT THE TOP."

Thing is, there's room for everybody at the top, but not everybody is gonna get there. That ain't your fault, but they're gonna take it out on you. Not all of 'em, but some of 'em, fo' sho'. The ones that don't think they can get where you goin', the ones that's jealous and frustrated about their own got-damn *missteps* and *failures*, the ones that don't wanna try no more or think they was handed a short stick. Those are the ones that will wish you didn't get where you did. Oh, they might smile and pat you on the *got-damn* back, but then as soon as you turn around, they'll be smack-talkin' you to anybody who'll listen. That shit gets rough, and you start to wonder who's really your friend and who's a fake-ass mothahfuck-ah. Who can you trust, and who'll throw you under the bus the first chance they get? Damn, it gets lonely when you don't know who to trust. That's why you gotta stick with your tried-and-true.

I've had the same *got-damn* group of friends since I was in high school. I love those mothahfuckahs like brothahs. Then of course I got Rhonda and my little girl Je'Niece, and I made a few more solid friends over the years too. That's all y'all need, though, and that might be all you gonna get. You see, the thing about big success is that even though it might not change *you*, it changes how other folks see you, and that's where the trouble starts. All you can do is keep doin' you, and the real ones are gonna stay with you.

> ***The worst part of success is trying to find someone who is happy for you.***
>
> —Bette Midler

DO THIS TODAY: *It can hurt to find out a friend is really jealous of you. But you gotta understand that their jealousy is caused by their own underlying issues and it ain't your fault. Think about your circle. Are your closest people seriously excited for your success? If not, maybe today's a good day to have a heart-to-heart with 'em about it.*

July 11th

"IF IT'S ANOTHER GUY'S NIGHT, STEP OUTTA THE WAY."

I don't care how high you been ridin, it can't be your night every *got-damn* night. Sometimes, you gotta let somebody else shine. You gotta step aside and give him the stage, 'cuz he's ready to go, he's in the flow, and he's gotta do his thang. Times like that, you just stand backstage and listen to the crowd roarin' for him, and feel that energy, knowin' that he's feelin' it too. Then he comes back, and he's pumped. You give him a high five, fist bump, bro hug, all of that, and he's grateful to you 'cuz you believed in that mothahfuckah. That feels good.

Now, imagine if it's his night and you pacin' backstage, feelin' some kinda way about folks laughin' and throwin' their hollahs at him instead of you? Damn, you know what that is, brothah? That's jealousy. That's ugly, and God don't like ugly. That kinda attitude is not only gonna block your blessings, it's also gonna make you a lot of mothahfuckin' enemies. How do you think that other guy's gonna feel when he comes off of his big show, and you back there givin' him the stink-eye, makin' him feel like he stole somethin' from you? He didn't steal nothin' from you, mothahfuckah. There's plenty of success to go 'round. Be happy for him, and you gonna get that back, don't you worry about it.

> ***Here's to celebrating light where we find it. And making light where we don't.***
>
> —John Green

DO THIS TODAY: *Like Bobby McFerrin's singing, "Don't Worry, Be Happy," stop worryin' if somebody one-upped you today. Be happy for 'em, 'cuz gratitude builds latitude. Today, I want you to congratulate somebody on somethin' they did right, even if it's just unloadin' the dishwasher or perfectly parallel parkin' their car.*

July 12th

"DON'T EVER MAKE NOBODY FEEL SMALL."

I used to have this uncle, whenever he'd come around, I'd feel myself shrink down like I was nothin' and nobody. He'd ask me questions he knew I couldn't answer. He'd try and get me to fuck up, say somethin' stupid, then he'd grin like he was smart as hell and I was stupid. Sometimes he'd say he was proud of me, or he'd bring me a football for my *got-damn* birthday, somethin' nice, but I couldn't stand the fool even when he was bringin' me presents. He made me feel small, and that's the worst mothahfuckin' feelin' in the world. I never wanna make somebody feel like that, ever, 'cuz that shit's somethin' they will never forget. If it weren't for my mama and my grandparents makin' sure I knew I was strong, that man coulda really fucked me up too. It's a damn good thing he never had kids of his own.

Now, I ain't sayin' I never done nothin' to make somebody feel that kinda way. We all make mistakes. Sometimes we do it without even thinkin'. But when I realize I done it, I turned it right back around and apologized, then I made damn sure it didn't happen again. 'Cuz that's the kind of thing that can really stay with somebody for a long, long time.

> ***I've learned that people will forget what you said, people will forget what you did, but people will never forget how you made them feel.***
>
> —Carl W. Buehner

DO THIS TODAY: *Be honest. Is there someone you can admit to belittlin' right now? Maybe at work or even with family. Let me help you curb that shit. Next time you feel like you wanna criticize, try this instead: Say, "I need some air," or, "Give me a minute," and take yo' ass to the bathroom or somewhere more private. Take a serious look at yourself and ask yourself why you wanna cut somebody down. Take a breath, then go back and say somethin' nice.*

July 13th

"YOU BETTER WATCH YOUR MOUTH. YOU NEVER KNOW WHO'S LISTENIN'."

You ever go to a peewee basketball game, and some of them kids look like they gettin' swarmed by bees. They runnin' around, wavin' their arms and shit, lookin' like they don't even know which hoop they supposed to be aimin' at. Well, apparently when you're at one of them games to watch your mothahfuckin' nephew, it ain't a good idea to say shit to your brothah while you up in them bleachers. Maybe you say, "Ouch, that kid ain't goin' pro any time soon." Or, "Damn, my grandmama in a wheelchair got more game than that little chubby one on the left." Oh, your brothah might think it's funny, but he's shushin' you for a *got-damn* reason. It might be loud in the recreation center gym, but folks can hear, and you have no idea whose mothahfuckin' pops is sittin' right by you. And sometimes, that little chubby one got a big mothahfuckah for a daddy, and he just got outta prison, and he's waitin' for you outside. You see what I'm sayin'? Keep it to your damn self, 'cuz that shit can come back to you and hurt like hell.

Now, I'm jokin' about that peewee basketball game, but your words, man, they mean somethin'. Imagine if the little kid you's makin' fun of heard you? It could hurt him real bad and not stop hurtin' for a long time. Same goes for adults, 'cuz some grown-ass men and women ain't strong enough to take your nasty remarks and be okay either. If you can't say somethin' nice, don't say nothin' at all.

> ***Be mindful when it comes to your words. A string of some that don't mean much to you, may stick with someone else for a lifetime.***
>
> —Rachel Wolchin

DO THIS TODAY: *Remember, words can either hurt or help. Maybe you thought it was nothin', but to them it was more, maybe their lives will never be the same again. Use your words, as a positive force in the world.*

July 14th

"YOU FIGHTIN' WITH SOMEBODY, IT'S HALF YOUR FAULT."

If you fightin' with somebody, you have the full power to end it instantly. All you gotta do is drop it and walk the fuck away. If they still standin' there fightin', then they a crazy mothahfuckah 'cuz they'll be fightin' all alone. It takes two to tango, so the sayin' goes. Now, I ain't never tangoed, but I got myself into a few fights and they never seem to end well. Why do we wanna go and start shit in the first place? Well, sometimes we don't start it, the trouble just comes to us. I get that. You can't control the mothahfuckahs that wanna come at you. You can't always control how some family member's gonna react to somethin' you did or said. Sometimes, it ain't even you, it's just something's *goings on* with the other person and they're takin' it out on you. But remember, it takes two. If you just stop respondin' to 'em, they'll eventually shut the hell up. That goes for in person, on the phone, email, and on the social medias. Remember, walkin' away don't mean you gave up, it just means you're the bigger person...and you don't want no negative energy comin' in there and fuckin' you up.

> ***Conflict cannot survive without your participation.***
>
> —Wayne W. Dyer

DO THIS TODAY: *You can't argue by your damn self, so the best thing to do is back off. Practice these couple of lines so you can use 'em when you need 'em: "How 'bout we just agree to disagree?" "Hey, let's not get into a fight over this. It ain't worth it." "If you feel that strongly, then I'm gonna back down." If none of these feels right, think of your own way to end an argument and have it ready for when you need it.*

July 15th

"SHOW SOME MOTHAHFUCKIN' RESPECT AND EXPECT IT BACK."

Everybody deserves some respect. What does that mean? Well, it means two things and I'm gonna tell you which one is owed to everybody, and which one's gotta be earned. One type of respect is when you show somebody due regard for their feelin's and give 'em some common courtesy. It's like acknowledgin' that they're people just like you, and you treat 'em with a bit of dignity. Every mothahfuckah deserves that, from the folks you pass on the street to the ones fixin' your car, to the president of the *got-damn* United States. They have a right to it, and so do you. So, expect other folks to give you the same courtesy. When they don't, you gotta kick their ass. No, no, no. I'm just kiddin'. But don't stay around folks that don't give you no respect.

Then there's another kinda respect that's gotta be earned, and not everybody's gonna have that respect from you. You give the second kinda respect to somebody who's done something remarkable. Like, I have got the utmost respect for Redd Foxx, Michael Jordan, Shaquille O'Neal, Oprah, Barack Obama, Serena Williams. Oh, there's more than that, includin' this comic that kept comin' back to the stage again and again when we was just startin' out. He was givin' it his all, and I respected that...but you see what I'm sayin'. Those folks worked hard, done some difficult and great things. I respect 'em. That's the second kind, and that shit's earned.

> ***We all require and want respect, man or woman, black or white. It's our basic human right.***
>
> —Aretha Franklin

DO THIS TODAY: *Everyone's entitled to look at the world differently and share their views. Try listenin' to somebody talk about their opinion today either in person or on a podcast or radio program, an opinion you know is* **opposite from yours***. Pay attention, don't get mad, just listen...you may learn somethin'.*

July 16th

"'ARE YOU OKAY?' ARE THE BEST *GOT-DAMN* WORDS YOU CAN SAY TO SOMEBODY."

You wanna stop a grumpy mothahfuckah, defuse the situation, deflect an oncoming toe-to-toe before it even gets started, ask 'em "Are you okay?" Folks ain't expectin' it, and it disarms 'em quick. But you gotta say it like you mean it. No, actually, you gotta really mean it. You see, most of the time when folks is snippy at you, when they be startin' some shit, it ain't even *about* you. They already got their panties in a bunch before you even walked in the *got-damn* door. So, instead of engagin' in their crazy, ask. As 'em if they alright.

I used to go to this diner called Tempo Time after Monday nights at the Cotton Club. Me and Ride (my friend Adrienne, best singer in the world) and the rest of the comics, we'd go there and get breakfast after the show, about two o'clock in the mornin'. This one time, we walk in, and the waitress had an attitude. She was shakin' her head, rollin' her eyes, tellin' us, "We ain't got no sausage," like she don't give a shit. Well, I just calmly smiled nice, and I said, "Hey, Lucille. Are you okay?" *Got-damn* if she didn't break down into tears. It was like a mothahfuckin' pipe burst. And she says, "I'm sorry, I'm sorry. I just got word my grandmama in the hospital, my furnace done broke on me this mornin', and I'm stuck here can't do nothin' about nothin'." Me and the gang, we told her don't worry, it's gonna be okay. We weren't in no hurry, and we didn't need no sausage. We knew how it was. Boy, you could see the relief come across her face. It was like all she needed was someone to see her. After we's done with our meal, she brought us a piece of pie on the house, and we made sure we tipped her well. She had to get her heater fixed and all.

> ***Good words are worth much, and cost little.***
>
> —George Herbert

DO THIS TODAY: *Think about somethin' you can say today and every day that will uplift somebody. Don't be fake. You gotta be both positive and sincere.*

July 17th

"KEEP TREATIN' FOLKS LIKE YOU DON'T WANT 'EM, AND PRETTY SOON YOU WON'T HAVE 'EM."

You can't go cuttin' folks off, blockin' 'em out, puttin' 'em down, and then expect 'em to be there for you when you need 'em. Sure, it maybe works one or two times 'cuz they don't know no better, or they're tryin' to give you another chance. But do it over and over, and if they're worth a damn to themselves, they'll be nowhere around, and you'll be standin' there wonderin' where's everybody gone. You might try and blame them, too, sayin' they abandoned you when you was needin' 'em. But you better take a long hard look at yourself and understand why they up and left you. Chances are, you been treatin' them like they's disposable. POOF! Are you a magician? 'Cuz you sho' know how to make folks disappear.

Sometimes we push folks away not because of what they done, but because we runnin' from our own problems. Maybe they gettin' a little too close, seein' the bad and the ugly, and it makes us uncomfortable. Or, maybe they startin' to call us out on our shit and we don't wanna deal with it. If you're puttin' up walls, kickin' folks to the curb, or if you just notice they're droppin' off, don't blame them. Take a good hard look at yourself and figure out what you been doin' to make that happen. Always remember to stop and breathe. Deal with one problem at a time. That way you can clear your head and make rational decisions.

> ***People are lonely because they build walls instead of bridges.***
>
> —Joseph F. Newton

DO THIS TODAY: *You got folks that you dropped out on, maybe found somethin' to dislike about 'em so you don't feel so bad about kickin' 'em to the curb? Pick one of those people and decide if it would be in your best interest to make it right and reconnect with 'em.*

July 18th

"YOU DON'T WANNA BE AROUND FOLKS THAT MAKE YOU FEEL LONELY."

Bein' with other folks is a basic human need, right up there with water and shelter and food. We all gotta feel connected in some way. But what if the folks that's around you make you feel lonely. How they doin' that? Well, maybe they so into themselves that you ain't important to 'em. Or, maybe they make you feel small, they put up walls, or they make it pretty *got-damn* clear that they don't want you to tell 'em about your nothin'—not your problems or your victories or your feelin's, nothin'. Damn, that can be even lonelier than sittin' by yourself.

You ever see them families that put in their TV dinners and they all sittin' around with their tray tables watchin' TV while they eat? Or maybe you in a restaurant and there's a couple out together and they both lookin' at their phones instead of at one another. Even worse is when one of 'em is on their phone and the other one's just sittin' there lookin' into their soda, lookin' out the window, wishin' the person they's with would at least try and connect. That right there, that's some lonely mothahfuckahs. Then there's the ones that just make you feel lonely 'cuz they don't ever seem to care about what you doin', what you sayin'. You don't wanna be around them folks, so just cut 'em loose. Start fresh. You'll feel less lonely all by yourself. And when y'all do that, make sure you ain't the mothahfuckah that's on the phone and not listenin'.

> ***I used to think the worst thing in life was to end up all alone. It's not. The worst thing in life is to end up with people that make you feel all alone.***
>
> —Robin Williams

DO THIS TODAY: *Turn everything off and eat a meal with someone. Talk, laugh, and enjoy your food. Light a candle if you have to, 'cuz candles make folks sit longer. It's a* **got-damn** *fact.*

July 19th

"WE ALL GOT SOUL MATES, AND Y'ALL WILL KNOW WHO THEY ARE 'CUZ YOU CAN FEEL IT."

Now, I ain't about to get all mushy on ya'. When I'm talkin' about soul mates, I'm not just referring to the romantic kind. We all got more than one soul mate out there. We got the kind you marry and live happily ever after, and we also got the kind that just feels like we've known 'em forever. These are the friends who you can ride in a car with for a long time and not talk, not play the radio or nothin', you can just be still together. These are the folks that understand what you're feelin' when you don't say nothin' at all. We're just comfortable with 'em at a whole different level. Now, that don't mean there's no bumps in the road. Hell, there's dips in the road sometimes and avalanches and shit. But if you're soul mates, you get over 'em and around 'em and you just know that it'll be alright. Everybody needs to connect with at least one of these kinda folks in their life. It makes livin' so much better.

How do you find your soul mates? You just be you. You ain't gonna find 'em by spendin' your time lookin'. You're gonna find 'em by doin' what you love and doin' good with your life. Before you know it, you'll have some of them folks takin' your journey alongside you, and they'll make you feel like you at home no matter where you're at on the road. Soul mates share the same energy as you. Maybe they reignite a long-lost dream, stir things up so you can connect with your soul purpose. But once that's done, sometimes soul mates move on. They ain't always tryin' to get that yummy. It's just how it *T-I-Iz.*

> ***A bond between souls is ancient—older than the planet.***
>
> —Dianna Hardy

DO THIS TODAY: *Hold up, we said soul mates not Soul Train. Your soul mates ain't always bringin' the party. Sometimes they bring hard lessons for you to learn. Do you have a soul mate that challenges you? How have they helped you grow?*

July 20th

"SOMETIMES YOU GOTTA WEED THE GARDEN."

You got friends that come into your life sometimes, and they're good for a while, but then you outgrow 'em. Sometimes that means you're risin' up and they ain't goin' nowhere. Other times, it means y'all just don't mesh well. Thing is, you can love the hell outta somebody, but that don't mean they're right for you or you're right for them. When you realize that, it's time to let 'em go. If you don't, the negative energy between y'all is just gonna muck up your flow and theirs too.

I had this friend, and he was wild. We'd go out, party, hit the clubs. But then one time he called me up and he said he's gonna pick me up and take me out. When we got there, an old girlfriend of his slid on over and the two of them spent the whole night together and I's sittin' there by my lonesome. Ya' see, I was only there 'cuz he needed two things—somebody to drive him home, and somebody to tell his wife he was with that night. Hell, naw, I ain't gonna be nobody's scapegoat. I sat there at a table watchin' the band, sippin' my one beer all night, thinkin' about all the other times he did that shit to me and I didn't barely notice it until now. That's when I realized I'd outgrown him. He was the life of the party and that's where he was gonna stay. I had other shit to do, and other folks that would show up for me when I needed 'em, somethin' this mothahfuckah never did, unless there was free drinks. Once I cut him loose, damned if my other relationships didn't get better. I got rid of the weeds and they stopped chokin' out the flowers.

> ***You don't let go of a bad relationship because you stop caring about them. You let go because you start caring about yourself.***
>
> —Charles Orlando

DO THIS TODAY: *Get your rake and your mulch, it's time to change the landscaping. Who do you need to weed the fuck out? Try these steps to free yourself. One, identify the toxic person. Two, establish boundaries. Three, be strong. Four, get a new tribe, folks who lift you up, not tear you down.*

July 21st

"I CAN'T STAND KIDS CALLIN' THEIR PARENTS BY THEIR FIRST NAME. IT'S DISRESPECT."

I called my granddaddy "Thurman" *one time*. He taught me that lesson right quick. He was Granddaddy, then there was Big Mama and my mama. I called my daddy "Pops" until I lost complete respect for him. I was an adult by then, and I never saw him no more anyway. He never was no daddy to me. But now, you hear kids callin' their folks Janet and Fred, and you go lookin' sideways, and they're like five years old holdin' their smartphone and got a diamond stud in their ear, hand on their hip. I walk over and smack the hell outta Janet and Fred. How'd they let that shit get that far? You ain't your kid's best friend, and if you still a kid, your folks ain't your homies. Show 'em some respect, and if you got kids, demand they show you some.

Kids who walk all over their folks won't hesitate to do it to their teacher, their boss, the authorities. Is that the kinda kid you wanna raise up in this world? Is that the kind of adult you wanna be? If your folks gave up eighteen years of their life to raise you, show 'em you appreciate 'em. They may not have done it perfect, but they tried. And if you like who you are, then they did somethin' right. At the very least, you can call 'em Mom and Dad.

> ***Don't use the sharpness of your tongue on the mother who taught you to speak.***
>
> —Ali ibn Abi Talib

DO THIS TODAY: *Ephesians 6:2–3 says, "Honour your father and mother that it may go well with you and that you may live long in the land." You betta' stop messin' with God. He ain't playin' wit y'all. Repeat after me, "Hey, Mom and Dad, Mommy and Daddy, Pops and Madea, Mother and Father." You get my drift. Think about why you wanna show them your respect.*

July 22nd

"IF SOMEBODY'S ASKIN' YOU TO GIVE UP WHAT YOU LOVE FOR 'EM, THEY AIN'T WORTH IT."

You should never have to sacrifice who you are, the things and the folks that make your heart sing, for anybody. Period. Let me tell you, I had this girl I was datin' before I met Rhonda. We hung around each other a lot, she was alright. But before we was even outta high school, she was houndin' me already. "When you gonna get serious, Bernard? When you gonna stop jokin', focus yourself on a real job?" Boy, when I'd hear her say that shit, my heart would drop right down into my gut. I could feel her jackin' up my energy. She didn't want me to chill with my boys no more either. I couldn't have that. I was gonna break it off with her, but she beat me to it. I thank God every day, though, because that's when I met Rhonda.

Thing that makes it hard, though, is when it's your own family that's not so good for you. It kills you to push away from your blood, but sometimes you just gotta give yourself some space and make it clear why you doin' it. When they see you successful, after all their mothahfuckin' naysayin', they'll change their tune. Then they can come back around if you feel like it's okay. But if you were to give up your dreams for somebody, or cut it off with your true soul friends, you gonna end up resentin' 'em, and it's gonna fall apart anyway. Why not spare yourself the grief and stop it before it gets that far.

> ***No good can ever come from deviating from the path that you were destined to follow.***
>
> —Robert Greene

DO THIS TODAY: *Emotional manipulators and controlling people can fuck up your happiness and drain your joy. Do this one thing: distance yourself from one of them right now. Don't subject yourself to that asshole. Let the doorknob hit 'em where the dog shoulda bit 'em!*

July 23rd

"SET YOUR BOUNDARIES AND DON'T LET NOBODY CROSS 'EM."

When we're little kids, makin' friends and hangin' out with our cousins, what we're doin' is figurin' out how to be with other people. These first friendships are so *got-damn* important, 'cuz they gonna teach us how to set our boundaries and how to respect the other kids' boundaries too. They gonna teach us how to care about somebody and care about our own *got-damn* selves. As we become adults, we realize that we're still dealin' with the same shit, just on another level. Settin' boundaries never stops, you just gotta know when to shut they ass down, and I hope you learned that when you was a kid. If you didn't, you gotta start learnin' it now. Let me give you an example from myself so you can see what I'm sayin'.

Y'all know how I like to tell mothahfuckin jokes about my family and shit. That's all in fun, and hell yeah it's some real shit mixed in there too. But guess what? Don't you ever bring yo' ass to me tryin' to talk about my damn family and crackin' jokes. Are you crazy? That's a fucked up, "Imma beat yo' ass" moment! Tell jokes about your own *got-damn* family, that's how it's s'posed to be. That's a boundary I ain't gonna never let anybody cross—the "messin' with my family" boundary. Hell, no. But lemme tell ya', a mothahfuckah will go as far as you let 'em. It's up to you to draw the line.

> ***When we fail to set boundaries and hold people accountable, we feel used and mistreated.***
>
> —Brené Brown

DO THIS TODAY: *Is your coworker constantly tryin' to push more work on you? Maybe your mother-in-law keeps tellin' you how to take care of your own got-damn* house *or your roommate keeps walkin' around buck-ass naked. Know your triggers. Determine how far you'll let strangers, friends, family, and coworkers go. If they cross the line, be assertive and direct with them. It's for everybody's own good.*

July 24th

"THE BEST FRIENDSHIPS ARE WHEN NOBODY EXPECTS NOTHIN' OF EACH OTHER EXCEPT TO BE THERE."

If you got one friend pullin' all the damn time, they gonna get tired. Either that or the one gettin' pulled is gonna get sick of bein' behind, sick of needin' the one in front to keep 'em goin'. That kinda friendship is off balance, and it ain't gonna last. Let me ask you somethin'. Do you like your boss? Maybe you do, maybe you don't, but at the very least, you know your boss is above you. That mothahfuckah's got control over you. There's an order to things, and that works for work. But when there's an order like that in a friendship, where one friend is bein' like the boss and the other one like the employee, I'm gonna tell you again, that shit's gonna get tired real quick, and somebody's gonna end up hurtin'.

True friends boost your courage and happiness and help you adjust to change. Your ride-or-die homies. They gonna challenge you, and it ain't always gonna be smooth sailin', but you know they'll always be ridin' shotgun helpin' you get where you goin'. You gonna be the same for them, too, when they sittin' in the driver's seat. You can go for miles and don't even need to say nothin'. Just be there, that's all. That's a real friend.

> ***Don't walk in front of me; I may not follow. Don't walk behind me; I may not lead. Just walk beside me and be my friend.***
>
> —Albert Camus

DO THIS TODAY: *Listen to "That's What Friends Are For" by Dionne Warwick. Now that it's stuck in your head, think about what it's sayin'—about countin' on your friends, havin' somebody on your side, in good times and bad. Now, think about your homies. Are they ridin' next to you?*

July 25th

"STOP TRYIN' TO FIND YOUR PERFECT MATCH AND START BEIN' THE ONE THEY'RE ALL LOOKIN' FOR."

Are you swipin' left and right, searchin' for the perfect match on the Bimble and the Tenders and all of that jazz? I get it, I do. This is a different time and age. Maybe I'm old school, but I don't think you can tell too much about a person if you ain't face to face. The point is that maybe you gotta stop searchin' to find what you been lookin' for. How much time are you spendin' messin' around on them apps, or out at the clubs lookin' for the person that's gonna complete you? Knock it the fuck off. Complete yourself. When you do that, when you makin' yourself happy doin' your thing, that's when you gonna start gettin' all the attention. Everybody's gonna swipe on *you*.

I got this buddy always moanin' and groanin' about how nobody swipes him back and shit. I'm thinkin', it's 'cuz you got this whole energy about you that screams mothahfuckin' desperate. What you got to offer, mothahfuckah? You sit around eatin' cheesy puffs, wipin' them nasty orange fingers on your phone while you playin' *Fortnite*. Get up off your ass and do somethin', be somebody, put your effort into livin'! It's time to rethink who you are and what you're all about. I told him to go on and volunteer doin' somethin' he likes, join a *got-damn* club, do a group sport, anything to bring your energy up and have some fun. That's when somebody gonna find *you*.

> ***Far too many people are looking for the right person, instead of trying to be the right person.***
>
> —Gloria Steinem

DO THIS TODAY: *Mary J. sang about searchin' for a "Real Love." Is that you? What type of person attracts you? Ask for what you want and visualize that* ***you are*** *the type of person who attracts that kind of partner. Then, put yourself out there. Go to special events, house parties, weddings. Everyone's energy is open at these events.*

July 26th

"LEARN TO COMMUNICATE, *GOT-DAMMIT.*"

Communication is key, and that's a mothahfuckin' fact. Do you know how many times you gotta communicate throughout your day, every *got-damn* day? Check this out: The average person is gonna hear somewhere about twenty-five thousand words a day! Damn, that's a lotta talkin'. Shoot, it's even more if you like my buddy De'Shawn. His wife talkin' at him all damn day, even in his mothahfuckin' sleep. For real though, you gonna spend somethin' like 75 percent of your day communicatin' about somethin' or other. That's a lotta time. Maybe it's just, "Hey, wanna get a sandwich?" Or it could be bigger, like decidin' if you gonna quit your job and go work the night shift up at your buddy's pizza place. Maybe it's talkin' to customers or textin' with your grandma. Whatever it is, if you awake for sixteen hours, that's...what is that? Like twelve mothahfuckin' hours of communicatin' every single day.

You doin' something that much, and you ain't good at it, you got some trouble fo' sho'. But if you learn to say what you mean, and learn to really hear what other folks is sayin', you gonna be alright. Your life is gonna be smooth, and you'll see things startin' to fall into place for you. I always say, if you can talk to folks, you can do just about anything. That's a *got-damn* fact. Remember the old adage, "A closed mouth doesn't get fed."

> ***The way we communicate with others and with ourselves ultimately determines the quality of our lives.***
>
> —Tony Robbins

DO THIS TODAY: *If you don't know how to communicate, you never gonna get what you want. Stop expectin' other folks to read your* got-damn *mind. Right now, think of one thing you been holdin' back from somebody. Tell it to 'em today.*

July 27th

"I'LL TRUST YOU UNTIL YOU GIVE ME A REASON NOT TO."

My mama always told me, "Bean, I'll trust you until you give me a reason not to." Well, I went a long mothahfuckin' time before I gave her a reason. Boy, I think I was in grade school when I done it. I don't know why I done it, but it was like somethin' possessed me and I couldn't help myself. When my mama found out I stole that baseball from the neighborhood shop, and she had to come pick me up, she didn't say a word. I could feel it comin' from her, the disappointment. I couldn't handle that. I knew from that day forward, she'd never be able to trust me the same. Oh, I might earn some of it back, but it would never be clean again. I was a nine-year-old criminal, and I'd have to live with that shame.

I never wanted to feel that way with nobody else, ever, so I did my best to always tell the truth. Always try to be on the straight and narrow. Sure, there was a few times I told a little white lie, but I always felt bad about it. Then there's Rhonda. That damn woman could tell if I was talkin' out the side of my mouth every time. She'd take one look at me and raise that eyebrow, hand on the hip, and I'd correct myself so fast. Some folks got that radar that can just sense a lie before it even come out. Shoot, Rhonda kept me on the level, and that's where I stayed for the rest of my mothahfuckin' life, thank God.

> ***Trust is like a vase...once it's broken, though you can fix it, the vase will never be the same again.***
>
> —Walter Inglis Anderson

DO THIS TODAY: *"Trust me, I know what I'm doin'." Folks say that shit when they don't know what the hell they doin'. Trust is crucial for the survival of friendships, love relationships, and workplace connections. How you gonna build trust? Be open and transparent from the beginning. Be dependable, consistent, and reliable. If you ain't been that way, start now and get your trust groove back.*

July 28th

"JUST BECAUSE YOU LOVE SOMEBODY DON'T MEAN THEY'RE GOOD FOR YOU."

All you need is love. Ain't that a bunch of bullshit? Love will get you as far as the bus will take you, if you got yourself a ticket. Love don't put food on the table, it don't keep the house hot in the winter and cool in the summer. Love don't make it so you can get along. I seen plenty of folks that stay together far too long, just 'cuz they're in love. Every day they're rippin' each other's throats out, screamin' and hollerin' just 'cuz somebody left the toilet seat up or ate all the *got-damn* Hot Cheetos. Then ten minutes later, they're makin' the mattress springs sing like Sister Berta in the church choir. But how long is that gonna last?

Anyway, sometimes it can feel like you took two steps forward and three steps back. There are ups and downs in every relationship. You might be able to keep it together, but there gotta be terms. You gotta communicate better, stop holding onto old shit, find your harmony. You either gotta get it together or let it go. 'Cuz if you fightin' like WWF, goin' up and down and round and round, it's mothahfuckin' exhausting. You gonna wear each other out before you realize you ain't good for each other. I get it, you got passion. But as you get older, you understand that a little peace goes a long way. You wanna be with that person who is gonna make you feel safe, make you feel like you're home. That's the kinda love that lasts.

> ***Letting go doesn't mean that you don't care about someone anymore. It's just realizing that the only person you really have control over is yourself.***
>
> —Deborah Reber

DO THIS TODAY: *If you're in a relationship right now, how's it goin'? What makes a good relationship for you? Define it, commit to it, and never accept nothin' else.*

July 29th

"FAM, YOU GOTTA STAY HUMBLE."

Humility is rare nowadays. We all gotta post our shit on the social medias, countin' the thumbs ups and the little hearts, readin' all the mothahfuckin' comments and shit. Damn, when I was a kid, if somebody was followin' you, you ducked down the alley to tried and shake the sumbitch. Now, everybody's wantin' *more* sumbitches followin' 'em. I don't understand it. But I think that's why there ain't nobody that's humble no more. If you're humble, you ain't braggin' on yourself all the *got-damn* time.

How you gonna accomplish that when everybody who's anybody says you gotta post your shit and get other folks to like it? *Got-damn*, it was hard enough for me to get my homeroom to like me, let alone all the folks in the world that have access to the mothahfuckin' internet. Keep up with Kardashians? I can barely keep up with the Joneses that live in the apartment above me. How the hell am I s'pose to compete with that shit? The answer is that you ain't s'pose to. You can still post up fo' sho', but aim your posts higher. Talk about shit that's upliftin', talk about a cause, make folks laugh, maybe sing and entertain 'em. Look at mothahfuckin' Will Smith's social medias. That man is makin' folks take a look at somethin' higher all the damn time, encouragin' folks to work on themselves. That's what I'm talkin' about. He could use his platform to brag on hisself all damn day, but he ain't doin' that, and he's one successful sumbitch. See, you can put yourself out there and stay humble at the same time, just like my boy Will Smith. Try some damn humility. It'll do you good.

> ***Do nothing from rivalry or conceit, but in humility count others more significant than yourselves.***
>
> —Philippians 2:3

DO THIS TODAY: *If your staff successfully reaches a goal, do you take credit all the* ***got-damn*** *time, or do you back up and let them take it once in a while? Check yourself. Quit tryin' to boost your ego? Pride can be some dangerous shit.*

July 30th

"EVERYBODY THAT COMES INTO YOUR LIFE IS GONNA CHANGE YOU IN SOME KINDA WAY."

It can't be helped. It's like dominoes all lined up, if you flick one, it touches the next one, and that one touches the next, and they all fall down in a pattern that's already been laid out on the mothahfuckin' table. Everybody that touches your life is gonna cause somethin' to shift, and it's gonna change you whether you like it or not. How they change you, well, that's up to you.

You know how some folks say everybody comes into your life for a reason, a season, or a lifetime? Well, I think that's a load of bullshit. Folks come to you because you are attractin' them to ya'. Not intentionally, I ain't sayin' that, necessarily. But it's like your dial is tuned into the frequency they're broadcastin', and they're either comin' at you like Tom Joyner's *Mornin' Show*, given' you a mothahfuckin' wake-up call. Or they comin' in like Terry Gross on *Fresh Air*, tryin' to teach you somethin'. Then there's the ones that come at you like smooth jazz radio legend Denise Jordan Walker, all smooth and shit, makin' you feel nice and mellow. So, which station you got yourself tuned into? Well, that's exactly who you gonna get. And when they get to you, everything they sayin', doin', the way they been treatin' you, all that's gonna have some kinda impact on who you are and where you're goin'. Like them dominoes.

> ***No love, no friendship can cross the path of our destiny without leaving some mark on it forever.***
>
> —François Mauriac

DO THIS TODAY: *Ask yourself what kinda folks you want in your life. Do you want some kinda change? Be a reflection of that. Straight up! If you want respect, be respectful. If you want truth, be truthful. If you want love, show love. You get me? Start today.*

July 31st

"WE DON'T NEED A MILLION FRIENDS. JUST ONE GOOD ONE, THAT'S ENOUGH."

What does it mean to have a good friend? It means you never gonna feel alone. It means you got somebody who's always got your back. That sumbitch is your ride-or-die. They got your weddin' ring in their breast pocket, your car keys when you been drinkin', and your bail money just in case. I know when you're young, you thinkin' you need a bigger circle. Sure, maybe you need enough to play a little full-court three-on-three. I see that.

But as you get older, you're gonna be happy playin' one-on-one. 'Cuz life gets busy, you know. You get into your career, maybe get married, have some kids, and you ain't got time to keep up with all of them relationships 'cuz you got a lotta *got-damn* responsibilities. That shit gets hard, and if you tryin' to see all of them guys enough to maintain what you had, you gonna run yourself down 'til you got no energy left for the ones that's most important to you. So, yeah, sometimes a tight circle is the strongest. My Chi-Town brothah Kanye West said it best with his song "Real Friends." Not all relationships is perfect, but Kanye believes your "real friends" always show you who they are. That's facts.

> ***A single rose can be my garden...a single friend, my world.***
>
> —Leo Buscaglia

DO THIS TODAY: *So, who's your real ones and who you got hangin' on that you wouldn't mind lettin' drop off? It's time to unfollow, remove, block, delete numbers of, back off from anybody who's sappin' your energy.*

August 1st

"YOU WANNA BUILD GOOD RELATIONSHIPS, YOU GOTTA LISTEN."

Listenin' ain't just about hearing the words somebody's sayin'. Naw, it goes a hell of a lot deeper than that. Listenin' is about you lookin' at somebody and really seein' 'em. It's like you're sayin' to 'em, "I hear you, and what you're sayin' is important." Most folks don't really care about changin' your mind, they just wanna be heard. When you stop half-ass listenin' and pay attention, folks are gonna trust you more. More information, less conflict, that's what good listenin' does. It's about respectin' them as a human bein', and as soon as you ain't doin' that, you better check yourself or the person doin' the talkin' is gonna check you.

When I was a kid, my mama would say, "Bean, look at me when I'm talkin' to you." Why you think she said that? I'll tell ya', it was to make sure I'm listenin', and make sure I'm seein' her so that I understand fully what she's tryin' to tell me. It's a good rule, and I still thank my mama for teachin' me that. When you look at somebody while they're tellin' you somethin', you see the expression in their face and you connect with 'em on a whole different level. Now we got our faces in our phones and don't even look up. It's a damn shame all the real connection we're missin' by doin' that. It's time we all shut up, look up, and listen.

> ***When we listen, we hear someone into existence.***
>
> —Laurie Buchanan, PhD

DO THIS TODAY: *Today, I want you to practice lookin' at folks when they talkin' to you. I don't care who it is, the bus driver or your mama, stop what you doin' and look at their face while they say what they sayin'. See if you feel more connected when you do.*

August 2nd

"IF IT PROWLS LIKE A WOLF AND HOWLS LIKE A WOLF, IT'S A MOTHAHFUCKIN' WOLF."

Stop ignorin' the warnin' signs that somebody's a nasty sumbitch just because you want somethin' they doin' "for you" to work out. All you're doin' is avoidin' the mothahfuckin' inevitable. Before you know it they gonna come on up and do some of that nasty shit to you that you been turnin' a blind eye on, 'cuz a wolf can't stay in that sheep's clothing very long before they start to sweat. They start slippin' up. You maybe start to notice more and more of that wolf's fur peekin' out, and still maybe you don't step back 'cuz maybe you think there's something nice for you if you just hold on a little bit longer. Maybe they're sayin' they gonna get you money, fame, a big step in your career, connections. Lemme tell you right now, if they're blowin' smoke up your ass, eventually it's gonna catch fire and you gonna get burned.

I'm just tellin' it like it *T-I-Iz*, and you better be seein' it like it *T-I-Iz*, and not changin' shit around to fit your own mothahfuckin' narrative. Listen here, them folks that will do whatever they can to cover up who they really are, they're stirrin' up some bad kinda juju and they gonna block your blessin's quicker than a sin. It can't end up good. So, if you see them red flags, you start hearin' the howlin', get yourself far enough away that the wolf can't smell you no more. When folks start showin' you who they really are, you bettah believe that shit.

> ***Don't let getting lonely make you reconnect with toxic people. You shouldn't drink poison just because you're thirsty.***
>
> —Anonymous

DO THIS TODAY: *Don't react to toxic people. Not givin' them a reaction when they desperately seek it is far more powerful. What wolves do you have in your life right now? How are you gonna get them to back the hell off?*

August 3rd

"CAREFUL NOT TO PICK UP OTHER FOLKS' NASTY HABITS."

If you hang around somebody long enough, you gonna start to pick up their little habits. It's kinda like if you head down south and stay there too long, you start callin' folks "sugah" and sayin', "I'm fixin' to." Even more than their cute little sayin's, you could pick up their politics, their faith, their business sense, or maybe even their taste in clothes, food, or entertainment. Along with all of this stuff, which could be good or bad, you could be pickin' up some nasty shit—like maybe bein' late, lyin', their negativity, their bad attitudes. Could be worse, too, like drugs and robbin' and shit. And other folks can always tell if you're gettin' into the wrong mothahfuckin' crowd. You start changin' in little ways. Teachers is a mothahfuckah for seein' it. Damn, they know the minute you walk into school, your pants is hangin' a little bit lower on your ass. "Mister McCullough, let's talk after class." They know with one mothahfuckin' look.

If you're hangin' around them kinda folks, the stealin', druggin' kind, get the fuck away right now. You know better than that. If I was your mama, I'd smack you upside the head 'til the white meat shows. You don't wanna stoop to their level, 'cuz that place is really mothahfuckin' hard to climb out of once you in it too deep. If you just noticin' your friends maybe gettin' into some ways you don't like, you can try to be the one raisin' them up, bein' the positive influence. Maybe your force is stronger than theirs. But if it gets to be too much, then just get the hell away from them sumbitches too. You got to save yourself.

> ***If you attach to the negative behavior of others it brings you down to their level.***
>
> —Guru Singh

DO THIS TODAY: *Bad seeds can bring a good person down. The reverse is also true. Look around, do you like who you see? If not, moonwalk your ass to the next exit.*

August 4th

"NO AMOUNT OF FRIENDS OR FANS IS WORTH SACRIFICIN' WHO YOU ARE."

Now it seems like everybody got fans, followers, whatever you wanna call 'em. In my day, those was called groupies and you only had 'em if you were doin' somethin'—if you were in a band, a movie star, doin' comedy, modelin', pro sports, shit like that. Nowadays you can get a million followers for puttin' a video of you sittin' on the *terlet* on the mothahfuckin' internet. Fine, I'm cool with that. I ain't gonna be one of them older dudes that's bitchin' about pop culture. I go with it. Gettin' myself a TikTok pretty soon, you know. I'm hip with the jive. Anyway, it's all good to get them followers, them fans, but you can't let 'em change who you are. Oh, I know too well, it's easy to fall into the trap of sayin', "Well, that's what the fans want, that's what I'll give 'em." Naw, the fans want to see your authentic self, 'cuz that's what's makin' you stand out, makin' you different enough to get all of that mothahfuckin' attention.

If you're spendin' more time worryin' about how you look than who you with and what you doin', if you got your face in that phone *conversatin'* with your fans more than you talkin' to the folks that's in the room, more than you goin' out, more than you laughin' and havin' big adventures, more than you doin' what you love, then you sacrificin' your soul. You can't keep that up, 'cuz pretty soon you gonna feel real empty inside. Fame don't last forever, but you sure as hell gotta live with yourself until the day that you die.

> ***Do not let the roles you play in life make you forget who you are.***
>
> *—Roy T. Bennett*

DO THIS TODAY: *Do it now. Hey Alexa, hey Siri, play David Bowie, "Fame." That was the cut back in the day. Truth is, real fame is backed by a history of doin' good work, not achievin' status. What do you love and do best? Focus on it. That's what you wanna share with the world.*

August 5th

"DO LITTLE NICE THINGS FOR FOLKS TO SHOW 'EM THAT YOU SEE 'EM."

Doin' somethin' nice don't gotta be a big, grand gesture. It takes almost no effort for you to hold the door open for somebody, let a mama with three cryin' kids cut the line at the supermarket, bring in the trash cans for your neighbor when you walk up. It's not about what it was that you done, or that it even necessarily spared them folks a big effort, it's about sendin' the message that, "Hey, somebody sees you." Somebody cares enough to do a little thing. That's all.

I remember this once when I was out mowin' the damn lawn, and I just kept on goin' and mowed the neighbor's too. I noticed it was gettin' longer than usual. Didn't know what was *goings on* if there was anything, but somethin' told me to do it. Took me maybe twenty minutes. Later that evenin' I get a knock on the door and it was my neighbor lady. She had tears in her eyes and a loaf of banana bread for me. She said her husband had a stroke and he was still recoverin', and it made her feel blessed when she saw that grass all cut and tidy. Somebody musta told her it was me, or she deduced it on her own 'cuz my grass was cut, too, I s'pose. Boy, the look on her face made me feel better'n that banana bread tasted, and that's sayin' a lot, 'cuz that was some delicious mothahfuckin' banana bread.

> ***One small action of love can do far, far more for a soul than all the most beautiful words in the world.***
>
> —Eileen Caddy

DO THIS TODAY: *Get on board the love train. Do some random act of kindness today to make someone's day. Tip extra, give up your seat on a crowded bus or train, make the pot of coffee for everybody when you get up, be on time for once in your life,* got-dammit*. Little things mean a lot, so get busy with 'em.*

August 6th

"LIFT UP OTHER FOLKS WHENEVER YOU CAN, AND YOU'RE GONNA GET LIFTED, TOO."

Thing is, when you're tryin' to rise and you recognize and support the sumbitches tryin' to rise up around you, it's gonna be easier for all y'all to make it. It's like you make the energy around you static, positive, lighter, and the path opens up for everybody. But if you knockin' folks down, climbin' up on 'em, tryin' to stop their blessin's, all you're doin' is buildin' up a whole lotta muck around you. That shit's like quicksand and it'll end up pullin' you down hard. You can't do fucked-up things to folks and expect to live a wonderful life. It don't work like that. The key to success is givin' back, not holdin' back.

I knew this guy in the entertainment business once. Man, that sumbitch was somethin' else. He'd talk you up to your face and then turn around and stab you in the mothahfuckin' back. He trampled every sumbitch that ever tried to help him out, then he'd smack talk about how they wasn't good enough. Lemme tell you somethin', that sumbitch's karma caught up with him. He landed his ass in jail for fraud, thought he could get away with cookin' some books 'cuz he's thinkin' he's better than everybody else, includin' the law. In the meantime, all the folks he was hurtin' along the way got lifted as soon as they ditched his ass. In fact, some of 'em started liftin' each other up too. A few of 'em shocked folks by how fast they found success after that. But they did it together, and boy am I proud of 'em too. See, you gotta help each other, recognize one another's talents, and y'all will get where you goin'. There's room for everybody at the top, and it's good to have company.

> ***Love one another and help others to rise to the higher levels, simply by pouring out love. Love is infectious and the greatest healing energy.***
>
> —Sai Baba

DO THIS TODAY: *You can't stop nobody from reachin' their goals. The only one that shit stops is you. If you been like that in the past, change it right now. Think about who you can build up or inspire. How are you gonna take steps to make that a reality?*

August 7th

"IT AIN'T WHAT'S IN YOUR WALLET THAT MATTERS, IT'S WHAT'S IN YOUR SOUL."

My granddaddy always used to say, "You can't take it with you." That's right, all of them gold chains and fancy cars, that ain't gonna mean nothin' when you standin' at the pearly gates. You can't buy your way into heaven. Only way to get there is to do good in your *got-damn* life. Is that mothahfuckin' Hummer gonna keep you warm at night? Are your Gucci sunglasses good company? Now, I ain't sayin' you shouldn't have nice things. Damn, I got myself a nice little Jaguar when I started doin' pretty good for myself. But I didn't hurt nobody to get it, didn't take no money out of my daughter's college fund or short my family on the shit they needed. I enjoyed that car, but it was never more important to me than my people.

I knew this sumbitch once that had a nice-ass truck. I mean the mothahfuckah never used it to haul shit, it was just for show. He'd pull into a parkin' lot and if he'd see some old guy in a beat-up car, he loved thinkin' that he was better'n him, for real. He'd say shit, too, but just out of earshot, you know. I couldn't hang around with that mothahfuckah no more. He was toxic as hell. No kinda truck or nothin' else would make me wanna hang out with him again. What I'm tryin' to tell ya' is, don't choose your friends by how they look or what they drivin', or even if they got themself a boat or a pool and shit. That's all fun for a minute, but if they don't got a good heart, a good vibe to go along with it, none of that is worth it in the end.

> ***Some of the people who are showing off their speed are headed in the wrong direction.***
>
> —Mokokoma Mokhonoana

DO THIS TODAY: *Take a hard look at yourself. Do you have low self-esteem issues or feel inferior next to other people? The solution is to improve your confidence and become more accepting of yourself, not buyin' more shit to try and show 'em up. Take a look at your friends too. If they was to lose all their material shit, would you still like 'em?*

August 8th

"WHAT ARE YOU FIGHTIN' FOR? RELAX AND JUST WORK IT OUT."

Lord, I swear folks is fightin' over the stupidest shit nowadays. You post on social medias that you like pizza and you'll get twelve people arguin' over whether or not pizza's good for you, if Pizza Palace is paying livin' wages, if you should eat pineapple with pepperoni. *Got-damn*, just stop it, y'all. You got nothin' better to do?

I know, I know, there's some shit that's gotta be dealt with. Not everything is pizza. Maybe you talkin' to your roommate about how you gonna split the bills, or you havin' some kinda debate about politics or human rights. All of that shit's important and you can't always just walk away. But there's a way to talk about it that's not confrontational, not angry or violent. I seen some folks get violent about the stupidest shit, like who drank all the Crown Royal or who lost the mothahfuckin' remote. One time I saw this beefy sumbitch get so mad that another mothahfuckah whipped into his parkin' space that he punched a dent in *his own* mothahfuckin' car! What the hell is that? You don't need to lose your shit over stuff like that, or ever, really. You're wastin' your *got-damn* energy. It's so much better to take a breath and stay chill, keep your heart rate down, you know. Plus, it's scary as fuck when you stayin' real calm while somebody else is freakin' the fuck out. They don't know what to do with that. See what I'm sayin'? Most situations can be figured out if you just keep a level head.

> ***A mild answer turns away rage, but a harsh word stirs up anger.***
>
> —Proverbs 15:1

DO THIS TODAY: *Make a commitment to handle things differently than before. Every problem has a solution, but you can't hear it if you're cussin' somebody out. Get comfortable with feelin' uncomfortable.*

August 9th

"EVERYBODY AIN'T GONNA LIKE YOU, AND THAT'S OKAY."

It's stressful to always be tryin' to make everybody like you all the damn time. You gotta stop doin' that shit. Not everybody's gonna like you. I don't mean to sound rude as a mothahfuckah, but I gotta tell you the truth. It's just like havin' a chocolate chip cookie. Chocolate chip is good, mm-hm, with a big old glass of ice-cold milk. But not everybody's gonna like chocolate chip the best. Maybe some folks is allergic to chocolate, or they just prefer the oatmeal raisin. That's okay. That's more chocolate chip for me.

When you learn about business and marketing and all of that jazz, the first thing they wanna know is, "Who's your target market?" If you say everybody, all of them bigwigs will laugh up in your face, 'cuz they know it's gonna fail. Not everybody can use everything, period. You gotta pick a target and try'n appeal to 'em specifically. If you stretch beyond that, well great, but that's a bonus and didn't require a particular extra effort. But if you go and spend all your advertisin' budget tryin' to appeal to every single body, you gonna crash and burn. Why? 'Cuz not everybody likes or needs everything...or everybody. You see how that translates? Hand to God, some folks is gonna hate you just 'cuz you're too damn likeable. For real, you can't win 'em all over, so best to stop tryin' and just be yourself. The ones who like you just for that are all you need. You'll get along just fine without the rest.

> ***I'm not concerned with your liking or disliking me. All I ask is that you respect me as a human being.***
>
> —Jackie Robinson

DO THIS TODAY: *If you ain't bein' hated on, you ain't doin somethin' right. When folks start talkin' smack behind your back, the reality is they really wanna be you or get what you got. Look at it as a compliment and keep on steppin'. Who have you been tryin' to win over that just don't like you? Let 'em go right now, and free up your energy for the folks that really care.*

August 10th

"YOUR FRIENDS ARE GONNA HAVE A BIG IMPACT ON OUR LIFE, SO CHOOSE 'EM WISELY."

You're known by the company you keep. That's somethin' I heard when I was a boy at church, I think. And I think that's partially right. I think you're also made by the company you keep, 'cuz the folks you spend the most time with is gonna have the biggest impact on who you are and what you doin' with your life. Shit, it's better to have no friends at all than have ones that's gonna steer you off your path, get you into trouble, or make you feel some kinda way about yourself. But the right kinda friends, they can get you up when you feel yourself veerin' off. I know, sometimes you thinkin' you didn't choose those friends, they chose you. Maybe they lived next door to you growin' up when all the kids on the block had to just hang together 'cuz of proximity and shit. You might be askin' God why He put 'em there if He didn't want y'all hangin' out. Well, maybe they's there just to teach you somethin', maybe make you stronger and show you what you do and you don't want outta life. At any rate, just 'cuz you played kick the can with 'em when you's growin' up don't mean you gotta stick with 'em if they go sour. You gotta keep decidin' who you wanna be, and if the folks around you ain't fittin' with that, change 'em out. For real, I ain't playin'.

> ***Life is partly what we make it, and partly what it is made by the friends we choose.***
>
> —Tennessee Williams

DO THIS TODAY: *My granddaddy used to say, you'll be lucky if you have one or two true friends in life. That's facts. Like attracts like, and you wanna choose friends who have goals and dreams, 'cuz they gonna live longer and have happier lives than the poor sumbitches that don't. So, get on the phone, call one of your true ones, and get to dreamin'.*

August 11th

"IF YOU GET A BAD FEELIN' ABOUT SOMEBODY, LISTEN TO IT."

Sometimes when you meet somebody, you get a feelin' in your gut like you better off stayin' away from that sumbitch. But then your brain starts tickin', and maybe somethin' they're sayin' sounds good. They're smooth talkin', drawin' you in, and maybe you convince yourself that they're alright after all. Naw. No. Hell no. Listen to your *got-damn* gut. It's tryin' to tell you to back off. It's the same kinda feelin' you get when you step out into the grass and there's a mothahfuckin' big-ass snake. You step the hell back. Yeah, they got a slick tongue and you might be tempted to get a closer look...but all y'all know what happened to Eve when she listened to the snake instead of her God-given instincts. BAM—nekkid forever.

Shoot, and that's how some of them slimy folks make you feel—buck nekkid, vulnerable, weak. If you'd have just listened to the warnin' signs, the feelin' in your gut you can't really explain, you'd have been clear of all of that nasty venom. If you pay attention and do what it's tellin' you to do, you gonna be alright. Otherwise, you gonna find yourself bare-assed, kicked outta the garden, God disappointed in you. You just gotta trust yourself enough to let your inner knowledge guide you sometimes instead of always listenin' to your head, 'cuz that mothahfuckah can talk you into some shit you didn't really wanna do.

> ***If something on the inside is telling you that someone isn't right for you, they're NOT right for you, no matter how great they might look on paper.***
>
> —Mandy Hale

DO THIS TODAY: *Follow your first mind. We all have it, and that shit never guides you wrong. Here's how to recognize it: slow down and clear your head, quiet your thoughts, and notice the sensations in your body. Tune in to you, and you'll find the solution, no doubt about it.*

August 12th

"IF YOU GOT AN ISSUE, BETTER TO WORK IT OUT NOW THAN LET IT BOIL OVER."

We let shit stew all the *got-damn* time. We think by sittin' on it that we're avoidin' the conflict. Well, that is a mothahfuckin' lie. You gotta catch that shit when it's just on simmer.

The thing is, the longer you sit on somethin' that's buggin' you, the bigger you gonna start to make it. Boy, you gonna be thinkin' up shit that ain't never even crossed their minds. You gonna think the worst, that's fo' sho'. But sometimes the sumbitch don't even know there's somethin' up. Then one day, you completely lose your shit on 'em. Damn, they're blindsided, so they come back at you. They're sittin' there like, "What the fuck?" Then you spit it out. You like, "You mothahfuckah done messed with my girl. I saw them text messages on there, you sumbitch." He shakes his head like he has no idea what the fuck you talkin' about. Then a light comes on. "You mean those texts from LAST YEAR? When we was plannin' your surprise mothahfuckin' birthday party?" Shit. That's right. Yo' boy did plan that shit with your girl. That's what them sneaky mothahfuckin' texts was about, and you let that shit eat you up for months after you saw 'em on her phone. All that time you been buildin' up some nasty-ass energy and you coulda cleared it up just by addressin' it right away. Damn, that's a bitch. And even if it woulda been true, you coulda cleared him outta your life a long time ago. Confront it straight away and move the hell on.

> ***To go sit down with people you've got a misunderstanding with is a big step. It shows that you have no hate in your heart, and you really wanna resolve it.***
>
> —Snoop Dogg

DO THIS TODAY: *Find a quiet space, focus on your thinkin' and feelin' about a conflict you got* **goings on**. *Follow that by comin' up with a plan of action to resolve it. Make a commitment to gettin' it done.*

August 13th

"SPEAK TO EVERYBODY LIKE YOUR MAMA'S LISTENIN'."

If I ever spoke to anybody with disrespect when I was a kid, whether it was the trash man or the pastor, my mama woulda whooped my ass. She said everybody deserves to be spoken to with the same kinda courtesy. And you know what? She's right. Just because you a trash man, a janitor, a newspaper deliverer, the bus driver, street sweeper, or even the guy that's holdin' a paper cup on the curb by the walkin' bridge, that don't mean folks should treat you like you nothin'. Man, you more than nothin'. You the one and only mothahfuckin' you, and just that deserves some *got-damn* respect. Whenever I see folks talkin' to anybody like that, it makes me hurt in my heart, 'cuz I know what it feels like. I done all kinda jobs before I made it as a comedian, deliverin' furniture, workin' a fryer at a fish place, drivin' the bread truck, and the worst part of them jobs was when some ignorant sumbitch thought you's nothin', thought you's dumb, or thought you's below him just because you wearin' coveralls. That's some bullshit right there. Funny thing is, I'd like to see some of them sumbitches now. Think they'd remember me?

> ***I don't trust anyone who's nice to me but rude to the waiter. Because they would treat me the same way if I were in that position.***
>
> —Muhammad Ali

DO THIS TODAY: *Try a new approach today. Work on bein' friendly, showin' some* got-damn *courtesy and some respect. Be kind in traffic, smile at your waiter, be courteous with your coworkers. Pretend you know that the corner store cashier is gonna be a celebrity in ten years and talk to her like you would talk to a future star. You can do it, your mama taught you right.*

August 14th

"KEEP ON YOUR FAMILY TRADITIONS, AND IF YOU AIN'T GOT ANY, START SOME."

I had a lot of traditions when I was growin' up. We'd bless the table before we ate our dinner, and before we went to bed, we said our prayers. We always had pancakes on Sunday mornin' and we made sugar cookies and played charades every Christmas Eve. Every Friday night, Grandpa Thurman took us with him to play the ponies. You know, it's all about the traditions.

We live in such a crazy mothahfuckin' world right now. Most folks have gone and left their traditions behind 'em, and I think it's a damn shame. 'Cuz the thing about traditions is they help us hold onto values that's been passed down from generation to generation. Why do you make the sugar cookies? Who started that tradition? Oh, great grandma Roberta started that 'cuz one year she had nothin' else to eat in the damn house, so she baked them cookies with her children and they all ate cookies with frostin' for dinner and all eight of them kids was so happy that night, all hopped up on sugar and shit, you know. Had to play charades to help 'em get that energy out. Every year after, the family kept on doin' it. See, there's a story, and a connection to your past, and that's important. Then y'all carry that into your next generations. It feels good to be part of somethin' bigger than yourself, somethin' that goes far, far back and nobody can take it away from you.

> ***Traditions are the guideposts driven deep in our subconscious minds. The most powerful ones are those we can't even describe, aren't even aware of.***
>
> —Ellen Goodman

DO THIS TODAY: *Reach out to a senior member of your family. Ask questions about past family traditions, like Friday fish fries at Big Mama's house. That crispy-ass fried catfish and spaghetti was no joke. Now's your chance to keep them traditions alive. You feel me?*

August 15th

"REAL FRIENDS PUSH YOU A LITTLE."

Now, I don't mean that you should go on and make friends that make you feel uncomfortable. That ain't what I'm sayin' at all. You gonna feel comfortable with your friends, bein' around 'em, but a good friend ain't gonna let you just slide through your life without doin' nothin'. They won't let you throw away your gifts 'cuz you lazy, unmotivated, too comfortable in your situation to step outside the mothahfuckin' box and try'n make the the best life you can for yourself. Fake friends be frontin', sayin' all the right things then leave when the goin' gets tough. If you start gettin' successful, they wanna hang for selfish reasons but they never pushed you or helped you get where you got. Fuck it, they want to use you. A good friend won't let you set your goals too low or hold you back. Hell naw, a good friend is gonna challenge yo' ass, even if that means shit might change between y'all.

You know, some folks is afraid of change, afraid that when their dreams start comin' true, they gonna lose their way of livin', maybe lose some of their friends, their routine's gonna get all shook up. Sometimes the folks you love, they don't mean to, but they hold you back 'cuz they don't want that shit to change, they ain't ready for it. It ain't their fault. They can still be your friend and all. But you know the real ones when they sometimes piss you off, sometimes they fightin' with you to do somethin' they know is right for you. If you got them kinda friends in your life, the real ones, you one blessed sumbitch. Hold onto 'em.

> ***Don't make friends who are comfortable to be with. Make friends who will force you to lever yourself up.***
>
> —Thomas J. Watson

DO THIS TODAY: *True friends accept you for you. They'll be there through thick and thin. They'll also cuss yo' ass out when you need it. Think of somebody close to you that gave you a hard time at some point. If you can, thank 'em for it.*

August 16th

"SOME SUMBITCHES ARE GONNA WANNA KEEP YOU DOWN."

You ever fall in with a sumbitch like that before? Maybe they real chill when you first workin' together, and you on your best mothahfuckin' behavior. You still in *recognisance* mode, gatherin' information, sittin' back and learnin' from 'em. You humble, so they don't think you know jack shit. They like it like that. Them mothahfuckahs like it when you down there and they way up here. Maybe you even on the same *got-damn* team, they ain't even your boss or nothin', they just bossy as hell. They got that kinda attitude that's proud and they need to feel superior to boost their mothahfuckin' ego. So maybe you let 'em at first, and they smile at you, buy you drinks, pat your back. They like you, as long as you nod and smile. As long as you a yes-man. But as soon as you speak up, have an opinion that's different than theirs, or you challenge they ass on somethin', watch 'em spit venom. They'll turn on you so fast your head'll spin. They got this subtle way of keepin' you down, keepin' you complacent. So if you go in bein' more concerned with folks likin' you than followin' your path, than havin' your say at the got-damn table, that sumbitch is gonna keep you down with a smile and a condescendin' pat on your back. Put him in his place, 'cuz you can't never let somebody keep you from your path.

> ***They like you more when you don't challenge them. They prefer to have an upper hand over you.***
>
> —Mitta Xinindlu

DO THIS TODAY: *One thing about those damn tables, they always turn. Here's how you handle a fool: respect yourself first. Stop being too nice, and don't be afraid of other people's opinions. Stand up for what you deserve, period. Commit that to memory. Next time somebody tries to go there with you, keep that in mind, and you gonna be okay.*

August 17th

"YOUR HEARTBREAK AIN'T THE END OF YOUR LIFE. IT'LL GET BETTER."

Most folks thinkin' of heartbreak as a romantic love that fell off, somebody left you and you feelin' devastated. Can't imagine livin' a day without 'em. That's one kind. But there's other kinds of heartbreak too. It can happen when a friend crosses you and you can't trust 'em, or when your child hurts you, when your mama passes on, or when your dreams get shattered. I know, all of that shit hurts, and that's okay to feel all kinds of ways when you goin' through it. But that's just it, you gotta go through. Then you come out the other side, 'cuz the fact of the matter is, it ain't the end of your life. You got more shit to do.

Man, if I'd have shut down every time my heart was broken, I'd have stayed sixteen. That's when my mama died. Then a year later, my brothah. Then it was like everybody I loved was fallin' off—grandmama, one of my best friends, even my mothahfuckin' deadbeat dad...and all he left me was the funeral bill. Anyway, I had to keep on goin', and it made me stronger. Made me realize that when folks is sad, bringin' a smile to their face, damn, that's powerful. I mean, I knew since I was little that was gonna be my superpower, after I saw my mama smile through her tears lookin' at a comedian on the TV. But it wasn't 'til I went through losin' all them folks that I realized it for real. Ya' see, your heartbreak can either shut you down or it can teach you somethin' and lift you up. It's your *got-damn* choice.

> ***Yes, the heart breaks. But, it also heals.***
>
> —Yasmin Mogahed

DO THIS TODAY: *It's always darkest before dawn. You gotta pass the test, just hold on. I promise you the days that break you are the days that make you. Think about somethin' really hard that you made it through. See, you got through that, and it gave you strength to take on the next challenge. Keep movin' forward. You got this.*

August 18th

"BE CAREFUL OF THE SUMBITCH THAT DON'T TRUST NOBODY."

If you paranoid that everybody's out to get you, shit, that's a mothahfuckin' reason I'm not gonna trust *you*. It's the first red flag, and I'm out. 'Cuz if somebody ain't trustin' other folks, they probably ain't gonna trust you, either. And if they ain't trustin' you for no good *got-damn* reason, they gonna be findin' reasons that ain't there. Then, you gonna find yourself in a really uncomfortable position. It's like the mighty O'Jays is tellin' it to you straight: they're backstabbers, and they might be smilin' in your face, but only 'cuz they wanna take your place. So, I'm just tellin' you, if somebody's never trustin' nobody, ask yourself if they're somebody you can trust.

I worked with this sumbitch one time, always cool to my face but then I find out he's talkin' behind my *got-damn* back. Then I thought about this guy, and realized he's a nervous mothahfuckah, guarded, didn't trust nobody. Turns out he's lyin', cheatin', stealin', takin' credit that wasn't his. I got my ass away from that crazy mothahfuckah and turns out that was a good thing. It wasn't too long before somebody higher up caught wind, and that sumbitch got fired, blacklisted, all of that. I thank God every day I finally saw the signs and broke my association with his ass. He didn't trust nobody 'cuz he couldn't be trusted. Now I learned my lesson and I know what to look for. You can listen to me or figure that shit out for yourself. Hell of a lot easier to listen to me.

> ***A man who trusts nobody is apt to be the kind of man nobody trusts.***
>
> —Harold MacMillan

DO THIS TODAY: *Think about the folks you doin' business with. Are they trustworthy? If they are, you'll be able to weather almost any storm. But on the flip side, if they ain't, even a mild breeze will capsize that relationship and you might just go down with the ship. Do you need to change some shit up right now, while the ocean's still calm?*

August 19th

"WE'RE ALL PEOPLE, YOU GOTTA SEE THAT."

I know there's differences between folks. We do shit different sometimes, and that's okay. Thinkin' about the differences that makes us who we are, those are all good. You know, Black women gonna have their hair and nails did, they gotta look fine all the *got-damn* time. You could have nothin' but a bottle of ketchup in the fridge, and they goin' up to Lee's Nails to get them acrylics on. That's right, it's okay, I love that about Black women. And White folks, they gonna take their lunch break, grab a bite with the crew or open up their plastic crate of kale salad, and back to work right on time. Black folks, you can't find their ass during lunch break. They done found a dark place to take a mothahfuckin' nap, and they gonna come back when they good and ready. That's a difference and we can respect that.

I know I mess around about it, but that's all it is is messin'. If you start to go further than that, if you startin' to look at some folks like they ain't good enough 'cuz of their color, their religion, their traditions, how much money they makin', who they love or their mothahfuckin' gender, any of that, you better check yo'self. You cut a sumbitch, he gonna bleed red. That's it. When you start seein' folks as the soul that's just wearin' a meat suit, one that they didn't go and pick out for themselves even, you gonna feel somethin' change. You gonna feel more connected.

> ***In recognizing the humanity of our fellow beings, we pay ourselves the highest tribute.***
>
> —Thurgood Marshall

DO THIS TODAY: *Expand your circle. Get involved in new activities so you can meet new people outside of your clique. Volunteer, join a travel club, or attend a cultural event you might not normally attend. Be open and receptive to new faces and races.*

August 20th

"YOUR SHIT CAN GET HEAVY. LET SOMEBODY ELSE CARRY IT ONCE IN A WHILE."

Asking for help can save your life and help your relationships too. Your whole perception of things can change in a positive way. It's hard to take help. I know it. We been conditioned all our lives to pull our own damn selves up by our bootstraps, make it on our own, be a man. We been taught that askin' for help is a sign of weakness. I'm gonna tell you right now, it's the strongest thing you can do. It takes courage to admit that you can't do it all. Nobody can do everything all the *got-damn* time. Even Batman had Robin. You catchin' my drift? You ain't less of a person. You ain't less of nothin' if you let somebody carry your load for a minute, or at least let 'em take a side or a corner. Don't be a mothahfuckin' martyr. Nobody likes that shit.

You ever get somebody askin' to help you, and you keep turnin' 'em down? It kinda makes 'em feel bad. Makes 'em feel like you don't want 'em. But when you say, "Yeah, man. C'mon and jump in. I appreciate you," when you let somebody help you out like that, you're allowin' them the opportunity to do somethin' good, and that's a blessin' for them too. It's a mothahfuckin' double blessin'. You feelin' some relief, they feelin' good, everybody blessed. That's what it's all about. And it's all good, 'cuz you know when somebody else is needin' somethin', you gonna help them out. It's the got-damn circle of life.

> ***People become attached to their burdens sometimes more than the burdens are attached to them.***
>
> —George Bernard Shaw

DO THIS TODAY: *If you need help with somethin', stop standin' around like Ned in the third grade and ask for it. People can't read your got-damn* ***mind****. What are you gonna ask for help with today? Just humble yourself, open your mouth, and do it.*

August 21st

"YOUR TIME IS THE BEST THING YOU CAN GIVE SOMEBODY."

When you sittin' there lookin' at your empty hands, don't think that you got nothin' to give. You got more than you think, 'cuz you got time. That's one thing everybody's got, even if it's limited. If you breathin' right now, and you readin' this, you got time. Now, I know you might be thinkin', "I'm so busy right now. I got work and studyin' and I gotta take my grandma to get her hair did." Alright, you takin' your grandma to the beauty shop, that's already givin' the best kinda gift—your mothahfuckin' time. That's what I'm talkin' about. She's gonna appreciate that more than any kinda material shit you can give her.

But I get it. We all think that we got too much to do and not enough time. But that's some bullshit, because we all got the same amount of time. You can't use it up, it ain't like a roll of toilet paper. There's always more in front of us, and we *choose* how to spend every mothahfuckin' minute. Yeah, I get that once the minutes slip behind you, you can't get 'em back. That's what makes spendin' your time with somebody the most valuable gift you can give 'em. Your time is priceless.

> ***When you give someone your time, you are giving them a portion of your life that you'll never get back. Your time is your life. That is why the greatest gift you can give someone is your time.***
>
> —Rick Warren

DO THIS TODAY: *Runnin' here, runnin' there, we always runnin' somewhere. Makes it easy to forget how important it is to spend time with people. Forgettin' this can cause conflicts, folks driftin' apart 'cuz they don't feel valued. Decide today to spend time with those you value most and make some memories you can treasure.*

August 22nd

"SAY WHAT YOU NEED TO SAY."

I know we ain't used to bein' blunt. We've gown up hearin' parents, teachers, grandparents, and aunties tellin' us to keep it to ourselves. You know, you wanna tell that little sumbitch Terrence down the street that he's dumber than a stump. You know he about one fry short of a Happy Meal, but hell, naw. If you say that, you gonna get a smack upside the head and sent to bed without dinner. In a different way, you can't go tellin' your folks your dreams when you a kid, 'cuz they just gonna tell you, "Bean, get your head outta the clouds." Or, "You better have a plan B." They even gonna tell you all the reasons why that shit ain't gonna work, and that's gonna bum you out. Maybe so much that you won't tell nobody nothin' no more. Why would you go on and tell somebody your hopes and dreams if you think they just gonna smash 'em to bits? If more people followed their dreams, folks' lives would change, society would be better. Hell, the whole *got-damn* world would improve. We can't be lettin' nobody shut that shit down.

Then there's the way you grow up where you ask, but you do not receive. Maybe you was poor, maybe your folks ain't that great and they didn't give a shit. Whatever it was that stopped you from gettin' what you asked for, it scarred you. Now you keepin' your mouth shut. And that's a damn shame, 'cuz now there's gonna be folks that'll listen if you talkin'. So, open your mouth. You got nothin' to lose and everything to gain. All you gotta do is start askin', start sayin', and put yourself out there.

> ***When you give yourself permission to communicate what matters to you in every situation you will have peace despite rejection or disapproval.***
>
> —Shannon L. Alder

DO THIS TODAY: *What have you been holdin' your tongue about? You might have to overcome some old trauma to do it, but it's time—you gotta say it. Once you start speakin' up, it's gonna be easier to do it again and again.*

August 23rd

"GIVE 'EM THE HELP THEY'RE LOOKIN' FOR, NOT THE HELP YOU THINK THEY NEED."

When my mama died, we had a parade of food comin' into our house every mothahfuckin' day. Casserole dishes, foil pans, Tupperware filled with homemade dinners filled our fridge. It was nice. It helped us out, and it made my family feel like folks cared. But there was this one sumbitch that kept tryin' to get us to come to his *got-damn* grief therapy group. Shit, we didn't wanna go to no group. We was dealin' with it together. But that mothahfuckah wouldn't let up. He kept sayin' it was gonna help us. Help us? You wanna help us, then cut our damn lawn, clean the gutters, give my grandmama a ride to her foot doctor. But, naw, he wanted to help in the way he wanted to help. It was always about him, not about us and what we needed. It was about that sumbitch pushin' his thing onto us. He was always about him.

When you really wanna help somebody out, ask what they need, then listen and respond. It's pretty straight-mothahfuckin'-forward. When your boss needs a report on her desk in twenty minutes, what's she gonna say when you come in with a vanilla cappuccino instead, just 'cuz you thought that would be somethin' she'd need. Fuck no, she needs the *got-damn* reports and you gonna need another mothahfuckin' job. You see what I'm sayin'? So, if your girl is feelin' some kinda way and she just wants you to hold her, but instead you sittin' there comin' up with ideas to fix shit. She don't want that. Shut the fuck up and wrap your arms around her and wipe her mothahfuckin' tears. Give her the help she's askin' for.

> ***When we give cheerfully and accept gratefully, everyone is blessed.***
>
> —Maya Angelou

DO THIS TODAY: *Make a commitment to go through today payin' closer attention to what folks* ***actually*** *need. And if you don't know, ask. It's not about you, it's about them.*

August 24th

"TREAT YOUR FAMILY RIGHT."

I got some friends that's so close to me, they just like family. These sum-bitches always been comin' to the family barbeques, the picnics, the holiday gatherin's. I got their kids' pictures up on my fridge and shit. These people's got my back and I got theirs. They family, you can call 'em framily—you know, your "friend family." That's your ride-or-dies. Then there's your blood, and y'all know that's thick as a mothahfuckah. All of those folks, you gotta treat 'em right all the damn time, not just when it's convenient or when you need 'em, 'cuz those kinds of relationships are like gold nuggets you just done panned outta the river. Why is it panned gold? Because you can't buy it, and it comes to you in your flow.

What does it mean to treat your family right? It don't mean to buy 'em shit. None of that crap is worth a damn. It means you gotta be there for 'em. Answer the damn phone when they callin' you. Give 'em your time when they need you. Have talks on the phone, get behind their hopes and dreams, and *got-dammit*, help 'em move. You know somebody's got you when they show up to put your mothahfuckin' couch on a truck when it's ninety-seven degrees and humid. That's love right there. It don't take much to be there for your people, just give 'em your time and be real with 'em. All the time, no exceptions.

> ***Blood is thicker than water.***
>
> —Medieval Proverb

DO THIS TODAY: *Remember that '70s Sister Sledge song, "We Are Family"? That was sho' 'nuff the truth. A lot of them damn sisters in that group too. But just like the Jacksons, the Isley Brothers, and the Osmonds, family was the thread that kept everything together. Family keeps you standin' strong. Connect with your family today: call your sister or granddad, shoot 'em a text, make a plan to do somethin' together. Let 'em know you care.*

August 25th

"DON'T GO TELLIN' EVERYBODY ALL OF YOUR PERSONAL BUSINESS."

Your business is your business. Ain't nobody else gotta be all up in it. It's crazy, the world we livin' in, where everybody's airin' out all their shit to anybody that's on the mothahfuckin' interwebs. Used to be that folks just gossiped around the water cooler or on the front stoop with the neighborhood gang. Now, all of our dirty laundry's hangin' out everywhere, flappin' in the wind. It's embarrassin', and it can get you into some deep shit on so many different levels.

I seen this lady, she's always postin' shit about her husband. She's sayin', "Here we go again. This the 997th reason Byron gonna die before me. He's so dumb, today he decided to rub hisself down with baby oil 'cuz his skin's so dry like a mothahfuckin' elephant and shit. Then he got in the damn shower. Yeah, oily feet and wet tile, he ended up on his damn ass. Now I gotta take care of his dumb ass. He got hisself a broken hip." You see what's goings *on* here? This woman done belittled her husband, the one that she's s'pose to have his back. Do you think that's lookin' bad on him? Hell, naw. That shit's lookin' bad on *her*. I see folks puttin' their love lives on status posts, tellin' everybody about their relationships and shit, where they goin' on vacation, and who got fucked up. Even good shit, you don't gotta put it all out there either 'cuz that kinda good shit could make folks feel like you braggin', and sometimes it makes 'em jealous. That shit can lead to a negative situation too. So, keep some of it to yourself. It's nobody else's business.

> ***The good and wise lead quiet lives.***
>
> —Euripides

DO THIS TODAY: *Blah, blah, blah. Your mouth has no damn filter. You tell yo' business, their business, and you'd tell my business if you knew it. Keep it up and folks won't tell you shit, they'll be lookin' for the exit when you walk in. Next time you feel the urge to talk, stuff some gum in your mouth and chew. And if you got posts out there on the social medias that's tellin' too much, delete those sumbitches right now. They could come back and kick you in the ass.*

August 26th

"IF SOMEBODY'S TELLIN' YOU A WHOLE LOTTA SECRETS, THAT'S A RED FLAG."

Secrets are cool when you little, and you under the tent fort you built in your livin' room, and your cousin whispers you somethin' that's just for you, and they swear you not to tell. They done said somethin' about your grandmama's underwear and shit. You giggle and cross your heart. That's a cool secret. But when you in a business relationship, and you got somebody tellin' you shit then sayin' you can't tell nobody else, that's not a cool secret at all. They doin' it more than once, then they sayin' you can't even tell the other folks on your *got-damn* team? Naw, that's some bigger mothahfuckin' bullshit. You better keep your eyes on that sumbitch, and don't get caught up in their messed-up drama. It might make you feel kinda special at first, but at the end of the day, bein' that sumbitch's secret-keeper is gonna come up and bite you in the ass.

What happens when other folks find out you been in on it the whole damn time? You gonna be instantly associated with the sumbitch. They gonna start thinkin', "What the hell is Bernie hidin' from us too?" Then you gotta understand that if they been tellin' you secrets, they probably tellin' other folks secrets too. And why it's all gotta be secrets in the first place? You ain't got no transparency, mothahfuckah? The only folks that gotta keep secrets is ones that got somethin' to hide. That's shady as hell. You gotta start seein' that for what it is and get the hell away. Just tell 'em, "Hey, don't tell me shit 'cuz I ain't good with keepin' it to myself." They won't tell ya' then, that's for damn sure.

> ***Whoever gossips to you, will gossip about you.***
>
> —Spanish Proverb

DO THIS TODAY: *Block that troublemaker on your phone and social media, now. If you don't, they'll drag you to filth with 'em. They're a sinkin' ship, mothahfuckin' quicksand, cow manure. Ain't nobody got time for that. (Thank you, Ms. Tamar.)*

August 27th

"MAN, WHEN YOU SAY 'I DO,' YOU SAYIN' IT TO THE WHOLE DAMN FAMILY."

You better make sure that when you walkin' down the aisle, you gonna get along with the folks that's sittin' on both sides of the church. 'Cuz you about to spend a whole lotta your life with all of them all. What do you know about 'em? If the answer is "not much at all," then you best be gettin' your learnin' on right mothahfuckin' now. There's a number of reasons for this. The first one bein' what I already mentioned; you gonna be spendin' time with 'em. Holidays, birthdays, dinner every mothahfuckin' Sunday. You get the picture. But the other thing is that they family and how they get on in it, that's gonna tell you a little bit about your partner too. How do they treat their mama? If they got siblings, how do they get along? Damn, if they an only child, how's that playin' out too? It's also gonna tell ya' if they folks is gonna be too involved. You gonna have a mother-in-law that's all up in your business, tellin' you how to raise your child and keep your house? You gonna have a father-in-law lookin' down his nose at you, makin' you feel some kinda way? That shit can drive a *got-damn* wedge into your relationship real fast. That's why I'm sayin', don't rush into nothin' until you assess the situation. Them folks that's gonna be part of your new family, they could also be amazing and you like 'em even more than your own mothahfuckin' family. You wanna know that too.

> ***Love is not maximum emotion. Love is maximum commitment.***
>
> —Sinclair B. Ferguson

DO THIS TODAY: *That's right, come one, come all: Loose Tooth Willie, Auntie Cleopatra and her seventh husband, nephew Tiny with his six-foot-six ass, bumpin' his head on the doorway. Aww, your new family, just more to love. Okay, if you still datin', I want you to assess. Can you live with 'em? If not, you better not make your partner choose, 'cuz that's somethin' that they'll never let you forget.*

August 28th

"EVERYBODY'S GONE THROUGH SOME SHIT YOU DON'T KNOW NOTHIN' ABOUT."

Whenever you meet somebody, you startin' a relationship with them in a story that's already in progress, and chances are good that they ain't gonna share every *got-damn* detail of it with you in their first mothahfuckin' encounter. You ain't gonna step up onto the bus, and the driver's got a bad attitude, but as you payin' your fee, he says, "I got kicked outta my house when I was sixteen, lived in a shelter. Some bad sumbitch beat me up when I's eighteen and stole everything I had. I struggled to find a job 'cuz I had no address, until finally I had an aunt that took me in. Then she up and died, left me with a coupla her children to raise...so, sorry I'm a little grumpy today." Fuck, no. If that bus driver's got a bit of an attitude, instead of bein' an asshole to 'em, maybe just step off and don't let it affect you. Give him a smile and a nod. You could even say, "Thanks. I appreciate you, man." Oh, boy, that goes a long mothahfuckin' way with folks. Same goes for your friends, your business associates, your banker, real estate agent, and your *got-damn* cab driver. Even your partner, your kids, you ain't them so you don't know all of their struggles all the damn time. Give 'em some respect, some courtesy, and make 'em feel like it's okay. You don't need to go addin' to their stress, 'cuz you have no idea what's on they mothahfuckin' mind or what kinda weight they carryin' with 'em.

> ***I think we all have our demons and our various shortcomings, and it would be nice if people felt more gently about other people, but also about themselves.***
>
> —Michelle Huneven

DO THIS TODAY: *You start tryin' to understand somebody, that's how you build a bridge. Who's in your life that gets you all worked up? Imagine they got a note attached to 'em that says some hard shit they've gone through. Imagine it just happened. How're you gonna treat 'em now?*

August 29th

"IN BUSINESS, GOOD CONTRACTS MAKE GOOD RELATIONSHIPS."

I don't care how chill you are with somebody, you gotta set up the relationship in a professional way from the get-go or things could get sour real fast. Deals on a handshake could end with a backhand, 'cuz once money is involved, folks can change. Or maybe they come across somebody that tells 'em they can do this for 'em, or that for 'em, or maybe they got a little bit more experience than you do. That "friend," that business acquaintance you thought was chill, could turn on you in a heartbeat. You just don't know. You gotta watch fast talkers and wishy-washy mothahfuckahs. You can't trust em'. Don't fall for their sob story of how everybody always leaves 'em and shit. Folks leavin' their ass 'cuz they found 'em out, and they could leave, 'cuz that sumbitch didn't have no contracts. When folks show who they are, believe 'em.

The other thing a real contract does is set up expectations. What is it exactly that you gonna be responsible for? What is the other guy gonna be responsible for? And how y'all gonna split up the money? If you set that out right away, there ain't no questions, no wiggle room. It just makes mothahfuckin' sense. And if that person you workin' with don't want no contracts, or they pushin' it off or makin' it seem like it's no big deal, you better start askin' some *got-damn* questions. 'Cuz if they a stand-up person, they gonna want them contracts too. They gonna understand why they need 'em, and since they got nothin' to hide and no tricks up their sleeve, they gonna be all for it. So, do not hesitate. Get that shit in writing.

> ***Be careful who you trust. The devil was once an angel.***
>
> —Ziad Abdelnour

DO THIS TODAY: *Stay on top of your game. Who do you need contracts with right now? Find a template online and create one or call a lawyer if you need to. It's time to protect your ass and establish a good business relationship.*

August 30th

"YOU'RE GONNA DISAGREE SOMETIMES, AND THAT'S OKAY."

Havin' disagreements don't make a bad relationship. It ain't that you disagree, it's how you do it that's important. As a matter of fact, disagreements can help you grow, help you become a good *got-damn* listener, help you understand somebody better. If you goin' on always agreein' about everything, chances are really mothahfuckin' good that one of y'all is just lettin' their shit go to keep the peace. That can only last so long before you gonna blow. So, rather than focusin' your energy on never havin' an argument, you gotta learn how to do it right. So, here we go. Imma teach you how to disagree without fightin'.

First, when some shit comes up and you feelin' some kinda way, stop and take a mothahfuckin' breath. I know it sounds cheesy as hell, but do it. That shit works. Next, listen. Period. Listen to what they're sayin' and ask 'em to explain more if you do not understand. Third, check yourself. If your argument comes from your ego, jealousy, or fear, just drop it right there. You gotta let that shit go. Fourth, if you got yourself some legitimate reasons to disagree, lay 'em down in a calm and rational way. But hold up, if the person you disagreein' with is not bein' calm and rational, just stop. The conversation's gotta wait 'til everybody's in a decent frame of mind to talk without losin' their shit. If y'all do that, you gonna be good, and hand to God, you gonna see your relationships gettin' a whole lot bettah.

> ***You don't have to win every argument. Agree to disagree.***
>
> —Regina Brett

DO THIS TODAY: *Who are some of the funniest comedians of all times? Now, I hope your ass includes Bernie Mac on that list. But, it might not. Sometimes, folks have different opinions from yours. You ain't gotta go be ignorant about it. When neither one a y'all gonna change the other's mind, that's when you stop arguin' and move on!*

August 31st

"A SOLID VESSEL NEEDS BOTH AN ANCHOR AND A SAIL."

Not everybody in your life is gonna be puffin' you up, hypin' you with your dreams, pushin' you toward your goals. That don't necessarily mean they bad for you, as long as they ain't draggin' you backward. Now, I didn't get myself on a boat too often, but I will say if you got a sail-boat with no anchor, you gonna find yourself driftin' out in the middle of the water at some mothahfuckin' point. The anchor is a good thing. Keeps you moored when you need to stay put for a while. What I'm tryin' to tell y'all is that we need folks in our lives that help us sail, and other folks that keep us grounded when we need it. I know I've appreciated both in my life. Sometimes that "both" comes from one person and other times it's from multiple different people. You got the hype man that's pumpin' you up, and the practical sumbitch that makes you stop and think about the *logisticals* of the situation. You need 'em both.

Rhonda always done that for me, all in one. There was times when she was encouragin' as a mothahfuckah, lettin' me practice on her, goin' to my shows, sittin' there dreamin' with me. Then there was times when I got caught up in the dreamin', and she talked with me about, "How, exactly, we gonna make that happen?" No judgment, no puttin' me down, just anchorin' me to the earth long enough to figure out a real kinda plan. Sometimes when you a dreamer like me, you need somebody to set you on your course a little bit. That way, you gonna get where you wanna go a helluva lot faster.

> ***I don't need a friend who changes when I change and who nods when I nod. My shadow does that much better.***
>
> —Plutarch

DO THIS TODAY: *If you got somebody in your life that's never hypin' you up, think about what they* **are** *sayin' to you. Maybe they're your anchor. Change the way you look at 'em, and the way you feel about 'em is gonna change. Maybe you'll start listenin' to what they got to say and lettin' them help you be better.*

September 1st

"IF YOU LET SOMEBODY MESS WITH YOU THE SAME WAY TWICE, MAYBE YOU THE FOOL."

My brother Darryl was ten years older than me. He was bigger than me, stronger than me, and he was a bad mothahfuckah. I loved the hell outta him, though. Damn, all I wanted was for him to pay some attention to me. When he did, it was like I was walkin' on air. I remember this one time, though, I had taken some money I earned helpin' the neighbor lady out with her groceries, and I bought myself a Mars bar at the corner store. Oh, man, I was excited. We didn't get no store-bought treats that often. But I had that candy and I saw my brothah and I was so excited, I offered him a piece. Well, he took that candy bar and he didn't break off no piece. He ate the whole mothahfuckin' thing. Left me one tiny bite, then he smiled and patted my head and took off. I was devastated, callin' him all kinda names under my breath. Next time I had some money, wouldn't you know, I did the same *got-damn* thing again. I let my brother eat my candy. Boy, did I feel like a dumbass right about then. He got me twice, but he also taught me a really valuable lesson that I won't never forget. Now that I think about it, Darryl taught me a lot of lessons like that. Maybe that's what he was there for, you know. He made me tough, made me think about shit when I was young. That way, I wouldn't have to be the fool when it was really important.

> ***Fool me once, shame on you. Fool me twice, shame on me.***
>
> —Chinese Proverb

DO THIS TODAY: *We live and we learn. Like checkin' the gas tank after you let your brothah take your car. Next time, you gonna tell your brothah "hell no," or you gonna make sure he fills it up. Your lesson is learned when you decide not to do something again 'cuz it caused you problems in the past. Get wise. What have you learned from recently that you ain't gonna repeat?*

September 2nd

"FORGIVE, BUT DON'T FORGET."

Forgiveness is one of my favorite mothahfuckin' topics. You get me started and maybe you can't get me to stop, but I'll try to keep it brief. Why is forgiveness so important? Because when you forgive somebody, it heals your own ***got-damn*** soul. Sure, it might make the other sumbitch feel a little bit better, but mostly it's makin' you free from that bullshit that's holdin' you down. Why you carryin' the weight of what somebody did to you? All that's doin' is lettin' it keep on hurtin' you. Put it down and you gonna walk a helluva lot easier.

Lots of folks might be thinkin' that forgivin' somebody is a sign of weakness, that forgiveness be like givin' up. Hell, naw. It ain't like that at all. It takes a strong mothahfuckah to forgive, and that don't mean you gonna forget about it and let that kinda shit happen again. You gonna forgive, but you gonna take the lesson that experience taught you and use it to make your life better. Maybe that means distancin' yourself from somebody, or maybe it means not puttin' yourself in situations like that again. It could mean takin' a look at yourself and seein' what part you played in the shit that went down so you can own it. Whatever the lesson, you learn it, be grateful for it, forgive, and move on. Forgiveness is freedom, and that's the truth.

> ***Forgive but do not forget, or you will be hurt again. Forgiving changes the perspectives. Forgetting loses the lesson.***
>
> —Paulo Coelho

DO THIS TODAY: *Who do you need to forgive? Write that person's name down and put "I forgive you" next to it. Repeat that step a couple of times each week. You're doin' that to free your mind so you can grow. Don't let grudges hold you down, they cause stagnation.*

September 3rd

"DON'T FIGHT OVER MONEY. IF YOU GOT SOME, GREAT. IF YOU DON'T, YOU'LL GET SOME."

Big Mama and Grandpa Thurman were married for a long mothahfuckin' time. They weren't never not married, I think. Least it always felt that way. One time, we was at a church picnic, and some young couple just new in love asked my grandmama, "What's the secret to a marriage that lasts as long as yours?" Big Mama took a sip of her sweet tea, and she looked this woman straight in the face, and she says, "Don't talk about money. If you got some, great. If you don't got none, don't worry, you'll get some." That was it. That was her mothahfuckin' words of wisdom. But that shit's true. Just look at the data—married couples fight over money more than anything else. Who's makin' more, who's spendin' more, how we gonna get more? All of that shit can really get up in between two people that love each other. It's a damn shame. And what folks don't realize is if they're worryin' about it all the *got-damn* time, they're basically prayin' for bad financial shit to happen. What Big Mama was sayin' was, don't worry your head over it all the damn time. Trust that you gonna have each other's best interests in mind. Trust that God will provide. Do what you can with what you got and be calm knowin' that there's more gonna come when you need it.

> ***Money may not buy love but fighting about it will bankrupt your relationship.***
>
> —Michelle Singletary

DO THIS TODAY: *Walk through things carefully. Money is an emotional topic, and how you deal with it can affect your family tree for generations. Stop, sit down, and have a long talk with your significant other. Put everything on the table. Once you understand each other fully, you can work toward overcoming things together, and you don't have to bring it up all the time.*

September 4th

"ALLOW FOLKS TO CHANGE, 'CUZ WE ALL JUST OUT HERE TRYIN' TO BE BETTER."

Sometimes we get so stuck on the idea of how somebody's always been, that we get blinded to their changes when they go through 'em. We can't imagine them bein' any other way than how we know 'em, so we block it out. We don't do that shit on purpose but it happens, and you better believe other folks is doin' it to you too. But the bottom line is, everything is gonna change at some point, and everybody can change if they wanna change. We gotta understand that and allow it, 'cuz if we don't, we end up blockin' other folks' blessin's.

The folks you know, they changin' all the time. Maybe your little girl grows up and now she's a mama. It's hard to look at her any other way than as your little girl, for a while, 'til her baby starts cryin' and you hand that little sumbitch back. "Oh, you want yo' mama, here ya' go. There, that's better." She the mama now. But yeah, it's gonna take you a while to change how you lookin' at her. Same thing happens when you get successful at your career and shit, or if you change careers. I was a stand-up comedian and that's it for a while. But then I wanted to be an actor and have my own show. It took a minute for folks to take me serious as an actor. "Bernie Mac, he a comedian." Well, I shut 'em up real quick. I think they got themselves a shock and eventually, they caught on. I'm tryin' to tell you here that you gotta keep your eyes and ears open, and if somebody makes a shift in their life, don't hold 'em to their past. It's gone, and they get to reinvent themselves every *got-damn* day, and so do you.

> ***I believe people change. I think that they can learn from mistakes.***
>
> —Kevin Plank

DO THIS TODAY: *You know you a badass when somebody somewhere is still discussin' the old you, 'cuz they don't have access to the new you. Change is a mothahfuckah. You gotta meet it with a positive attitude, learn to let go of set ways and become flexible. Who's in your life that's changed lately? Try to get to know the new person they've become.*

September 5th

"IF EVERYBODY'S DOIN' SOMETHIN', BUT YOU KNOW IN YOUR HEART IT AIN'T RIGHT, DON'T DO IT."

If your friends go on and jump off a cliff, you gonna do it too? Yep. When I was a young teenager, the answer was probably, "Yep." It's normal. Every kid wants to fit in. But I wasn't like that for long. I learned real young how to stand my ground, stand up for what's right, 'cuz at the end of the day, you're the only one you gotta live with for the rest of your *got-damn* life. You gotta think for yourself and take responsibility for your own mothahfuckin' life.

I think that's why most folks follow the crowd, though. They wantin' somebody else to blame when the shit hits the fan. "It wasn't my decision. I didn't do it. It was him...and her...and all of them that did it in front of me." Hell, naw. You had all of them chances in front of you to see what was gonna happen, and you did it anyway. If that's the case, then you deserve whatever it was at the bottom of that jump. On the other hand, if you see what's goin' down and you stop, maybe you gonna switch it up, and the folks behind you gonna follow you instead. You get to be the hero then. How 'bout them apples? And if they don't stop with you, well then at least you know you doin' what you need to do. You ain't responsible for them, 'cuz they get a chance to make their own choices just like you did. It's called free will, and God didn't give you that by no accident. Use it.

> ***Be yourself and set the trend. Don't follow.***
>
> —YG

DO THIS TODAY: *Choosin' your own path means decidin' what's right for you at every moment. That means not choosin' somethin' based on what people usually do, not followin' the* **got-damn** *crowd. What are you doin' that's not really "you?" Feel free to stop doin' it—now.*

September 6th

"WHEN YOU MAKE A MISTAKE, APOLOGIZE AND TRY'N FIX IT!"

I know it's hard to say, "I'm sorry." It's hard like a mothahfuckah to admit you did somethin' wrong, screwed up, fucked shit up, or hurt somebody. It's all about takin' responsibility for your actions. When you do that, it's gonna work out okay, or at least it's gonna work out how it's supposed to. Also, when you apologize, you make the person on the other end of that feel like you see 'em. It softens 'em up a bit too. 'Cuz chances are, they don't wanna be in that situation with you either.

I remember this one time, I fucked shit up real bad with Rhonda. I went out late, you know, and I didn't come home for dinner. It wasn't the first time, neither, and she was workin' real hard and raisin' our little girl, Je'Niece. Anyway, I get in real late and I ask what's for dinner. She said, "We already ate." I was like, "I want some pork chops." She lookin' at me like, "You know where the kitchen is, cook 'em yourself." Well, I was gonna show her. I threw them chops in the pan, salt and pepper, and I fried 'em 'til the whole *got-damn* house was fulla smoke. Then I ate 'em, too, choked 'em down with plenty of water. Tasted like ashes. But I refused to admit I was wrong. All night, we didn't speak to each other, felt like hell. Next day, I come in and I'm still feelin' that tension in the air. I take a breath, and I say, "I'm sorry, Rhonda. I'm gonna do better." You could see the damn tension rush on outta her body like a mothahfuckin' exorcism. She said, "I'm sorry too. And you ain't ever makin' no pork chops again. Stay outta my damn kitchen." You see, life is better when you address it and move on.

> ***When you realize you've made a mistake, make amends immediately. It's easier to eat crow while it's still warm.***
>
> —Dan Heist

DO THIS TODAY: *Next time somethin' happens, take a deep breath and with sincerity, say, "I realize I hurt your feelings, and I'm sorry." That acknowledges that you know it was you and leave it at that! Who you got to apologize to today?*

September 7th

"NOBODY'S PERFECT, SO STOP EXPECTIN' PERFECTION."

Lemme ask you a question. Are you perfect? If you sayin' yes, then you better check yourself, 'cuz you an arrogant sumbitch. Now, I ain't talkin' about, "God made each of us perfect in his eyes." That ain't what I'm talkin' about here. I'm askin' if you got zero flaws. Are you a flawless individual? Ain't none of y'all can answer yes to that. So, if you ain't perfect, why you expectin' folks around you to be? Seems like nowadays, folks makes one little mistake, or there's one little thing you don't like about 'em, so you cast 'em off like they some kinda last year's style. Get over your *got-damn* self. People may be flawed, but that's what makes 'em human. That's what gives us a chance to grow, to learn to love somebody despite the little things we don't maybe love about 'em. Maybe they need you in their life to help 'em learn something, to make a change.

Now, I ain't sayin' that you gotta hang around somebody that's got somethin' major wrong that you can't stand. That's just askin' for trouble. If they a big liar, a cheater, doin' shit that's makin' you feel uncomfortable. Maybe you can kinda back offa them folks. But if this person is a good soul, they make you laugh and you enjoy their company, if you don't like the fact that they wear pleated khakis with gym shoes and that's why you can't chill with 'em, maybe you better take a long hard look at yourself.

Even the best needles are not sharp at both ends.

—Chinese Proverb

DO THIS TODAY: *Perfectionism comes from your fear of makin' a mistake, and last I checked ain't nobody perfect, not even you. What's not perfect about yourself? Be real now. Once you got that, tell yourself it's okay and you're good just like you are...and so's everybody else.*

September 8th

"YOU GOTTA BE FRIENDS, NOT JUST LOVERS, OR IT AIN'T GONNA WORK FOR VERY LONG."

When you just startin' out with somebody, you wanna see if them sparks is flyin'. You lightin' up that room, makin' each other feel some kinda way. You know what I'm sayin'? You got chemistry, can't take yo' hands off each other. I know how that goes. I was young once too. But what happens when that spark fizzles the fuck out? What happens when you spendin' seven minutes makin' flames and then you got the rest of the twenty-three hours and fifty-three minutes of the day left over to fill with somethin'? Are you gettin' along for the rest of that mothahfuckin' time? That's why it's important that you got more in common than some hormones up in there. You gotta actually *like* each other, for real. You gotta make each other laugh. You gotta like doin' some of the same things. Maybe you like the same music or the same restaurants. That's a good start right there. Maybe you like the same kinda movies, or you both like to go to Comic-Con, the opera, or the mothahfuckin' demolition derby. Whatever it is, make sure you like spendin' actual time together doin' real shit. You gotta be able to chill with your partner, not just heat it up with 'em. You gotta have good conversations, good food, and good *got-damn* times or it's gonna get real old real fast, and you gonna start to feel lonely. Y'all gotta like each other, 'cuz "All you need is love," is a load of bullshit. "Why can't we be friends?" Sing it with me, now. That's more like it.

> ***It is not a lack of love, but a lack of friendship that makes unhappy marriages.***
>
> —Friedrich Nietzsche

DO THIS TODAY: *Friendship should be a top priority with your partner. Did you stop havin' fun? Start again, now. At least once a week, do somethin' together that's a blast! Maybe even read a page from this book to each other and get your laugh on. If you ain't got a partner right now, do fun shit by yourself. You enjoyin' life, and that's all that matters.*

September 9th

"FOLKS THAT STICK OUT MIGHT JUST BE RISIN' TO THE TOP."

The kids that's a little bit odd, a lot of times they gonna be the ones that get successful when they grow up. Maybe it's 'cuz they learn to take hard knocks and get back up again. Or maybe it's that they had somethin' special to begin with. You think Stevie Wonder stuck out in school? Hell, yeah, he did. Probably got teased on the sly too. Little kids can be nasty sumbitches. But li'l Stevland Morris soon had a surprise for their asses. He was signed to Motown Records when he was eleven, and by the age of thirteen he was the youngest person to have a number-one hit on *Billboard*'s Hot 100 charts.

You wanna be friends with them cats that stick out, though, fo' sho'. First off, different sumbitches is more interestin' than the kids who wanna just be like everybody else. They got cool shit to talk about. They get excited and they don't give a good *got-damn* who's watchin'. Second, they probably need a friend, so they gonna be real loyal unlike them fake-ass mothahfuckahs that's just usin' you for your ride. Third, their quirks and shit, that's their gifts, and them kids is gonna turn into the next Zuckerburgs and Bezoses, for real. They gonna move on up 'cuz they the kind of folks that CEOs and shit notice for thinkin' outside the box. Hell, that's the only way they know how to think. Here's the deal, the kids who's stickin' to the status quo won't never be nothin' but status quo. So, you get yourself hangin' around the creative types, the different thinkers, the weird kids. Don't write somebody off 'cuz they different. Write 'em *in*, and maybe you learn somethin' and maybe you start gettin' on their kinda level too.

> ***You can't blend in when you were born to stand out.***
>
> —R. J. Palacio

DO THIS TODAY: *Is there somebody you know that you been writin' off 'cuz they stick out? How can you make an effort to get to know them better? You might just find the kinda friend you never knew existed!*

September 10th

"JUST BECAUSE YOU DON'T LIKE SOMETHIN', DON'T MEAN IT AIN'T GOOD FOR SOMEBODY ELSE."

I got things that I do not like. I can't stand sandwiches. Gimme a red hot or a piece of chicken, a cheeseburger, pizza—that's alright. But a sandwich with cold cuts and shit? No thanks, I'll pass. But I ain't gonna put you down 'cuz you wanna get a mothahfuckin' sandwich. As a matter of fact, I had a friend one time that cried big ole tears over a *got-damn* salami sandwich from Henry's Deli. Shit musta been real good, but hell if I was gonna take a bite. He can have the sandwich, 'cuz it takes all kinds to make a world.

I know this kid, he loves him some computer games and shit. And apparently he's really mothhafuckin' good at it too. I guess you would be good if you did somethin' for about twelve hours a stretch, hyper focused. The kid's gettin' good grades, takin' care of his shit, workin' at a job too. But when he's off, he plays games. His folks is always sayin' he's good for nothin', that them games is gonna rot his brain. Now, video games ain't my particular cup of tea neither. But I'd never get down on a kid like that, especially if he got manners, workin', keepin' his shit together. Funny, that kid started his own Twitch stream and he's makin' more money than he knows what to do with. His folks gotta eat their words, and that shit don't taste too good. Worse than a sandwich.

Who are you to judge what's best for someone? Pay attention to what you thinkin'. Your judgments could be based on your insecurities that you projectin' onto someone else. Instead, try and understand 'em, and if they ain't harmin' nobody, at the very least you can just let 'em be.

> ***By judging others, we blind ourselves to our own evil and to the grace which others are just as entitled to as we are.***
>
> —Dietrich Bonhoeffer

DO THIS TODAY: *Who you been castin' your judgment on? Next time you wanna judge, picture a stop sign in your head reminding you to stop the thought and then change it to something more positive.*

September 11th

"HAVE SOME MOTHAHFUCKIN' MANNERS."

Show some got-damn respect. Stop bein' bossy, and good gawd stop raisin' your voice. We can hear you just fine. Just bein' polite, that'll get you a long *got-damn* way in this world. I'm sure somebody taught you some manners when you was a kid. Say "please" and "thank you." Don't talk with your mouth full. Open the door for folks. Put your got-damn *napkin* on your *lap*. When you meet somebody, shake their hand firmly—none of the namby-pamby weak-ass shake, that includes women too. Firm handshake, period, and look 'em in the eye. This shit might not seem like a big mothahfuckin' deal to you, but try *not* usin' manners and see if y'all got any friends left after a while. See if you get anywhere in your job, get a raise, get a promotion, move up the ladder. Use no *got-damn* manners and you might not have a job left at all. Can you imagine if you workin' at a department store, and somebody comes up to you to ask you a question, and you look at 'em and say, "What?" Hell, naw. You gotta say, "Hi, I'm Bernard. What can I help you with?" It's basic customer service skills.

It seems like good manners is gettin' rarer and rarer. I see kids walkin' and lookin' at they phones, bumpin' into folks and not sayin' "excuse me" or nothin'. Some of 'em get an attitude, as if it's that old lady's fault you crashed into her ass 'cuz you can't see where you goin'. Kids is backtalkin' their teachers, actin' like they own the place. I ever did that, my granddad woulda' beat the livin' tar outta me. Now, the parents is goin' in and defendin' their little sumbitches. It's a damn shame. Manners shows respect, and you gotta have respect for other folks if you wanna get anywhere in this world.

> ***Good manners will open doors that the best education cannot.***
>
> —Clarence Thomas

DO THIS TODAY: *Make an extra effort to say "please" and "thank you," to use good etiquette at the dinner table, say "excuse me," and hold the* **got-damn** *door open for folks. See if it boosts your confidence and makes folks treat you a little different too.*

September 12th

"DO YOUR RESEARCH."

When you goin' to meet a potential business associate, or you goin' on a job interview or some shit like that, do your *got-damn* research before you go. You gotta know who it is you're talkin' to. If you do that, you can make conversation with 'em that makes 'em feel good, like you really interested in the company and you know what you settin' yourself up to get into. You also got plenty of material to talk about, and the conversation ain't gonna go dry. However, if you do not do this, you could very well end up puttin' your foot in your *got-damn* mouth.

This principle doesn't just go for work-related things. If you goin' to meet your girlfriend's parents for the first time, you definitely gotta do your homework. Ask her everything you can about 'em. What do they do for a livin', what's their hobbies, are they married to each other? What's their position on global warming, sex on TV, Obamacare? Is any of 'em a vegetarian? You gotta ask those things so you can avoid a potential misstep. Or, if you like to stir shit up, so you know exactly which buttons to hit. You hear what I'm tellin' you? It's better to go in with knowledge than to run in there blind. It gives you the mothahfuckin' upper hand, 'cuz you prepared as a mothahfuckah. That's how you impress folks with your confidence. That's all confidence is, anyway. Knowin' that you know what you need to know.

> ***Know your business and industry better than anyone else in the world. Love what you do or don't do it.***
>
> —Mark Cuban

DO THIS TODAY: *It's easy as hell to do your research. Check up on somebody you workin' with, gonna work with, or somebody you know, just to get some practice at it. But remember, other folks can research yo' shit too. Watch the things you postin' online. You don't want that shit to come back and bite you in the ass.*

September 13th

"YOU DON'T REALLY KNOW SOMEBODY 'TIL YOU SPEND THREE DAYS IN A CAR WITH 'EM."

If you really wanna know somebody, take a mothahfuckin' road trip with 'em. There's just somethin' about the open road that's gonna tell you a whole lot about somebody's personality that you maybe wouldn't have seen otherwise. It's gonna tell you if they patient—that's when y'all are stuck behind a mothahfuckin' traffic jam so thick folks is stopped, barbeque grills out, lawn chairs, and shit. Is the person you in the car with gonna go with the flow, or pitch a *got-damn* fit when they know damn well there ain't nothin' you can do about it?

Then there's sharin'. When you on that long stretch of road where there ain't nothin' for miles and miles, and they get out the last bag of chips, are they gonna give some up for you? 'Cuz your stomach's growlin' like a sumbitch. Are they gonna eat 'em all? Sharin'.

Next, you got flexibility. On a three-day car ride, sometimes you get a little detour. Or maybe you see the sign for the biggest mothahfuckin' pie in the world. That's some *Guinness Book* shit, and you wanna go see it. Is your ridin' partner gonna say, "Hell, yeah. Let's go to the big-ass pie!" Or will they moan and groan and tell you, "Hell, no. We got a schedule."

Finally, are they gonna let you drive? Sometimes somebody just has to have that *got-damn* control and won't let you take the wheel for nothin'. That's tellin' right there. Over those three days, you gonna get tired. You gonna get bored. You might get stinky, hungry, and you definitely gonna have to pee. Everything is gonna get tested, but if you get through it, *got-damn*, you know it's meant to be.

> ***Every moment of your life is either a test or a celebration.***
>
> —David Deida

DO THIS TODAY: *Have you ever taken a long-ass road trip, train ride, or bus ride? How did you handle it? Was you patient, did you go with the flow? Self-reflection here can help you adjust your own* got-damn *attitude.*

September 14th

"TAKE CONSTRUCTIVE CRITICISM IN STRIDE."

You don't know everything, and neither do I. At some point, you ain't gonna be the smartest person in the *got-damn* room. Some of y'all know what that feels like already. Maybe you know it better than you should. Y'all know who you are, stop lyin' to yourself. I'm just messin' around. It's good thing, especially as you gettin' started on your path. There's gonna be folks that know a lot more than you do about what it is you doin'. If them folks tell you somethin', if they givin' you some feedback, you better shut your mouth and listen. Constructive criticism from experts is a mothahfuckin' gift. Take it. Use it to make yourself better.

When I was a teenager, I thought I was gonna go up on an open mic at one of the Chicago clubs and kill it. I stepped out on that stage and I told my jokes, and I'm tellin' you, that place was quieter than a morgue at midnight. I looked out there and all I saw was bug-eyes. I walked to the back, and there was this old comic back there. He was pretty much retired, just came out once in while for the hell of it. He looked at me and did a slow shake of his head. He said, "Hey, kid. You can't go out there and just make cracks at the audience right off the bat. You gotta talk about what you know." Now, my tension was all high, fight-or-flight mode and shit. But my mama taught me to be respectful, so I just nodded. On that bus ride home, I thought about what he told me. Started thinkin' more about my life and what was funny. I looked over and saw a sumbitch, kinda tired, lookin' over at me. I says, "I know I'm Black. Shit, I'm so Black I leave smudges on coal." That sumbitch laughed, and I knew that old comic was right, all I had to do was listen.

> ***I like criticism. It makes you strong.***
>
> —LeBron James

DO THIS TODAY: *Criticism hits those blind spots. It's funny, you can feel self-conscious if somebody critiques you, but truthfully, it just means there's somethin' about you that's worth takin' the time to criticize. What kinda criticism have you received lately? How could it help you become better? Don't miss the blind spots.*

September 15th

"IF YOU MAKE A PROMISE, KEEP IT."

I know maybe way too much about broken promises. You see, my daddy left when I was a little kid. I can't even remember a time when he was around. But he'd call up once in a while, talk to me on the phone, then he'd promise me he'd pick me up on Saturday and we'd go to a ball game, a movie, or even just for a drive. Boy, I'd get excited, 'cuz that's my daddy and I was too young to really understand what a sumbitch he was quite yet. Anyway, I'd get on my best clothes, get some coins outta my piggy bank and put 'em in my pocket, and I'd wait on the stoop with all this excitement runnin' through me. I'd wait, and I'd wait, and I'd wait, and that sumbitch would never show. Either that, or he'd roll in six hours late with some mothahfuckin' excuse, then he'd talk to my mama and leave in a huff. He never wanted to see me in the first place. He's just usin' me, you know.

What that taught me is not to trust folks, and that ain't always a good thing. It also taught me never, ever to make a promise that I wasn't plannin' on doin' my mothahfuckin' best to keep. I understand that sometimes you try, and somethin' stops you from pullin' through. But if that's a rare occasion, folks will forgive it, 'cuz they know you a man of your word. If it's all the *got-damn* time though, you better check yourself. Maybe you bit off more than you can chew, so you can't fulfill all of your promises. Or, maybe you know you ain't gonna do it and they's just empty words. Whichever it is, you gotta quit makin' promises you can't keep.

> ***Your word is your honor. If you say you're going to do something, then do it.***
>
> —Joyce Meyer

DO THIS TODAY: *Do you agree to things, even though you know you can't do them? How often do you cancel personal plans at the last minute? Have people stopped asking you for help or support? Maybe 'cuz they know they can't count on you to give it. Those are all signs that you don't keep your word. How are you gonna change that?*

September 16th

"TAKE TIME OUT TO DO FUN SHIT WITH THE PEOPLE YOU LOVE."

It's so easy to get caught up in the grind. You got a million mothahfuckin' things to do, and you get home to finally kick your feet up and you're feelin' tired. You just wanna watch some television, read a magazine, take a nap. Or maybe you one of those folks that can't sit down, always got a project goin'. You fixin' the sink, washin' your car, clippin' the hedges, reorganizin' the DVDs by alphabetical order. You the kinda person always sayin' there's shit to get done. I gotta tell both y'all to just stop. Take a look around you. You got family, a partner, kids, friends. Ask yourself if they gonna look back ten years from now, smile, and say, "Oh my God, you remember that time me and Bernie cleaned out the sock drawers?" Hell, naw. You ain't buildin' memories if you always workin', always cleanin', or if you layin' around bein' lazy as a mothahfuckah. You want good relationships, you wanna feel good about your *got-damn* life, grab your people and do somethin'.

You got shit to do all around you, even if you livin' out in the middle of nowhere, USA. You got nature shit to do out there. In the cities, there's all kinda shit from museums and restaurants to gettin' on them electric scooters and goin' for a whiz around town. If you don't know what to do, let your people decide and be open to what they sayin'. You might find somethin' fun you never knew was out there. If you tend to get caught up and the day gets away from you, you gotta schedule it.

> ***Enjoy your popcorn and enjoy the show. It's just a movie, so have fun!***
>
> —Martin Lawrence

DO THIS TODAY: *Put it in there on your calendar. F-U-N S-H-I-T. Put it in there just like that, and you won't forget. I swear you gonna see all of your relationships get better, you gonna be happier, and that feels real good.*

September 17th

"DON'T POINT OUT SOMEBODY'S FLAWS UNLESS YOU REALLY TRYIN' TO HELP 'EM."

Most folks already know what's wrong with 'em. If they got a cowlick on the back of their head makin' their hair stand all up funny, they know that shit. If they fat, they know they fat. If they can't do math, if they a bad mothahfuckin' driver, if they ain't got a ton of patience, most folks know all of that shit about themselves already. You goin' and pointin' it out, that's just gonna make 'em feel bad about it.

I had this buddy in high school, name was Chris. That poor sumbitch had the most pimply face you ever seen. Looked like he got stung by a whole nest of hornets. He didn't let it stop him and shit, but he knew it wasn't lookin' too good. Sometimes, the kids in school would say some stupid shit. Girls maybe didn't look at him as much as they shoulda. I was over at this kid's house one day, and his own mama came in, shakin' her head. "Boy, you got some serious acne, and you'd be a handsome kid too. Damn shame." He put his head down and she walked on through the room. All I could think was, "What in the actual hell?" She wasn't offerin' no help, no advice, no appointment to the skin doctor, nothin'. Just sayin' shit just to say it. I could tell it affected him too. Words can hurt just as bad when they ain't intended to. We gotta be careful of that.

> ***Whenever you are about to find fault with someone, ask yourself the following question: What fault of mine most nearly resembles the one I am about to criticize?***
>
> —Marcus Aurelius

DO THIS TODAY: *Sticks and stones may break your bones, but words will never hurt you. That shit needs some* **got-damn** *adjustment. Words have the power to destroy, but words can also be positive, healing, and uplifting. Starting today, think about how you communicate. Are your words helping or hurting?*

September 18th

"YOU ONLY KNOW THE PARTS OF SOMEBODY THAT THEY WANT YOU TO SEE."

What you get of somebody, it ain't all of 'em. It's only what they want you to see. It ain't like they lyin', nothin' like that. It ain't about keepin' secrets. There's a lot of reasons somebody ain't sharin' everything about 'em. Mostly it's about protectin' themself from the shit that they don't wanna keep as a part of themself. Sometimes folks has worked real hard to reinvent themself, and they wanna forget who they used to be. If they went through some fucked-up shit, or if they done some fucked-up shit, why would they wanna pull all of that back out? They'll tell ya' when they feel the time is right. But pushin' somebody to tell ya' more than they want to, it's a good way to hurt 'em, and get yourself pushed away quick.

There's another part of this that you gotta be cautious of, though. If they keepin' some stuff down and they ain't quite worked it out yet, that can get ugly. I went with this girl once, she about near broke her ankle tryin' to run away from the ice cream truck. Never told me she got hit by one when she was a kid, twice. Whenever she heard that music playin', she'd start shakin', runnin' like a banshee. I had to cut her loose, 'cuz I liked my Fudgsicles better than I liked her. You see what I'm sayin'? You just gotta be prepared, 'cuz there's always gonna be some things you don't know about folks, and if you stay with 'em long enough, it'll come out. Then you gotta decide if it's worth workin' through.

> ***Sometimes people think they know you. They know a few facts about you, and they piece you together in a way that makes sense to them.***
>
> —Leila Sales

DO THIS TODAY: *Stop tryin' to force someone to reveal themselves to you. If you care about 'em, give it time and let them build trust. Everybody's holdin' back a part of themselves at first. What are you holdin' back? How can you work on openin' up about that?*

September 19th

"DON'T EVER TRUST NOBODY THAT CAN'T GET ALONG WITH A DOG."

Dogs are the best mothahfuckin' judge of character. They don't get it wrong. You ever have some poor sumbitch come into your house, and you got the sweetest, kindest, big-ass mutt in the world. I mean, your baby can put her head in his mouth and just come out with a face full of slobber. But that sad sumbitch comes in, and that same dog sits there like a mothahfuckin' statue—ears back, hair on his ass raised up. Watch out for that sumbitch, 'cuz that dog knows somethin' we don't. He never had nobody teachin' him not to listen to his *got-damn* instincts.

I had this acquaintance one time, and we all was goin' over to another friend's place to play some cards, have a coupla beers, you know. It was a Saturday night. Well, I walked in and this sumbitch walked in right behind me. Soon as I step inside, I see this big old beefy mutt standin' there. I put my hand down, told him to c'mere, and he run up and licked me all the fuck over, all slobbery and shit, but he was a good dog. Then this other sumbitch walk up behind me, and the dog's hair stood up. Hand to God, this dog starts growlin' under his breath. The sumbitch was like, "Hey, hey. Put your damn dog away. I don't like mothahfuckin' dogs." Don't like dogs? Who don't like dogs? They a man's mothahfuckin' best friend. Well, our buddy put the dog away, then about two hours later, we was kickin' that sumbitch out 'cuz he was cheatin' at Texas hold 'em. That dog had a smug look on his face too. For real. We shoulda listened to him. He knew what's up.

> ***If your dog doesn't like someone, you probably shouldn't either.***
>
> —Jack Canfield

DO THIS TODAY: *Have you ever experienced when a dog senses somethin' about somebody that you didn't see at first? Stop and listen, 'cuz that hound can guide you away from negative folks and situations, even if you don't know the reason. You can actually tune into your own senses like that by practicin' daily meditation.*

September 20th

"YOU AIN'T ALWAYS GONNA MISS 'EM WHEN THEY GONE."

When I started shootin' lots of films and television out in Hollywood, I'd already been married to Rhonda for a long time. Now, I missed her when I was gone. I missed home too. I'm a Chicago boy all the way down to my mothahfuckin' Bulls jersey. For real. Anyway, I missed Rhonda, but I know she didn't always be missin' me. Same with Je'Niece. I'd be callin' Rhonda all the damn time, and she ain't pickin' up the phone. I know she out gettin' her hair did and gettin' some *got-damn* sushi with Je'Niece. I don't like no sushi. You eat that shit and you hungry again in an hour, and don't you ever let that blob of green shit touch nothin' or your lips gonna burn for two mothahfuckin' weeks. Hell, naw. They can have their sushi. Do that shit without me.

My point is, they was lovin' their girl time. I knew that, and I knew that them not missin' me every second of the mothahfuckin' day did not mean that they didn't care. It just means they was smart enough not to go on and beat themselves up every day about somethin' they could not help. Missin' me wasn't gonna bring me back there. I had a movie to make, a TV show and whatnot. I wasn't gonna come back, so why get all sappy about it? That's a healthy mothahfuckin' relationship.

> ***The truth is: as I have plenty of great people in my life, my needs are emotionally met. I am not yearning for feelings from people that are not here.***
>
> —Nikola Grace Radley

DO THIS TODAY: *You can't put your life on hold waitin' on somebody. Don't stop doin' the things you love with the people you love. If you missin' somebody right now, I suggest you keep livin' every day to the fullest, and leave the door open so others can join in.*

September 21st

"LEARN HOW TO GOLF."

I been known to play a few rounds of golf in my day. I like it for a lot of reasons...it's relaxin', you get to be out in the fresh air walkin' around with your friends, you can wear some fly threads too. I got myself some pink plaid pants and a mothahfuckin' sweater vest. Only place you can dress like a leprechaun on crack and nobody's gonna look at you funny. But the biggest reason I learned to play golf is that lots of business deals go down out there on the green. Connections are made, bonds get formed, and shit gets worked out. There's somethin' about bein' out there in an open field of grass that takes folks' walls down, and they can talk for real. Movie deals, contracts, all of that shit happens on the green. Just make sure you get to it before you hit the cocktails on the ninth hole. Golf is about business relationships, and that's gonna help you get where you wantin' to go.

The other thing I like about golf is it's kind of a meditation. You get out there on the green, and when you walkin' all that way, it clears your head. Then when you linin' up that drive or that putt, you got razor focus on it, and you ain't thinkin' about nothin' else. When I come off of the course, I feel like a new man, and sometimes I even walk off with answers to situations I didn't even know I was thinkin' about. Now, some of y'all might find this kinda thing when you doin' other activities—maybe hikin', bikin', runnin', or surfin'. I know other sports like that's also very meditative, but I'd bet that not too many business deals goin' down on a surfboard.

> ***I love coming in for quick pops. You come in. You score. You leave. You're on the golf course. It's great. You don't carry any story.***
>
> —Samuel L. Jackson

DO THIS TODAY: *Locate your nearest golf course and plan a time to go play a round or just hit the driving range, maybe with a few friends or coworkers. If you really can't do that, then go for a walk someplace there's grass or sand. It will get you in a similar frame of mind.*

September 22nd

"BE PREPARED TO SEE THE FOLKS CLOSEST TO YOU AT THEIR WORST."

The ones we know's gonna stand by us no matter what, love us unconditionally, those are the ones that get it bad when we dip down. For me, that person's been Rhonda since I can remember. I think I been that person for her too. If you got somebody that you love unconditionally, you probably seen 'em screamin' like a mothahfuckah, seen 'em cryin' so hard they can't breathe, heard 'em say things you hopin' Jesus ain't hearin'. You seen 'em with no makeup, wig off, dirty sweatpants and slippers, shufflin' in like they just come up offa *The Walkin' Dead*. Maybe even smellin' like it too. That's 'cuz somethin' inside of 'em snapped, they hit a low, they feelin' like hell, and they know they can let it all out around you and you still gonna love 'em.

Sometimes, they even gonna take it out on you. Maybe they ignore you, or they get on you for shit they'd normally let slide. They might call you names, yell at you, tell you to leave 'em the hell alone. If they your real one, if you both love each other without a single *got-damn* string attached, it ain't gonna matter what they say or do. You gonna be okay, just give it time and maybe a little bit of space. 'Cuz they don't mean that shit, for real. So, you gotta detach and not let it affect you. At the end of the day, they just showin' you all their ugly, and it makes your relationship stronger. If you can love 'em like that, oh brothah, you gonna love 'em like crazy when they at their best.

> ***But I have seen the best of you and the worst of you, and I choose both.***
>
> —Sarah Kay

DO THIS TODAY: *You want a piece a me? Sorry, this is a package deal. You can't separate which part of me you want to deal with and return the rest. You gotta deal with everything, the good, the bad, and the fucked up. Learn how to manage all the moving parts to build trust, happiness, and a new outlook on the situation.*

September 23rd

"SOMETIMES YOU JUST GOTTA APPRECIATE YOURSELF."

Appreciation is a funny thing. It's good to tell folks you appreciate 'em, and show 'em too. But what about your own *got-damn* self? What happens when you start to feel like you ain't appreciated? All the shit you do for folks, and this especially true once you got some of your own kids. You pretty much do everything for this tiny human that can't do shit for themselves. I ain't sayin' you don't wanna do it. Most of the time, you do. But sometimes you so tired, you just wanna lay down on the mothahfuckin' couch, eat potato chips, and watch reruns of *The Andy Griffith Show*. But naw, not tonight, brothah. You got diaper duty and laundry duty and maybe you get a couple hours of sleep in there. Then, your significant other gets up in the mornin' actin' cranky, tellin' you to hurry yo' ass up or you gonna be late to work, you feel totally and completely unappreciated. Well, lemme tell you somethin', I'm sure you's appreciated. It's just that your significant other is tired too. And the child, well they can't tell you nothin' yet.

Sometimes this happens at work too. You workin' yo' ass off, and the boss never says, "Hey, Bernie. Thanks. You doin' a great job, man." Maybe your boss is workin' his ass off too. Maybe he's tired. You lookin' for that bit of appreciation, and when it don't come, you start feelin' some kinda way. But all you gotta do is stop and think, "Am I doin' this for the praise? Or am I doin' my best for my own *got-damn* self?" The best answer is that you doin' it for yourself, 'cuz you like the feelin' of doin' your best. All you gotta do is appreciate yourself.

> ***Simply give to yourselves that which you need—which is love and appreciation without judgment.***
>
> —Réné Gaudette

DO THIS TODAY: *Are you feelin' underappreciated? Take a minute to think about all the things you appreciate about yourself.*

September 24th

"GROWIN' OLD CAN GET UGLY, BUT WHEN YOU LOVE SOMEBODY, IT'S ALL GOOD."

Growin' old is a mothahfuckah. But like my granddaddy always used to say, "It's better than the alternative." Grandpa Thurman would get up every mornin' and read the obituaries. If his name wasn't in there, then he got up from the table and got dressed for the day. Growin' old is somethin' else. He had hairs growin' out his ears and his nose and none comin' out the top of his head. His nostrils got wider, his pants got shorter, and he started complainin' about all of his aches and ailments more than he complained about "those got-damn kids today." My grandmama, she was gettin' older too. She put her teeth in a cup when she went to bed at night and woke up with her hair wrapped and her wig on the dresser. She had spindly hairs growin' outta her chin that she'd pluck with a tweezer when she remembered. Then she lost her legs to the diabetes, and she was stuck up in that wheelchair. But Big Mama and Thurman, they still held each other's hand. They played gin rummy and ate butter cookies on a Saturday night. I'd catch my granddad watchin' my grandmama leavin' the room sometimes, and I could tell he didn't care one bit about any of the stuff that changed about her. They loved one another just like they was seventeen, except maybe not so frisky, you know. That's how it's supposed to be. If you marry somebody for the right mothahfuckin' reasons, if you fall in love with the soul of the person, well, that's never gonna change. You gonna keep seein' 'em just the same way, no matter how broken, how "ugly," how wrinkled, or how ill they might become.

> ***Getting old is a fascinating thing. The older you get, the older you want to get!***
>
> —Keith Richards

DO THIS TODAY: *Imagine your life when you're old and gray. How has your physical appearance changed? You could even use one of those aging apps to get an idea. Now, visualize yourself in your life in twenty or thirty years. How are you gonna change your mindset to meet that vision of yourself as you age?*

September 25th

"FIND YOUR NATURAL FIT INSTEAD OF TRYIN' TO SQUEEZE INTO SOMEBODY ELSE'S BOX."

Worst thing you can do to yourself and the folks around you is try to stuff yo' ass into someplace you don't quite fit. It's gonna be uncomfortable at best, and it's gonna be a mothahfuckin' disaster at worst. In that kinda circumstance, you gotta ask yourself why you there in the first place. Maybe it's a job at a place that don't quite have the same values as you got. Or it could be a church, a community organization, a college, or even just a *got-damn* social group. You get in there and you try real hard to make it work. You do everything you can think of, but you never quite feel like a part of it. Maybe you feelin' on the outside, not fittin' in. Or maybe you don't wanna fit in 'cuz you really don't like those sumbitches. So, again, ask yourself, "Why am I here?" Are you goin' to that small private school in mothahfuckin' Ohio 'cuz you wantin' to make your Uncle Stanley proud? Don't do that shit. He ain't the one livin' at that place every *got-damn* day. He already done made his choices, he needs to leave you the hell alone. You workin' as an engineer 'cuz your mama told you that was a respectable job? Shoot, you gonna hate it and you gonna resent your mama. Don't try to fit the mold someone else laid down for you, 'cuz that ain't gonna be you. Then if you squeeze in there and stay there, you ain't gonna be out there lookin' for the fit that's right. You gonna get stuck, and that's the worst mothahfuckin' feelin' in the world.

> ***Stay true to yourself. An original is worth more than a copy.***
>
> —Suzy Kassem

DO THIS TODAY: *I know sometimes it feels like there's a gap between what you wanna be and what the world and other people think you should be. The pressure to "fit in" can be rough, but you can't forget who you are. What are your core values? What's most important to you in your life? Keep those goin' and you gonna be a stand-out, not a fit-in, and that's okay. What makes you unique is gonna make you successful.*

September 26th

"TODAY IS THE HISTORY OF TOMORROW."

I never set out to "change lives" and shit. I just wanted to make folks laugh, 'cuz I knew deep down that was my gift. But you're readin' this right now, so maybe I'm changin' your life for the better and a whole bunch of other ones too. Maybe when folks lookin' back they'll search up Bernie Mac history and that's what they'll find. "Bernie Mac made a difference," and shit, right next to a picture of me smilin' holdin' my *got-damn* cigar and a mothahfuckin' smile on my face.

You see, the truth is, no matter what you do right now, you're changin' lives. Maybe it starts with changin' your family's lives just by bein' born. Then as a kid maybe you make a friend or even an enemy and that's changin' other folks' lives. Then maybe you grow up to be a doctor, a video game designer, a singer, a schoolteacher, a postal carrier. Whatever you doin', it's gonna touch lives. What you're doin' every *got-damn* day, that's changin' the future. And if you doin' it big enough, thinkin' about the bigger picture sometimes, then maybe you end up part of the bigger shit they call *History* with a capital *H*.

> ***Never underestimate the valuable and important difference you make in every life you touch, for the impact you make today has a powerful rippling effect on every tomorrow.***
>
> —Leon Brown

DO THIS TODAY: *Do something out of the ordinary for somebody. Treat your coworker to lunch today, and I don't mean Mickey D's. Splurge on your partner. Or why not surprise that new high school graduate with this book to help them navigate through life's ups and downs? It's the thought that counts and the results that matter.*

September 27th

"OTHER FOLKS' ISSUES AIN'T JUST DRAMA."

Don't go tossin' somebody's issues off just 'cuz they don't seem important to you. "Oh, I don't wanna deal with your drama." Or, "I don't do drama." Her issues ain't just drama. What do you think this is, daytime television? When your niece is cryin' 'cuz her boyfriend cheated on her with the *got-damn* hostess up at Applebee's, it might seem like another episode of *Gossip Girl* to you, but to her, that shit's for real. You gotta learn how to have some mothahfuckin' empathy. If someone's comin' to you for help, maybe even just for a hug, and you wave 'em off 'cuz you ain't thinkin' their troubles is important, what kinda message is that sendin' to them? It's sayin' either, "You dumb if you got yourself worked up about that." Or, it's sayin', "I don't care enough about you to worry myself with your shit." Either one of them messages don't make her feel better, it only makes you look like a selfish, egotistical sumbitch. Are you a selfish, egotistical sumbitch? I didn't think so, so don't start actin' like one.

If somebody comin' to you with their problem you think is trivial, check yourself. When's the last time you had a tantrum 'cuz somebody kept leavin' the lights on usin' up electricity? Was that drama? When did you get upset about somethin' at work, maybe somebody ain't pullin' their weight? Was *that* drama? No? So, why's their issue drama and yours is not? Like I said, check yourself, then engage. Listen to 'em. Ask questions, then let 'em know you here for them. Sometimes that's all they need, and they gonna be okay.

> ***I need drama in my life to keep making music.***
>
> —Eminem

DO THIS TODAY: *Take the attention off of you for a minute. Do you notice the subtle signals people give when they need or want your help? Tell yourself, "It's okay for me to not think about me for a while. All my shit will still be there when I get back to it." You'll draw people closer 'cuz you've opened up your heart.*

September 28th

"MAKE SURE YOU TREATIN' YOUR TEAM LIKE THEY ALL IMPORTANT."

One of the worst mistakes you can make when you workin' with a team is to start actin' like you playin' one on five. Especially when you know damn well you couldn't win without that quick sumbitch that's runnin' point. Just 'cuz you hittin' the most slam dunks, don't mean the rest of the team is nothin'. How many of those slammers would you have hit if nobody woulda pass you the ball, mothahfuckah? Without your team, you gonna be disqualified before you even get started. It's time you began to appreciate all of the folks that's workin' together for the win. 'Cuz I'm gonna tell ya' somethin'. If you ain't with 'em when you winnin', they sure as hell ain't gonna be there for you when you lose.

Now, I ain't sayin' that you can't never be the one to call the plays. Hell, when I had the *Midnight Mac* show, had my Macaronis and the Mac Man Band, y'all can tell just by them names who was in charge up in there. Yeah, I might have been callin' the shots, but all of them knew how much I appreciated them. They could always come to me with an idea, and I'd listen. They could tell me if they had a problem and I'd try'n do somethin' about it. And I knew that we sure as hell wouldn't have a show without every one of 'em. We was a team, and that's how it's done. Same went for every time I was on a movie set or a television show. You can't even go on and film if just one of them actors don't show up. Even one of the crew. It takes all of them different talents to make it all work. You gotta respect that and act accordingly.

> ***If you want to go fast, go alone. If you want to go far, go together.***
>
> —African Proverb

DO THIS TODAY: *You gotta appreciate all the gifts your other team members bring to the table. You need all y'all to win this game. Unity is strength. How strong is your team?*

September 29th

"IT'S OKAY TO KEEP WORK RELATIONSHIPS AT WORK."

You ain't gotta be friends with your boss, your receptionist, your co-worker that always brings in the mothahfuckin' donuts. You ain't gotta invite them over for Sunday dinner, your kids' birthdays, your graduation parties, and you ain't gotta add them to your holiday card list. It's okay to set up your *got-damn* boundaries. You just gotta know where you wanna draw the line. With some folks, I like 'em enough to make it a work-and-cocktails relationship. I see you at work, and maybe after work for a drink, but that's it. If I see you outside of work or Crowley's Bar on the corner, I ain't gonna recognize you at all, mothahfuckah. I'm just gonna keep on walkin'.

Then there's a select few that I'll grab a bite with, maybe you come to our New Year's Eve party. But those folks gotta be chill, not the kind that always gotta talk shop even off the clock. Then there's the ones you meet at work, but they quickly become part of your circle 'cuz somethin' just clicks with y'all. These are the ones that you gonna stay friends even if one of you leaves the company. Thing is, you can choose where you wanna draw the line with each of 'em. But you also gotta remember that other folks is gonna draw their line too. So, don't be lookin' at somebody sideways if you don't get invited to their wedding, their gender reveal party, or their kid's bar mitzvah. It's okay.

> ***Balance is not better time management, but better boundary management. Balance means making choices and enjoying those choices.***
>
> —Betsy Jacobson

DO THIS TODAY: *Friend or acquaintance? Everybody who smiles in your face ain't your friend. You gotta know the difference. Make a mental list of your friends and acquaintances and draw that line between 'em.*

September 30th

"GRAB A DRINK OR A COFFEE WITH FOLKS WHEN YOU CAN."

If you be travelin', make sure to touch base with the folks you know who's livin' in the places you goin'. Get a cup of coffee or a drink, catch up. What they say about "it's who you know" that can make or break you, well that shit's true as a mothahfuckah. And I ain't talkin' about just higher-ups, folks with celebrity status, or the ones that can do somethin' for ya'. 'Cuz more often than not, when you get to know somebody, they still on their way up too. Or if you already up, they gonna feel good that you touchin' base with 'em. Keepin' up your relationships is part of your path to success.

You know, one time somebody I worked with out in LA come 'round to Chicago for some reason or another. He called me up, said he was here, and we played a beautiful round of golf together. You might know him—name is Samuel L. Jackson. And it's a good thing he called, 'cuz if I woulda found out he was in my city and didn't let me know, there woulda been some *got-damn* hell to pay. 'Cuz it makes ya' feel good when you get a chance to show somebody around your hood, be the host and shit. It's nice, and that's how you build solid connections with folks.

> ***I was taken by the power that savoring a simple cup of coffee can have to connect people and create community.***
>
> —Howard Schultz

DO THIS TODAY: *Start right where you are by buildin' on the relationships you already have—friends, classmates, coworkers, acquaintances. Start on Facebook, LinkedIn, Instagram, TikTok. The information you receive is crazy, from tips on job opportunities to new business connections. Also, you can catch up on where they livin' now so you can give 'em a buzz when you travelin' nearby.*

PART FOUR:
PLENTITUDE

You can have everything you want in this world. It's there and God will give to you, as long as you doin' what you need to do to make it happen for yourself.

A lot of people have this misconception that there's only so much to go around, and if they're struggling to grab what they want, it won't be there later. That couldn't be further from the truth. I know what it's like to struggle. When Bernard and I were first starting out, I was in nursing school and working at a grocery store. Bernard worked a number of different jobs, and sometimes when he was in between, it got harder than I'd like to remember. We ended up on food stamps, and I know that was a low point for Bernard. But there is no shame in getting a little bit of help when you need it, as long as you're doing everything you can.

When I got my nursing degree, I was the breadwinner for a while. That's okay, though, because that's what you do. When one of you puts down the burden for whatever reason, the other one picks it up. That's how we got through it, together. But the one thing we never lost sight of was that everything we wanted was waiting down the line, all we had to do was follow the path God had planned for us. I was good at that, and Bernard was too. He was just a little bit "bigger" about it. Nursing is a quieter profession than being a big-time comedian, but I loved it, and I was happy going to work on most days. Even when you love something, there's gonna be days when you don't wanna go. That's just being human. But overall, I had a really good career, that was my path. That and being a mom to Je'Niece and a partner to Bernard. I knew all along he was going to see his dreams come true. He had too much of himself into it for them not to. He always had a solid understanding of who he was and where he was going.

When he got there, oh boy, it took me a minute to adjust. Bernard and Je'Niece, too, I suppose. The first time I took Je'Niece to the mall and told her to pick out school clothes, she was looking at me like I was crazy. Up until then, we were shopping at discount stores. You know, we made it work. But that first mall trip was something else for Je'Niece. Then, when we moved into the nice condo downtown, Bernard wanted Je'Niece to have a driver take her to school. She wasn't too comfortable with that quite yet. It was hard for her to deal with her friends and the kids in school thinking she changed because she got money all of a sudden. She hadn't changed, but their perception of her did. That took some time for her to get used to, I know that.

When Bernard started making some money, he told me that when he made his first million dollars, I could quit my job at the psychiatric hospital. I'd worked there for a long time, and it was a good job. But now we were living out in the suburbs, and it was taking me an hour to drive to work and an hour home. I was tired. In the winter I'd be leaving in the dark and getting home in the dark too. I remember one day I was looking in one of my purses and I pulled out a couple of paychecks! Je'Niece looked at me and said, "Mama, you didn't cash those yet?" I thought to myself, *Oh, my lord. Are we doing that well that I didn't need to cash my checks?* It kind of hit me hard that maybe we were doing well enough for me to finally quit my job. After all, things were getting a bit challenging at work. I was actually hit a couple of times by patients and my nerves were wearing thin. I loved my job but I didn't like those bruises.

I told Je'Niece I was gonna talk to Bernard. I told him about my paychecks, that I forgot to cash them, and we didn't even realize the money wasn't there. Finally, I said, "You made your first million. You promised I could retire."

Can you believe he told me, "No, not yet."

I said, "What? You told me when you made that first million dollars I could quit! Well, hello, I checked the bank account and you did it!"

He again said, "Not yet. Let's build a cushion, 'cuz you never know."

I knew what he meant, as much as I hated it. I agreed because neither one of us wanted to go back to the struggle we had overcome. But Je'Niece would have none of that. She went to her father and she talked some sense into him. I retired from nursing, and wouldn't you know Bernard just kept going and going with his career. We've never had to worry about money again, thank God. It took our little Boops, who was already a woman by then, to assure us that abundance was right there for us and we didn't need to worry anymore.

Slowly but surely we began to get used to this new wealth. Bernard brought his first luxury car, a white Acura Legend. Oh, and I became a shopaholic for about six months. I ordered everything from the home shopping networks. You know, they had everything from a gadget that would peel your potatoes for you, to real cubic zirconia earrings. And you could buy it at three o'clock in the morning. Okay y'all, this was before there was such a thing as Amazon. Anyway, I know they were tired of delivering to my house. Either that or the delivery drivers must have thought I was running some kind of illegal operation or something. I finally did settle down though, once I got that outta my system.

The bottom line is, even though we had a few moments of doubt that might have held us back for a minute, ultimately we believed in the abundance that God put on this earth for us, for all of us. We had faith that we were on our path, and we kept putting one foot in front of the other. You can do the same thing too. You just need to believe it.

October 1st

"IT'S ALL RIGHT THERE FOR YOU, BUT YOU CAN'T GRAB IT IF YOU DON'T REACH OUT."

Remember the TV show *Good Times*? I loved the dad on that show. Even though the Evans family lived in the projects, he was never lazy, always kept a job, and didn't like handouts. They had enough to eat and they was happy too. Laziness can be taught, but so can ambition. One thing I can't stand is the sumbitch that's layin' around on his ass whinin' and cryin' that nothin's ever workin' out for him. Fool, nothin's workin' out for you 'cuz you ain't workin'! You sittin around on yo' ass mad as hell 'cuz your aid check is late, then you gotta be first in line at the food pantry. All that and they still only gave you a chicken, a box of Corn Flakes, and three apples. Then you had the nerve to say, "They can forget about me usin' my gas to come back here again." You sound like a got-damn *fool*. Now, I ain't talkin' about folks that's got legitimate reasons to need assistance, 'cuz they grateful for it. I'm talkin' if you able-bodied, can walk, talk, see, and hear, and you got your head on straight, ain't no reason you layin' around not workin'. I don't wanna hear about this shit no mo'. 'Cuz a free ride'll only take you right back to where you started.

Then there's the folks that go to work every day at their humdrum job, do the routine day in and day out. That guy's a good enough guy, but he just can't seem to cut a break. That's 'cuz he ain't jumpin' and leapin' outside the box, workin' extra hard to pursue somethin' he loves. If he's bored with his life and he ain't doin' nothin' to light him up inside, he ain't on his path. That's why he ain't gettin' nowhere. It's time for that sumbitch to reach higher!

> ***When you stop making excuses and you work hard and go hard, you will be very successful.***
>
> —DJ Khaled

DO THIS TODAY: *Stop that woulda, coulda, shoulda mess. Don't nobody owe you nothin'. How you gonna reach a little bit higher today? Even a baby step is settin' the gears in motion. Get off yo' ass and move.*

October 2nd

"THERE'S ALWAYS ANOTHER APPROACH. DON'T GIVE UP."

Ain't nothin' sadder than a dream that gets tossed in the trash. What a *got-damn* waste. I bet you if all of them dreams got taken out and smoothed out and rebooted, the world would be a better mothah-fuckin' place. Listen, you gonna fail. You gonna fail a lot, and that's okay. It's a good thing. 'Cuz every time you fail it makes you rethink the way you goin' about it. Gettin' mad and quittin', that's like that sumbitch that would stomp off the basketball court when you was a kid 'cuz he ain't kickin' your ass. He's sayin' you cheatin' and shit, sayin', "Imma take my ball and go home." Let's see where that li'l punk is today. Probably shootin' hoops all by his damn self, still livin' at his mama's house.

Thing is, we get so set in our plan sometimes that we forget there's more than one way to do things. In fact, there's probably an infinite number of mothahfuckin' ways to do shit. You just gotta start openin' up to 'em. I know, we start in school learnin' that there's this way and you gotta do it this way or you not gonna pass the test. Well, this ain't school no more, mothah-fuckah. This real life up in here. In real life there ain't no wrong and no right, it's just, "Do it line up with who I am and my purpose?" That's what's right. You fall down, you think if you still on the track. If you still on the track, you get up and jump them hurdles.

> ***When it is obvious a goal cannot be reached, don't adjust your goal, adjust your action steps to reach it.***
>
> —Confucius

DO THIS TODAY: *Do you have a goal that feels like it's just outta reach? Do you feel stuck? Maybe you need to change your approach. Try aiming high but starting low. Take small steps then slowly increase. Make sure you have a clear goal and know what you want. Without a clear goal, you can't put together a clear plan to achieve it.*

October 3rd

"YOU GOTTA ENJOY THE FRUITS OF YOUR LABOR. AIN'T NO SHAME IN THAT."

Psalms 128:2 from the New Living Translation says, "You will enjoy the fruit of your labor. How joyful and prosperous you will be." *Hallelujer!* Ain't that the truth? Now, your first priority is to do what sets your soul on fire. All the wonderful shit that flows into you because you doin' everything right, that's like residuals. But it can be some fine things, and you ought to enjoy 'em.

I remember when Rhonda and Je'Niece and I were lookin' to move to a bigger house in the suburbs. I was drivin' around with Dollah, my driver, and we went to go look at this house. When the real estate agent let us in, right there in the foyer was a massive bear! He was dead, stuffed, you know. But damn, we bought that house and I wanted the owner to leave the bear, but he wouldn't let it go. I told Dollah I was gonna get me a lion. That would be the shit. A month later I called him up and he couldn't believe, I told him I got it. Okay, I might have been pullin' his chain on that one, but I did get me a nice house, nice car, and once I made my first million, Rhonda retired from her job up at the psychiatric hospital. We had everything we needed and most of what we wanted, and we was helpin' folks when we could. I did not feel bad about any of it 'cuz Rhonda and me, we worked hard for everything we got. Now, that don't mean I was too big to take home the ketchup packets from Red Lobster. You gotta be smart about shit, you know?

> ***Certain things should be yours to have when you work your way to the top.***
>
> —Redd Foxx

DO THIS TODAY: *A farmer don't plant a seed and walk away. He waters it, takes care of it, and it grows. Then he harvests the got-damn* **results**. *You ain't seein' no farmer lettin' their crop rot in the mothahfuckin' field. You feel me? You deserve everything you got when you work hard for it. Find a way to enjoy the fruits of your labor.*

October 4th

"DON'T ASK WHAT YOU WANNA BE, ASK YOURSELF WHAT IS YOUR PURPOSE."

Before you even goin' to kindergarten, big folks is askin' you, "What do you wanna be when you grow up?" You're five years old, how many things you think you know there even is to be at five years old? If you grow up in the hood, you gonna be like, "A policeman, a fireman, a pastor, a bus driver, or a mothahfuckin gangster." Or you gonna be whatever your folks is. But what I want to know is how come nobody ever asks you as a little kid, "What's your purpose?" You know why, 'cuz yo' parents was still tryin' to figure out their purpose. They don't know, they tryin' to survive every day robbin' Peter to pay Paul takin' care of yo' ass. I heard my boy Nick Cannon once say: "My vocation is my vacation. I love what I do." Now that's what's up. To me that's knowin' your purpose. You gots to find what you love to do. Here's how you know when you've found your purpose. You'll do that shit for free. That's right, I said for free, that's how much you love it. Ain't nobody gotta force you to go to work, yo' ass will be the first one there and the last one to leave. You'll be lighting up that place with so much positive energy, folks gon' swear you high as hell. But you on a natural high and that shit is contagious. It's good for inspiring others. So follow your heart's desires. That is where your blessings lie also.

> ***When you are deciding on next steps, next jobs, next careers, further education, you should rather find purpose than a job or a career.***
>
> —Chadwick Aaron Boseman

DO THIS TODAY: *Go get that damn shovel, 'cuz you gotta dig deep. Take a look inside of yourself and go deeper. Now ask yourself what really makes you happy? Can you feel it? You should be able to see it clearly. Once you identify that feeling, what made you feel it, that's your purpose. Now, run with it.*

October 5th

"CELEBRATE!"

I ain't sayin' this shit just because today is my birthday. Okay, maybe I am, but what's it to ya'? It's my birthday and if I wanna celebrate, that's my *prerogative*. But if y'all wanna just take a moment to think about how blessed this earth became when I was put on it, go on right ahead and do that now.... Alright, that's good.

I know we always celebratin' birthdays and holidays, even them ones that's made up like National Muffin Day and shit. It's fun and all that jazz. Holidays are great times for traditions and gatherin' together, feelin' special. But what I'm tellin' you ain't necessarily about that kind of celebrations. Listen up, I'm tellin' you this: don't work so hard that you forget to celebrate your victories. You know, like a high five and a chest bump when MJ hits the three at the buzzer! There's always gonna be another game, a championship playoff, a next season. It's easy to keep your head down and keep lookin' toward the next goal. But you gotta take that minute to celebrate your successes along the way, or you might just get so run down from workin' all the *got-damn* time. Could you even imagine an NBA game where the players didn't jump up and down, fist bump, and slap each other on the ass? What a borin' mothahfuckin' game, then. Nobody would watch it. But when they're out there pumpin' each other up, pumpin' up the crowd, it elevates all of that energy around 'em. Sometimes, that energy makes the win.

> ***Once you start celebrating the little victories in life, you will realize just how infinite they truly are.***
>
> —Alicia Emamdee

DO THIS TODAY: *Create a new birthday tradition and write it on your calendar so you don't forget. Use the day as an opportunity to celebrate all of your successes throughout the year, then make a wish and set your focus on where you hope to be by this time next year.*

October 6th

"SOMETIMES YOU DON'T KNOW WHAT YOU GOT 'TIL YOU AIN'T GOT IT NO MORE."

It shouldn't take losin' somethin' for you to appreciate it. But honestly, that's the case for most folks and a lotta things. I bet you takin' the air you breathe for granted until your jackass brother holds your head under water until your eyes bug outta your head. That's right, I'm speakin' from experience. I never begged Darryl to take me back to the community pool again. But I had a newfound appreciation for air, that's fo' sho'.

Back then things was tight, so we looked for different ways to have fun. For example, my mama couldn't afford to get us all bikes, so my cousin had to share her bike with me. Why you laughin'? I ain't had no problem with that, I was all li'l man. Just 'cuz that bike was pink with a white basket with flowers on it and that long-ass yellow banana seat, that didn't mean nothin'. Shit, that bike was my motor coach, my Buick deuce and a quarter. That bad boy took me everywhere. I made it the "in thing" to ride a girl bike in my neighborhood. But that all changed the day my cousin left the bike on the damn driveway and a car rode right over it. My bike was destroyed, demolished, fucked up. *Got-damn*, I'm sweatin' now even thinkin' about it. That bike was my first love. I cried more than my cousin. That ugly-ass cry too, 'cuz I knew we wasn't gettin' another bike. But I knew then and there that if I ever got my own got-damn *bike*, I'd never leave it on the mothahfuckin' driveway.

> ***When the well's dry, we know the worth of water.***
>
> —Benjamin Franklin

DO THIS TODAY: *Try not usin' somethin' today that you use all the* ***got-damn*** *time. Maybe it's your car, or your coffee pot, your computer, phone, or TV. Maybe it's the hot water in your shower. Or maybe you don't call that friend you talk to every day. See how it feels to do without it for a day, and maybe you appreciate it a little more tomorrow.*

October 7th

"GRATITUDE BRINGS ALL THE BLESSIN'S TO THE YARD."

Remember every year when you was in grade school, you'd have to make a placemat with all of the things you thankful for written on all them different colored leaves, or the feathers of a handprint turkey, or a Pilgrim hat? Yeah, every kid's is pretty much the same: I'm thankful for Mama, Big Mama, cookies, my pet frog Princess, ice cream, God. You know, standard thankful list kinda stuff. It was cute, and it kinda got us thinkin' about the folks and the things in our lives that made us happy. But the problem is then we get older, and we still just rattlin' off "thankful lists." Okay, it's not like doin' that's a bad thing, but it ain't gonna help you in the same way that real gratitude will.

Real gratitude will change a sumbitch at his very core, and it'll change yo' life. Real gratitude don't leave you feelin' like you owe somebody somethin', it makes you feel connected to 'em in a deeper way. Real gratitude feels good. It's all about creating a cycle of good that brings everybody on up together. 'Cuz you know what? Doin' good for you, that makes the other person feel good too. It's a win-win situation. So if somebody wants to hold the damn door for you, or help you out with a project, or give you a ride, accept that shit with appreciation in your heart. Gratitude creates latitude.

> ***Be thankful for what you have; you'll end up having more.***
>
> —Oprah

DO THIS TODAY: *Tune in to everyday details of your life and notice the good things you might sometimes take for granted, like Mr. Andrews who always gets your mail for ya' or those beautiful flowers growin' under your window, the sound of smooth jazz on the radio, or your warm cozy bed at night. It's amazin' what you start to notice when you focus on feelin' grateful.*

October 8th

"ALL YOU GOTTA DO IS TAKE ONE STEP AT A TIME, OTHERWISE YOU GONNA TRIP."

When you in the army you learn real quick how to take one step at a time. You hear that mothahfuckin sergeant shout, "ATTENTION! Forward, march. Left, left, left, right, left." Mess that shit up and yo' ass is doin' a hundred pushups. Not only you, but the entire platoon. They gonna fuck yo' skinny ass up latah with the rock socks for that shit. But why they takin' all of that so serious? 'Cuz you gotta learn how to take one mothahfuckin' step at a time, that's why.

You ever try to take two or three steps at once? You gonna fall on yo' ass like a mothahfuckah. Settle the hell down. Where you tryin' to get to so fast you gotta go leapin' all over the *got-damn* place like a ballerina on crack? Shit, if you go takin' too many steps at once, you might end up gettin' where you wanna go eventually, but you gonna drag yo' ass through the door all beat up and bruised. You gonna feel like you been hit by a truck and dragged through the *got-damn* mud. But if you take one step at a time, follow the path, and watch for the next foothold, you gonna get there. Trust that, and you will. It took me two mothahfuckin' decades to really hit my stride, and look at how that done for me. So, put your shoes on 'cuz it's time to get steppin', and I don't mean my smooth Chi-Town steppin', you know we smokin' on the dance flo'. Naw, it's time for you to take three steps forward and no steps back.

> ***You don't have to see the whole staircase, just take the first step.***
>
> —Rev. Dr. Martin Luther King, Jr.

DO THIS TODAY: *First, remove any blocks from the past where you were hurt, or you fucked up and it still bothers you. Second, take time to heal and repair. Third, move forward. Forgive yourself, don't push yourself too hard or too fast, and accept where you at right now. You stand a better chance of success 'cuz you focused and movin' in one direction.*

October 9th

"YOU CAN'T LIVE IN ABUNDANCE IF YOU ALWAYS THINKIN' YOU AIN'T GOT NOTHIN'."

It's time to train your brain to start thinkin' everything is there for you, instead of moanin' and groanin' about the shit you don't have. If I'd have done that, I bet you dollars to donuts that I woulda never accomplished half the shit that I did. 'Cuz brothah, if you think you ain't got nothin', I bet you I had more nothin' than you have...or at least the same amount of nothin'. We was so poor, we was told the music from the ice cream truck was the sound of the Devil's henchmen comin' to snatch up naughty children. *Got-dammit*, I spent half my childhood summers hidin' in my closet, just 'cuz my granddaddy didn't wanna fork over no quarter for mothahfuckin' Push-Up Pops. But you know what? I never really thought about the fact that we was poor. We had enough to eat, mostly. But we made up for any emptiness in our bellies by puttin' laughter in there. A good laugh tasted better than any old Push-Up anyway.

Thing is, if I was sittin' around moanin' and groanin' all the time about what I didn't have, I'd have been a miserable sumbitch. That's called livin' with a lack mindset. You start doin' that, and that's what you gonna have—an abundance of lack. Ya' see, whatever you thinkin' about most, that shit is gonna manifest in your life, so you bettah make damn sure you thinkin' about the positive.

> ***The mind has a powerful way of attracting things that are in harmony with it, good and bad.***
>
> —Idowu Koyenikan

DO THIS TODAY: *Fill your mind with thoughts of abundance, success, love, happiness, wealth, time, anything you desire. Know that it's all already there for you. Go put your rose-colored glasses on so you can see it.*

October 10th

"THE MORE YOU DO FOR OTHER FOLKS, THE MORE YOU GONNA GET BLESSED."

What does the Bible say? Give and it shall be given to you. That's right, God said the way you gonna get shit is by givin' it away first. I know, if you tryin' to use logic, it don't make no sense. But this ain't logic, this is above all of that. This is God, and He don't play. Well, Luke may have said it, but it's the words of God, and still…He don't play. You can see it right there, He's tellin' you straight up that you start givin', you gonna get it back and for real. And when God gives gifts, it's gonna be bigger than what you gave, you can bet yo' ass on that one.

But here's where it gets tricky. You can't give with your hand out. That's not the right *got-damn* attitude. You gotta bless folks without expectations of nothin' in return. You gotta give with a good heart, 'cuz you want to help and you a generous sumbitch. You can't expect nothin' comin' right back from the person you givin' somethin' to. Hell, naw. That ain't how it works. You just gotta trust that God and the Universe is gonna provide for you in some kinda way when the time is right. So, while you knowin' you gonna receive from givin', you can't start doin' it for that reason. It's kinda like when you a kid and you go visit that lonely old neighbor of yours, but you only goin' for the butterscotch candies he always got in a dish by the couch. It's nice he gets a visit, but you ain't gettin' the same thing out of it as if you goin' just 'cuz you care. So you gotta give with the right intentions, then you gonna set yourself up to receive.

> ***When you focus on being a blessing, God makes sure that you are always blessed in abundance.***
>
> —Joel Osteen

DO THIS TODAY: *Think about why you doin' the nice stuff you been doin'. Is it for the praise? Is it to get somethin' back? Start helpin' folks anonymously so you get the feelin' of doin' good just for the sake of doin' good.*

October 11th

"DO WHAT YOU LOVE, 'CUZ THAT'S WHAT'S GONNA GET YOU EVERYTHING YOU NEED."

When I say everything, I don't really mean everything...like everything in the whole mothahfuckin' world. That would be impossible. I mean that when you're groovin' in the path that God laid out for you, and you doin' it 'cuz you been watchin' for all the signs and the open doors and you been workin' your ass off, then you gonna end up bein' surrounded by an abundance of all the good things you wish for yourself. It might take some time, but that's okay, 'cuz you trust that it's comin'. In the meantime, you feelin' okay 'cuz you doin' what you love, so you been havin' a good time without all the other stuff. You got an abundance of joy floodin' through yo' ass, and damn, that makes you rich as a mothahfuckah.

When you feelin' rich without all the material things, you livin' in the mindset of abundance, and guess what? That's when you gonna start reelin' in more abundance. I know it don't seem fair, it's like you gotta have some to get some, but that's the *got-damn* way that it works. But the good thing is that doin' what you love is free as my cousin Abraham on a Saturday night. Havin' that feelin' that you content and got everything you need, that's free too. That's all you need, and that all comes natural when you livin' your passion, 'cuz that shit's your gift, and God intended for you to use it. That's gonna keep you on the path, and that path is paved with mothahfuckin' gold.

> ***Doing what you love is the cornerstone of having abundance in your life.***
>
> —Wayne W. Dyer

DO THIS TODAY: *Wanna stop workin'? Then do what you love and you'll be gettin' paid but never* **workin'** *a day in your life. Live for your truth and be consistent with who you really are. Do not wonder for another damn moment what your life would be like if you lived your passion. Instead, identify the first step right now to go out there and start livin' it.*

October 12th

"ABUNDANCE OF EVERYTHING'S LIKE A NATURAL RESOURCE THAT AIN'T EVER GONNA DRY UP."

I know a lot of folks that get frustrated when they seein' other folks succeed. Jealousy is a mothahfuckah fo' sho'. But it ain't always jealousy that makes 'em upset. You see, we been trained to think that some folks get the goods and others get left dry. We been raised up to think that if there's a whole lotta folks around the dinner table, there won't be any biscuits left for you. That's the wrong way to think, 'cuz the abundance that's out there in this Universe, it ain't like biscuits. You ain't gonna get to the bottom and nothin' left but crumbs, then you lookin' at yo' brothah side-eyed 'cuz that sumbitch took two. Naw, that basket of biscuits just keeps on refillin' itself.

I remember when I was a kid, I was at a church picnic and there was a table full of desserts. Oh boy, made my mouth water. But I couldn't have none 'til I finished my dinner, then I got into a game of kickball and I forgot. When I finally made it back there, all that was left was three molasses cookies and I could see some of the other kids comin'. I grabbed up them cookies and stepped aside, thinkin' I'd won. Then my little heart dropped into my stomach—here comes Sister Ophelia with a big ole tray of sliced chocolate cake. She looked at me and says, "Uh, uh, Bean. You got all them cookies." I shoulda been patient and shoulda trusted that there was gonna be more desserts, maybe taken one cookie and then I coulda got that cake too. You see what I'm sayin'? The dessert table's always gonna get refilled, so settle yo' ass down and don't go grabbin' everything you can.

> ***When people are genuinely happy at the successes of others, the pie gets larger.***
>
> —Stephen Covey

DO THIS TODAY: *Are you confident that the Universe has more than enough of everything for every soul on it? It's like a big buffet, and every time somebody takes a plate, it gets refilled straight away, for real. You just gotta believe it.*

October 13th

"IF YOU WANT IT, YOU GOT TO KNOW THAT YOU DESERVE IT 100 PERCENT."

In order for things to line up for you to receive the things that you want, you gotta know that you deserve 'em. I ain't talkin' in a selfish kinda way. I'm talkin' you know that you done everything you needed to do, and that as a human bein', you deserve what this world has to offer you. 'Cuz lemme tell you somethin', if you don't think you deserve it, you sure as hell ain't gonna get it. That's how it works.

I remember when Je'Niece was little and I was workin' hard at my day job, then goin' to the club to do open mic comedy at night. I came home exhausted, but Rhonda got up and she made me somethin' to eat. She was tired, too, workin' as a nurse all day and takin' care of Boops, that's what we called her. I wrapped my arms around my wife and said, "Baby, I don't deserve you." She backed the hell up and wrinkled up her face. "You sure as hell do," she said. "Why would I want somebody that didn't deserve me? You think I'm somebody who'd settle?" I never thought of it that way before, but I did from then on. Whenever somethin' comes to me, I know I deserve it. That's the kinda confident you gotta be in yourself. Just like I know I deserve to be a bestsellin' author 'cuz I put down the foundation, you gotta know you deserve to be and have whatever the hell it is you wanna be and have 'cuz you did the work too.

> ***You were created in the image and likeness of God. So you share the Divine qualities of love, abundance, health, beauty, and goodness. We all do.***
>
> —Doreen Virtue

DO THIS TODAY: *Imagine you at a family dinner, table full of good ole soul food dressin', sweet potatoes and collard greens. Now, ask yourself if everybody standin' around that table deserves to eat. Y'all thanked the Lord for blessin' that food to all y'all bodies, includin' yours. Everybody's deservin' of abundance.*

October 14th

"APPRECIATE THE DOWN TIME FOR WHAT IT IS AND MOVE ON."

Y'all, I hate to say this, but I was not a big fan of livin' in LA. I'm a Chicago man at the core of my bein'. But one of the reasons I didn't like it might be a little bit surprisin'. You know how they say it's beautiful out there, seventy-three degrees and sunny every day. They's right. Seventy-three degrees and sunny every mothahfuckin' day. When I was out there long, long stretches at a time shootin' the TV show, I found myself prayin' for a rainstorm that never did come. I used to enjoy the rainy days when you had a good excuse to just stay in and do nothin' much. You see, when you live in the Midwest, we got the rain and the snow and the sleet and maybe you complain about it a little bit when it gets too much, but then the sun comes out and everything's beautiful again. Damn, that makes it worth it.

When you got a time in your life that's not goin' so good, you gettin' down on yourself, or maybe it's just a little bit stagnant and you feel like you just coastin' along, that's just a mothahfuckin' rainy day. You gotta grab yo' blankets and a book and make the best of it, learn what you gotta learn, and relax into it. Know that the sun's gotta come out again, and when it does, boy, it's gonna feel so good. And that rain, shoot, it made the flowers pop up and bloom like somethin' else.

> ***Unless you have bad times, you can't appreciate the good times.***
>
> —Joe Torre

DO THIS TODAY: *Think of a time that you went through a rough patch and somethin' good came out on the other side. Remember no storm lasts forever. Keep shinin' yo' light. You got this!*

October 15th

"WHEN YOU CAN SEE IT YOU CAN BELIEVE IT, AND WHEN YOU BELIEVE IT YOU CAN ACHIEVE IT."

You know a lot of folks, that'll have them "dream boards" and shit. They take some big piece of paper and cut out pictures of what they want their life to be like, the things they wanna have, and stick 'em on there kinda like a *got-damn* collage. Maybe they put a yacht on there, an office with big windows, a pretty lady and some pretty kids, stacks of money. Whatever it is, they'd be puttin' that on there so they can look at it all the time. I used to think they was some crazy sumbitches, but now I understand where they comin' from. When you can see somethin' so clear, it's like you lookin' into the future, and you can really start feelin' it comin'.

Now, I ain't doin' no arts and crafts and shit. That just ain't my thing. But I'd lay in my bed at night, or if I'm drivin' a long way in the car or I'm out on the golf course, and I'd imagine that shit in my head. Sometimes if it's before bed, I end up dreamin' it. Then I wake up and I'm wonderin' if that was a dream or did that shit really happen? That's when you know it's comin' up for you, for real. You can see it like that, and you start believin' in it. You know it's on your path and then suddenly the steps to get there start to kinda unfold in front of you and you take 'em, 'cuz you can see the destination right up there ahead of you.

> ***Dreams are the things which we conceive, and we can achieve them if only we would believe.***
>
> —Sai Marie Johnson

DO THIS TODAY: *The Dollar General's got poster boards, so go get yours. No joke, that vision-board shit really works. You ain't gotta tell nobody what you doin', either. Build your vision board and put it in a place where you can see it everyday. A closet, behind your bathroom door, next to your bed. You'll manifest best when you see it, 'cuz you'll start to believe it.*

October 16th

"IF YOU WANNA SUCCEED IN BUSINESS, YOU GOTTA FILL A GAP THAT NEEDS FILLIN'."

You could make the most amazin' mothahfuckin widget in the whole *got-damn* world, I mean that sumbitch does twenty-seven things at once, don't need no charge-up and fits in your *got-damn* pocket. But if nobody wants it, if it costs too much money, or if there's already something out there that's workin' just fine, you ain't gonna be able to sell it to save your life. You gotta bring things to the world that the world's been needin' or wantin', or somethin' that's gonna catch folks' eyes and make 'em realize they never knew they needed it before, but now they do!

One thing I love about comedy is that folks always wanna be entertained, it's a never-endin' demand. It ain't like, "Oh, hell. I laughed my ass off yesterday, so I don't need to laugh no more. I'm good." Mothahfuckah, folks wanna keep on laughin'. They gonna keep on goin' to the movies, listenin' to music and podcasts, readin' books, all of that. Even when times is rough, they wanna be entertained to escape. When times is good, they do it to celebrate. So, I'm glad to do what I do, 'cuz that gap ain't never gonna be completely filled. I just keep pourin' and pourin'. There's other kinda things like that too. Food is one of 'em, folks always gotta eat. Funeral homes is another one. What? That shit's the truth right there, for real. Just look for the need or the want, and fill it and *boom*, you gonna be successful.

> ***Progress isn't made by early risers. It's made by lazy men trying to find easier ways to do something.***
>
> —Robert A. Heinlein

DO THIS TODAY: *Let's say you could put anything out into the world right now, what would it be? Tap into your imagination and see what you come up with. Ask yourself, "Who needs this in their life right now?" Define your market, and do it for them, then take the risk. 'Cuz now you ain't doin' it just for you, and that's gonna be a key to your success.*

October 17th

"SOMETIMES YOU GOTTA TAKE WHAT'S ON THE TABLE AND BE GRATEFUL, THAT'LL GET YOU STARTED."

All or nothin'? That's a bunch of bullshit, lemme tell ya' that right now. If my grandmama offered me a piece of chocolate cake after Sunday dinner, and I told her, "Yeah, but all or nothin', Big Mama." You bet yo' ass it'd be nothin'. You take what's bein' offered, and you appreciate it. You do that, and you gonna be offered some more at some point. That's how it works. Now, let's go back to the cake. My grandmama offers me a slice and I say, "Yes, please." Then I eat that cake and I say, "Wow, Big Mama, that's the best cake I ever had. I appreciate you." She gonna feel good, and maybe she gonna offer you an extra slice too. Even if she don't, that's okay, 'cuz everybody's feelin' good now and you got a belly full of cake.

But what if you don't like what's on the table? Well, I ain't tellin' you to take that. Leave it the hell alone, it ain't meant for you. There's somebody else that loves what's bein' served, so let 'em have it. They gonna appreciate it a helluva lot more. That's not the shit I'm talkin' about. I'm talkin' about the chocolate cake. Think about it like this: if I'd have turned it down when I was asked to to comedy at the funerals, or at the little dive clubs in the city 'cuz they was too small, then I'd have never gotten the bigger gigs. When it comes to doin' what you love, there ain't no small offers, only egos too big to take 'em.

> ***Take what is offered and that must sometimes be enough.***
>
> —Richard K. Morgan

DO THIS TODAY: *You gotta play the hand that you been dealt. It's time for you to accept the cards and figure out how to use 'em to your advantage. Acceptance is faith that you goin' the right way toward happiness. Know that when this hand's played, there's gonna be another round. How you gonna play?*

October 18th

"IF YOU DON'T HAVE IT, DO WITHOUT."

This was a piece of advice my mama used to give me, and she was right. You go without somethin' for a while and you realize you doin' okay with what you got. I think we get so used to havin' all the extras, the luxuries, that we forget there's a whole lotta shit we can do without. Remember when we used to have a phone that stuck to the wall with a cord? I think we paid nine dollahs a month, and if you charged up the long distance, you was gonna get yo' ass whooped. We didn't need no cell phones payin' four hundred dollahs a month and shit. We didn't have no cable TV, streamin' service, radio you can talk to and shit. Didn't have no video games. We didn't have no four cars a family. You had one car, and your cousins and uncles all come over to use it too. We didn't have no closets full of clothes. We had one outfit for school, one for church, and one for play. And lawd if you didn't change into your play clothes after school, and Big Mama catches you out in the street playin' stickball in your school clothes, you gonna need new pants 'cuz she gonna beat yo' ass 'til it come right through. But my point is that we got so much *got-damn* shit nowadays that we can get along just fine without. I know, 'cuz I did it. So instead of borrowin' money you ain't got, instead of rackin' up credit cards, try just gettin' along with the things you need and a few of the things you want. Chances are, you gonna feel a little freer like that, anyways.

> ***Blessed is he who expects nothing, for he shall never be disappointed.***
>
> —Alexander Pope

DO THIS TODAY: *Make a list of things you been wishin' for and divide it into needs (the shit you can't survive without, for real) and wants (anything else). It's gonna become clear real quick.*

October 19th

"YOU GOTTA STOP THINKIN' YOU A DIME A DOZEN AND START THINKIN' YOU ONE IN A MILLION."

If you go through life thinkin' like, "Who am I to think I am as funny as Richard Pryor?" Or whatever it is you thinkin', you ain't never gonna be what it is you wanna be. Period. You might be thinkin' everybody's got the same idea as you, the same invention, the same singin' voice, the same talent for cookin' crepes, but what if they don't? What if yours is just a little bit better, but you didn't even try 'cuz you thought you was just the same amount of good as the other folks doin' it? You gotta know that even when there's folks that's good, you can both be good in a different kinda way.

Redd Foxx, Richard Pryor, Jackie Gleason, they was all some of my heroes and my idols growin' up. Man, them sumbitches was so funny, they coulda caused me to wanna stop my career in my tracks, thinkin' I'll never be as good as them. But I didn't do that, 'cuz I knew it wasn't about bein' better than them, it was about bein' me. I didn't need to be Richard Pryor 2.0, I just had to be Bernie Mac. And I stuck to my guns on that, even when I was makin' the leap from the Chitlin' Circuit to the mainstream. They wanted to smooth me out, but soft Bernie was not gonna cut it. Bernie Mac without the *got-damn asshole mothahfuckah* wouldn't be Bernie Mac, and that woulda took away my *one-in-a-millionness*. And that thing you got that's makin' you just you, it's your gift so don't let that shit go.

> ***Ride the energy of your own unique spirit.***
>
> —Gabrielle Roth

DO THIS TODAY: *Create your own path, connect with who you really are. Your dreams, likes, and dislikes. No more assumin' shit based on what "the world" wants you to do. When you connect with your true self, you'll be a pro at choosin' your own path in a real and honest way.*

October 20th

"SHARE YOUR GIFTS WITH THE WORLD."

You could have the best mothahfuckin' singin' voice on the *got-damn* planet, but how you gonna get blessed if all you doin' is singin' in the shower? You gotta get it out there and share it with the world, otherwise it's just gonna go to waste. You know what happens to a wasted talent? It turns into a dead weight that holds you down while you tryin' to swim to the top.

There was this woman, she sang in the choir at the Burning Bush Baptist Church where my granddaddy was deacon. Her voice was sweet as hell, brought tears to your eyes. It was full of all the feelin's, sorrow and joy and everythin' in between. Sometimes I only went to church just to hear her sing. I thought, boy, that woman was blessed, and she was. She had this gift and *got-damn* it was powerful. She shared it with the church folks, but that was about it. I don't know why she didn't take it no further than that. Maybe she had some shit goings *on* inside of her that made her think she couldn't or shouldn't do nothin' else with it, like a recordin' deal or workin' on the stage and shit. Maybe she had low self-esteem, maybe she had a fear of success or was thinkin' money was the devil's work, who the hell knows. But I found out later that she was so poor, she was gettin' her food from the church pantry and ended up livin' in the shelter. Now, why the hell she couldn't use that gift to lift herself up outta there, I wish I knew. You don't wanna go and waste your gifts like that. Use 'em. That's why God gave 'em to you.

> ***Why hide your talent in the closet of complacency when you have greatness within you?***
>
> —Robin Sharma

DO THIS TODAY: *We're all born with gifts, it's just that some folks never open their package. What are you afraid of? Be afraid and do it anyway. Make a commitment to open your gift to the world.*

October 21st

"YOUR FAITH'S GOTTA BE BIGGER THAN YOUR FEARS."

Havin' faith means you got complete and total trust, so much that you hold somethin' to be true even if you can't see it, touch it, taste it, hear it. You just know it. You gotta have that kinda faith that everything is workin' out exactly as it's supposed to. I think that's why folks need religion in their lives, they need God, and it don't really matter which religion it is at the end of the day. I ain't gonna get into that. But what it gives you is a belief that no matter what happens, it's gonna be alright. It's that kinda faith that gives folks hope even in the face of fear. It's the mothahfuckin' light at the end of the tunnel. If you can see that, you know you gonna be okay. And that dark spot can be scary as hell if you can't see no light at all. You ever been alone in the dark in a place that you know some bad shit has happened, like the mothahfuckin' alley behind Tony's Pizza where Crazy Jimmy got mugged last week? Yeah, you be shakin', nothin' but yo' white-ass teeth chatterin' in the dark.

That faith is somethin' bigger than yourself, and it's givin' you both the light and the hand to hold in the mothahfuckin' dark. You ain't gonna feel alone if you got God sittin' there with you. I'd rather have Him than some sumbitch that's also scared as hell, shakin', tryin' to hold onto you with his clammy-ass hand. I mean, I ain't sayin' I wouldn't help that sumbitch too. But I'd be like, "Hey, Buddy. Here's God and He's right here for ya'. He's all powerful, all seein', and He knows the way. So, hold His hand and shit."

> ***Never allow your faith to fail.***
>
> —Donnie McClurkin

DO THIS TODAY: *Before you even start your day, I want you to say to yourself, "Everything's always workin' out for me," and believe it like you never believed nothin' else in the world. It's workin' just how it's supposed to work. Trust the process and you gonna like the results.*

October 22nd

"TIME DON'T MEAN NOTHIN', SO STOP WORRYIN' ABOUT IT."

You ain't gotta be on anybody else's timeline but your own, *got-dammit*. Who's to say you gotta be outta yo' mama's house at eighteen, graduatin' college at twenty-two, and successful in your career by the time you thirty, married with some kids and shit? If you tryin' to fit yourself into that kinda box, all you doin' is settin' yo'self up for disappointment. It's gonna make you anxious, depressed, and frustrated as hell if you ain't hittin' them marks. But who set them marks? It sure as hell weren't God, 'cuz He knows everybody's movin' at their own mothahfuckin' pace.

Listen, do a tree take the same amount of time to grow as a dandelion? Do a baby horse grow up and start walkin' on its own at the same *got-damn* age as a baby human? Nature don't get that shit wrong. And that dandelion ain't gonna look at that tree and feel some kinda way about it, and that tree ain't throwin' no shade. Hell, naw...and no pun intended. They just do what they do and they don't care about what nobody else is doin'. That's none of they business. Just like what "everybody else" is doin' is none of your *got-damn* business. Time don't mean shit, and as soon as you start rushin' 'cuz you think you gotta make some kinda life deadline, that's when you start makin' mistakes. My mama, she'd say, "Measure twice, cut once."

> ***If a man does not keep pace with his companions, perhaps it is because he hears a different drummer. Let him step to the music which he hears, however measured or far away.***
>
> —Henry David Thoreau

DO THIS TODAY: *Don't let society's timelines fuck up your thinkin'. The truth is there is no "right way" and there is no perfect timeline. Are you confident that you're on your path, and that everything's gonna work out? Make your own timeline.*

October 23rd

"DON'T GO MESSIN' SHIT UP. JUST LET IT BE."

I remember bein' in the kitchen when I was a kid and my grandmama's cookin' some gumbo or somethin', and it smells good up in there. And she's got all them bottles and cans of spices and shit, and she'd be pourin' this and dashin' that, and my stomach's rumblin'. Then I hear, "Good Lawd Jesus Mary and Joseph!" That's Big Mama's way of cussin'. She done wrecked the soup 'cuz she's puttin' too much of this or that, maybe shook a little more pepper than she shoulda, or salt. It was good as it was, all she had to do was let that shit simmer. Now everybody gonna be chokin' it down, drinkin' milk and shit to stop the burnin' in their mouth. Then maybe next time she makes the gumbo, nobody's gonna trust it. They gonna think twice before takin' a bite.

We do that shit, though. All the mothahfuckin' time. We get onto somethin' that's good, somethin' that's workin', and then we try to add more and more and more, and we end up fuckin' it up. Maybe we just get too excited, and the good ideas is rollin' off one after another. Sure, all of them might be good ideas, but do they all go in the same *got-damn* pot? No, they do not. If you got somethin' that's workin', leave it the hell alone and let it work. Then, when the time is right, you get out that other idea and start a new pot cookin'. That way you always gonna have somethin' on the stove, and it's all gonna be delicious.

> ***Let things flow naturally forward in whatever way they like.***
>
> —Lao Tzu

DO THIS TODAY: *Listen to the song "Take Your Time" by the S.O.S. Band! Now, S-l-o-w t-h-e f-u-c-k d-o-w-n. Period. You mess shit up when you zoomin' all over the place. Still yourself and make a commitment to handle things one at a time. You'll get far better results that way.*

October 24th

"IT'S THE SMALL THINGS YOU DO UNDERNEATH THE RADAR THAT MAKE A DIFFERENCE."

In this day and age, seems like everybody's broadcastin' every mothahfuckin' thing they doin'. "Went to the gym today, benched 230. Back day!" Why do I need to know that shit? I used to go to the gym, didn't want nobody to see me. I'd sneak the hell in, do my shit, and get the hell out. Didn't wanna talk to nobody, and I sure as hell didn't want nobody to see a picture of me in my sweaty-ass shirt and my athletic shorts. Put some damn clothes on, mothahfuckah. I don't wanna see yo' nipples. Anyway, it used to be that gettin' in that workout was somethin' you did for yourself to make yourself better, healthier, lookin' good. It still is, but now folks is showin' it off. But you don't gotta do that. Sometimes, it's the small things you doin' every day, things that nobody really knows you doin', that build up to the big wins.

Take this dude Charles. I met him while workin' at Wonder Bread. This man was swole like a big-ass balloon. He was like Popeye the Sailor Man bustin' outta his shirt and shit. One day I asked him. I said, "Popeye, I mean Charles, man, folks never see you at the gym. Where do you work out?" He said, "Man, I ain't goin' to no gym. I do it in my basement." That really stuck with me. Do you know when God blessed Rhonda and me with our house, the first thing I did was install a gym in my basement. That's why I look all buff as a mothahfuckah, fo' real. Y'all not gonna see me at nobody's gym, that's shit's all under wraps, then it takes folks by surprise. Same for practicin' my comedy, workin' on new film roles, helpin' out the needy and all of that. Do it quietly and then it's gonna make a big impact.

> ***Everyone sees the glory moments, but they don't see what happens behind the scenes.***
>
> —Allyson Felix

DO THIS TODAY: *Today, do all of your shit without postin' about it nowhere or tellin' nobody what you did. Just be proud of yourself and know what you done is gonna help get you where you wanna go. Let folks know by your results.*

October 25th

"YOU ALREADY GOT EVERYTHING YOU NEED TO SUCCEED."

When you was a baby, you didn't know nothin' different but bein' just who you were. It was livin' with other folks that taught you how to be self-conscious, hold back, not trust folks, shut down your creativity, stop dreamin', all of that. Now, if you got a good family unit, good friends, you gonna keep as much of yourself as possible, but probably not all of it. 'Cuz then the rest of society creeps in, and strangers can be a sumbitch. So, maybe you still confident and creative, but you lost your ability to dream big. Damn, that's been a mothahfuckin' roadblock for ya', I know. Well, here's the deal. It ain't actually gone. It's still there, you just gotta get rid of the other shit that's blockin' it.

The thing is that God wants you to have all of your qualities. So He's gonna align the Universe to give you signs and lessons. If you see 'em, and you learn 'em, you can return yourself to the real you—the one that's got all he needs to follow his path. I lost my confidence for a while. Life hit me hard. But you know what got me back? My granddad passed. I stood up at his funeral and started imitatin' Grandpa Thurman, and I's makin' folks laugh again. I guess my eyes was open just enough to see the sign, and I thank God for it. So, if you lost one of your qualities, all you gotta do is open your eyes to seein' what's bein' thrown down at you, and don't worry. You gonna pull it out again, 'cuz it's been there all the time, waitin' on you.

> ***Your vision will become clear only when you can look into your own heart. Who looks outside, dreams; who looks inside, awakes.***
>
> —Carl Jung

DO THIS TODAY: *You can choose to seek all the answers in distant lands and experts, or you can choose to believe that everything you need is already inside you. Today, look inside and be confident you know what's best for you.*

October 26th

"BE RESPONSIBLE FOR YOUR LIFE, BUT ALSO LET GO OF THE WHEEL."

I know this might sound like a *got-damn* contradiction, but life's full of 'em, ain't it? You gotta takes personal responsibility for your choices and your actions, but at the same time, you gotta let go of the results. When you think on it, you gonna see it makes perfect mothahfuckin' sense. You heard of the sayin', "Let go and let God." Yeah, it means to let go of the results and let God's plan roll itself out.

You can't go tryin' to control every mothahfuckin' thing in yo' life or every other person. 'Cuz the reality is, you can't. And if you try, it's gonna be a helluva lot of *got-damn work* and you gonna end up goin' batshit crazy. You can lead a horse to water, but you can't make him drink. That shit means that you can do what you do, you can teach somebody somethin', you can set it up right, but you can't force the mothahfuckin' results. You know, I could set my sister's kids up with private got-damn school and get 'em a tutor, but I can't make 'em learn shit if they don't wanna...or if they's dumb as a doorknob. It just is what it is, and I gotta be good with doin' what I can and let go of the rest. Same goes for your own life. If you doin' everything you need to be doin' to make somethin' work, and it don't, you just gotta trust that there's a different plan for you, and in the end it's gonna work out better than you ever imagined. Believe that.

> ***The two things in life you are in total control over are your attitude and your effort.***
>
> —Billy Cox

DO THIS TODAY: *Once you believe that everything is workin' out for you, you gonna let go of the wheel, 'cuz you got trust in the process. What have you been tryin' to control that ain't none of your business controllin'? Let go of it now.*

October 27th

"BELIEVE IN MIRACLES."

If you ain't believin' that a miracle could happen to you, well then how the fuck you gonna notice it when it does? Y'all know the story about the poor beggar that's sittin' under the statue of the Virgin Mary at the fountain in front of the church and he's prayin', "Please, Lord. Let me win the lottery. I just wanna win the lottery, please." Then all of a sudden he hears a voice, and it says, "Son, you gotta buy a ticket." You see what I mean right here? You gotta buy that mothahfuckin' ticket, and you buy that ticket 'cuz *you believe* you can win. That would be some kinda miracle. But you sure as hell won't win if you never play. Oh, Sistah Benita can tell you a little about that. She was askin' everybody to pray for her gettin' a new husband. Then one day she met the man of her dreams. They courted for a year and a half before they decided to get married. She bought the dress and they paid for the banquet hall. However, when they went to apply for their marriage license, they told her she can't get one, 'cuz she still married to her first husband. *Got-damn*, that woman was blockin' her miracle that whole damn time—she never bought the ticket.

Believin' in miracles is like havin' hope that amazin' shit can happen to you for no reason except that you deserve it. How do you deserve it? You trust that it's gonna work out the way that it should...and you put in the *got-damn* work. You buy the mothahfuckin' ticket.

> ***Miracles happen every day, change your perception of what a miracle is and you'll see them all around you.***
>
> —Jon Bon Jovi

DO THIS TODAY: *You know miracles exist. You can see 'em when somebody receives an unexpected blessin', or they accomplish somethin' amazin' as hell. You're here readin' this right now, ain't you? I think that's a got-damn* **miracle**. *Miracles happen every moment, the trick is to remember, realize, and appreciate them. What miracles have happened in your life already?*

October 28th

"YOU CAN'T FAIL IF YOU DON'T TRY."

Most folks get lazy, get comfortable with doin' nothin', 'cuz they scared they won't succeed. Failure is a mothahfuckah. Some folks wanna kick its ass and other folks run the hell away from it and hide. But failin' ain't somethin' to be afraid of, for real. We just been taught that it is the worst mothahfuckin' thing you can do. That's a load of bullshit. All that thinkin' does is make folks afraid to even try.

But let's think about hidin' for a minute here. Remember when you was a kid and you's playin' hide and seek with yo' cousins. Everybody acted like they didn't wanna be the seeker. You tryin' to rig the "Eenie, Meanie, Minie, Moe" and shit so you don't get picked. But for real, nobody wanted to sit in the damn closet for twelve *got-damn* minutes while they cousin's runnin' all over the place lookin' in all the shit screamin' and tryin' to find folks. Hell naw, it's way more fun to be the one lookin'. You might not find everybody, but at least you doin' somethin'. When you hidin', you ain't doin' jack shit. You bored, get tired, and you wastin' your *got-damn* time and your mothahfuckin' talents. So, stop hidin' in the closet. What's the very worst thing that could happen if you try to do somethin' you been wantin' to do? The only failure is when you fail to even try.

> ***The only man who makes no mistakes is the man who never does anything.***
>
> —Theodore Roosevelt

DO THIS TODAY: *Why you hidin' on the couch watchin' the boob tube all day, playin' video games and shit? You hidin', you already failin' at life. Figure out what it is you hidin' from, then get off yo' ass today and do somethin' extraordinary. Try, and know it's a win even if you fail.*

October 29th

"THE MORE YOU YAKKIN', THE LESS YOU WORKIN'."

We all know that sumbitch that's talkin' all the damn time. It ain't all bad. Maybe he's talkin' about his hopes and dreams, his plans, what he's accomplished. Or maybe he's tellin' you all about how he taught his Golden Retriever to go fetch him a coffee at mothahfuckin' Starbucks. He's the guy that calls you on the phone or walks up to your desk and you pretend like you on another call. Do not look that mothahfuckah in the eyes or you gonna get stuck talkin' to him for the next thirty-seven minutes about his new got-damn Bonsai hobby. How you gonna get any work done? As a matter of fact, how the hell does ***he*** get any work done?

Shut the hell up and do yo' job. Folks waste more time tellin' you what they gonna do than they do actually doin' it. That's one way to pause your got-damn progress. Why? 'Cuz the more you talkin', it's doin' two things. One, it's takin' time away from action. Two, it gives folks an opportunity to shoot you down. Now, there's a time and a place. You brainstormin' on a project? Great. You gotta new idea and you wanna bounce it off a trusted confidant? Fantastic! But first off, don't keep beatin' a dead horse. Second off, if it ain't got nothin' to do with you or the person you tellin', either one, then maybe curb your ***got-damn*** enthusiasm. Third, consider whether you're takin' up the other person's time or if they really want to hear all about the new shade of taupe you painted your three-seasons room. If they lookin' sideways like they tryin' to ease out of the conversation and they lookin' at they laptop, back the hell off. They got better shit to do, and so do you, probably.

> ***You are what you do, not what you say you'll do.***
>
> —Carl Jung

DO THIS TODAY: *Has anybody said to you, "Let someone else get a word in?" That means yo' ass is talkin' too much. It's time to start focusin' on the vibe the folks you talkin' to are throwin' back. If their body language says they done listenin', then it's time for you to stop talkin' and maybe go do somethin'.*

October 30th

"DON'T LET NOTHIN' CATCH YOU OFF GUARD. YOU GOTTA BE READY FOR ALL KINDA CRAZY."

The thing that's mothahfuckin' insane about life is that at any minute there's about a million different things that could happen. Is there a higher probability that some shit's gonna happen over other shit? Yes. Like there's a higher chance that you gonna get a knock on your *got-damn* door and it's gonna be the mothahfuckin' Amazon delivery driver than a barbershop quartet singin' you a rap-battle rendition of "Mack the Knife" in their skivvies. But, there's always *a chance* that some crazy shit is gonna happen to you right...now! Or right...now! You gotta be ready for it, and don't be afraid of it. That crazy shit is supposed to happen, so embrace it.

Now, you might say, "How the hell is it a good thing when my drunk-ass neighbor drives his *got-damn* Cadillac Escalade right through my mothahfuckin' front window?" Yeah, I can see how you might not be thinkin' that's a blessin'. But you gotta be patient. Maybe 'cuz of that you go stay with your wife's sister for a while while yo' house is gettin' fixed. When you there, she got a neighbor comes by and you get to talkin'. They get excited about somethin' you got goin', and they daddy just passed and left 'em with a shit ton of money. They invest in your opportunity, and you both realizin' a dream. You see what I'm sayin' here? Don't discount nothin', 'cuz all the crazy plot twists is part of the story, and that's what makes it interestin'.

> ***If you do not expect the unexpected you will not find it, for it is not to be reached by search or trail.***
>
> —Heraclitus

DO THIS TODAY: *It's better to be prepared for an opportunity and not have one than to have an opportunity and not be prepared. The best way to get to thinkin' in this mindset is to see the end result in advance, that way nothin's gonna surprise you. Can you see your end result? Now you can see how the opportunity's gonna help you get there.*

October 31st

"REINVENT YOURSELF WHENEVER YOU CAN."

Halloween is the best mothahfuckin' time to reinvent yourself. You just pick out whatever the hell you want to be, and for one night, you become that. When you's a little kid, man, you really thought you *was* that superhero, rock star, sheriff of the Old West. You'd be runnin' around shootin' folks with your plastic cowboy pistol. You be grabbin' your cousin and throwin' his ass in the jail and shit. Damn, that's when you really knew how to become a new mothahfuckin' character, just like that. The crazy shit is, you can still do it, you just forgot how.

I ain't sayin' to be fake, or to be somebody you ain't. That wouldn't be true to yo'self. But if you don't like who you are, if you don't like the way you behavin' or how you puttin' yo'self out into the world, you can change that shit right now. Decide who it is you want to be, how you want to behave, then figure out what it is you need to change to transform into that person. Take off old shit that ain't workin' and put on new. You could be a mothahfuckin' pharmacist your whole life, and suddenly you feelin' like you don't like it no more. You gettin' bored, it ain't fulfillin'. Okay, what character you wanna be now? You wanna be a pianist? Take off your mothahfuckin' white coat, sit down at a piano, and start to learn. Take some lessons, and start callin' yourself a pianist. Keep at it, and pretty soon you be tinklin' the ivories down at the local piano lounge. You can, you just gotta remember how to be that kid at Halloween.

> ***Every great dream begins with a dreamer. Always remember, you have within you the strength, the patience, and the passion to reach for the stars to change the world.***
>
> —Harriet Tubman

DO THIS TODAY: *Dress up for Halloween. You don't gotta go buy a fancy costume, but think of somethin' real good, somethin' that gets you excited, and dress the hell up. Go to a party, hand out candy, or even go mothahfuckin' trick-or-treating. Enjoy whoever or whatever you become for the night and really get into it. Trust me, it's gonna be fun.*

November 1st

"GRAB SOME FRIENDS AND PULL 'EM ONTO YOUR PARTY BUS."

When you start seein' some success, when you receivin' those blessin's, you gotta pull in the folks that you care about and let 'em come along too. I ain't sayin' to give nobody a free ride. All a free ride'll do is make folks lazy. I'm sayin' if there's some folks that helped you along the way, or if they're good folks with talents that could work with what you doin', open up them doors and get 'em on. There's plenty of seats, and you gonna have a lot more fun if you're doin' it together.

Let me tell you somethin'. It's the worst thing in the mothahfuckin' world when you see somebody you helped out about a million times *before* they made it, gave 'em your time and your talent, maybe even some of your money to help 'em rise up. Now, they up there doin' good, and *got-dammit* that sumbitch brought some other folks up with 'em instead of you. Not because them other folks was there for 'em before they hit it big, but 'cuz these sumbitches got somethin' they want. Maybe it's money or clout. Maybe they just thinkin' they better than you now that they're a big shot. *Got-damn*, you don't wanna be one of them sumbitches. When you got folks that's good to you, folks that helped you, you gotta share your blessin's with 'em.

> ***The strength of the team is each individual member. The strength of each member is the team.***
>
> —Phil Jackson

DO THIS TODAY: *Think about anybody that might've helped you get where you at now; a family member, friend, coworker, associate. Can you bring 'em back onto your team in some kinda way? If so, ask 'em if they want in!*

November 2nd

"YOU GOTTA GET INTO YOUR FLOW."

When you workin' real hard and things is comin' fast and easy, boy, that's when you say you in the flow. You know, in a river, the flow is the current, and it's movin' you in one direction. Everything moves in the flow with the river. When you in the flow, it means you on your right path and things is comin' to you easy and natural. You headin' toward success, so why the hell would you wanna turn around and start swimmin' upstream? The answer is, "You don't." Then how is it that so many folks seems like they're doin' just that? Well, it ain't that they chose to do it, but somethin' threw 'em off course and they couldn't make themselves right again. Trust me, I been there, done that.

When I was in my early twenties, I took a gig doin' stand-up for a fancy event. Folks was sittin' at tables with nice tablecloths and real silverware. Lots of folks too. Maybe three hundred. Boy, it was my big opportunity, and I tanked it that night. It pretty near killed me. It turned me a around and for a minute there, I was strugglin' like a mothahfuckah, swimmin' upstream. I was doin' all kinda jobs that wasn't meant for me. But I kept watchin' for the opportunities, and when one slammed right into me, I took it, and I was back! Nothin' feels better than layin' on your back, lookin' up at the clouds, lettin' that river carry you.

> ***Those who flow as life flows know they need no other source.***
>
> —Lao Tzu

DO THIS TODAY: *Think back to a time when you had such precision focus while doing somethin' you loved that time seemed to fade away. How did that feel? That's when you were in your flow. Flow is complete absorption in your experience. It's a beautiful thing 'cuz you feel productive, happy, and 100 percent focused.*

November 3rd

"IF IT'S MEANT FOR YOU, IT AIN'T GONNA FEEL LIKE A STRUGGLE."

The struggle is real. I hear y'all, I been through it. But it's the times that you really strugglin' and feelin' like you gettin' nowhere that maybe you strayed off of the path you was meant to be on. If somethin' is meant for you, if you workin' through God's plan, it ain't always gonna be smooth, but it sure as hell ain't gonna feel like drivin' through hell nekkid on a Big Wheel. It's gonna be work, but it ain't gonna be like gettin' your head slammed in the door of a mothahfuckin' '77 lime green Pinto repeatedly. If you feelin' like that, jump out, mothahfuckah. You goin' the wrong way! Abort mission! Abandon ship! You lost as a mothahfuckah, and you gotta get yourself right.

When you're really doin' what you meant to be doin', you gonna know it. Bein' on the right path at the right time don't mean yo' ass is gonna be obstacle free. But those obstacles will be nothin' more than bumps in the road, and the idea of giving up won't feel like the right option at all. Quittin' will make you feel sick to your stomach. You'll be driven from somewhere within yourself to find another way to make it work so you can continue on toward your dream. That's when it's meant for you. Remember, God is good, and he wants you to succeed. He ain't gonna make the right path the darkest one.

> ***You can do anything as long as you don't stop believing. When it is meant to be, it will be. You just have to follow your heart.***
>
> —Keke Palmer

DO THIS TODAY: *You got somethin' you doin' in your life that feels like hell? Does it feel like you don't wanna go at it no more? Make a decision to let that shit go and move on to somethin' that lights you up. The right path ain't the most difficult one.*

November 4th

"MAKE SURE YOU STAYIN' HEALTHY, OR NONE OF THE REST OF IT MATTERS A GOOD *GOT-DAMN*."

You could have every mothahfuckin' thing in the world, but if you ain't feelin' good enough to enjoy it, what's it worth? They say, "If you ain't got your health, you ain't got nothin'." That's the truth. You know if you ever been sicker'n a dog, layin' up in your bed with the Vicks VapoRub slathered all over your *got-damn* chest, head poundin' and body achin'. All you can manage to do is keep one eye open to watch the Sox game. Then your kid runs in the room and turns off the mothahfuckin' TV right in the middle of a *got-damn* pitch. When you sick like that, you at the liberty of other folks and you feelin' helpless. It don't matter what you got, you can't enjoy it. It don't matter what you done in yo' life, 'cuz all you can think about is not dyin' right there...from boredom.

All kiddin' aside, you gotta take care of yourself, 'cuz God only gave you one body and you gotta wear it 'til your soul leaves this earth. I know there's some crazy mothahfuckin' medical advances *goings on* here, and doctors can fix a lot of shit. But it's a helluva lot easier to *not break that shit* in the first place than to try'n fix it.

> ***To keep the body in good health is a duty. Otherwise, we shall not be able to keep the mind strong and clear.***
>
> —Buddha

DO THIS TODAY: *What do you got* ***goings on*** *that shouldn't be ignored no more? You get constant headaches? Make a doctor appointment. You ain't gettin' no exercise? Get cho' ass off that couch and walk. I don't mean walkin' to the refrigerator either. Put yo' shoes on and move. Start slow if you have to. You always tired? Get more sleep. You see where I'm goin' with this. Whatever ain't right with your body, start fixin' it now.*

November 5th

"MONEY DON'T BUY HAPPINESS, BUT IT HELPS YOU WRITE YOURSELF AN ORDER."

You shouldn't be doin' it for the dough, but when you're doin' it and the dough comes in, you realize that when you have some, you suddenly got a little bit more control. Money won't make you happy, but it can help you open up some doors that sure as hell might.

There's folks out there that grow up thinkin' cash is king, and other folks actin' like it's evil as the Devil himself. Both of those are fucked up. Money ain't the be-all end-all, that's fo' sho'. Money can do things to folks, make 'em greedy, depressed, jealous, make 'em do shit they never thought they'd do. But scoffin' at money don't work neither. In this world, you need a little bit of it to get along—ask anybody that's gone without it for a while. Hell, nobody that's been dirt poor to where they got no heat and no food would ever say they don't need no money. That kinda shit's comin' out of the folks that's never had to do without.

Here's what money buys: security. Havin' it and knowin' that more is comin' gives us peace of mind as we face the uncertainty about what lies ahead in this changin' *got-damn* world. That peace of mind sure is important to even think about bein' happy. Plus, money can buy us some things that brings joy—like takin' our kids to Disney World or somethin' like that. So, how you gotta look at it is that, yeah, you gotta do what you passionate about, but you also gotta figure out how you gonna make some money doin' it. That's the business side, you know. You gotta be smart about that too.

> ***Wealth is not about having a lot of money; it's about having a lot of options.***
>
> —Chris Rock

DO THIS TODAY: *What do you love to do, what's your passion? Now, write up a little mock business plan showin' how you gonna bring in some cash doin' it.*

November 6th

"FROM START TO FINISH, YOU THE ONE'S GOTTA LIVE WITH YOURSELF."

Whatever it is you doin' with your life, at the end of the day when that sun is settin', you gotta get into bed with your own mothah-fuckin' self. You gonna like that sumbitch? You gonna love him? Or are you gonna regret it so hard that you wish you could sneak out on yourself before the sun come up? Maybe it's somewhere in between, and that's where you got the space to fix the shit that's muckin' it up.

We all make mistakes; I know that as much as the next sumbitch. But you ain't gotta keep on beatin' yourself up over 'em. You gotta learn from 'em, then you'll be able to live with yourself, respect yourself, and be proud. One time when Boops was little, her toys was spread out all over that little apartment of ours. I kept on tellin' her to pick 'em up, but she didn't. So, I bagged 'em up and I threw 'em in the trash. Boy, she was heartbroke. I regretted doin' that, felt like a horrible sumbitch. But I learned somethin' important. I learned not to react out of a hot minute where I let my temper take control. It was a lesson I needed so I wouldn't make that kinda mistake on somethin' even bigger later on. I learned to think more careful about my choices before I acted on impulse. Damn, that's a tough one for a lot of folks, but I learned it. At the end of the day, I like who the hell I am, and that's the only thing you can take with you.

Eventually stardom is going to go away from me. It goes away from everybody and all you have in the end is to be able to look back and like the choices you made.

—Matt Damon

DO THIS TODAY: *Do you like yourself? If you was your own roommate, would you kick yourself the hell out? If the answer is abso-fuckin'-lutely, then figure out what you gotta fix and fix it. Remember nobody will think you're somebody if you don't think so yourself.*

November 7th

"YOU GOTTA KNOW THAT YOU ALREADY ARE EVERYTHING YOU WANNA BE."

When you plant a tiny seed in the ground, that little sumbitch has got everything it needs to become a mighty tree already inside of it. Same goes for you. Everything you are and everything you gonna be is already a part of you. It's in your cells, your brain, your very mothahfuckin' bein'. It's all there, it just needs to get the right *got-damn* conditions to grow. Ya' see, you can't go and plant a tomato seed and end up with a mothahfuckin' rose bush. Everything that's tomato is in the tomato seed, the stem and the leaves, the seeds, the juice; and that ain't gonna change no matter what kinda water or plant food you givin' it. But I'm gonna tell you somethin' straight. If you try'n make that tomato seed sprout into a rose bush, you gonna mothahfuckin' kill it. Same thing with you. Who you are, it's all inside a' you at this very mothahfuckin' moment just like the seed, and if you try'n make yo'self into somethin' you ain't, it's gonna kill ya'.

Your destiny and shit, the fulfillment of all your desires, it's all there in yo' soul, like the ingredients of who you are and who you gonna be. All you gotta do is own it. I knew I was a comedian when I was real young, and I declared that shit from day one. I was sayin' it to anybody who'd listen, and I didn't care who believed me and who didn't. *I believed me*, and you can see the *got-damn* results of that right here.

> ***I've always been famous, it's just no one knew it yet.***
>
> —Lady Gaga

DO THIS TODAY: *Go on and listen to the song "Believe in Yourself" from* The Wiz*. It's tellin' you to believe in yourself right from the start. You can learn all the techniques in the world, but if you don't believe you can do it, that shit won't work. Don't limit yourself no more.*

November 8th

"KNOW WHAT'S IMPORTANT TO YOU AND BUILD EVERYTHING ELSE AROUND THAT."

What's at the core of who you are as a human bein' and how you get along in this world is your values. Most of the time, you learnin' those from your folks, your family, the people that done raised you and helped form your young mind. Or maybe they didn't teach you right, and you formed your values later tryin' to undo what they done. However you got 'em, your values is kinda like your moral compass. You gonna refer to 'em all the damn time whether you realize it or not. You gonna weigh your decisions against what's most important to you. You gotta be careful though 'cuz values can sometimes be lost. For instance, I can't get used to how these new-breed millennials and Gen Zs are talkin' to their mamas. Where did they learn so much disrespect, callin' them by their first names and cussin' at them like it ain't nothin'. They musta learnt that in them damn streets.

Our values are a choice, and they dictate how we speak, what we say, who we choose as friends, how we make a livin', and just about every damn thing we do. If we live according to our values we can look to them as guideposts when making decisions. Small decisions like who you followin' on social media, or which one of my jokes you laughin' at (all of em' I hope) to big decisions like who you choosin' as a mate or where you movin' to. Follow your values, they won't guide you wrong.

> ***It's important to know what really matters in life. Your sanity, your health, your family, and the ability to start anew.***
>
> —Les Brown

DO THIS TODAY: *What are your values? Make a list of the top ten most important things to you. Refer to that list when you're questionin' a decision or an opportunity. Is it in line with what's most valuable to you?*

November 9th

"SOMETIMES THE BEST THING TO DO IS NOTHIN' AT ALL."

We've been programmed from a young age that sittin' there doin' nothin' is akin to doin' the Devil's work. You caught sittin', yo' mama's gonna find somethin' for you to do, and it's probably not gonna be fun. So, when we find ourselves coastin', we feel some kinda guilt about it. We feel like we gotta keep rollin' all the damn time. But that ain't the truth. We need time to stop and regroup once in a while.

Thing is, if you did the right shit to put a plan into motion, sometimes if you try and hurry it up, try and poke and prod at it while it's unfoldin', you gonna wreck the whole ***got-damn*** thing. It's kinda like my mama's sponge cake. She used to make that and we'd put crushed strawberries on it, mmhmmm, boy that was good. She told me the trick to a sponge cake is that you gotta leave it alone in the oven while it's bakin', or it ain't gonna rise right. Well, you think little Bean was gonna leave it the hell alone? Hell to the no. I was smellin' that sweet cake cookin', and I was gettin' antsy. Not only did I open the mothahfuckin' oven, I poked that shit with a fork to see if it was done yet. Soon as that fork touched that puffy, soft cake, that shit deflated like a mothahfuckin' beach ball with the stopper popped. It fell right flat, and I slammed that oven and ran off, dove into my bed actin' like I's takin' a nap. When my mama opened up the oven, I think the whole block could hear her scream. I learned my lesson right quick. If it's still cookin' leave it the hell alone. All you gotta do to get that sweet, sweet reward is do nothin' at all.

> ***Don't underestimate the value of doing nothing.***
>
> —A. A. Milne

DO THIS TODAY: *The Bible tells you numerous times to "be still." When we choose to be patient, we are really choosing peace. Impatience brings about stress. Patience teaches us to pause, accept the present moment as it is, and just breathe. Today, let things unfold as they will.*

November 10th

"DON'T LET YOUR SUCCESS CHANGE WHO YOU ARE."

I know I got successful, but I'm fairly sure there ain't nobody that'd say I changed what it was that was important about me. Sure, I got myself a few new clothes and shit, a bigger house out where it's quiet and you can hear yourself think. But when it come down to my values, my attitude, the way I treat my friends and family, that shit didn't change one mothahfuckin' bit. Why would I go and do that? It's the real me that got me this far, I don't wanna go and screw that up. It don't make no sense.

But it happens, I know it does. I seen some sumbitches, they start makin' money, start seein' their face on the mothahfuckin' billboards and shit, up on the marquee. They think they hot shit, start treatin' their families like they nothin', treatin' their wife like she can be replaced and shit. You better believe that wife gonna leave his ass, and he gonna find himself alone with his money and his mothahfuckin' signs. I bet my wife Rhonda's sisters got nervous about that and shit, when I started gettin' famous. But they didn't have nothin' to worry about. When I was gone, I'd be callin' Rhonda every chance I get just to tell her I miss her. She's the best *got-damn* thing ever happened to me. Pretty soon, Bede, Stuff, and Chami—that's what I call her sisters Bridgett, Mary, and Charoni—they seen it too. I was the same mothahfuckah that done took their sister to the prom. Same one that walked her down the aisle and held her hand when little Boops was born. You can't go changin' the person who got you the success in the mothahfuckin' first place, so just make sure you check yourself.

> ***Never let success get to your head and never let failure get to your heart.***
>
> —Ziad K. Abdelnour

DO THIS TODAY: *Instead of takin' all the spotlight, it's time for you to share it. I want you to make a list of every person that contributed to your success. Take a look at that and know you did not do this alone, and that shit is humbling.*

November 11th

"DON'T FORGET WHERE YOU COME FROM."

Once you leave a place, it can be too easy to forget about it, especially if it's holdin' some bad memories for ya'. But you gotta remember that, even if that place was harsh and dark, it was the soil you grew up out of. The experiences you had there, they brought you what you needed to become who you are today. Do you like yourself? Are you happy with where you at in yo' life? Then you gotta express gratitude for the past, 'cuz it made you what you are.

I don't go thinkin' about my little apartment above the Burning Bush Baptist Church in a sketchy part of the south side of Chicago, or the rodent-infested place I shared with Rhonda when we first got married, and start thinkin', "I just wanna forget about all of that." Hell naw, I wanna remember it like it was yesterday. That's part of who I am. Sometimes I remember so I can hold onto the sweetness of a moment, and other times I remember so I don't go repeatin' the same *got-damn* mistake. Then sometimes, I remember so I have a point of reference for what I wanna keep or what I don't want no more in my own life goin' forward. If you forget all of that and try'n erase it, you throwin' away all of your lessons, all of the foundation you built the rest of your mothahfuckin' life up on. So, remember it, and be grateful. If you got on out of a neighborhood that was rough, even go on back and do somethin' to help it out.

> ***There are two things we should all care about: never to forget where we came from and always praise the bridges that carried us over.***
>
> —Fannie Lou Hamer

DO THIS TODAY: *Don't forget your roots. People say that when they feel a person is actin' big headed, snobby, thinkin' they are better than those that they grew up with. Truth is someone may have paved the way for you. How you gonna pave the way for the next generation?*

November 12th

"YOUR JOB AIN'T TO *PRODUCE*, IT'S TO *EXIST* IN THE BEST MOTHAHFUCKIN' WAY POSSIBLE."

It ain't your mission in life to be "productive." Hell, naw. You ain't no robot in a *got-damn* factory churnin' out widgets as fast as you can. But somehow, we got it into our thick skulls that we always gotta be "productive," always gotta be doin' somethin'. That word "idle," it's like it was created by the mothahfuckin' Devil himself the way some folks look at it. If they ain't busy, they think they bein' lazy. It ain't right, and it seems to be worse over here in Western civilization. We always gotta be doin', we don't know how to just be.

The Italians, they know how to *be*. They got a sayin' over there: *Il dolce far niente. It is sweet doing nothing*. And no, I don't know Italian. I looked that shit up. Anyway, over there in Italy, they go for long-ass lunches with like seven mothahfuckin' courses. Then they sip espresso and talk about big ideas and shit. Then they take a nap and maybe they go back to work, maybe not. Them folks over there, they know how to be.

Once again, I ain't sayin' it ain't important to get shit done and to take care of your business. But there's a time for workin', and there's a time to just relax and literally do mothahfuckin' nothin'. You ain't lazy, and that most definitely ain't "wasted time." It's time you get to spend just bein' a human, and that's more than good enough, it's mothahfuckin' fantastic!

> ***I think in the Western world we have gotten overly identified with doing, and we've kind of forgotten about the art of being.***
>
> —Shakti Gawain

DO THIS TODAY: *Nothin'. That's right, set aside some time to just* **be** *today, whatever that looks like for you. Layin' in a hammock, lingerin' over a meal, whatever it is, don't feel no shame in doin' not much of nothin' for a while.*

November 13th

"RESET YOURSELF TO THE FACTORY DEFAULT."

We sure as hell were not put on this mothahfuckin' planet just to suffer. I know that for a *got-damn* fact. Why do you think Jesus died on the cross? You think He done that so you could go on and live a life of pain and hardship? No, he did not. God put you here to be full of His joy, full of life, and to live in His mothahfuckin' abundance. Joy, that right there is your *got-damn* natural state of bein'. But it's like we been tricked into thinkin' it ain't. We been reprogrammed to think that you gotta get ripped up inside before you can feel somethin' good. "No pain, no gain," and shit like that. Hell to the mothahfuckin' naw. Sometimes I wonder what *got-damn* masochist started that kinda ridiculous rumor. Maybe Satan himself, 'cuz that sumbitch likes to see folks suffer. Okay, if you goin' through some shit, you gotta push through it. But that's different than expectin' that you can't be happy *without* the mothahfuckin' pain. That's ridiculous. God wants you to be happy, healthy, safe. You the one fuckin' it up.

> ***Our most natural state is joy. It is the foundation for love, compassion, healing,and the desire to alleviate suffering.***
>
> —Deepak Chopra

DO THIS TODAY: *Hit your factory reset button right now. What "new programming" do you need to wipe away in order to start fresh and live a life of joy? You might wanna work on deletin' the following apps: negativity, fear, self-doubt, anger, insecurities, fear of abandonment, fear of lack, and low self-esteem. See if you start runnin' better.*

November 14th

"WHEN YOU TACKLIN' A PROBLEM, FIRST ASK YOURSELF IF IT'S SOMETHIN' YOU REALLY WANNA BE SOLVIN'."

Some of y'all have gotten to the point that you see any kinda problem, and you rollin' up them sleeves and divin' right it. It's like a mothahfuckin' compulsion. You gotta solve that shit, and you gotta do it now, and you gotta do it first. Slow down, mothahfuckah. Check with your heart. Does it feel good to work on this project? Is it takin' away from somethin' else you wanna be doin'? Is it your *got-damn* problem to solve? 'Cuz here's the thing right there: if you workin' on somethin' that isn't meant for you, then you takin' away somebody else's opportunity. Maybe that door was open, but you want the one that's meant for *you* to walk through it.

It's kinda like when I was at this house party once back in high school, and me and my friend Billy done gone upstairs lookin' for the bathroom. There was this bedroom door open and I walked right on by. But Billy, man, he walked in. That chick in there, she was waitin' for some action and she was smokin' hot...but she wasn't waitin' for no Billy. That sumbitch ended up with a broken mothahfuckin' nose from that chick's *got-damn* boyfriend, looked like the Incredible Hulk. You see what I'm sayin'. If it don't check out completely, if it ain't in your flow, then leave it the hell alone. You ain't gotta go fixin' everybody's else's shit all the time.

> ***All questions need to be explored from our hearts first and then embraced by our heads.***
>
> —Andrea T. Goeglein

DO THIS TODAY: *Think about somethin' that you been tryin' to figure out or tryin' to fix. Ask yourself right now, "Is this my problem to solve?" Then ask yourself, "Is it serving a purpose in my life?" If the answer is no to either one of those questions, then it's time to let it go.*

November 15th

"DON'T EVER WISH BAD ON NOBODY, NOT EVEN FOLKS YOU THINK DESERVE IT."

Don't be wishin' bad shit on folks, 'cuz now you done gone and created a fucked-up situation for yourself. Karma's gonna come back around and kick yo' ass. I know, you been trained in the brain by all them movies, video games, and even by Grandmama who's always sayin' "an eye for an eye" and shit. They all tellin' you that you gotta seek revenge, or you gotta at least wish that some bad shit happens to the folks that done you dirty. But when you start doin' that shit, you're no better than they are, for real. Just leave the situation alone, their shit's gonna come back around on 'em without your help. Here's what I'm talkin' about.

You crusin' in your car on a beautiful Sunday afternoon. Just chillin' listenin' to some old school and enjoyin' the ride. You happen to look up in your rear-view mirror and this stupid-ass fool has sped up behind you riding your tail. Ain't that a bitch? They damn near touchin' yo' bumper tryin' to intimidate you to move over, then he jumps in front of you. Your relaxin' ride has just come to a halt, 'cuz now you pissed as hell. You either gonna go the hell off, or you can remain cool. 'Cuz here's the thing: You have no *got-damn* idea why he's in such a hurry. Maybe his wife's in labor. Maybe his mama at the hospital dyin'. Maybe he's got some bowel issues and he needs to get to a terlet fast. You have no idea. But it don't matter, 'cuz it ain't got nothin' to do with you. How you handle it, that's got everything to do with you. So, are you gonna be a jackass? 'Cuz either way, you only got your own karma to deal with.

> ***How people treat you is their karma; how you react is yours.***
>
> —Wayne W. Dyer

DO THIS TODAY: *Remember, rotten fruit will fall on its own. You ain't gotta shake it. A***cceptance** *is the key to movin' forward with your life. What do you got in your life that's still eatin' at you? Try to reframe it and let it go so you can close the wound.*

November 16th

"SOMETIMES YOU GOTTA BE WILLIN' TO LOSE IT ALL TO GET BACK YOURSELF."

I had this friend that was stuck in a nasty-ass marriage. Boy, was that sumbitch unhappy. That woman was eatin' his soul and spittin' it out 'cuz she didn't like the taste. But he hung in there strugglin' to make it work doin' the right thing, you know, tryin' not to sing the blues. But I bet that got-damn Johnnie Taylor was all up in his head singin', "Cheaper to Keep Her," 'cuz there's money involved, of course. Mothahfuckin' money, that shit can get a hold on you and make you do shit you know's makin' you miserable. Ya' see, he couldn't stand the thought of that woman takin' half of all he worked real hard to accomplish. The big-ass house with the pool and bar, the cars, the jewelry, the vacation homes, and the collection of rare mothahfuckin' Black Santas. Okay, maybe I made that last one up, but you see what I'm sayin'. That shit can get ridiculous.

All of that material shit don't mean squat when you tradin' your happiness for it. You can get more shit, but what you can't get is all the time you spent bein' miserable as a pig at a barbeque. Brothah, you've been tryin' to make it work, but now it's time to start puttin' yourself first. Be a selfish-ass mothahfuckah about you, and that don't mean keepin' the money. It means keepin' your sanity. Then, go do somethin' to celebrate your freedom! Maybe you go deep-sea fishin' 'cuz she never would go with you or take a drive across country. It's time for you to be the truest version of you, and that's got nothin' to do with your stuff.

> ***It's better to have half of a million than all of nothing.***
>
> —Gary Davis

DO THIS TODAY: *Never be afraid of improvin' your life because of what you may lose. Fear of change is rooted in complacency. Right now, identify something you been complacent about. Ask yourself, "What if I fixed it?" You gonna quickly see the benefits outweigh the cost.*

November 17th

"GOD AIN'T GONNA DELIVER YOUR MAIL TO SOMEBODY ELSE'S BOX."

I heard a preacher once say, "Never be jealous of what God has done for somebody. What God has for you is for you, and He's never gonna deliver your mail to someone else's house." Ain't that the truth? So, why you lookin' at your neighbor sideways when he gets a new black Cadillac Escalade and you still drivin' that beat-up old Buick sedan? Remember, God said don't covet thy neighbor's shit. Why you thinkin' He said that? It ain't yours, it ain't your path, it ain't meant for you. Jealousy is a constant battle between heart and soul, but I got news for you. If you hung up on what your neighbor got that you ain't, then you done shut your own *got-damn* mailbox and duct-taped it. You blockin' your own mothahfuckin' blessin's.

So, instead of peekin' out the *got-damn* window then bitchin' underneath yo' breath about how Li'l Bigboy livin' next door is a sumbitch and don't deserve what he got, go on out there with a big smile and tell him congratulations! Be happy for that mothahfuckah 'cuz he must be doin' somethin' right, followin' his path. Let his abundance be an example that all you could want really is available if you open to it. Bottom line is, you gonna reap what you sow, so don't be a hater. Soon, you gonna welcome more joy as you celebrate other folks' successes with 'em.

> ***A competent and self-confident person is incapable of jealousy in anything. Jealousy is invariably a symptom of neurotic insecurity.***
>
> —Robert A. Heinlein

DO THIS TODAY: *Take your eye off their prize, you ain't got no idea what they gone through to get it. Break that cycle by takin' these three steps: 1. Shift your focus to the good in your own life. 2. Remind yourself that nobody has it all. 3. Learn to celebrate the success of others. Practice those steps and you gonna start lookin' in your own mailbox instead of yo' neighbor's.*

November 18th

"NOTHIN' BLINDSIDES YOU UNLESS YOU LETTIN' IT."

How the hell did this happen? You know you said it before. I've said it, fo' sho'. Maybe things is goin' along just fine and then, *BAM*! Some kinda shit pops up outta nowhere and smacks you back a coupla steps. You thinkin', "Where the hell did that come from?" That shit surprised the hell outta you. But it shouldn't have, mothahfuckah. You just got complacent, didn't have yo' eyes open wide enough to see the *got-damn* signs. That's what sometimes happens when things is goin' okay. You get comfortable, then you forget to use your peripheral vision. Ya' know, that's when you can see shit outta the corners of your eyes. Even when you focused on the goal, you need to keep that awareness *goings on* out there on the periphery, 'cuz when shit happens, there's always mothahfuckin' warnin' signs.

For example, I got a gig headlinin' at one of the clubs in Chicago before I hit it real big, and I was supposed to get paid a hundred and fifty dollahs. That was good money, and I was glad to have it, but I shoulda known that sumbitch wasn't gonna pay me no hundred and fifty dollahs. He had shifty eyes, that's one. I done heard other comics never got paid, that's two. He didn't give me no contract, that's three. I had three signs, but I was still shocked when my check was for fifty dollahs—the sumbitch forgot the *got-damn* one. Then he turned around and said no, I musta misunderstood. To hell I did, but I was too excited to be headlinin' that I missed the mothahfuckin' signs. You gotta watch for the signs so that shit don't happen to you.

> ***Nothing ever strikes without a warning.***
>
> —Danny Glover

DO THIS TODAY: *Work on your peripheral awareness in just an observant kinda way. Spend today noticin' what's happenin' in back, around, and underneath. Think about what you're pickin' up that you maybe wouldn't have noticed before.*

November 19th

"SPEAK STRAIGHT OR NOBODY GONNA UNDERSTAND WHAT YOU SAYIN'."

Folks gotta quit beatin' around the bush and straight up say what they mean. Nothin' I hate worse than to have to figure out what the hell somebody's tryin' to tell me, especially if they wantin' somethin'. You want somethin' from me *and* you want me to work my ass off to figure out what the hell it is? I'm gonna tell you right now, you ain't gettin' it. Speak straight, mothahfuckah. Tell it like it *T-I-Iz*. That's my motto in life. You want me to lend you a thousand dollahs 'cuz you haven't been payin' yo' rent and you about to get yo' ass thrown out? Lead with that shit! Don't come up in here sayin', "Oh, Bernie, man. You look great. Yeah, uh, I been havin' some rough luck and shit. Suzie got pneumonia. I haven't been able to work on a job site you know, since I stubbed my big toe back in March. Life's a bitch...but you seem to be doin' alright." Fuck that shit. First of all, come up and tell me what you want. Then if I feel like hearin' more, I'll ask, *got-dammit*. Second off, you about to get thrown out? Why the hell you ain't askin' me for some help three mothahfuckin' months ago before you got yourself into a real bad situation? Sometimes I just gotta shake my head.

Whether you askin' somebody for a favor, you got an idea at work, or maybe you askin' for a raise or you wanna ask out that girl you been havin' yo' eye on at church, say it straight. Folks is gonna know what you mean that way, and you gonna come off as an honest sumbitch. That kinda communicatin' is gonna get you farther than beatin' around the mothahfuckin' bush.

I will speak with a straight tongue.

—Chief Joseph

DO THIS TODAY: *Stop beatin' around the bush. Be more like a kid, they don't give a shit. What do you want? Ask for it. What you gotta say to somebody? Say it. See if that gives you your power back.*

November 20th

"YOU ONLY GOT TODAY, RIGHT NOW, SO LIVE IN IT."

Y'all know that one mothahfuckah still livin' in the *got-damn* past. His stories ain't all bad. Sometimes they pretty damn entertainin' and shit. Maybe he was captain of the football team back in high school. He was the star player, dated the head cheerleader, teachers all liked him. He could get away with anything in that town. Most of his good stories started with, "Here, hold my beer and watch this." He had buddies from the team that had his back and his whole future ahead of him. But that's where it stopped, right there. He never really did much of anything with the rest of his *got-damn* life. After high school, he played college ball, but he wasn't quite good enough to get into the pros. He never took his classes serious and didn't never figure out what else he was passionate about beside throwin' the pigskin. So, he works a job he don't like and he relives the mothahfuckin' "glory days" every chance he gets. He maybe says he ain't got no regrets, but that sumbitch has got plenty.

Then there's the other way of livin' in the past, where you went through some fucked-up shit, or maybe you made some bad choices, and you still lettin' it eat you up. That ain't who you are no more. Not the high school football star or the fuckup, or the one that had to get through some kinda tragedy that hurt 'em. You can't live in yesterday, so why you bringin' that version of yourself with you? You gotta live for today and that's it. Make more memories instead of rehashin' all the old ones. That's how you do it. That's how you find the pieces that make the whole mothahfuckin' you.

> ***Don't let yesterday use up too much of today.***
>
> —Will Rogers

DO THIS TODAY: *What's got you stuck in the past? Imagine that it's in a movie that you can't rewind, so you can't watch that shit no more. Let go of it now so you can stroll into the future with ease and confidence.*

November 21st

"NO DECISION IS EVER PERMANENT."

Once you realize this, oh brothah, it opens up everything to you. We let every mothahfuckin' decision of our lives weigh heavy on us, goin' back and forth about what to do 'cuz we think we gotta live with that forevah. You gotta relax right now, 'cuz you can make one decision, and maybe you change your mind and make a different decision at another time. It's okay. The only thing that's for sure in life is that shit's gonna change. Period.

Now, I ain't sayin' that there won't be no consequences for your choices. There sure as hell will, that's guaranteed. Every action's got a reaction. But what I'm sayin' is you don't always have to live with every choice forever. If ya' did, there wouldn't be half of all marriage endin' in divorce. Even in *got-damn* sports, you see it clear as the mornin'. I remember bein' at the Chicago Bulls games back in the day. Coach Phil Jackson, Michael Jordan, Scottie Pippen, Dennis Rodman, all those cats. Coach Phil would be on the sidelines scopin' shit out. It's the middle of the third quarter and Rodman's on the free-throw line. Plays have all been strategized and everyone's ready to rock and roll. As the team stands at the line, Coach Phil thinks of somethin', so he calls a time out. BAM! He changes the plan and of course, they won the mothahfuckin championships over and over and over again. Change is good.

> ***Nothing is permanent except change.***
>
> —Heraclitus

DO THIS TODAY: *What you been hemmin' and hawin' about 'cuz you thinkin' it's a huge* **got-damn** *decision? Ask yourself if it's somethin' that can be changed down the line. Most likely it is, so then go ahead and just decide. See if it takes a weight off your shoulders.*

November 22nd

"YOU GOTTA LET GO OF SHIT THAT AIN'T SERVIN' YOU IN ORDER TO MAKE SOME ROOM FOR WHAT WILL."

We all got shit holed up in our brains that ain't doin' us no *got-damn* good no more. I know, it's hard sometimes to get rid of it 'cuz we become attached, kinda like that old La-Z-Boy armchair that's worn through the tweed cloth, handle broke, but it's comfortable. We get comfortable sometimes with the shit that ain't workin' right no more. But some of that shit's got to go so you can bring in a replacement that's gonna do you better.

It's like we all got this box inside of us full of the tools we need at any given point in our lives. We got different tools for different jobs. Maybe when you a kid, you got fear of the dark and that's gonna keep you safe so you don't go snoopin' in dangerous places. Maybe you gotta stay right by yo' mama 'cuz yo' daddy up and left and you don't wanna get abandoned by her too. Maybe when you got older, somebody lied to you real bad so you put your guard up, can't trust nobody. Well, okay, you needed those tools at the time to make yourself feels safe. But you gotta take a new look at all of them tools now and decide if you still need 'em. Is that trust issue servin' you now or is it harmin' your ability to connect with folks? You see what I'm sayin'? You gotta clear out your toolbox. You ain't the same person you was before, so let that shit go. When you do, there's a spot there for somethin' new to go in.

> ***Abundance is a process of letting go; that which is empty can receive.***
>
> —Bryant H. McGill

DO THIS TODAY: *Real talk, no bullshit. The reason why folks don't become who they wanna be is 'cuz they too attached to who they been. What tools you got in your box that ain't servin' you no more? Start gettin' rid of 'em one at a time. It's a new day and a new opportunity to create a better life for yourself.*

November 23rd

"NO MATTER WHAT YOU DOIN', YOU CAN ALWAYS DO BETTER."

If you ever thinkin', "This is the best I can possibly get," then brace yo'self 'cuz you probably about to die. That's it. You done reached the highest level. You on the winner board and you gone and leveled up, mothahfuckah. See you on the othah side. Get the hell over yourself. You ain't the best you can get, 'cuz no matter how good you doin' at somethin', there's always somethin' else you can learn, somethin' you can improve. If it ain't your game, then maybe it's your got-damn *personality*.

It's okay to be an expert, but most experts keep on studyin' 'til the day they die. 'Cuz they know that there's new advances all the damn time, plus society's constantly changin' too. You just nail a comedy routine, then all of a sudden you can't make fun of folks no more. It ain't politically correct to be talkin' about grabbin' an ass, 'cuz that's harassment. You can't talk about the difference between Black folks and Caucasians, 'cuz that's racist. Can't talk about my cousin that stuttered so bad his bus driver thought he's makin' fun of him, wouldn't let him on the bus. That's against folks that's differently abled. I ain't want to go hurtin' nobody. So, I gotta work on some new jokes. Okay, I can do that, 'cuz it's my job to keep learnin' so I can make folks laugh now, today, not yesterday. 'Cuz last time I checked, nobody's livin' in *yesterday*.

> ***Man is not the only animal who labors; but he is the only one who improves his workmanship.***
>
> —Abraham Lincoln

DO THIS TODAY: *What can you improve on today? How's that new grill workin' out? Have you learned how to adjust the temp settin's yet so the meat won't be so damn hard next time? I know you perfect but, shit, we all got stuff we can improve on. Start workin' on yours.*

November 24th

"DON'T GO AND BLOCK UP THE FLOW OF WEALTH."

Did you know that some years ago, some of the top billionaires in the mothahfuckin' world made a pledge to give back? It was called The Giving Pledge. They all agreed to shed at least half of their wealth during their lifetimes or in their wills. But guess what happened? Since they made this pledge and started givin', their fortunes grew so much that now it's a problem, 'cuz their givin' can't keep up! You see, abundance flows naturally in and out of everybody's life, but then a lot of folks is gonna go blockin' it up and shit.

What happens if you block the water flow in a mothahfuckin' fountain? The whole thing's gonna get outta whack and shut down. You gonna get stagnant nasty-ass water sittin' in there, gettin' all gunked up. That's what's gonna happen if you holdin' onto all of yo' shit. I get it, there's "reasons" you can't let go. You ain't no mothahfuckin' millionaire. But that's the point. You got this book, so you probably got somethin'. Are you afraid you ain't gonna have nothin' pretty soon? Maybe you think you worked hard for what you got, so let them other sumbitches fend for themselves too. But that ain't how it works. You gotta know in your heart that the money fountain is gonna flow both ways, all you gotta do is open up the valve then bring yo' *got-damn* bucket.

> ***If you wake up deciding what you want to give versus what you're going to get, you become a more successful person. In other words, if you want to make money, you have to help someone else make money.***
>
> —Russell Simmons

DO THIS TODAY: *Stop being stingy. When you give, you open up the valve to also receive. Make your own pledge right now to loosen your purse strings. It could be somethin' as small as buyin' the drinks when you go out with your friends, or as big as sponsorin' the local little league team. Do it knowin' there's an endless supply.*

November 25th

"I DON'T WANNA BE HAPPY ALL THE DAMN TIME, I JUST WANNA BE CONTENT."

Everybody's sayin', "You gotta be happy." "How you gonna get happy?" They got the keys to happiness in their *got-damn* three-day miracle workshop. Fuck happy. Constant happiness would be 100 percent insane. You wanna walk around all the time with a big ole shit-eatin' grin on yo' face? Folks is gonna wonder, "What the hell is wrong with that boy? Bless his heart." You look like a crazy mothahfuckah. If you just happy all the damn time, you ain't gonna learn no lessons, you ain't gonna grow as a person or nothin'.

Naw, the key for me is I wanna be *content*. That means I ain't worried about too much, means I got some mothahfuckin' peace up in here. You see a guy that's content, he's got confidence. He's easy to be around. He knows everything's gonna work out alright, so that makes him comfortable in his *got-damn* skin. Sure, that sumbitch has happiness, but it ain't always about happy-happy-happy all the *got-damn* time! There's bursts of happiness all surrounded by mothahfuckin' peace. If you wanna be content, that ain't about gettin' everything you want. It's about not wantin' more than what you got. 'Cuz if you got that, you got gratitude. If you got that kinda gratitude, you got some good got-damn energy, and you on the right mothahfuckin' path.

> ***It's what you do with what you got. You got to make like that's a lot. It's what you do with what you got that pays off in the end.***
>
> —John Amos

DO THIS TODAY: *Create your happiness now. Don't be fooled by folks who seem like they have it all, shit, they ain't always content. Relax and breathe. Are you content right now with what you have, who you are, and where you at?*

November 26th

"DESPERATION IS THE OPPOSITE OF ABUNDANCE."

You might be thinkin' that the opposite of havin' everything is havin' nothin'. Well, you'd be right too. But the thing is, abundance don't mean havin' everything. Abundance is a mothahfuckin' mindset, not necessarily a physical state of havin' a lotta shit. Abundance is a state of knowin' you good, knowin' that everything you need is available to you. But lots of folks, when they ain't got that security and that knowin', them folks can start actin' desperate. Boy, if you ever know somebody who's comin' from a state of desperation all the *got-damn* time, you get what I'm sayin' here. Them folks have got some nervous mothahfuckin' energy. It's almost like you can see their skin vibratin'. They talk fast all the damn time, and they always got more ideas before you even have a chance to process the last ones. Them folks is desperate 'cuz they ain't got the faith that everything is there for 'em. They thinkin' they gotta grab and grab until they get a handful of somethin'. But the thing is, with them folks, even once they get that handful, they ain't gonna feel like it's enough. They never gonna feel satiated. That's why shit gets crazy with them folks. You ever heard somebody say that desperate times seek desperate measures? Well, folks like that, they livin' in desperate times all the *got-damn time*, so they do some shit that you'd never think of doin' if you feelin' content in your life. Desperation makes folks lie, cheat, steal, hurt the folks that's tryin' to help. You wanna stay the hell away from them folks, fo' sho'. You don't want this shit rubbin' off on you.

> ***It is a characteristic of wisdom not to do desperate things.***
>
> —Henry David Thoreau

DO THIS TODAY: *Are you desperate for somethin'? Watch your actions 'cuz bein' desperate is not a good look and it will never get you what you want. Plus, it can cause wishy-washy behavior and folks will start thinkin' you fulla shit. Rome was not built in a day. Slow your roll.*

November 27th

"YOU GOTTA HAVE YO' SHIT IN ORDER IF YOU WANT ABUNDANCE IN YO' LIFE."

The Universe has a serious kinda order to it. Could you imagine if it got all fucked up and we had some kinda winter right after spring and shit? The new little flowers comin' up would be like, "What the hell?" They die from the *got-damn* snow hittin' 'em. Look at babies. They gotta roll over before they sit up, then they scootch before they crawl, then they stand up and then watch the hell out! There's a got-damn *order* to everything. You ever see the leaves from a tree? They all lookin' alike if they's from the same tree. Order. You see what I'm sayin'? If you wanna be in sync with the Universe, you gotta have yo' shit in order too. You gotta make sure your bills is paid, right? The order is you owe somebody some money, you pay it. You don't, and the flow of abundance is gonna be like, "Hell, naw. We skippin' Jenkins's house. He don't know what the hell is *goings on*."

So, you gotta ask yourself why you ain't payin' that bill. You been livin' in a place of lack? Like, you been thinkin' you can't pay that 'cuz then you won't have no money for somethin' else you gonna need? Okay, maybe not, but pay some. Move it in the right direction. Pay more next time. Have faith in the divine order of things, that you gonna get that flow opened back up to receive all the wealth you gonna need. Get yourself ready. Clean that mothahfuckin' house, 'cuz God's gonna pop over on a surprise visit. You gotta be prepared.

You have to grow from the inside out. None can teach you, none can make you spiritual. There is no other teacher but your own soul.

—Swami Vivekananda

DO THIS TODAY: *Time to get your house in order. Set up a system to make sure yo' bills is paid on time. If you got some late ones, pay a little on 'em right now to show good faith. You gotta show that you can handle a little before God blesses you with a lot.*

November 28th

"IF YOU TRYIN', YOU GOTTA AT LEAST EXPECT THERE'S A CHANCE YOU GONNA SUCCEED."

Unless you four years old or you got a few screws loose, you ain't gonna sit there thinkin' real hard, tryin' to turn yo'self into a mothah-fuckin' orangutan with the power of yo' mind. Why? 'Cuz you know there ain't no chance of succeedin' at that kinda bullshit. You'd need some kinda Harry Potter magic and shit to make that happen. So, lemme ask you somethin'. Why you doin' all that work tryin' to launch your new business, get top salesman, become a fashion model, if you don't think there's a *got-damn* chance you gonna succeed? The answer is, *you do think there's a chance* or you wouldn't be tryin' at all.

I hate it when folks say shit like, "I know it's not likely, but...." Hell, no. If you got it in your head that it ain't likely you gonna succeed, you ain't gonna succeed. You just settin' yourself up for failure. So, that's when you gotta dig down deep and find that one little glimmer of hope, that little bit of a chance, and focus on that instead. You gotta remember, the plants that you waterin', those are the ones that's gonna grow. You ain't gonna water a plant that you know is gonna die. Why would you waste your water like that? So, tell yourself every step of the way that you gonna succeed. If you tryin', you know there's a chance, so take it as far as you can go. You never know which challenge success is on the other side of, so you just gotta keep goin'.

> ***Just try new things. Don't be afraid. Step out of your comfort zones and soar, alright?***
>
> —Michelle Obama

DO THIS TODAY: *A rising tide raises all boats. I love that, 'cuz that shit is so true. Is your tide high? If not, maybe you just need a li'l adjustment. How you gonna raise your tide so you're confident? Take a step toward doin' it today.*

November 29th

"STOP LOOKIN' AT THE *GOT-DAMN* COMMENTS."

Imagine you on your death bed and in yo' head you see the reaction of folks when they find out you gone. What do you see? If you say you thinkin' about all the mothahfuckin' comments on yo' social medias sayin', "Oh, the world lost somebody so talented, so young. Prayin' for his family." All of that shit? If that's what you thinkin' about, you better check yo'self right now. I get it, them comments feels good for a second. Makes you feel like a mothahfuckin' celebrity and shit. But them comments ain't your *legacy*. With one *got-damn* push of a button all of that could be deleted, wiped out, gone, poof, done. The question is, what did you do with your life?

Were you at peace with yourself? Were you so full of mothahfuckin' joy and abundance that it flowed over into other folks' lives? That right there is a *got-damn* legacy you wanna be leavin'. Are you more worried about the comments folks are leavin' or the impact you havin' on the world? Thing is, that shit can get up in your psyche and shit. You readin' the hate, it hurts, so don't do that shit either. I never read the reviews of my shows. If folks was laughin', I knew. 'Cuz there's always gonna be a sumbitch out there wants to cut you up. Don't give 'em the satisfaction. Just be confident that you on the right path, you doin' you, and just don't even read that shit.

> ***The internet isn't reality. The things people are typing are words in an app you can choose to ignore. Put your phone down, close your eyes, count to ten. Think about how you can make the world a better place in the real world. We need you out here.***
>
> —Lizzo

DO THIS TODAY: *Remember, haters gonna hate. They are the people who will broadcast your failures and whisper your success. Thanks for that, Will Smith. Take heed to what he said, he's talkin' from experience. Don't look at a single comment today.*

November 30th

"IT AIN'T ALL ABOUT WILLPOWER, IT'S MORE ABOUT ENVIRONMENT."

You gotta set yourself up to succeed. 'Cuz you could have all the mothahfuckin' willpower in the world, but if everything around you's settin' you up for failure, it's gonna be one helluva struggle. It's kinda like when you tryin' to eat healthier, but you open up the cupboard and that package of Twinkies is starin' back at you. It's gonna be a lot easier if them sumbitches weren't in there.

I had a friend in high school, smart as a mothahfuckah. Probably had the highest IQ of anybody I knew, but he's failin' school. I knew why too. He's livin' in a house that ain't never got no quiet. His grandmama tryin' to raise him, plus his mama there and she on drugs, then she got his sister's kids. He's workin' too. How you gonna study like that? Finally, there was this good teacher that tried to help him out. He found him a place to stay, an old man that needed a little bit of help, you know, gettin' in his groceries and keepin' the lawn nice. Once my friend moved in there, he started gettin' better grades, gettin' his homework turned in. That sumbitch graduated and went to college, now he a mothahfuckin' lawyer. But you see, no matter how much willpower he had in his house growin' up, focusin' on homework and shit was gonna be a struggle. The quiet, safe, clean environment made it a little bit easier.

> ***More often than not, relying on willpower alone is not enough to stick to your good intentions and achieve your goals. What you need is to change your environment so that good behaviors become automatic and bad behaviors harder to do.***
>
> —Max Weigand

DO THIS TODAY: *How can you change up your space to help you focus on success? Do one thing to move toward that today.*

December 1st

"CHECK THE FACTS. EVEN IF YOU TRUST SOMEBODY, THEY COULD BE WRONG."

Generally speakin', folks is trustworthy, you know? You can't be goin' around thinkin' everybody's a lyin' cheat. Thinkin' like that would drive you crazy. Thing is, it ain't always about trust. Folks make mistakes too. Maybe they tellin' you some kinda business information, and they think it's accurate, but they got it from a source that wasn't givin' it to 'em straight. So for the most part, trust folks, but if it's somethin' important, you gotta go do your own *got-damn* research too. Or maybe it means you cross-reference what they told you with somebody else who knows. You get two or three folks tellin' you the same thing, maybe it's all good. It could mean you talk to an expert. If yo' coworker tells you to buy stock in Willie's Widgets 'cuz they did, and they know it's gonna pay out fo' sho', you better call your *got-damn* financial advisor before you go buyin' in. You see what I'm sayin'?

I had this sumbitch once wantin' me to make a movie with 'em, put up some of my own money and shit. They tellin' me they got a top-notch crew, they got a home base in Atlanta, they got some fantastic projects under their belt already, and they been doin' this for twenty years. Mothahfuckah, if you been doin' this for twenty years, how come I can't find none of your shit anywhere? I find myself a *got-damn* web site that's got a PO Box that ain't no *got-damn* office in Atlanta, Georgia, and some fake-ass photos of some movies that's still *in production*! Can't find nothin' legitimate about you nowhere, then I ask around. Shoot, nobody done worked with you wants to work with you again. I done my research, 'cuz all of what he was tellin' me sounded real good, but you can put frostin' on a piece of shit and underneath it's still a piece of shit.

> ***Trust, but verify.***
>
> —Ronald Reagan

DO THIS TODAY: *Did anybody tell you somethin' lately that you just took at face value? Take a minute to cross-reference. Maybe you find out they chill, but if not, make sure you don't let it slide.*

December 2nd

"YOU GOTTA BE LOOKIN' YOUR BEST AT ALL TIMES. YOU NEVER KNOW WHO YOU GONNA RUN INTO."

Y'all can say you don't judge a book by its cover all you want, but the truth is, we all doin' it. You gonna look a sumbitch up and down, give 'em the once-over, 'cuz you assessin' his situation. Yep, you doin' it, and he's doin' it to you too. So, what is he gonna see when he's lookin' at you?

I tell ya', folks today ain't got no shame. They goin' up to the corner store in their pajama bottoms with some Tweety Birds all over 'em, flip flops, nasty-ass T-shirt that got the Cheeto cheese wiped on it. They lookin' like they just rolled outta they box under the *got-damn* overpass. They get the sodas and lotto tickets, go on out the door, and get up in their brand-new shiny black G Wagon. What in the actual hell? You drivin' a G Wagon and you couldn't put on no pants? It's a damn shame. I mean, what if you runnin' into somebody in that store that coulda opened doors for you? Hell, what if you run into me? Now, I ain't a judgmental sumbitch, but if you can't get outta your pajamas to go to the store, I don't think I'm gonna give you my business card and shit. Hell, naw. You gotta present yourself like you a mothahfuckin' gift. Your clothes, your haircut, your nails, your shoes, you gotta let 'em say, "Hey y'all, come open this package!" What you lookin' like on the outside is gonna give folks a little glimpse of what maybe's on the inside too. So, have some mothahfuckin' self-respect and clean yo' act up!

> ***To me, clothing is a form of self-expression. There are hints about who you are in what you wear.***
>
> —Marc Jacobs

DO THIS TODAY: *It don't matter what you doin' today, get yourself together. Wear clean clothes, nice shoes, brush yo'* got-damn *teeth. See how that changes your confidence level.*

December 3rd

"A FIRM HANDSHAKE TELLS FOLKS YOU GOT CONFIDENCE."

Nothin' worse than a sumbitch shakin' yo' hand for the first time and his hand's all loose and floppy. Gives me the mothahfuckin' willies, but it also says that he ain't got the confidence to hold firm and look me in the *got-damn* eye. Shakin' hands firm is somethin' my granddad taught me when I was just a young man. His hand was big, and he took my little one in it. He told me, "When you shake hands with folks at church, it's gotta be firm, but don't squeeze the hell out of 'em." Then he took my hand, and told me to look him in the eye. He went on and said if you got a handshake that's weak, you a sissy and you probably hidin' somethin'. If it's too strong, you tryin' to prove somethin', and that ain't good neither. Just firm, like you pickin' up a baseball and you about to throw it.

Boy, that's probably one of the best things I was ever taught. That day I went to church, and I was shakin' everybody's hand, and I learned a whole helluva lot about the folks in the Burning Bush Baptist Church. Brotha Franklin was a sissy, and Mr. Wilkins and Don the janitor. Mrs. Moseley had a clincher that almost broke my bones, so I was always suspicious of that woman after that. Then there was the folks that had a perfect shake. I'd stick with those folks, 'cuz I felt like I could trust 'em. That's what I'm sayin', though, your handshake is as important as a mothahfuckah. It's a part of somebody's first impression of you, so make sure it's good.

> ***It's all about having fun and smiling and shaking hands.***
>
> —Tone Lōc

DO THIS TODAY: *Practice your handshake with somebody. Ask 'em if it's good, or if it needs some improvement. Maybe you let 'em know about theirs, too, if they wanna hear it.*

December 4th

"BE CAREFUL WHAT YOU GO LOOKIN' FOR, 'CUZ YOU JUST MIGHT FIND IT."

I hear a lotta young folks goin' out to Hollywood, or New York, or Detroit, or Nashville, they gonna be film and music superstars. They be wantin' fame and fortune and all of that attention from the *got-damn* paparazzi. But them kids got no idea what it is they askin' for, and if they ain't passionate about what they doin' to get there, the fruits of that labor's gonna taste rotten as hell.

When you makin' wishes, sayin' prayers, and throwin' your hopes and dreams out there to God and the Universe, you gotta study up about what all of it's gonna mean. You wanna be a famous actor? That's gonna mean a lot of *got-damn* rejection, 'cuz you gonna put in for a lotta parts you ain't gonna get. Then if you do get the fame, that's gonna mean you ain't got no privacy no more. You gonna be livin' in a glass house, so you better be prepared to change yo' clothes in the basement. It's gonna mean you gonna have a lot of fake folks tryin' to get close to you, so you always gotta guess who's the real deal. It's gonna mean lots of time spent on sets, workin' crazy hours, travelin'. Could also mean you gotta stay fit, eat right, work out, keep yourself in shape. If you get that fame, it's probably gonna come with fortune. You gonna have to learn how to manage that money, make sure you don't flush it all away too fast. Lots of famous folks have their time, then they end up with nothin'. I ain't sayin' you shouldn't do it. I done it, and I wouldn't change a *got-damn* thing. But you gotta love the core of it so much that you gonna be able to deal with all the rest.

> ***Be careful what you set your heart upon for it will surely be yours .***
>
> —James Baldwin

DO THIS TODAY: *What's your goal? Do you know everything that comes with it if you reach it? If the answer is no, do some research. The more clearly you see everything about that goal, the easier you gonna achieve it...if you decide it's still what you want.*

December 5th

"IF YOU IMAGININ' THE WORST, THAT'S ALL YOU GONNA SEE."

Your imagination can be convincin' as a mothahfuckah, and we been taught to imagine the worst-case scenarios so we can prevent 'em from happenin'. But sometimes all that does is make us paranoid, scared, makin' all kinds of shit up in our heads that's statistically not very likely to happen. You ever go to bed right after watchin' a ***got-damn*** horror movie? You layin' there, eyes wide open, thinkin' that little *tick-tick* you hear way the hell downstairs is a sumbitch in a mothahfuckin' clown mask comin' to kill you and steal yo' watch. Your mind is a mothahfuckah, and it gonna create whatever you thinkin' about. If you'da gone to bed and you just watched *The Santa Clause 3*, you gonna be thinkin' that *tick-tick* is got-damn *Tim Allen* in a red suit instead of some Freddy Krueger shit.

I got a friend, she can't watch nothin' that's scary or depressin' as hell, 'cuz that shit fucks her up for days. It's like her mind can't separate it out from reality. I get it, though. The mind's a bit crazy like that. It don't always know what's real and what's made-up stories, especially when you watchin' in HD and shit. And, especially when them shows is so close to bein' real. That's when it gets scary as hell. Suddenly, every time you lookin' in a mirror at night, all you can see is Candyman and shit. You can't keep on thinkin' the worst is gonna happen, or you gonna be a nervous wreck and that energy is gonna block yo' blessin's, for real. If you think you gonna get mugged, you think your business is gonna fail, you think your partner gonna cheat, you thinkin' it into reality. Don't do that shit. Think better thoughts.

> ***The only thing you experience is what you created.***
>
> —Meir Ezra

DO THIS TODAY: *Do you have a worst-case scenario mindset? It's time to reprogram. Take one thing you always thinkin' the worst about and rewrite the script. Get that new visual in your mind and reference it often.*

December 6th

"WAKE UP EVERY MORNIN' AND SAY, 'THIS IS THE BEST DAY OF MY LIFE.'"

I had this friend of mine named Jay, and every mornin' that sumbitch would get up and say, "Today's the best day ever." Well…I ain't gonna lie. What he really said was, "Imma make today my bitch." And that sumbitch would too. He ain't come from nothin', neither. Grew up in the projects, no daddy and no mama, raised up by his no-good uncle that never did a *got-damn* thing for that boy but put a roof over his head. But Jay's attitude was mothahfuckin' inspirin'. First time I heard him say it, I'd crashed at his place for the night, and we woke up late, sun's shinin' and it's gettin' hot. He opens his eyes, rolls outta bed, and I wake up to him sayin' it out loud, "I'm gonna make today my bitch." Well, I didn't hear him right, and I's thinkin' he says he's gonna make *me* his bitch. I shot up outta bed and grabbed that mothahfuckah by the throat, and I says, "What did you say to me?" He got this big shit-eatin' grin on his face, and he says, "C'mon, Black. Let's make today our bitch." I eased up, and I said, "Whatchyou mean, mothahfuckah?" He gets this look in his eyes like they all lit up. That day was a great mothahfuckin' day. We did all sorts of shit, goin' down to the Navy Pier, we made some new friends that ended up bein' a connection for Jay and the construction business he's wantin' to start. We ate good food from some cheap Mexican street vendors. It felt good, and I learned somethin' from him. Every day you gotta look at it like an opportunity. If you doin' that, it is gonna be a good day every day.

> ***Every day I feel is a blessing from God. And I consider it a new beginning. Yeah, everything is beautiful.***
>
> —Prince

DO THIS TODAY: *Say it right now. This is the best day of my life! Or, if you prefer. I'm gonna make today my bitch. Now go and do it!*

December 7th

"YOU CAN'T BE IN CONTROL OF YOURSELF IF YOU GOT SUBSTANCES CONTROLLIN' YOU."

I ain't talkin' about pharmaceutical prescriptions given to you by a doctor to help you with a situation. I'm talkin' about overusin' and abusin' drugs and alcohol to the point it changes who the hell you are. How you gonna be responsible for your actions if you ain't got control of yourself? Well, most folks will use that as somethin' to blame so they don't have to take responsibility. But that's a *got-damn* copout. I ain't puttin' down folks that's got an addiction. They probably had somethin' in their life that lead 'em there, and I pray they get some help.

But what usin' drugs and too much alcohol does to you is it gives you an out. You can say, "That wasn't me, it was the drugs talkin'." You get to shift the responsibility, then guess what? You let go of your control. When you do that, you got nothin'. You ain't on your path no more. It's sad when I see that happenin' to folks with a bright mothahfuckin' future. You gotta trust that your own mind is much, much more powerful than any kinda substance. It can do greater things for y'all. You wouldn't let some other sumbitch control you, why you lettin' some drugs and shit do it? You gotta keep your power, that's the only way to find the kinda success you deserve. So, be the sober one, 'cuz that buzz is gonna last a minute, but you achievin' your dreams, that shit's gonna last a helluva lot longer.

> ***I like to be in control of how I look and how I feel and how I act.***
>
> —Billie Eilish

DO THIS TODAY: *Assess your use of substances right now. If you lettin' 'em take over too much of your control, put a pause on 'em. If you havin' trouble pausin', get help. It's one of the mothahfuckin' strongest things in the world to ask for help when you need it.*

December 8th

"YOU GOTTA PLAY MUSIC, IT'S LIKE THE SOUNDTRACK FOR YOUR *GOT-DAMN* LIFE."

There's somethin' a little suspicious about folks who never listen to no music. You ever get in the car with somebody, and they don't turn on no radio, and they ain't talkin', neither. It's strange. Or you got over to somebody's crib and they sittin' there gettin' you drinks and shit, and they don't put on no record? Hell, naw. You gotta at least have some background Muzak. Ya' see, the music is like the soundtrack to your mothahfuckin' life. You ever watch a movie without no soundtrack on? It's boring as hell, makes you wanna smack yo' head against the wall. You gotta have a soundtrack, mothahfuckah. It makes you feel alive.

Them musicians, they know they got that kinda power too. They make a song, write them lyrics and that music, and they know how they wanna move you with it. Sometimes, a particular song will remind you of a time in your life, bad or good, and you go to it when you wanna remember that feelin'. Other songs, we use 'em to rev us up, get us movin'. You put on a little Frankie Beverly and Maze when you about to clean the house, it keeps you wipin' and sweepin' and groovin' like you a *Solid Gold* Dancer. Then other times, you put on a song to help you wipe away some kinda pain you goin' through. That song helps you hit a reset in your soul. 'Cuz what good music does is it takes you on an emotional journey in just a few *got-damn* minutes. Use that, it's a mothahfuckin' gift.

> ***All you really have that really matters are feelings. That's what music is to me.***
>
> —Janis Joplin

DO THIS TODAY: *How you feelin' right now? Do you wanna highlight it or change it? Put on a song to fit the moment and for the next three minutes, let it make you feel some kinda way. Like the famous* Soul Train *sayin' goes, I wish you Love, Peace, and S-O-U-L.*

December 9th

"TOO MUCH OF A GOOD THING MIGHT PRETTY NEAR KILL YA'."

I love my job, but that don't mean I always wanna be doin' it. That's a common misconception about followin' your passion. Folks think, "Wow, you doin' what you love, must be fun all the damn time." Well, it is, mostly. But, you know, whiskey's fun until you drink seventeen shots and wake up on the flo' wearin' a boa and no pants. Livin' your passion, sure, it's fun. I wouldn't wanna do nothin' else with my life. But it starts to get un-fun when you been shootin' a show for seventy-two days straight, eighteen hours a day, no sleep, and you miss the hell outta your family. When it starts gettin' like that, it's time to put shit on pause and rethink how you doin' it.

Ya' see, life has this way of jumpin' up in your passions and turnin' 'em into money-makers. That's a mothahfuckin' good thing mosta the time. That's how you turn your passion into a career, but you can't let the money-machine take over. It's okay to say no to a project, not 'cuz you don't like it, but just 'cuz you needin' a break for a minute. It's also just fine to let the folks that's puttin' it together know that you wanna do it, but the timeline's gotta be a little bit longer, or you need every other weekend off to go home and visit your family. Whatever you gotta do, do it, 'cuz it would be a damn shame if you got burned out on what you love.

I feel sad when I'm overworked, and I just become a moneymaking machine and my passion and creativity take a backseat. That makes me unhappy. So, what did I do? I started to say no.

—Lady Gaga

DO THIS TODAY: *Bein' busy is kinda like a humble brag that you important. But if you really are "too damn busy," you ain't saying no enough. If you said no more, what could you say yes to? More self-care, more time with your family? More of workin' on your passion project? Allow your possibilities to inspire your "no."*

December 10th

"YOU DON'T ALWAYS WANNA BE THE SMARTEST MOTHAHFUCKAH IN THE ROOM."

If you always thinkin' you the smartest sumbitch you know, then you gotta start knowin' some more folks. How you gonna learn if you always the one that knows more than everybody else? Then it begs to ask the question, "Do you really know better than everybody else, or are you just full of your *got-damn* self?" Now, it's okay to be an expert in some kinda things, and maybe for them things you the one to go to for the final say. But you gotta open your eyes and see that other folks got talent too. Other folks have got gifts, and even if they ain't the smartest one in the room, that don't mean their contributions ain't valuable as a mothahfuckah.

You gotta learn how to collaborate, commiserate, compromise. You gotta learn how to listen, 'cuz maybe, just maybe, somebody's got the winningest mothahfuckin' idea ever, and you gonna miss it if you talkin' on your own shit all the *got-damn* time. When I had the *Midnight Mac* show, I's workin' with the dancers and the band, all of that, the Macaronis and the Mac Man Band. If my band leader, Shorty Ruff, if he had some ideas, I sure as hell listened to him 'cuz he's the music man. I am humble enough to admit that he's gonna know better than me when it comes to the jams. I know what I like, but he knows how to do it up right. Listen, if you take the best of everybody's best, you got a winner fo' sho', 'cuz you lettin' everybody shine, and that's openin' a door for abundance to flow on in, right there.

> ***As you navigate through the rest of your life, be open to collaboration. Other people and other people's ideas are often better than your own.***
>
> —Amy Poehler

DO THIS TODAY: *If you got a team, trust 'em. Listen to 'em. Learn to collaborate. If you ain't got a team, maybe bounce ideas off somebody and get feedback. You only gonna make yourself better. Teamwork is the best work.*

December 11th

"WHEN YOU MAKE IT TO THE TOP, YOU GOT FOLKS LOOKIN' UP TO YOU. YOU GOTTA TAKE THAT RESPONSIBILITY SERIOUSLY."

You get successful and chances are you got folks that's thinkin' you their mothahfuckin' role model. And if you got your success in anything that's entertainment, sports, music, video gamin', TikTokkin', you got a helluva lotta impressionable kids lookin' up to you too. They gonna be wantin' to be like you, so you gotta teach 'em how to act right, otherwise if they doin' what you doin' and it's some bad shit, that's on you. But if you got good values, you gonna be a good example, so just do you. Them kids is gonna wanna do it too. And maybe even more important, they gonna *know* they can.

I like to think that I can be that kinda hero for some kids back in my old neighborhood on the south side of Chicago. Y'all know they named a street after me? Yeah, it's Bernie Mac Street, right where our tiny apartment was up above the Burning Bush Baptist Church on the corner of West Sixty-Ninth Street. My publicist, Denise Jordan Walker, I called her DJ, damn, that girl had some kinda creative genius. DJ knew it was gonna be more than just a sign. Two-hundred folks come out to see it go up, includin' the Reverend Jesse Jackson...and a whole lotta little kids growin' up right where I did. If y'all could see the look on they faces, 'cuz that sign's tellin' 'em they can do it too. If my success is gonna inspire even one of them kids, I'm a happy sumbitch.

If you are given a chance to be a role model, I think you should always take it because you can influence a person's life in a positive light, and that's what I want to do.

—Tiger Woods

DO THIS TODAY: *Pretend you in front of a first-grade class. You gotta tell them kids everything about yourself, everything you do, and all of them kids is gonna do exactly what you doin'. What would you change about yourself knowin' that?*

December 12th

"ADD VALUE AND YOU GONNA BE SUCCESSFUL."

Why do you think every got-damn fast-food chain's got a "value menu?" 'Cuz folks want value. Well, what the hell is value? When you talkin' about goods, shit you buy, value is when you gettin' yo' money's worth. When I'm talkin' about addin' value, I don't mean that you gotta come with a side of fries. I don't mean you gotta throw your own money at it. I mean whenever you gettin' involved in some kind of endeavor, make sure you addin' somethin' beneficial to it. Otherwise, you just dead weight, and why would anybody want that?

Let's say you workin' at a fast-food restaurant. Hey, no shame in that, I worked my share of fry baskets in my day. Let's say you workin' there and you just goin' along cookin' the food, puttin' in containers, ringin' up customers. Okay, you doin' your job. You just gettin' along, and that's alright. But if you wanna be successful, you gotta add somethin' to it. When I was workin' at Dock's Fish Fry, I used my gift to bring in customers. Ya' see, I's always makin' folks smile when they come in for their food. So, I started standin' outside talkin' to folks, bringin' 'em in, tellin' 'em about specials and, "Mmhmmm, make sure you add some of them hush puppies. They make everything bettah." The boss noticed sales was up when I was workin', and that's how I got a promotion. Take that on into my career as a comedian, and I ain't just got fans. Anybody can have some fans and it don't help 'em a *got-damn* bit. But you givin' 'em a show, and a movie, and a television program, a live stage performance, and a book. That's value.

Convert your fans into your customers by adding value to what you do.

—Israelmore Ayivor

DO THIS TODAY: *Think about how you could add value to whatever you doin' today. Do you have a kickin' TikTok account? Maybe you start sellin' T-shirts with your tagline on 'em. You work at a retail clothing store? Create an extra-fly window display. You washin' the dishes for your mama, put 'em away too. You see what I'm sayin'? Add value.*

December 13th

"LEARN HOW TO SELL WHAT YOU GOT."

I wouldn't call myself no salesman. I'm a comic, an actor, a mothahfuckin' artist. I ain't no salesman, but I gotta know how to sell myself if I wanna work my craft and make some money for doin' it. When you think about it, seems like we always sellin' ourselves in some kinda way. I ain't sayin' you gotta hustle nobody, I'm just sayin' there's a way we puttin' ourselves out there for folks to either like or turn around and say, "Naw, not for me." When you an artist, you can create all the mothahfuckin' art you want, but if you ain't sellin' it, you starvin'. In the kinda world we live in, you gotta make some money if you wanna survive. Now, maybe you got yourself a sugah mama or a sugah daddy, and you got all the time in the world to create art without havin' to make no dough off it. But if you like most of the folks out there, you wanna make it your career so you don't have to work no survival job no more.

You gonna spend an average of thirteen years of your life workin'. That's a lotta *got-damn* time. You better make sure you doin' somethin' you like doin'. That means if you got a passion, and you can make some money doin' it, them thirteen years ain't gonna seem like you throwin' away all that time. So, you gotta hone up your salesman skills and learn how to sell what you got. It ain't a sellout, it's a sell up.

Good things happen to those who hustle.

—Chuck Noll

DO THIS TODAY: *What is your passion? Do you know how you're going to make a livin' doin' it? If the answer is no, do some research on it today. How are other folks doin' it? That can be a good place to start. You gotta hustle and flow.*

December 14th

"DON'T TRY AND READ THIRTY-SEVEN SELF-HELP BOOKS."

It's easy to get caught up in the self-help wave. You start feelin' a little better, doin' a little better, and you wanna see what the next guy has to say about it. Thing is, you could get thirty-seven different self-help books and they all gonna say a lot of the same shit, just in different ways. And lemme tell you, that shit can get confusin' as hell. I ain't sayin' not to get one or two of 'em. I ain't no therapist or somethin' like that, I'm just tellin' you what I know. So if you wanna cross check my ass, please do it, fo' sho'. But if you get bogged down in readin' more and more, first thing is it's gonna get confusin'. Second thing is you gonna spend more time readin' than doin'. You gonna let life pass you by if all you doin' is readin' about how to do it, instead of gettin' out there gettin' your hands dirty. You gotta put them principles into practice, y'all. That's why I got a "do this today" section at the end of every page.

So, you try the steps these books is tellin' ya', and if it ain't workin' out quite right, then it's okay to go on and get another book. But thing is, you gotta really try it for real. If you puttin' everything you have into some kinda method, some kind of advice, and you still feelin' like you ain't makin' no progress, then you gotta check in with your intuition. Is this advice still feelin' right? If it ain't, chalk that one up to a learnin' experience and move on. But be honest with yourself about whether you really tryin'. That's gonna make all the *got-damn* difference.

> ***Listen to advice but follow your heart.***
>
> —Conway Twitty

DO THIS TODAY: *Ignore the side conversations. Remind yourself to be positive. Follow your own damn heart no matter how ridiculous it might seem and despite the disapproval of folks around you. Followin' your heart will teach you a lot about courage.*

December 15th

"KNOW WHAT PART YOU PLAY, AND EVERYBODY ELSE'S PART TOO."

You gotta know the who, what, where, why, when, and how of whatever industry it is that you involved in. If you ain't understandin' how the *got-damn* machine works, then how you gonna know how to make it work for you? So, you study it like a mothahfuckah 'til you know it inside and out. That way, not only do you sound intelligible about it, you know who to go to to get what you need.

Lemme tell you somethin' about folks that wanna be an actor, 'cuz you know I spent some time on the big screen myself. Okay, so you know that an actor memorizes lines and goes on a set and maybe you know what the director's supposed to do. But do you know what the first AD supposed to do? How about the best boy, the grip, the head of craft services? Do you know who you supposed to talk to if you ain't got a call sheet? Who's the one that's meant to get your wardrobe to your trailer? What does the editor do? Shit, if you don't know this information, then you ain't ready. You gotta know all the damn parts so you know where you fit. Imagine if you a mechanic and you specialize in fixin' a carburetor. Cool, that's great, but what if you don't know what the fan belt does, where the brake lines are at, or how to put in the *got-damn* oil? I don't think I want you to fix my mothahfuckin' carburetor. You get my drift? You gotta know as much as you can about whatever business you thinkin' you goin' into, so you know how to do your job the best possible way. And *got-damn*, if you know what other folks doin' in that business, they gonna respect you for that, and them connections could be invaluable.

> ***A life is not important except in the impact it has on other lives.***
>
> —Jackie Robinson

DO THIS TODAY: *Learn about the industry you in or you wanna get into. Find out all the movin' parts, all the different roles folks play from start to finish, and take some good* ***got-damn*** *notes.*

December 16th

"EVERYBODY'S GOT A GOOD IDEA. WHAT MAKES YOU THINK YOURS IS A STAND-OUT?"

Everybody who's got an idea and they excited to tell y'all about it, they think that idea's good. They thinkin' it's the best thing since sliced bread. But did they actually do their homework? Is there about another million of the same ideas out there? I know, you don't wanna make yourself or nobody else feel small, don't wanna hold 'em down, that ain't what I'm talkin' about here. If you got an idea, that's great. That's the very first step, though. You gotta whole got-damn *staircase* still to go. But that's okay, you can do it.

Listen here. What if I come and tell you I got this sweet new invention. You ask me what the hell it is, and I say, "It's a doormat." A doormat? They gonna look at you like you a crazy sumbitch. Who gonna buy a doormat? Then I say, "It's a doormat that can sense who the hell's standin' on it and let ya' know if you wanna answer the door or pretend like you ain't home." Now there it is, I'd buy the hell outta that sumbitch. You price it right, and every mothahfuckah's gonna want one of them. Nobody likes to be taken by surprise, and you accidentally open up the door when yo' cousin Lenny comes around. He always lookin' for a handout and shit. That's a unique *got-damn* product right there. Same thing if you pitchin' a TV show idea, a movie script, a book, yo' music. What makes you stand out from all of the rest? That's your angle, and that's what's gonna make you successful.

> ***Business opportunities are like buses, there's always another one coming.***
>
> —Richard Branson

DO THIS TODAY: *Make a list of all the ways your idea, product, art, service is unique. That's gonna be your sellin' point. If you can't think of none, then you might wanna get creative and rethink what you got. Could be it needs some tweakin'.*

December 17th

"YOU WANNA FIND SUCCESS? STOP CHASIN' IT."

That might sound like a mothahfuckin' contradiction, but I'm gonna tell you why it ain't. First off, what's your idea of success? For most folks, it's havin' the reward that comes with winnin'. If you lookin' at it that way, success comes at the end of the road. But I'm gonna tell you, that couldn't be further from the truth. Success is part of the process. And that's a *got-damn* good thing too. 'Cuz if success is part of the process, then when you workin' toward somethin' you got a passion for, you already successful. Ya' see, it's built right in. However, if you chasin' success, then you livin' from a lack mindset. You chasin' it 'cuz you ain't got it yet. You gotta get to that destination 'cuz you ain't there yet.

Best thing you can do for yourself is quit chasin'. You know if you a chaser 'cuz you always got the next scheme to "make it big." You keep thinkin', *When this succeeds, I'll be happy*. You got a stack of plans that never get realized. You been puttin' up your own *got-damn* roadblock. Stop chasin' and start bein'. Don't say you gonna be happy, be happy. Don't say you gonna be successful, be successful. Keep yourself busy doin' what you love to do, and before you know it, you gonna realize you been a successful mothahfuckah all along. You know what happens when you make success a part of your personality? Abundance starts flowin' in, and you can't stop it for tryin'.

> ***Success usually comes to those who are too busy to be looking for it.***
>
> —Henry David Thoreau

DO THIS TODAY: *Stay focused on the future but use your time in the present. Imagine you on a road and you can see the horizon, but you also gotta be whistlin' while you walkin' and watchin' where you step.*

December 18th

"DON'T TELL NOBODY WHAT YOU WANT FOR NO CHRISTMAS THIS YEAR."

Now, don't get all up in my Christmas business. I mean, whatever winter holiday you celebratin', most of 'em's comin' with gifts. That's just the kinda society we livin' in nowadays. And right around this time of year, seems like everybody's askin', "What do you want for (insert Christmas, Hanukkah, Kwanzaa, or your favorite winter holiday)?" I get they don't mean no harm by askin' that. Shoot, I asked it a lotta times myself, especially to the family. The wife, Boops, the cousins, in-laws, you know. But when you gotta answer that question over and over, it does a couple of things to your mindset. First, it refocuses your brain on lack. You thinkin' you want this and you want that, rather than focusin' on all of your blessin's. Second, it sets you up for disappointment. You think you gonna get everything on that list of yours? Maybe, maybe not. But then you anxious thinkin' about it. Third, it makes it too easy on the giver. You want folks to take a minute to think about who you are as a human bein'. If they know you well enough, they gonna be able to figure out somethin' that's gonna make you happy. Fourth, givin' out lists takes the fun of the surprise outta the receivin'. That's half the joy is gettin' somethin' thoughtful, somethin' somebody took the time and care to think about and then wrapped it up nice and handed it to you, 'just 'cuz they know it's gonna make you smile. So, this year, when folks is askin' you what you want, tell 'em you happy just to have 'em in your life. But if they wanna give you a gift, make it a surprise. See how that refocuses all of that abundance energy this holiday season.

> ***It's the thought that counts.***
>
> —Adage

DO THIS TODAY: *Practice what you gonna say when somebody asks you what's on your Christmas list. Try this one or use your own variation: I'm already blessed, so I ain't askin' for nothin'. If you wanna surprise me with somethin' from your heart, I'll accept it gratefully.*

December 19th

"FOLKS DON'T JUST UP AND MAKE IT OUTTA NOWHERE, YOU JUST SEEIN' WHERE THEY AT NOW."

I'm sure some folks was lookin' at me when I started makin' it, goin', "Oh, Bernie Mac, where the hell'd he come from?" But I wasn't no instant star and shit. Back then, you couldn't just make one mothahfuckin' TikTok and—*BOOM*—famous. Okay, but that's my point too. You think somebody's just instantly famous, even on TikTok? Take a closer look. Some of them folks has had years of acting training, takin' classes at Second City and shit. Maybe they done theater they whole life, greasin' up them entertainin' chops.

I'm gonna give you an example. Billie Eilish, lots of folks thinkin' she was an overnight success. Sure, she young, but that don't mean she didn't work her ass off to get where she got. That little girl was actin' in homemade movies, singin' and dancin' since she was knee high to a grasshopper. Eight years old, she's singin' in the choir, and eleven years old, she's composin' her own music. Her timeline might'a been slid up a little earlier than most folks, probably 'cuz she grew up in a musical family, but that don't mean she didn't put her time in. She was workin' her passion for over a decade before she hit it big. Successes almost never just come up outta nowhere, they get built up over time. Just 'cuz you don't see the fin of a shark 'til it pops up outta the water don't mean he didn't swim up from the bottom.

> ***If you really look closely, most overnight successes took a long time.***
>
> —Steve Jobs

DO THIS TODAY: *Look up one of your favorite overnight success stories. Maybe it's a pop star, an athlete, a real estate tycoon. See if you can find out what they done to get where they at now. My guess is they put in a hell of a lot more groundwork than you realize.*

December 20th

"MAKE YOUR *GOT-DAMN BED.*"

After you stretch yo' ass out and put yo' feet on the floor, the first thing you should do in the mornin' is make your *got-damn* bed. I know, I'm soundin' like your mama, but I got a different kinda reason for tellin' you this. Your mama wanted you to make your bed to keep the mothahfuckin' house clean, 'cuz she's sick and tired of doin' all the shit herself. I could give a good *got-damn* about how clean your house is. You the one gotta live in it. I'm tellin' you to make your bed 'cuz it starts you out havin' accomplished somethin' within the first minute of openin' your eyes. That's gonna subconsciously make you feel good and set you up right for the whole rest of the day. I started makin' it a habit to make my bed right as I'm slidin' out of it. Even if my wife's still asleep up in there, I just tuck her right the fuck in, fluff them pillows around her, and it's all good.

You doin' this, you buildin' a habit. One thing most successful folks has in common, is they have good habits, shit they do every day (especially in the mornin') that's keepin' 'em on track. Makin' your bed is an easy one. How long's it take you? Thirty seconds? It's a good mothahfuckin' start. Anybody can do somethin' for thirty seconds, just ask my wife.

> ***It is only when you take responsibility for your life that you discover how powerful you truly are.***
>
> —Allanah Hunt

DO THIS TODAY: *Make your bed. If you already been doin' that, add another tiny habit right after that to help further your successful mindset. Maybe you wipe down your bathroom sink or floss instead of just brush, drink a glass of water 'cuz you gotta stay hydrated, y'all see what I mean.*

December 21st

"INCREDIBLE THING ABOUT THE WORLD IS THERE'S SO MUCH AMAZIN' SHIT TO DO."

I don't ever wanna hear you sayin' you bored, mothahfuckah. Not when there's so much got-damn amazin' shit to do in this great big world out there. All you gotta do is go out the door and open up yo' eyes. If you bored, if you ain't doin' nothin', well that shit's on you. I can't remember a time when I wasn't doin' somethin'. Now, I ain't sayin' you can't take a break once in a while just to relax, be a little bit idle and let your mind breathe. But generally speakin', I always got somethin' ***goings on***. 'Cuz you know I started out a comic, then I went on into actin' in movies and TV shows, but I also love music. Man, I've always wanted to cut me an album some day. And if I ain't workin' toward a specific new goal, I'm doin' other activities to have fun and maybe learn somethin', broaden my view, so to speak. Maybe I'm golfin', goin' to a play or a concert, playin' with the grandkids and grand-nieces and -nephews, goin' to a ball game, takin' a *got-damn* walk and lookin' at nature—that shit's fascinatin'. Anyway, when I get done with one goal of mine, I'm always keepin' my eyes open for the next thing, 'cuz there's always somethin' there waitin'. None of y'all path's a dead-end street. It keeps on goin' until you want it to stop. I mean hell, who woulda thought I'd go ahead and be an author? Damn, that's cool. So, the first thing you say after, "I did it!" is "What's next?"

> ***People ask, "What's the best role you've ever played?" The next one.***
>
> —Kevin Kline

DO THIS TODAY: *Stop thinkin' that when you reach your goal, that's it for you. Instead, think, "What's next?" Make a list, either on paper or in your brain, of all the amazin' shit you could choose from after you reach the goal that's on your plate right now.*

December 22nd

"DON'T GET SO SUCKED IN THAT YOU FORGET TO PUT YOUR HEAD UP ONCE IN A WHILE."

Sometimes you can get your head stuck so far up in your passion that you forget there's a whole lotta world out there, and you best not be lettin' it slide by without you. I see it all the damn time. Y'all know them folks, all they ever talkin' about, all they ever doin' is work. I get it, you excited about the new mothahfuckin' vitamin supplement you sellin' all made outta plants, vegan and cruelty free, it's gonna make me skinny and make sure my heart don't fail me. You love that shit and you wanna sell more of it. You got chutzpah, I'll give ya' that. But *got-damn*, can we watch the Bears game without you tellin' me how them vitamins fixed your damn colon? You keep beatin' somebody over the head with somethin' pretty soon they gonna tell you to knock it the fuck off.

Other thing is not so much about other folks, it's about you. Soon as you get that kinda tunnel vision, you ain't noticin' all the other shit that's goings *on* in the world. You wanna be good at what you doin', you gotta connect. You gotta keep in tune with the society you livin' in. You think I'd be a good comedian if all I did was talk about my jokes? Where the hell you think them jokes is comin' from? I'm gettin' 'em from my observations of the world. How am I gonna make a joke about White folks at basketball games if I ain't never seen one in person?

> ***We often engage the defense mechanism of tunnel vision, just to keep ourselves focused on our daily lives. This makes us terribly jaded in our perception of what is really around us.***
>
> —Vera Nazarian

DO THIS TODAY: *Go out somewhere and just watch. I like to call it people-watchin'. Parks is good for it, malls, airports, big-box stores, sports events. Be an observer and see what you see.*

December 23rd

"PAY ATTENTION TO YOUR DREAMS AND THEY GONNA TELL YOU SOMETHIN'."

If you wake up from a dream and it made you feel some kinda way, pay attention. 'Cuz when you sleepin', your brain's gonna process shit in a whole different kinda way. I remember a friend of mine told me about this dream she had right before a very important meetin'. In the dream she was sittin' on a bench waitin' for a train. It was a cold winter's day and this large man walks up and stands in front of her with his back to her. He opens his coat and she's suddenly on a train in a dark tunnel! There's two ladies talkin' to her on the train, very close to her face, askin' all kinda questions, bein' nosey and shit like an interrogation. She answers the ladies as best she can, then they suddenly disappear. In their place is a close friend who passed on some years earlier. ***Aw, hell naw, I'd be tryin' to wake my ass outta that dream right then***. Anyway, the passed-on friend looks at her slowly then asks her in all sincerity, "Why are you doin' this?" So, she tells him why. He smiles and shakes his head. He's happy with what she said. Then her dream ends right there. Thirty minutes later, she had the meetin' with this top executive that had the power to push one of her dreams into reality. Towards the end of that call, the executive asked the exact question that was in her dream, "Why are you doin' this?" She was floored, and she literally gave him the answer she gave the passed-on friend in the dream. The executive decided to back the project. That dream literally put her in line with her truth and gave her what she needed to bring her goals to fruition. Now, that's some deep shit right there.

> ***Reality is wrong. Dreams are for real.***
>
> —Tupac Shakur

DO THIS TODAY: *What kinda question you got that you been lookin' for an answer to? Let your dreamin' mind take over. Think about the question when you go to sleep tonight and see if you wake up with some clarity.*

December 24th

"BELIEVE IN MAGIC."

I know a lotta Christian folks gonna get all up in my business for talkin' about Santa on Christmas Eve, 'cuz I should be talkin' about the baby Jesus. Well, just sit yo' ass down and hear me out, now. I'm a man of faith. I was raised up in the Burning Bush Baptist Church, so trust me, I *know* the real meanin' of Christmas. But I also know what kinda joy the fairy tale part of the holiday brings to folks all over the world. Santa Claus hoppin' from house to house, droppin' toys under the trees of good little children, that's some kinda magical story that's good for your soul to hear.

Listen, I know y'all feelin' the magic of the Christmas season, even if you ain't Christian. It's twinkly lights, folks smilin', carolin', hot chocolate. Hell, I got some Jewish friends that loves Christmas so much, they watchin' all the Christmas movies on the Hallmark Channel. They put up them twinkly lights right next to they menorah. It's bringin' folks together and makin' 'em feel good. So go on and believe in the magical feelin', read *'Twas the Night Before Christmas*, watch them sappy movies, bake them cookies, and encourage the younger folks to believe in all of them fairy tales too. We all need a little more magic in our lives.

> ***Those who don't believe in magic will never find it.***
>
> —Roald Dahl

DO THIS TODAY: *James Brown said it best in his song, "Santa Claus Go Straight to the Ghetto." Y'all know that song. Shit, they play it on the radio every year. Put out some milk and cookies and add a slice of sweet potato pie while you at it. Maybe you celebrate with Santa Claus, or maybe you don't. Whatever kinda magical myth you know and love, it don't matter, 'cuz somebody's gettin' cookies, and a milk mustache too.*

December 25th

"YOU CAPABLE OF RECEIVIN' EVERY GIFT YOU BEIN' GIVEN."

Y'all know you've opened up a gift before, and you said, "Oh, no, no, no. I could never accept this. It's too much." Maybe it's a Rolex or a bottle of five-hundred-dollah cologne. Maybe you just think it's more than that sumbitch can afford. But who the hell are you to judge? If you receive somethin' and you sayin' that kinda shit back, you gonna make 'em feel bad. Make 'em feel like you don't want it, maybe they gettin' embarrassed 'cuz you think they ain't makin' enough money. There's shame attached to that kinda receivin', and shame is gonna fuck up your flow. You can receive every gift you bein' given with gratitude, period.

That goes for God's gifts too. That goes for everything the Universe been puttin' in your flow. Maybe He give you the gift of knowin' how to work out numbers like other folks know words; you can not only handle that gift, but you can thrive with it. You can use it in ways no other sumbitch can. That's your gift, and you gotta own it and be grateful for it. Same thing when He gives you a gift you ain't so sure about. Maybe it's somethin' that hurts at first, somethin' He gave you so you can learn somethin' important in your life. You can receive that too. And you can accept it with grace. Kinda like when Aunt Rita knits you an angora sweater with a picture of a cat wearin' real silvery tinsel on the front. You can accept it with grace and a smile on yo' face, 'cuz you know it was given in good spirit.

> ***God never gives someone a gift they are not capable of receiving. If He gives us the gift of Christmas, it is because we all have the ability to understand and receive it.***
>
> —Pope Francis

DO THIS TODAY: *Give thanks for all of your gifts and know that you are fully capable of receivin' all the gifts offered to you in the future. They're meant for you, ain't no mistake about that.*

December 26th

"YOU KNOW WHAT YOU CAN DO, YOU JUST GOTTA TRUST YOURSELF."

You were put on this earth a full and complete mothahfuckin' package. You got everything you need right there to make shit happen for yourself, some assembly required, and you ain't gonna fuck it up unless you ain't listenin' to your God-given instincts. You already know this in so many ways, if you payin' attention. Let's say you on top of a buildin' and you lookin' over at the next buildin', down at the space between the two, and it goes down about a dozen stories to an alley below. Don't ask me why you up there, you playin' Spider-Man or some shit. But you lookin' at that distance from one edge to the other, and you gonna know if you can make it or not. Ya' see, you know your body's own limitations. Same thing goes for your mind and your ability to do the things you wanna be doin'. You *instinctually* know what it is you capable of. Let's say you wanna launch your own business, but somethin's tellin' you to hold back. Listen to your gut, 'cuz maybe there's somethin' you ain't ready for. Maybe you don't know all the things you know yet, and if you do it now, you gonna fall down that crack. On the flip side, if your gut's tellin' you to go for it, then you ready as hell, so do it. You know what you can handle, and as the sayin' goes, God ain't gonna give you nothin' that's too much.

> ***No bird soars too high if he soars with his own wings.***
>
> —William Blake

DO THIS TODAY: *What limitations have you put on yourself? Ask yourself if they comin' from your own instincts, or are they comin' from something outside of you?*

December 27th

"LOTS OF FOLKS MAYBE THINK YOU CRAZY, 'TIL IT WORKS."

You wanna know some shit that folks thought was strange as hell when they were first introduced to the market? Bicycles, nail polish, cars, laptop computers, disposable cups, mothahfuckin' cheeseburgers. Most folks thought these inventions was crazy and wasn't ever gonna last. But some crazy sumbitch believed in 'em enough to do what it took to get 'em out there and show folks what they was missin'. Now, how you think the naysayin' folks is feelin' after sayin', "Nobody's gonna wanna eat with their hands in their cars." They wish they'd got on that drive-up cheeseburger train, that's fo' sho'.

When I was sayin' I was gonna be a comedian, back when I was in high school, I got a lotta flack from a lotta folks who thought I was a crazy sumbitch too. "You need to get yourself a real job," is what mostly they'd tell me. They was thinkin' tellin' jokes was just a party trick or a mothahfuckin' hobby. "You funny," they'd say. "But you ain't no Eddie Murphy." I didn't wanna be no Eddie Murphy, no offense to the man or nothin'. He's fantastic. I just wanted to be me and make some money doin' it. It's a good thing I didn't listen to those folks neither. 'Cuz now they eatin' their words, just like fifty million Americans a year is eatin' a mothahfuckin' cheeseburger. Every new idea sounds crazy 'til it works, then it sounds like success.

> ***The distance between insanity and genius is measured only by success.***
>
> —Bruce Feirstein

DO THIS TODAY: *Think of some crazy idea that you think fills a need, then Google it to see if somebody's doin' it. I bet they are, 'cuz there's a lot more out there bein' done than you even realize. If nobody's doin' it, consider takin' it on yourself. You ain't crazy if it works!*

December 28th

"IT DON'T FEEL THE SAME WHEN IT'S ALL HANDED TO YOU RIGHT FROM THE START."

What if some mothahfuckah handed you a trophy right now? It's a big-ass trophy, five feet tall, gold plated, and it's got your *got-damn* name inscribed at the bottom. Just above that, it says, "World Champion Freestyle Skydiving." You ain't never jumped outta no plane. You got it up on your fireplace and shit, and folks look at it and say, "Wow, that's amazin'." And you like, "Naw, somebody gave it to me." That's fucked up, right? It's makin' you feel like a mothahfuckin' fraud. That's how it must feel when you been given everything you want from the very start. I feel bad for them sumbitches, 'cuz they gonna feel all empty inside. You know who I'm talkin' about, right? This is the members of the "Lucky Sperm Club." Y'all know, the ones that just got gifted into the rich mothahfuckin' life. It's okay to have money, no shame in that, for real. But some of them parents don't teach their kids how to earn somethin', and that's doin' 'em a disservice. They gonna feel like they ain't worth nothin', like they ain't needed for nothin'. That's why all them rich kids has anxiety, depression, drug abuse, all of that shit. We started havin' money when Je'Niece was in high school, but hell if I was gonna give her everything she wanted. She had to learn how to take care of herself, learn what it felt like to accomplish somethin', and that was the best gift we coulda gave her.

> ***You measure the size of the accomplishment by the obstacles you had to overcome to reach your goals.***
>
> —Booker T. Washington

DO THIS TODAY: *Make a commitment right now to do somethin' that you gotta work hard to accomplish, even if that shit's just knittin' a scarf or puttin' together a piece of IKEA furniture. Pay attention to the feelin' you get when you done.*

December 29th

"STOP OVERTHINKIN' EVERY GOT-DAMN THING. THAT SHIT'S GONNA DRIVE YOU CRAZY."

Human bein's is the only got-damn animal on earth that's over-thinkin' shit. You think a dog's sittin' there goin', "Hm, I wonder if the cat hates me, or if he just has a problem with dogs in general. I wonder what I did to offend him. Think I should talk to him? Maybe it was that time I ate his food, but it smelled so good. No, he is the fuck not thinkin' about nothin' but, "Hey, what's that? A squirrel?" He already forgot the cat took a swipe at him two minutes ago. He's movin' on.

I remember there was this time when another actor said somethin' to me on a movie set, and that shit just rubbed me the wrong way. It was the end of they day, and I went to my hotel and damn if I couldn't stop thinkin' about it. I even called Rhonda and we talked about it for an hour, that shit was eatin' me up. Couldn't figure out why they was so angry with me. I kept thinkin' maybe I done somethin' wrong and fucked some shit up. I couldn't sleep and everything. Next day, I decide to ask 'em straight up...sort of. "Hey, uh, is everything okay, man?" I asked. That sumbitch looked at me like he had no clue what the fuck I was talkin' about. So, I say, "Yeah, um, yesterday, you asked me if I knew what the fuck I was doin' and shit?" He's still lookin' confused, then a big grin comes across his face, and he slaps my shoulder. I'm thinkin' there ain't nothin' funny, mothahfuckah. "You thought I was talkin' to you? I was rehearsing my next line." I couldn't believe it. I wasted all that time worryin' 'cuz I was overthinkin' somethin' that didn't mean nothin'.

> ***Men do not stumble over mountains, but over molehills.***
>
> —Confucius

DO THIS TODAY: *Think on somethin' that's been buggin' you lately. Once you get it, let your mind wander with it a bit. Whenever you go too far away from the solid facts, say, "Stop. Delete." Clear that page and start over.*

December 30th

"LIFE IS A CRAZY MOTHAHFUCKAH, BUT IT'S HARD TO CRY ABOUT IT WHEN YOU LAUGHIN'."

I ain't delusional. I know there's some real mothahfuckin' tragedies happenin' in the world every day. I ain't livin' in no La-La Land and I don't expect you to, neither. But if you thinkin' about all of that bad shit all the damn time, you gonna get overwhelmed real quick. It could make you not even wanna go on livin'. That's why I do comedy, you know. 'Cuz I love seein' folks forget about all the problems of the world for just a mothahfuckin' minute and laugh. When I'm lookin' out an an audience and everybody's roarin', folks doubled over, tears in they eyes from laughin' so hard, I know I done some good. And you know what? Lots of times they laughin' at the very things they might be cryin' about outside of that show. If you can laugh at it, you can get through it, and it's gonna be okay.

The other thing I see when I'm lookin' out at the crowd laughin' is that they all in it together. Laughter does that too. I used to tell jokes on the L train. Before I'd start one of my stories, everybody'd be mindin' they own business, not lookin' nowhere in particular, especially not at each other. But then I'd start it, and suddenly folks is lookin' up. They start laughin' and they lookin' at one another, noddin' they heads, clappin'. Isn't that somethin'? Laughter makes folks feel a little less lonely in this big ole world. Ya' see, nothin' is black and white, and there's two sides to every coin. Tragedy is comedy, and how you see it just depends on the way you lookin' at it.

> ***Life would be tragic if it weren't funny.***
>
> —Stephen Hawking

DO THIS TODAY: *This might be a hard mothahfuckin' thing to do but do it anyway. Think about somethin' that's brought you sadness in the past. Now, write a joke about it. See if doin' that helps lighten your spirit a little bit.*

December 31st

"EVERY END AIN'T NOTHIN' BUT A NEW START."

It's New Year's Eve! Congratulations, you made it through another year. How did it go for you? Right now a lot of folks is lookin' back on their year, rememberin' good times and bad. But they also lookin' forward, makin' resolutions, hopeful for a new start. That's right, no sooner does that clock strike midnight than it starts tickin' the seconds into next year. End, beginnin', almost like there ain't no kinda transition at all. That's the way it works, you know. It ain't like a line, it's more like a loop. You just keep goin' round and round, startin' and stoppin', old and then new, end and then beginnin'. That's somethin' that can really give you hope when you thinkin' an end is a bad place to be.

Relationships, you end one and there's instantly a new one. Maybe it's just with yourself for a while, but that's new too. It's a chance to choose how you wanna be with yourself, to work on lovin' yourself and knowin' what you want when the next one comes around. The music ends, the silence begins, and in the silence you refresh your mind. When your baby's born, your freedom ends...but a new kinda selflessness begins. Parenthood, that's a whole new chapter too. You see what I'm sayin'? You gotta embrace the infinite nature of everything. Ain't no stoppin', just movin' through it all and takin' it all in as it comes.

> ***Every beginning has an end and every end has a new beginning.***
>
> —Santosh Kalwar

DO THIS TODAY: *You at the end of this book, but this book don't have no endin'. Put your bookmark, your dollah bill, your little slip of paper, your grocery store receipt, at the first page now. Tomorrow you gonna start again, and this time maybe you get somethin' new out of it.*

Afterword

Bernie Mac is one of the greatest to ever do it. For me to have never met this man, I feel really tied to Bernie. Not just because we are both from Chicago, even though the style of comedy we both possessed is highly influenced by what I like to call "the crib," but being fathers, chocolate brothers, and storytellers.

I find myself talking about The Mac Man all the time, more or less because I adopted something from him that I thought was part of his genius. I don't care how big or small a role was in a TV show or movie, or even how long the stand-up set was, he always brought it on a memorable level. I actually call that The Bernie Mac Method.

Anytime you saw Bernie on screen or in person you were either quoting him or just laughing at the thought of whatever he did or said. His delivery was masterful, energetic, and just real. Think about its people that get standing ovations for impersonating him, verbatim, like literally doing his original voice and delivery along with the jokes. I've always wondered if that annoyed him. Most people think it's paying homage, which I get, but I've always wondered, "Is that really paying homage or cheating by doing something that always worked?" But honestly, that's just how great Bernie was and his impact...everybody wanted to have that confidence and presence on stage.

I had few moments in my life where Bernie had an impact on me. First was at his memorial, and I actually snuck in because it was a line around the corner. I don't know how I got in! But I got in. While sitting there and watching speaker after speaker I was sitting there talking to myself and God saying who I wanted to work with among all those great people. And honestly I did get to work with and have relationships with some of his amazing comrades in this business.

The second moment was at the Black Women Expo in Chicago. I was hosting some random something there and in between the performances I saw a sign for a panel that Rhonda and Je'Niece was doing. I walked in and I was the only guy there! It was the Black Women Expo, so it was full of amazing Black women. Anyway, when I tell you Je'Niece was hilarious, she was hilarious, honestly reminding me of her father. I was sitting there like, "Why doesn't she do comedy?"

Outside of the laughs, they talked a lot about what happened and who he was as a man. It was moments where I was crying tears of hurt and tears of joy. I knew after that, me and Je'Niece had to be friends, and that's exactly what happened. In my transition to Hollywood from Chicago it was moments Je'Niece was laying her dad's wisdom on me. I really don't think she understood the impact of that. That's why when I received The Bernie Mac Award at the Comedy Awards it was a full-circle moment.

I thrive to represent Chicago because it also represents our King Bernie Mac. I truly believe that I have the same spirit and drive and pray that he's looking down proud of me. His jokes. His words. And his presence will live on forever. Thanks, Bernie, for opening the doors for me to be myself and tell it like it is.

—Lil Rel Howery

Acknowledgments

Rhonda McCullough and Walker-Bryce Creative would like to collectively thank all the people close to Bernie who shared their stories: Je'Niece McCullough, Adrienne Locke, Bill Hawthorne, (Dollah Bill), and Phillip Seed (Shorty Ruff), plus Sinbad and Lil Rel Howery. We'd also like to thank the team that made this book a reality: our incredible agent Ian Kleinert and everyone at Permuted Press including and especially our amazing editor Jacob Hoye. Also, a big thanks to Jenna Walker, our Ball State University intern, for all of her hard work. Thanks to Chicago casting agent and friend Sharon King for her connections, as well Andre LaVelle and James David Shanks for their contacts.

Rhonda R. McCullough would like to acknowledge her daughter and granddaughter, Je'Niece and Jasmine, her sisters, nieces, nephews, friends, and extended family. Thank you for your support and strength as I've learned to navigate through life in a new way. Thank God for His blessings and thank you Bernard for everything.

Denise Jordan Walker would like to thank her children Jordan and Jenna, and mom Barbara for their unwavering patience and sense of humor as I worked in my undercover studio. Also thank you to my cousins Kevin, Dana, and Billy for their super support. Thank you for believing in me. Thank you to all the other special people who supported me in this journey: JJ, Sophia, Diane, Maysa, Stacia, Dr. Williams, Robin, Lisa, Raven Rose, and all of my family.

Melinda Bryce wants to thank her husband Jason and her kids Alfie, Kayden, and Megan, for being her muses and for making her laugh on the daily. Mom, you gave me confidence, and Dad, you gave me my voice. To my writing and film cohorts, thanks for the endless encouragement. I also want to give a huge shout out to all my friends and family. You're the real ones. You know who you are, and I couldn't have gotten where I am without you. I love you guys.

Finally, we all want to thank Bernie Mac. Bernie, none of this would have been possible without you. Thanks for sharing your advice and your humor with the world.